H. H. Wilson

RigVeda Sanhitá a Collection of Ancient Hindú Hymns

Translated from the Original Sanskrit

H. H. Wilson

RigVeda Sanhitá a Collection of Ancient Hindú Hymns
Translated from the Original Sanskrit

ISBN/EAN: 9783742807762

Manufactured in Europe, USA, Canada, Australia, Japa

Cover: Foto ©Angelika Wolter / pixelio.de

Manufactured and distributed by brebook publishing software
(www.brebook.com)

H. H. Wilson

RigVeda Sanhitá a Collection of Ancient Hindú Hymns

RIG-VEDA SANHITA.

A COLLECTION OF

ANCIENT HINDU HYMNS,

CONSTITUTING

THE FIRST ASHṬAKA, OR BOOK,

OF THE

ṚIG-VEDA;

THE OLDEST AUTHORITY FOR THE RELIGIOUS AND SOCIAL

INSTITUTIONS OF THE HINDUS.

TRANSLATED FROM THE ORIGINAL SANSKRIT.

By H. H. WILSON, M.A., F.R.S.

Member of the Royal Asiatic Society, of the Asiatic Societies of Calcutta and Paris, and of the Oriental Society of Germany; Foreign Member of the National Institute of France; Member of the Imperial Academies of Petersburgh and Vienna, and of the Royal Academies of Munich and Berlin; Ph.D. Breslau; M.D. Marburg, &c., and Boden Professor of Sanskrit in the University of Oxford.

Published under the patronage of the Court of Directors of the East-India Company.

SECOND EDITION.

LONDON:

N. TRÜBNER AND CO.,

60, PATERNOSTER ROW.

1866.

INTRODUCTION.

When the liberal patronage of the Court of Directors of the East-India Company enabled Dr. Max Müller to undertake his invaluable edition of the *Ṛig-Veda*, a wish was expressed, that its appearance should be accompanied, or followed, with all convenient despatch, by an English translation. As I had long contemplated such a work, and had made some progress, in its execution, even before leaving India, I readily undertook to complete my labours and publish the translation.

It might, else, have been thought scarcely necessary to repeat a translation of the first *Ashṭaka*, Ogdoad, or Eighth book, of the *Ṛig-Veda*; as that had been, already, more than once accomplished; partly, in English, by the Rev. Mr. Stevenson and Dr. Roer, and fully, in Latin, by the late Dr. Rosen. A translation in French, also, by M. Langlois, extending through four *Ashṭakas*, or half the *Veda*, has been recently published at Paris; but I was not aware, when I engaged to publish an English translation, that such a work had been commenced. At the same time, these translations do not seem to preclude, entirely, the usefulness of an English version. The earliest publication, the work of the Rev. Mr. Stevenson, extends only to the three first hymns of the third lecture, or section, out of the eight which the first book, or *Ashtaka*, consists of: Dr. Roer's translation is equally limited, stopping with two sections, or thirty-two hymns. Both translations were printed in India, and are procurable, with some difficulty, in this country. Dr. Rosen's translation of the first book is complete, as to the text; but his premature death interrupted his annotations. Although executed with profound scholarship and scrupulous exactitude, and every way deserving of reliance, as an authentic representative of the original, the Sanskrit is converted into Latin with such literal fidelity, that the work scarcely admits of consecutive perusal, and is most of value as a reference. The translation is, in fact, subordinate to an edition of the text which it accompanies on the same page; and the work is designed less for general readers than for Sanskrit scholars and students of the *Veda*. The principle followed by M. Langlois is the converse of that adopted by Dr. Rosen; and he has avowedly sought to give to the vague and mysterious passages of the original a clear, simple, and intelligible interpretation. In this it may be admitted that he has admirably succeeded; but it may be, sometimes, thought that he has not been sufficiently cautious in his rendering of the text, and that he has diverged from its phraseology, especially as interpreted by the native Scholiast, more widely than is advisable. The real value of the original lies not so much in its merits as a literary composition, as in the illustration which it supplies of the most ancient Hindu system of religious worship and social organization; and, unless its language be preserved as far as may be consistent with intelligibility, erroneous impressions of the facts and opinions of primitive Hinduism may be produced. It is, also, to be observed, that M. Langlois has made his translation from manuscript copies of the *Veda* and its commentary, which, whilst it has greatly enhanced the difficulty and labour of the task, and, so far, adds to the credit of the translator, suggests less confidence in the genuineness of the original—as the manuscripts are, all, more or less defective,—than if the version had been made from a carefully collated edition. The present translation possesses, at least, the advantage, over its predecessors, of an accurate text; and it will be the fault of the translator, if he does not benefit by it. In converting the original into English, it has been his aim to adhere as strictly to the original Sanskrit as the necessity of being intelligible would allow.

It may be almost superfluous to apprise the reader, that the oldest, and, nominally, the most weighty, authorities of the Brahmans, for their religion and institutions, are the *Vedas*, of which works four are usually enumerated: the *Ṛich*, or *Ṛig-Veda;* the *Yajush*, or *Yajur-Veda;* the *Sáman*, or *Sáma-Veda;* and the *Átharvańa*, or *Atharva-Veda*. Many passages are to be found in Sanskrit writings, some in the *Vedas* themselves, which limit the number to three;*

* Colebrooke on the *Vedas.*—*Asiatic Researches*, Vol. viii., p. 370.

and there is no doubt that the fourth, or *Atharva-Veda*, although it borrows freely from the *Rich*, has little in common with the others, in its general character, or in its style: the language clearly indicates a different and later era. It may, therefore, be allowably regarded rather as a supplement to three, than as one of the four, *Vedas*.

Of the other three *Vedas*, each has its peculiar characteristics, although they have much in common; and they are, apparently, of different dates, although not separated, perhaps, by any very protracted interval. The *Ṛig-Veda* consists of metrical prayers, or hymns, termed *Súktas*,—addressed to different divinities,—each of which is ascribed to a *Ṛishi*, a holy or inspired author. These hymns are put together with little attempt at methodical arrangement, although such as are dedicated to the same deity sometimes follow in a consecutive series. There is not much connexion in the stanzas of which they are composed; and the same hymn is, sometimes, addressed to different divinities. There are, in the *Veda* itself, no directions for the use and application of the *Súktas*, no notices of the occasions on which they are to be employed, or of the ceremonies at which they are to be recited. These are pointed out, by subsequent writers, in *Sútras*, or precepts relating to the ritual; and, even for the reputed authors of the hymns, and for the deities in whose honour they are composed, we are, for the most part, indebted to independent authorities, especially to an *Anukramaṇiká*, or index, accompanying each *Veda*. The *Yajur-Veda* differs from the *Rich* in being, more particularly, a ritual, or a collection of liturgical formulæ. The prayers, or invocations, when not borrowed from the *Ṛich*, are, mostly, brief, and in prose, and are applicable to the consecration of the utensils and materials of ceremonial worship, as well as to the praise and worship of the gods. The *Sáma-Veda* is little else than a recast of the *Ṛich*, being made up, with very few exceptions, of the very same hymns, broken into parts, and arranged anew, for the purpose of being chanted on different ceremonial occasions. As far, also, as the *Atharva-Veda* is to be considered as a *Veda*, it will be found to comprise many of the hymns of the *Ṛich*.* From the extensive manner, then, in which the hymns of the *Ṛig-Veda* enter into the composition of the other three, we must, naturally, infer its priority to them, and its greater importance to the history of the Hindu religion. In truth, it is to the *Ṛig-Veda* that we must have recourse, principally, if not exclusively, for correct notions of the oldest and most genuine forms of the institutions, religious or civil, of the Hindus.

These remarks apply to what are termed the *Sanhitás* of the *Vedas*,—the aggregate assemblage, in a single collection, of the prayers, hymns, and liturgic formulæ of which they are composed. Besides the *Sanhitás*, the designation *Veda* includes an extensive class of compositions, entitled, collectively, *Bráhmańa*,

---

* "By the followers of the *Atharvaṅa*, the *Ṛichas*, or stanzas of the *Ṛig-Veda*, are numerously included in their own *Sanhitá* (or collection)."—*Sáyańa Áchárya*, Introduction, Müller's edition, p. 2.

which all Brahmanical writers term an integral portion of the *Veda*. According to them, the *Veda* consists of two component parts, termed, severally, *Mantra* and *Bráhmańa*;[*] the first being the hymns and formulæ aggregated in the *Sanhitá*; the second, a collection of rules for the application of the *Mantras*, directions for the performance of particular rites, citations of the hymns, or detached stanzas, to be repeated on such occasions, and illustrative remarks, or narratives, explanatory of the origin and object of the rite. Of the *Bráhmańa* portions of the *Ṛig-Veda*, the most interesting and important is the *Aitareya Bráhmańa*, in which a number of remarkable legends are detailed, highly illustrative of the condition of Brahmanism at the time at which it was composed. The *Aitareya Arańyaka*, another *Bráhmańa* of this *Veda*, is more mystical and speculative than practical or legendary; of a third, the *Kaushítaki*, little is known. The *Bráhmańa* of the *Yajur-Veda*, the *S'atapatha*, partakes more of the character of the *Aitareya Bráhmańa*: it is of considerable extent, consisting of fourteen books, and contains much curious matter. The *Bráhmańas* of the *Sáma* and *Atharva Vedas* are few, and little known; and the supplementary portions of these two *Vedas* are, more especially, the metaphysical and mystical treatises

* As in the *Yajna Paribháshá* of *Ápastamba*, quoted by *Sáyańa*, "The name *Veda* is that of both the *Mantra* and the *Bráhmańa*;" and, again, in the *Mímánsá*, "The *Bráhmańa* and the *Mantra* are the two parts of the *Veda*: that part which is not *Mantra* is *Bráhmańa*;" this constitutes the definition of the latter.—*Introduction*, p. 4 and p. 22.

termed *Upanishads*, belonging to an entirely different state of the Hindu mind from that which the text of the *Vedas* sprang from and encouraged. Connected with, and dependent upon, the *Vedas* generally, also are the treatises on grammar, astronomy, intonation, prosody, ritual, and the meaning of obsolete words, called the *Vedángas*. But these are not portions of the *Veda* itself, but supplementary to it, and, in the form in which we have them, are not, perhaps, altogether genuine, and, with a few exceptions, are not of much importance. Besides these works, there are the *Prátiśákhyas*, or treatises on the grammar of the *Veda*, and the *Sútras*, or aphorisms, inculcating and describing its practices; the whole constituting a body of Vaidik literature the study of which would furnish occupation for a long and laborious life. A small part only is yet in print. None of the *Bráhmańas* are published; neither are the *Sútras* or *Prátiśákhyas*.[a] The *Upanishads* have been more fortunate in finding editors.[b] The texts of the *Sanhitás* of the *Veda* are in progress; as, besides the present edition of the *Rich*, an edition of the *Vájasaneyi* portion of

---

[a] Part of the first *Káńda* of the *Satapatha Bráhmańa* has been printed by Dr. Weber, concurrently with his edition of the text of the *Yajur-Veda*; and it is his intention to complete it.

[b] Some of the shorter *Upanishads* were printed, with translations, by Rammohun Roy; and five of those of the *Yajush* have been published by M. Poley: Berlin, 1844. The *Brihaddrańyaka* has been printed by the Asiatic Society of Calcutta, under the editorship of Dr. Roer, in their *Bibliotheca Indica*; and the *Chhándogya Upanishad* has been begun in the same series.

the *Yajur-Veda* has been commenced,—by Dr. Weber, at Berlin,—the publication of which has been, also, liberally aided by the Court of Directors.

The text of the *Sanhitá* of the *Sáma-Veda*, and a translation by the Rev. Mr. Stevenson, were published, some years since, by the Oriental Translation Fund; and a more carefully elaborated edition of the same, with a translation in German, and a copious glossary and index, has been recently published by Professor Benfey, of Göttingen. In time, therefore, we shall be well supplied with the *Mantra* portion of the *Veda*: but there is yet but a partial and distant prospect of our having the *Bráhmańa* printed, and being, thus, enabled, from adequate materials, to determine how far the whole may be legitimately considered as a constituent part of the *Veda*.

From a careful examination of the *Aitareya Bráhmańa*, with an excellent commentary by Sáyańa *Achárya*, it is sufficiently evident, that this work, at least, is of a totally distinct description from the collection of the *Mantras*, or the *Sanhitá*, of the *Ŗig-Veda*. Although, no doubt, of considerable antiquity, it is, manifestly, of a date long subsequent to the original *Súktas*, or hymns, from the manner in which they are quoted,—not systematically, or continuously, or completely, but separately, unconnectedly, and partially; a few phrases only being given, forming the beginning, not even of an entire hymn, but of an isolated stanza, occurring in any part of the hymn, or in any part of the *Sanhitá*; consequently proving, that the *Sanhitá* must have been compiled, and widely circulated, and generally studied, before such mutilated citations could be recognized, or verified, by those to whom the *Bráhmańa* was presented. It is evident, also, that the great body of the Brahmanical ritual must have been sanctioned by established practice, before the *Bráhmańa* could have been compiled; as its main object is the application of the detached texts of the *Sanhitá* to the performance of the principal ceremonies and sacrifices of the Brahmans, enforcing their necessity and efficacy by texts and arguments, and illustrating their origin and consequences by traditional narratives and popular legends, the invention and currency of which must have been the work of time,—of a very long interval between the *Sanhitá*, in which little or nothing of the kind appears, and the *Bráhmańa*, in which such particulars abound. Again, we find, in the *Bráhmańa*, the whole system of social organization developed, the distinction of caste fully established, and the *Bráhmańa*, *Kshattriya*, *Vaiśya*, and *S'údra* repeatedly named by their proper appellations, and discriminated by their peculiar offices and relative stations, as in the code of MANU. A cursory inspection of the *S'atapatha Bráhmańa*, as far as published, and of some of its sections in manuscript, shows it to be of a character similar to the *Aitareya*; or it may be even, perhaps, of a later era: and we may venture to affirm, in opposition to the consentient assertions of Brahmanical scholars and critics, that neither of those works has the slightest claim to be regarded as the counterpart and contemporary of the *Sanhitá*, or as an integral part of the *Veda*; understanding, by that expression, the primitive record of the religious belief and observances, and of the archaic institutions, of Hindu society.

Whilst acknowledging, with occasional exceptions, the early date of the *Bráhmaňas*, and accepting them as valuable illustrations of the application of the primitive hymns and texts of the *Sanhitá*, we must look to the latter alone, as a safe guide, in our inquiries into the most ancient condition of the Hindus; and we must endeavour to convey a more precise notion of what is meant by the designation, as it is exemplified in the *Veda* which has been taken as the text of the following translation, and which, as has been shown, may be regarded as the source and model of the other works similarly named.

According to the credible traditions of the Hindus, the *Súktas*, the prayers and hymns—now collected as a *Sanhitá*,—had existed, in a separate and individual form, long before they were assembled and arranged in the order and connexion in which they are now met with. In the *Ṛig-Veda* the number of *Súktas* is something above a thousand, containing rather more than ten thousand stanzas. They are arranged in two methods. One divides them amongst eight *Khaňdas* (portions), or *Ashṫakas* (eighths), each of which is, again, subdivided into eight *Adhyáyas*, or lectures. The other plan classes the *Súktas* under ten *Maňďalas*, or circles, subdivided into rather more than a hundred *Anuváкas*, or sub-sections. A further subdivision of the *Súktas* into *Vargas*, or paragraphs, of about five stanzas each, is common to both classifications. The hymns are of various extent: in one or two instances, a *Súkta* consists of a single stanza; in some, of a number of stanzas; but the average number, as follows from the above totals of one thousand hymns and ten thousand stanzas, is, of course, about ten. The hymns are composed in a great variety of metres, several of which are peculiar to the *Vedas*, and the variety and richness of which evince an extraordinary cultivation of rhythmical contrivance. In general, a hymn is addressed to a single deity, but, sometimes, to two; and, occasionally, the verses are distributed among a greater number. The divinities are various; but the far larger number of the hymns in this first book of the *Rich*, and, as far as has been yet ascertained, in the other books, also, are dedicated to Agni and Indra, the deities, or personifications, of *Fire* and the *Firmament*. Of the one hundred and twenty-one hymns contained in the first *Ashtaka*, for instance, thirty-seven are addressed to Agni alone, or associated with others; and forty-five, to Indra: of the rest, twelve are addressed to the Maruts, or Winds, the friends and followers of Indra; and eleven, to the Aświns, the sons of the Sun; four, to the personified dawn; four, to the Viśwadevas, or collective deities; and the rest, to inferior divinities;—an appropriation which unequivocally shows the elemental character of the religion. In subsequent portions of the *Veda*, a few hymns occur which seem to be of a poetical, or fanciful, rather than of a religious, tendency; as one, in which there is a description of the revival of the frogs, on the setting in of the rainy season; and another, in which a gamester complains of his ill success: but we shall better appreciate the character of such seeming exceptions, when we come to them. Each *Súkta* has, for its reputed author, a *Ṛishi*, or inspired teacher, by whom, in Brahmanical phraseology, it has been originally *seen*, that is, to whom it was revealed; the *Vedas* being, according to later mythological fictions, the uncreated dictation of Brahmá. For the names of the *Ṛishis*, except when incidentally mentioned in the hymn, we are indebted, as above remarked, to an index of the contents of the *Veda*, which also specifies the metre and the number of stanzas of each hymn, and the deity worshipped. It is an old book, and of high authority; but, inasmuch as it is of later composition than the text, it may not, always, be regarded as of unquestionable correctness. Most of the *Ṛishis* are familiar to the legends of the *Puráńas*, as Gotama, Kańwa, Bharadwája, Vasishṭha, Viśwámitra, and others. To some of these a number of hymns are attributed; to others, of less note, and, perhaps, only of imaginary existence, one or two only are ascribed. The arrangement of the *Súktas* by *Ashṭakas* does not seem to depend upon any fixed principle. Of that by *Mańḍalas*, six out of the ten "circles" comprise hymns by the same individual, or by members of the same family: thus, the hymns of the second *Mańḍala* are ascribed to Gṛitsamada, the son of S'unahotra, of the family of Angiras; those of the third, to Viśwámitra and his sons, or kinsmen; of the fourth, to Vámadeva; of the fifth, to Atri and his sons, who are of rather equivocal nomenclature; of the sixth, to Bhara-

DWÁJA; and, of the seventh, to VASISHṪHA and his descendants. The *Ṛishis* of the first and the three last *Maṅḋalas* are more miscellaneous; the hymns of the ninth Circle are, all, addressed to SOMA, the Moon-plant, or its deified impersonation. This arrangement has been considered as the older and more original of the two; the distribution into *Ashṫakas* being intended for the convenience of instruction; forming, through their subdivisions,—*Adhyáyas* and *Vargas*,—so many lectures, or lessons, to be learned by the scholar. The inference is not improbable; but we are scarcely yet qualified to come to any positive conclusion. The more usual division of the manuscripts is that into *Ashṫakas;* and in neither case is the principle of classification so unequivocally manifested as to suggest reasonable grounds for a departure from the established practice.

The absence of any obvious dependency of the *Súktas* upon one another is sufficiently indicative of their separate and unsystematic origin. That they are the compositions of the patriarchal sages to whom they are ascribed is, sometimes, apparent from allusions which they make to the name of the author or of his family: but these indications are of unfrequent recurrence; and we must trust, in general, to tradition, as preserved by the *Anukramaṅiká*, for the accuracy of the appropriation. Their being addressed to the same divinity is a less equivocal test of community; and they, probably, were composed, in many instances, by the heads of families, or of schools following a similar form of worship, and adoring, in preference, particular deifications. Besides the internal evidence afforded by difference of style, the hymns, not unfrequently, avow a difference of date; and we find some ascribed to *ancient Ṛishis*, while others admit their being of *new* or *newest* composition. The great variety of metres employed shows, also, a progressive development of the powers of the language, which could have been the effect only of long and diligent cultivation. There can be little doubt, therefore, that they range through a considerable interval; although, as far as respects their general purport, they belong to the same condition of belief, and to a period during which no change of any importance took place in the national creed. The same divinities are worshipped in a similar strain, and, with one or two doubtful exceptions,—which are, possibly, interpolations, or which may admit of explanation,—offer nothing that is contradictory or incongruous. This is the more remarkable, as there can be little doubt that the hymns were taught, originally, orally, and that the knowledge of them was perpetuated by the same mode of tuition. This is sufficiently apparent from their construction: they abound with elliptical phrases; with general epithets, of which the application is far from obvious, until explained; with brief comparisons, which cannot be appreciated without such additional details as a living teacher might be expected to supply; and with all those blanks and deficiencies which render the written text of the *Vedas* still unintelligible, in many passages, without the assistance of the Scholiast, and which he is alone enabled to fill up by the greater or less fidelity with which the traditional explanations of the first *vivâ voce* interpreters, or, perhaps, of the authors of the hymns themselves, have come down to his time. The explanation of a living teacher, or of a commentator, must have been indispensable to a right understanding of the meaning of the *Súktas*, in many passages, from the moment of their first communication: and the probability is in favour of an oral instructor, as most in harmony with the unconnected and unsystematic currency of the hymns; with the restricted use of writing,—even if the art were known in those early times (a subject of considerable doubt),—and with the character of Sanskrit teaching, even in the present day, in which the study of books is subordinate to the personal and traditional expositions of the teacher, handed down to him through an indefinite series of preceding instructors.

At last, however, there arrived a period when the antiquity of the hymns, the obscurity of their style, the peculiarities of the language, and the number to which they had multiplied, with the corresponding difficulties of recollecting and teaching them, and, possibly, also, the perception, that some venerable authority on which their growing claims to superior sanctity might be based was wanting, suggested, to the progressive advancement of the literature of the Brahmans, the expediency of rescuing the dispersed and obsolete *Súktas* from the risk of oblivion, and moulding them into some consistent and permanent shape. The accomplishment of this object is traditionally ascribed to the son of PARÁŚARA *Ṛishi*, KṚISHṆA

DWAIPÁYANA, thence surnamed VYÁSA, *the Arranger;* a person of rather questionable chronology and existence, who is supposed to have flourished at the time of the great war between the rival families of KURU and PÁŃḌU, to the latter of which he was attached. The account that is usually given of his proceedings shows that his especial province was that of superintendence,—possibly under the patronage of the *Rájá* YUDHISHṭHIRA, after his triumph over the KURUS,—and that various other learned persons, already familiar with the hymns of the respective *Vedas*, were employed to prepare each several *Sanhitá*, or collection: thus, PAILA was appointed to collect the *Súktas* of the *Ṛich;* VAIŚAMPÁYANA, the text of the *Yajush;* JAIMINI, the hymns of the *Sáman;* and SUMANTU, those of the *Atharvaṅa*. Each of these became the teacher of his own collection, and had a succession of disciples by whom the original collection was repeatedly subdivided and rearranged, until the *Sanhitás* of the *Ṛig-Veda* amounted to sixteen or twenty; those of the *Yajur-Veda*—distinguished as twofold, termed the Black and the White *Yajush*—amounted to forty-two; and those of the *Sáma-Veda*, to twenty-four. There were, also, various *Sanhitás* of the *Atharva-Veda;* and, besides these, there were numerous *S'ákhás*, or branches, of each *Sanhitá*, studied in as many separate schools.* The precise nature of these distinctions is not very satisfactorily known at

* Colebrooke on the *Vedas*.—*Asiatic Researches*, Vol. iii., p. 373. *Vishṅu Puráṅa*, Book III., Chap. iv.: p. 275.

present, as they have almost wholly disappeared; but they consisted, apparently, of varieties of form, (not of substance), containing the same hymns and formulæ arranged in a different order, according to the conceptions of the teacher respecting their historical succession or liturgical value, or according to differences in the mode of their recitation,—some being recited audibly, some repeated inaudibly, and some being chanted or sung. Various readings, also, seem to have been followed by different schools, although not to such an extent as materially to affect the identity between the original and its descendant. Of the *Sanhitás* of the *Ṛig-Veda* the only one now in use is that ascribed to a teacher named Vedamitra or Śákalya. Whether the authorities which profess to detail the multiplicity of these compilations be entitled to entire confidence may be matter of question; but the traditions are concurrent and consistent; and there can be little doubt that there was a time at which the collection, and classification, and study, of the religious poems, which, even then, bore the stamp of antiquity, did form an important and popular branch of the literature of the Brahmans, and must have been pursued, with extraordinary diligence, zeal, and ability, through a protracted interval, anterior to the rise of philosophical speculation, mythological fable, poetical legends, and traditional history.[a]

[a] The foundation of the *Vedánta* philosophy, and the compilation of the *Itihásas* and *Puránas*, are, also, ascribed to *Vyása*. It would be out of place to enter into any examination of the question here,

The interest evinced in the collection and preservation of their ancient hymns and formulæ is the more remarkable from their having, as far as we can yet judge, afforded little countenance to the religious and social institutions which, no doubt, were fully matured at the date of their compilation. It is yet, perhaps, scarcely safe to hazard any positive assertion respecting the system of religious belief and practice taught in the *Ṛig-Veda*, or the state of society which prevailed when its hymns were composed; and it were still more indiscreet to risk a negative, and deny its sanctioning the leading features of the Brahmanical institutes, until we shall have examined it throughout, and ascertained, beyond dispute, that no such sanction is to be found in it. In offering any opinion on these points, therefore, it must be understood that they are derived solely from what is actually before us,—the *First Book* of the *Ṛig-Veda*, now translated,—and that they are subject to confirmation, or to contradiction, according to the further evidence that may be produced. It is true that we have a somewhat wider field for speculation, in the other three books, translated by M. Langlois, and in detached portions from other books, which have been translated and published by other Sanskrit scholars, especially by Mr. Colebrooke, Professor Burnouf, and Dr. Roth. The latter, however,

beyond the remark, that there seems to be little satisfactory evidence for the tradition; several of the *Purāṇas* being, in fact, ascribed to other persons. The tradition may have originated in the impulse given to the general cultivation of Sanskrit literature by the school, or schools, of *Vaidik* criticism.

from their partial and isolated state, are, necessarily, imperfect authorities; and, of the former, it may be observed, that they do not seem to offer anything materially at variance with the tenour of the first *Ashṭaka*. It will be sufficient, therefore, for the present, to confine ourselves to the evidence at hand, and deduce, from it, a few of the most important conclusions to which it appears to lead, regarding the religious and mythological belief of the people of India,—whose sentiments and notions the *Súktas* enunciate,—and the circumstances of their social condition, to which it occasionally, though briefly, adverts.

The worship which the *Súktas* describe comprehends offerings, prayer, and praise. The former are, chiefly, oblations and libations: clarified butter poured on fire, and the expressed and fermented juice of the *Soma* plant, presented, in ladles, to the deities invoked, —in what manner does not exactly appear, although it seems to have been, sometimes, sprinkled on the fire, sometimes, on the ground, or, rather, on the *Kuśa*, or sacred grass, strewed on the floor; and, in all cases, the residue was drunk by the assistants. The ceremony takes place in the dwelling of the worshipper, in a chamber appropriated to the purpose, and, probably, to the maintenance of a perpetual fire; although the frequent allusions to the occasional kindling of the sacred flame are rather at variance with this practice.* There

* It is said, in one place, however, that men preserved fire *constantly kindled* in their dwellings (Hymn LXXIII., v. 4: p. 195).

is no mention of any temple, nor any reference to a public place of worship; and it is clear that the worship was entirely domestic. The worshipper, or *Yajamána*, does not appear to have taken, of necessity, any part, personally, in the ceremony; and there is a goodly array of officiating priests,—in some instances, seven; in some, sixteen,—by whom the different ceremonial rites are performed, and by whom the *Mantras*, or prayers, or hymns, are recited. That animal victims were offered on particular occasions may be inferred from brief and obscure allusions in the hymns of the first book;* and it is inferrible, from some passages, that human sacrifices were not unknown, although infrequent, and, sometimes, typical. But these are the exceptions; and the habitual offerings may be regarded as consisting of clarified butter and the juice of the *Soma* plant.

The *Súkta* almost invariably combines the attributes of prayer and praise. The power, the vastness, the generosity, the goodness, and even the personal beauty, of the deity addressed are described in highly laudatory strains, and his past bounties, or exploits, rehearsed and glorified; in requital of which commendations, and of the libations or oblations which he is solicited to accept, and in approval of the rite in his honour, at which his presence is invoked, he is implored to bestow blessings on the person who has instituted the

* In the second *Ashtaka*, we have two hymns on the occasion of the *Aśwamedha*, a sacrifice of a horse. (See Translation of M. Langlois, Lecture III., Hymns v., vi.)

ceremony, and, sometimes, but not so commonly, also on the author, or reciter, of the prayer. The blessings prayed for are, for the most part, of a temporal and personal description,—wealth, food, life, posterity, cattle, cows, and horses, protection against enemies, victory over them, and, sometimes, their destruction, particularly when they are represented as inimical to the celebration of religious rites, or, in other words, people not professing the same religious faith.* There are a few indications of a hope of immortality and of future happiness: but they are neither frequent nor, in general, distinctly announced; although the immortality of the gods is recognized, and the possibility of its attainment by human beings, exemplified in the case of the demigods termed Ṛibhus,—elevated, for their piety, to the rank of divinities. Protection against evil spirits (*Rákshasas*) is, also, requested; and, in one or two passages, Yama and his office as ruler of the dead are obscurely alluded to. There is little demand for moral benefactions, although, in some few instances, hatred of untruth and abhorrence of sin are expressed, a hope is uttered that the latter may be repented of, or expiated; and the gods are, in one hymn, solicited to extricate the worshipper from sin of every kind. The main objects of the prayers, however, are benefits of a more worldly and physical character. The tone in which these are requested indicates a quiet confidence in their being granted, as a return for the benefits which the gods are supposed to derive, from

* Note a, p. 138.

the offerings made to them, in gratifying their bodily wants, and from the praises which impart to them enhanced energy and augmented power. There is nothing, however, which denotes any particular potency in the prayer, or hymn, so as to compel the gods to comply with the desires of the worshipper;—nothing of that enforced necessity which makes so conspicuous and characteristic a figure in the Hindu mythology of a later date, by which the performance of austerities for a continued period constrains the gods to grant the desired boon, although fraught with peril, and even destruction, to themselves.

The next question is: Who are the gods to whom the praises and prayers are addressed? And here we find, also, a striking difference between the mythology of the *Ṛig-Veda* and that of the heroic poems and *Puráńas*. The divinities worshipped are not unknown to later systems: but they there perform very subordinate parts; whilst those deities who are the great gods—the *Dii majores*—of the subsequent period are either wholly unnamed in the *Veda*, or are noticed in an inferior and different capacity. The names of S'IVA, of MAHÁDEVA, of DURGÁ, of KÁLÍ, of RÁMA, of KRISHŃA, never occur, as far as we are yet aware. We have a RUDRA, who, in after times, is identified with S'IVA, but who, even in the *Puráńas*, is of very doubtful origin and identification, whilst, in the *Veda*, he is described as the father of the winds, and is, evidently, a form of either AGNI or INDRA. The epithet KAPARDIN, which is applied to him, appears, indeed, to have some relation to a characteristic attribute of S'IVA,—

the wearing of his hair in a peculiar braid: but the term has, probably, in the *Veda*, a different signification, —one now forgotten,—although it may have suggested, in after time, the appearance of S'IVA, in such a head-dress, as identified with AGNI. For instance, KAPARDIN may intimate his head being surrounded by radiating flame; or the word may be an interpolation. At any rate, no other epithet applicable to S'IVA, occurs; and there is not the slightest allusion to the form in which, for the last ten centuries, at least, he seems to have been almost exclusively worshipped in India, —that of the *Linga* or *Phallus*. Neither is there the slightest hint of another important feature of later Hinduism, the *Trimúrti*, or triune combination of BRAHMÁ, VISHṆU, and S'IVA, as typified by the mystical syllable *Om*; although, according to high authority on the religions of antiquity, the *Trimúrti* was the first element in the faith of the Hindus, and the second was the *Lingam*.*

The chief deities of the *Veda* are, as has been noticed above, AGNI and INDRA. The former comprises the element of *Fire* under three aspects: 1st, as it exists on earth, not only as culinary, or religious, fire, but as the heat of digestion and of life, and the vivifying principle of vegetation; 2nd, as it exists in the atmosphere, or mid-heaven, in the form of lightning; and, 3rd, as it is manifested in the heavens, as light, the sun, the dawn, and the planetary bodies. The *Sun*, it is true, is acknowledged and hymned as a divinity,

* Creuzer, *Religions de l'Antiquité*, Book I., Chap. I.: p. 140.

the soul of all moveable and immoveable beings; and his manifestations are already known as Ádityas, including several of the names preserved in the *Puráńas*, as Vishńu, Mitra, Varuńa, Aryaman, Púshan, Bhaga, and Twashtri, who are nothing more than the Sun diversified as presiding over each month of the solar year. Still, however, the sun does not hold that prominent place, in the *Vaidik* liturgy, which he seems to have done in that of the ancient Persians; and he is chiefly venerated as the celestial representative of Fire.

If we advert more particularly to the attributes of Agni, we find that confusion, in them, which might be expected from the various characters he fills. As the fire of sacrifice, he is the servant of both men and gods, conveying the invocations and the offerings of the former to the latter; he is the *Hotri*, or priest, who summons the gods to the ceremony; the *Purohita*, or family priest, who performs the rite on behalf of the master of the house. Personified as a divinity, he is immortal, enjoying perpetual youth, endowed with infinite power and splendour, the granter of victory, of wealth, of cattle, of food, of health, of life; he travels in a car drawn by red horses; he is the source and diffuser of light, the destroyer and reviver of all things. He is known under many and various appellations; and many inferior deities are considered to be merely his manifestations. The acts and attributes of other deities are, not unfrequently, ascribed to him (p. 179): he may assume the form or nature of any other divinity

(p. 184) who is invoked to a ceremonial rite. He is identified with YAMA, VARUṆA, MITRA, with the Sun, and with the eternal VEDHAS (p. 190). A curious series of allusions, evidently of a remote antiquity, identifies him with AṄGIRAS, who, in the *Veda*, as well as in the *Purâṇas*, is a patriarch and *Ṛishi*, and the founder of a celebrated holy family, to members of which many of the hymns of the *Veda* are attributed. AṄGIRAS is, in one place (p. 3), used instead of the repetition of the name AGNI; and, in another, AGNI is expressly called the first and chiefest AṄGIRAS (p. 79). The meaning of this myth is, apparently, explained in another passage, in which it is said that the AṄGIRASAS first made sure of AGNI, whence subsequent votaries preserved his fires and practised his rites (p. 187); which clearly intimates that this priestly family, or school, either introduced worship with fire, or extended and organized it in the various forms in which it came, ultimately, to be observed. The tenour of the legend, as it was afterwards expanded in the *Brâhmaṇas* and heroic poems, equally intimates the latter, and refers the multiplication, or universality, of the occasions on which fire constituted an essential element of the worship of the Hindus, to AṄGIRAS and his descendants.[a] Of the attributes of AGNI, in general, the meaning is sufficiently obvious: those of a physical character speak for themselves; and the allegory conveyed by others is, either, palpable enough, as when

[a] See the passage of the *Mahâbhârata*, cited in note d, p. 3.

Agni is said to be the son of the Wind, or springs, naturally, from Hindu notions, as when he is said to be both the father and the son of the gods,—nourishing them, like a father, by the oblations he bears to them, while the act of offering those oblations is the duty of a son. The legend of his hiding in the waters, through fear of the enemies of the gods, although alluded to in more than one place (pp. 58, 177), is not very explicitly narrated; and its more circumstantial detail is, probably, the work of the *Bráhmańas*. The allusions of the *Súktas* may be a figurative intimation of the latent heat existing in water, or a misapprehension of a natural phenomenon which seems to have made a great impression, in later times, —the emission of flame from the surface of water, either in the shape of inflammable air, or as the result of submarine volcanic action.*

The deification of Indra is more consistent, as he has no incongruous functions to discharge. He is a personification of the phenomena of the firmament, particularly in the capacity of sending down rain. This property is metaphorically described as a conflict with the clouds, which are reluctant to part with their watery stores, until assailed and penetrated by the thunderbolt of Indra. As in all allegories, the language of fact and fiction is apt to be blended and confounded in the description of this encounter; and the cloud, personified as a demon named Ahi or Vṛitra, is represented as combating Indra with all the attri-

* See the legend of *Aurva*, *Vishńu Puráńa*, p. 290, note.

butes of a personal enemy, and as suffering, in the battle, mutilation, wounds, and death. In the versions of the conflict found in later works, and in the heroic poems and *Puráńas*, the original allegory is lost sight of altogether; and VṚITRA becomes a real personage, an *Asura*, or king of *Asuras*, who wages a doubtful war with the king of the gods. This contest with the clouds seems to have suggested, to the authors of the *Súktas*, the martial character of INDRA on other occasions; and he is especially described as the god of battles, the giver of victory to his worshippers, the destroyer of the enemies of religious rites, and the subverter of the cities of the *Asuras*. A popular myth represents him, also, as the discoverer and rescuer of the cows, either of the priests or of the gods, which had been stolen by an *Asura* named PAŃI or BALA. Like AGNI, he is the possessor and bestower of riches, and the granter of all temporal blessings, when devoutly worshipped, and when propitiated by the *Soma* juice, which seems to be more especially appropriated to him, and which has the effect of inspiring him with animation and courage. Some of his attributes are, obviously, allegorical references to the locality of the firmament; as when he is said to have elevated the sun, and fixed the constellations in the sky; to be more vast than heaven and earth; and to have sundered them, when originally united (p. 169). Of another, which refers to him in the guise of a ram, no very satisfactory explanation is given; although, as remarked by M. Nève, the metamorphosis suggests some analogy between him and Jupiter Ammon. His taking part in the wars of tribes and princes, and ensuring the triumph of those he befriends, belongs to the poetical part of the personification, and arises, no doubt, from that character for personal valour derived from his metaphorical defeat of Vṛitra, and the real instrumentality of the electricity of the atmosphere, in the descent of fertilizing showers.

The Sun, Súrya or Savitṛi, occupies a much less conspicuous place, in Hindu worship, than we should have anticipated from the visible magnificence of that luminary, and his adoration by neighbouring nations. We have, in the first book, only three *Súktas* addressed to him, individually; and they convey no very strikingly expressive acknowledgment of his supremacy. Like Agni and Indra, he is the giver of temporal blessings to his worshippers; he is the source of light, moving, with exceeding swiftness, between heaven and earth, in a chariot drawn by two white-footed horses, or, as it is sometimes said, by seven,—meaning the seven days of the week. He is said to be the healer of leprosy, which may have given rise to the more modern legend of his having cured Sámba, the son of Kṛishṇa, of that disease; if it be not an unauthorized graft upon the original stem. He is represented as golden-eyed and golden-handed; mere figures of speech, although a legend is devised to account for the latter.

The text of the *Veda*, in one remarkable passage in the first book, recognizes a difference of degree in the relative dignity of the gods, and even in their age; enunciating veneration to the great gods, to the lesser, to the young, and to the old (p. 71). Among the lesser gods, an important share of adoration is enjoyed by a group avowedly subordinate to INDRA,—involving an obvious allegory,—the MARUTS, or Winds, who are naturally associated with the firmament. We have, indeed, a god of the wind, in VÁYU; but little is said of him, and that, chiefly in association with INDRA,—with whom he is identified by scholiasts on the *Veda*. The MARUTS, on the contrary, are frequently addressed as the attendants and allies of INDRA, confederated with him in the battle with VṚITRA, and aiding and encouraging his exertions. They are called the sons of PṚIŚNI, or the earth, and, also, RUDRAS, or sons of RUDRA; the meaning of which affiliations is not very clear, although, no doubt, it is allegorical. They are, also, associated, on some occasions, with AGNI; an obvious metaphor, expressing the action of wind upon fire. It is, also, intimated that they were, originally, mortal, and became immortal in consequence of worshipping AGNI, which is, also, easy of explanation. Their share in the production of rain, and their fierce and impetuous nature, are figurative representations of physical phenomena. The Scholiast endeavours to connect the history of their origin with that narrated in the *Puráńas*, but without success; and the latter, absurd as it is, seems to have no better foundation than one proposed etymology of the name,—"Do not (*má*) weep (*rodih*),"—which is merely fanciful, although it is not much worse than other explanations of the name which commentators have suggested (p. 225, note a).

The ÁDITYAS, or lesser Suns, are especially the sons of ADITI, who has, in general, the character of mother of the gods, identified, in this part of the *Veda*, with Earth, or even with the Universe; in which case she is, evidently, allegorical. Little is said of the Ádityas collectively; but some of them are individually addressed. There is no separate hymn to Vishńu; but he is mentioned as Trivikrama, or he who took three steps or paces, which Mr. Colebrooke thought might have formed the groundwork of the *Pauráńik* legend of the dwarf *Avatára*. It may have been suggestive of the fiction: but no allusion to the notion of *Avatáras* occurs in the *Veda*; and there can be little doubt that the three steps, here referred to, are the three periods of the sun's course—his rise, culmination, and setting.* Mitra is never addressed alone: he appears amongst the Viśwadevas (or gods collectively), or associated with Varuńa and Aryaman. He is said, by the Scholiast, to be a divinity presiding over the day, and, in combination with Varuńa, a dispenser of water. Varuńa occupies a rather more conspicuous place in the hymns: he is said to be the divinity presiding over the night; and, in that capacity, probably, the constellations are called his holy acts, and the moon, it is said, moves by his command. The title of king or monarch, *Rájá* or *Samrát*, is very commonly attached to his name. With Mitra, he is called the lord of light; and he supports the light on high, and makes wide the path of the sun: he grants wealth, averts

* It is expressly so stated by *Durgáchárya*, in his commentary on the *Nirukta*.—See Burnouf, Introduction to the 3rd vol. of the *Bhágavata Puráńa*, p. xxii.

evil, and protects cattle; in all which we have no trace of the station assigned to him, in later mythology, of sovereign of the waters. In one rather obscure passage, however, it is said of him, that, abiding in the ocean, he knows the course of ships; but he is, also, said, in the same stanza, to know the flight of birds and the periodical succession of the months. The notions entertained of VARUŃA, beyond that of his connexion with the sun, do not appear to be very precise. ARYAMAN is never named alone; most usually, with MITRA and VARUŃA: we have a text identifying him with the sun; and he is said, by the Scholiast, to preside over twilight. PÚSHAN, besides being occasionally named, has, in the first book, a hymn to himself, the main purport of which is to solicit his protection on a journey, particularly against robbers: he is said to be the divinity, or, rather, perhaps, the *Áditya*, or sun, presiding over the earth. The connexion of the personified dawn, or USHAS, or, rather, many dawns, or USHASAS, with the sun forms a natural portion of solar adoration: several hymns are addressed to her, the language of which involves no mystery, but is dictated by the obvious properties of the morning, not unfrequently picturesquely and poetically described.

Demigods who are, much more frequently than any of the preceding (except the MARUTS), the objects of laudation, are the two AŚWINS,—the sons of the Sun, according to later mythology, but of whose origin we have no such legend in the *Veda*, as far as we have yet gone. They are said, indeed, in one place, to have the sea (*Sindhu*) for their mother: but this is explained to intimate their identity, as affirmed by some authorities, with the sun and moon, which rise, apparently, out of the ocean. They are called Dasras,—destroyers, either of foes or of diseases; for they are the physicians of the gods. They are, also, called Násatyas,—in whom there is no untruth. They are represented as ever young, handsome, travelling in a three-wheeled and triangular car, drawn by asses, and as mixing themselves up with a variety of human transactions, bestowing benefits upon their worshippers, enabling them to foil or overcome their enemies, assisting them in their need, and extricating them from difficulty and danger. Their business seems to lie more on earth than in heaven; and they belong, by their exploits, more to heroic, than celestial, or solar, mythology. They are, however, connected, in various passages, with the radiance of the sun, and are said to be precursors of the dawn, at which season they ought to be worshipped with libations of *Soma* juice.

The Sabeism of the Hindus—if it may be so termed—differs entirely from that of the Chaldeans, in omitting the worship of the planets. The constellations are never named as objects of veneration or worship; and, although the moon appears to be occasionally intended under the name *Soma*,—particularly, when spoken of as scattering darkness,—yet the name and the adoration are, in a much less equivocal manner, applied to the *Soma* plant, the acid asclepias, actual or personified. The great importance attached to the juice of this plant is a singular part of the ancient Hindu ritual: it is sufficiently prominent even in this portion of the *Ṛig-Veda:* but almost the whole of the *Sáma-Veda* is devoted to its eulogy; and this is, no doubt, little more than a repetition of the *Soma Maṅḍala* of the *Ṛich*. The only explanation of which it is susceptible is, the delight, as well as astonishment, which the discovery of the exhilarating, if not inebriating, properties of the fermented juice of the plant must have excited in simple minds, on first becoming acquainted with its effects. This, however, is, of course, wholly different from any adoration of the moon or planets, as celestial luminaries, in which they do not appear to have participated with the sun.

INDRA and SAVITṚI thus have their respective satellites, dependent upon, and identifiable with, their principals. AGNI does not seem to have any subordinate multiples, except in the rather anomalous deifications called ÁPRÍS, which, although including certain female divinities and insensible objects, such as the doors of the sacrificial hall, are considered to be impersonations of AGNI. BRAHMAṆASPATI, also, as far as we can make out his character from the occasional stanzas addressed to him, seems to be identifiable with AGNI, with the additional attribute of presiding over prayer. The characteristic properties of this divinity, however, are not very distinctly developed in this portion of the *Veda*.

Of RUDRA, also, the character is equivocal; but it may be doubted if it partakes, in any remarkable degree, of that fierceness and wrath which belong to the RUDRA of a later date. He is termed, it is true, the slayer of heroes; but so is INDRA. The effects of his anger upon men and animals are deprecated: but he is, also, appealed to as wise and bountiful, the author of fertility, and giver of happiness; and his peculiar characteristics are, evidently, his presiding over medicinal plants and removal of disease,—attributes of a beneficent, not of a malignant and irascible, deity. As above remarked, the MARUTS, or winds, are termed his sons; and this relationship would assimilate him to INDRA. There is, also, a class of inferior deities, termed RUDRAS, who, in one passage, are worshippers of AGNI, and, in another, are the followers of INDRA; being the same as the MARUTS. So far, therefore, RUDRA might be identified with INDRA: but we have the name applied, unequivocally, to AGNI, in a hymn exclusively dedicated to that divinity (p. 70). The term denotes, according to the Scholiast, the 'terrible AGNI:' but there is no warrant for this, in the text; and we may be content, therefore, with the latter, to regard RUDRA as a form or denomination of fire.

Of the other divine personifications which occur in this first book, the particulars are too few to authorize any unexceptionable generalization. Some of them are such as every imaginative religion creates; personifications of earth, ocean, night, and of inanimate things. Female divinities make their appearance: but they are merely named, without anything being related of them; and we have, as yet, no sufficient materials on which to construct any theory of their attributes and character. The only exception is that of IḶÁ, who is called the daughter of MANUS, and his instructress in the performance of sacrifice; but what is meant by this requires further elucidation. The VIŚWADEVAS, or universal gods, do not appear, in this part of the *Veda*, as the particular class which is referred to by MANU, and in the *Puráńas*, but merely as the aggregation of the divinities elsewhere separately named, or INDRA, AGNI, MITRA, VARUŃA, and the rest.

We thus find, that most, if not all, the deities named in the hymns of the *Ŕich*—as far as those of the first *Ashtaka* extend,—are resolvable into three: AGNI, or fire; INDRA, or the firmament; and the Sun. Or, indeed,—as the sun is only a manifestation of fire,—we might resolve all the forms into two, AGNI and INDRA. We may, however, consent to take the assertion of YÁSKA, that there are, in the *Veda*, "three gods: AGNI, on the earth; VÁYU or INDRA, in the sky; and SÚRYA, in heaven; of each of whom there are many appellations, expressive of his greatness, and of the variety of his functions." There is nothing, however,—confining our negation to the present portion of the *Ŕich*,—to warrant the other assertion of YÁSKA, that "all the gods are but parts of one *átmá*, or soul, subservient to the diversification of his praises through the immensity and variety of his attributes."* The *Anukramańiká* goes further, and affirms that there is but *one deity*, the *Great Soul (Mahán Átmá)*; quoting, however, in support of this doctrine, a passage which, in its proper place, applies only to the Sun, who is there called (p. 304) "the soul of all that moves or is immoveable;"

---

* *Nirukta, Daivata Káńda*, I., 4, 5.

an expression which is, probably, to be figuratively, not literally, apprehended.

The notion of a soul of the world belongs, no doubt, to a period long subsequent to the composition of the *Súktas*. Whether their authors entertained any belief in a creator and ruler of the universe certainly does not appear from any passage hitherto met with; but, at the same time, the objects of the early worship of the Hindus — fire, the sky, the *Soma* plant, even the sun,—are addressed in language so evidently dictated by palpable physical attributes, or by the most obvious allegorical personifications, that we can scarcely think they were inspired by any deep feeling of veneration or of faith, or that the adoration of such mere and manifest elements contemplated them in any other light than as types of the power of a creator. However extravagant the expressions, we can scarcely imagine them to have been uttered in earnest, particularly as proceeding from men of evident talent and observation, endowed with more than common intellectual activity and acuteness of perception.

Leaving the question of the primary religion of the Hindus for further investigation, we may now consider what degree of light this portion of the *Veda* reflects upon their social and political condition. It has been a favourite notion, with some eminent scholars, that the Hindus, at the period of the composition of the hymns, were a nomadic and pastoral people. This opinion seems to rest solely upon the frequent solicitations for food, and for horses and cattle, which are found in the hymns, and is unsupported by any more positive statements. That the Hindus were not nomads is evident from the repeated allusions to fixed dwellings, and villages, and towns; and we can scarcely suppose them to have been, in this respect, behind their barbarian enemies, the overthrow of whose numerous cities is so often spoken of. A pastoral people they might have been, to some extent; but they were, also, and, perhaps, in a still greater degree, an agricultural people, as is evidenced by their supplications for abundant rain and for the fertility of the earth, and by the mention of agricultural products, particularly, barley (p. 67). They were a manufacturing people; for the art of weaving, the labours of the carpenter, and the fabrication of golden and of iron mail, are alluded to: and, what is more remarkable, they were a maritime and mercantile people.

Not only are the *Súktas* familiar with the ocean and its phenomena, but we have merchants described as pressing earnestly on board ship, for the sake of gain (p. 152); and we have a naval expedition against a foreign island, or continent (*dwípa*), frustrated by a shipwreck (p. 307). They must, also, have made some advance in astronomical computation; as the adoption of an intercalary month, for the purpose of adjusting the solar and lunar years to each other, is made mention of (p. 65). Civilization must have, therefore, made considerable progress; and the Hindus must have spread to the sea-coast, possibly along the Sindhu or Indus, into Cutch and Gujerat, before they could have engaged in navigation and commerce. That they had extended themselves from a more northern site, or that they were a northern race, is rendered probable from the peculiar expression used, on more than one occasion, in soliciting long life,—when the worshipper asks for a hundred *winters* (*himas*); a boon not likely to have been desired by the natives of a warm climate (p. 176). They appear, also, to have been a fair-complexioned people, at least, comparatively, and foreign invaders of India; as it is said (p. 259) that Indra divided the fields among his *white*-complexioned friends, after destroying the indigenous barbarian races: for such, there can be little doubt, we are to understand by the expression *Dasyu*, which so often recurs, and which is often defined to signify one who not only does not perform religious rites, but attempts to disturb them, and harass their performers: the latter are the *Aryas*, the *Arya*, or respectable, or Hindu, or *Arian* race. *Dasyu*, in later language, signifies a thief, a robber; and *Arya*, a wealthy or respectable man: but the two terms are constantly used, in the text of the *Veda*, as contrasted with each other, and as expressions of religious and political antagonists; requiring, therefore, no violence of conjecture to identify the *Dasyus* with the indigenous tribes of India, refusing to adopt the ceremonial of the *Aryas*, a more civilized, but intrusive, race, and availing themselves of every opportunity to assail them, to carry off their cattle, disturb their rites, and impede their progress,—to little purpose, it should seem, as the *Aryas* commanded the aid of

Indra, before whose thunderbolt the numerous cities, or hamlets, of the *Dasyus* were swept away.

We have no particular intimation of the political condition of the Hindus, except the specification of a number of names of princes, many of which are peculiar to the *Veda*, and differ from those of the heroic poems and *Puráńas*. A few are identical; but the nomenclature evidently belongs to a period anterior to the construction of the dynasties of the Sun and Moon, no allusion to which, thus far, occurs. The princes named are, sometimes, described as in hostility with each other; and the condition of the provinces of India occupied by the Hindus was, no doubt, the same which it continued to be until the Mohammedan conquest,—parcelled out amongst insignificant principalities, under petty and contending princes.

Upon a subject of primary importance in the history of Hindu society, the distinctions of caste, the language of the *Súktas*—of the first *Ashíaka*, at least,—is by no means explicit. Whenever collectively alluded to, mankind are said to be distinguished into five sorts, or classes, or, literally, five men, or beings (*pancha kshitayah*). The commentator explains this term to denote the four castes, *Bráhmańa*, *Kshattriya*, *Vaiśya*, and *S'údra*, and the barbarian, or *Nisháda*: but Sáyańa, of course, expresses the received impressions of his own age. We do not meet with the denominations *Kshattriya* or *S'údra* in any text of the first book, nor with that of *Vaiśya*; for *Viś*, which does occur, is, there, a synonym of man in general. *Bráhmańa* is met with, but in what sense is questionable. In the neuter form, *Brahma*, it usually implies prayer, or praise, or sacrificial food, or, in one place, preservation (p. 274); in its masculine form, *Brahmá*, it occurs as the praiser, or reciter, of the hymn (p. 204), or as the particular priest, so denominated, who presides over the ceremonial of a sacrifice (p. 24): and in neither case does it necessarily imply a *Bráhmańa* by caste; for, that the officiating priests might not be *Brahmans* appears from the part taken by VIŚWÁMITRA at the sacrifice of S'UNAHŚEPA, who, although, according to tradition, by birth a *Kshattriya*, exercises the functions of the priesthood. There is one phrase which is in favour of considering the *Bráhmańa* as the member of a caste, as distinguished from that of the military caste (p. 279): "If you, INDRA and AGNI, have ever delighted in a *Bráhmańa*, or a *Rájá*, then come hither:" but even this can scarcely be regarded as decisive. A hymn that occurs in a subsequent part of the *Veda* has, however, been translated by Mr. Colebrooke, in which the four castes are specified by name, and the usual fable of their origin from *Brahmá*, alluded to.* Further research is necessary, therefore, before a final sentence can be pronounced.

From this survey of the contents of the first book of the *Rig-Veda*, although some very important ques-

---

* In the *Purusha Súkta*, in the eighth *Ashtaka*, we have this verse: "His mouth became a priest [*Bráhmańa*]; his arm was made a soldier [*Kshattriya*]; his thigh was transformed into a husbandman [*Vaiśya*]; from his feet sprung the servile man [*Súdra*]."—Colebrooke on the Religious Ceremonies of the Hindus, *Asiatic Researches*, Vol. vii., p. 251.

tions remain to be answered, it is indisputably evident that the hymns it comprises represent a form of religious worship, and a state of society, very dissimilar to those we meet with in all the other scriptural authorities of the Hindus, whether *Bráhmańas*, *Upanishads*, *Itihásas* (or heroic poems), or *Puráńas*. Various notions, and personifications, and persons have, no doubt, been adopted from the *Veda*, and transmitted to subsequent periods, although, not unfrequently, with important modifications; but the great mass of the ritual, all the most popular deities, possibly the principal laws and distinctions of society, and the whole body of the heroic and *Pauráńik dramatis personæ*, have no place, no part, in the *Súktas* of the *Ṛig-Veda*. That the latter preceded the former by a vast interval is, therefore, a necessary inference: for the immense and complicated machinery of the whole literature and mythology of the Hindus must have been of gradual and slow development; and, as many of the genealogical and historical traditions preserved by the *Rámáyańa*, *Mahábhárata*, the poems, plays, and *Puráńas*, are not likely to be mere inventions, but may have had their foundations in fact, then the course of events, the extension of the Hindus through India, the origin and succession of regal dynasties, and the formation of powerful principalities, all unknown to the *Sanhitá*, are equally indicative of the lapse of centuries between the composition of the *Súktas* and the date of the earliest works that are subsequent to the great religious, social, and political changes which, in the interval, had taken place. If the hymns of the *Sanhitá* are genuine,—and there is no reason why they should not be so; if there is any shadow of truth in the historical portions of the *Rámáyaña* and *Mahábhárata*,—and there must be some; a thousand years would not be too long an interval for the altered conditions which are depictured in the older and in the more recent compositions. Considerations deduced from the probable progress of Hindu literature are calculated to confirm this view of the distance that separates the age of the *Veda* from that of the later writings, and, in this manner, to lead to an approximation to the era of the former. The *Súktas* themselves are, confessedly, the compositions of various periods,—as we might conclude from internal evidence, —and were, probably, falling into forgetfulness, before they were collected into the *Sanhitás*. We then have a succession of schools engaged in collecting, arranging, and remodelling them, after which come the *Bráhmañas*, citing their contents in a manner which proves that their collective compilation had become extensively current and was readily recognizable.

After the *Bráhmañas* come the *Sútras*, rules for the application of the passages cited in the *Bráhmañas* to religious ceremonies; the works of authors to all of whom a high antiquity is assigned, —ÁPASTAMBA, KÁTYÁYANA, and others, who quote the *Bráhmañas* as their authorities. Of the philosophical *Sútras*, the *Sánkhya*, which seems to be the oldest system, is, perhaps, independent of the *Veda*; but the *Púrva* and *Uttara Mímánsás* are, declaredly, intended to expound and elucidate the philosophy and the practices of the *Veda*, and are, therefore, necessarily subsequent to the *Sanhitá* and *Bráhmaña*, although attributed to names of ancient celebrity,—JAIMINI and VYÁSA. These works were, possibly, contemporary with the liturgical aphorisms; the *Vedánta Sútras* being, also, posterior to the *Upanishads*. Now, all these writings are older than MANU, whose cosmogony is, evidently, a system of eclecticism compiled from the *Upanishads*, the *Sánkhya*, and the *Vedánta*, and many of whose laws, I learn from Dr. Müller, are found in the liturgical *Sútras*. Yet MANU notices no *Avatáras*, no RÁMA, no KṚISHṆA, and is, consequently, admitted to be long anterior to the growth of their worship as set forth in the *Rámáyaña* and *Mahábhárata*.

There is, in MANU, a faint intimation that Buddhistical opinions were beginning to exert an influence over the minds of men,—in the admission that the greatest of virtues is abstinence from injury to living beings,—which would make his laws posterior to the sixth century B.C.' But, conjecturing the probable dates of the heroic poems to be about the third century B.C., we cannot place MANU lower than the fifth, or sixth, at least; beyond which we have the whole body of philosophical and *Vaidik* literature. This would carry us, for the age of the *Bráhmaña*, to the seventh, or eighth, at the least; and we cannot allow less than four or five centuries for the composition and currency of the hymns, and the occurrence of those important changes, both civil and religious, which the *Bráhmańa* exhibits. This will bring us to the same era as that which has previously been computed, or about twelve or thirteen centuries B.C. Mr. Colebrooke, from astronomical data, would give the *Súktas* a higher antiquity; as he places their aggregation, or *Sanhitá*, fourteen centuries B.C., a date not far from that which is here suggested.[a] All this is, no doubt, to be received with very great reservation; for, in dealing with Hindu chronology, we have no trustworthy landmarks, no fixed eras, no comparative history, to guide us. In proposing the above dates, therefore, nothing more than conjecture is intended; and it may be wide of the truth. We can scarcely be far wrong, however, in assigning a very remote date to most, if not to all, the *Súktas* of the *Ṛig-Veda*, and in considering them to be amongst the oldest extant records of the ancient world.

The text which has served for the following translation comprises the *Súktas* of the *Ṛig-Veda* and the commentary of SÁYAŃA *Achárya*, printed, by Dr. Müller, from a collation of manuscripts, of which he has given an account in his Introduction.[b] SÁYAŃA *Achárya* was the brother of MÁDHAVA *Achárya*, the prime minister of VÍRA BUKKA RÁYA, *Rájá* of VIJAYANAGARA in the fourteenth century, a munificent patron of Hindu literature. Both the brothers are celebrated as scholars; and many important works are attributed to them,—not only scholia on the *Sanhitás* and *Bráh-*

---

[a] *Asiatic Researches*, Vol. vii., 283, and Vol. viii., 483.

[b] *Ṛig-Veda*, Preface, p. vii.

maṅas of the *Vedas*, but original works on grammar and law; the fact, no doubt, being, that they availed themselves of those means which their situation and influence secured them, and employed the most learned Brahmans they could attract to VIJAYANAGARA upon the works which bear their name, and to which they, also, contributed their own labour and learning. Their works were, therefore, compiled under peculiar advantages, and are deservedly held in the highest estimation.

The scholia of SÁYAṄA on the text of the *Ṛig-Veda* comprise three district portions. The first interprets the original text, or, rather, translates it into more modern Sanskrit, fills up any ellipse, and, if any legend is briefly alluded to, narrates it in detail; the next portion of the commentary is a grammatical analysis of the text, agreeably to the system of PÁṄINI, whose aphorisms, or *Sútras*, are quoted; and the third portion is an explanation of the accentuation of the several words. These two last portions are purely technical, and are untranslateable. The first portion constitutes the basis of the English translation: for, although the interpretation of SÁYAṄA may be, occasionally, questioned, he undoubtedly had a knowledge of his text far beyond the pretensions of any European scholar, and must have been in possession, either through his own learning, or that of his assistants, of all the interpretations which had been perpetuated, by traditional teaching, from the earliest times.

In addition to these divisions of his commentary, SÁYAṆA prefaces each *Súkta* by a specification of its author, or *Ṛishi*; of the deity, or deities, to whom it is addressed; of the rhythmical structure of the several *Ṛichas*, or stanzas; and of the *Viniyoga*, the application of the hymn, or of portions of it, to the religious rites at which they are to be repeated. I have been unable to make use of this latter part of the description; as the ceremonies are, chiefly, indicated by their titles alone, and their peculiar details are not to be determined without a more laborious investigation than the importance or interest of the subject appeared to me to demand.

I have, perhaps, to offer, if not an excuse, a plea, for retaining the original denominations of the divisions of the *Veda*, as *Sanhitá*, *Maṇḍala*, *Ashṭaka*, *Adhyáya*, *Anuváka*, *Súkta*, and *Varga*, instead of attempting to express them by English equivalents. It appeared to me, however, that, although the terms Collection, Circle, Book, Lecture, Chapter, Hymn, and Section might have been taken as substitutes, and, in a general sense, were allowable, yet they in no instance exactly expressed the meaning of the originals, and their use might have conveyed erroneous impressions. I have considered it advisable, therefore, to treat the original terms as if they were proper names, and have merely rendered them in Roman characters. I do not apprehend that any great inconvenience will be experienced from the use of these original designations, their conventional purport being readily remembered. I have, also, specified the metre that is employed in each *Súkta*, in order to show the variety that prevails. The description of the different kinds will be found in Mr. Colebrooke's Essay on Sanskrit and Prakrit Prosody, in the tenth volume of the *Asiatic Researches*.

H. H. WILSON.

1st *July*, 1850.

ṚIG-VEDA SANHITÁ.

FIRST ASHṬAKA.

FIRST ADHYÁYA.

ANUVÁKA I.

SÚKTA I. MAṄḌALA I.

The first *Súkta* or Hymn is addressed to AGNI. The *Ṛishi* or author is MADHUCHCHHANDAS, the son of VIŚWÁMITRA. The metre is *Gáyatri*.

1. I glorify AGNI,* the high priest of the sacri- Varga I.

* A great variety of etymologies are devised to explain the meaning of the term *Agni*, the most of which are, obviously, fanciful, but the import of which expresses the notions entertained of his character and functions. On earth, he is invoked (*níyate*) the first (*agra*) of the gods; in heaven, he is the leader (*agraṇí*) of the hosts of the gods; he is the first of the gods (*prathamo devatánám*); he was the first-born of the gods (*sa vá esho'gre devatánám ajáyata*). In these derivations, *Agni* is compounded, irregularly, out of *agra*, first, and *ní*, to lead. It is also derived from *anga*, body; because he offers his own substance, in the lighting of the sacrificial fire.' The author of a *Nirukta*, or glossary, called *Stháuláshṭhívin*, derives it from the root *knú*, with the negative prefixed (*aknopayati*), he who does not spare the fuel. Another compiler of a glossary, *Śákapúṇi*, derives the word from three roots, *i*, to go, *anj*, to anoint, and *dah*, to burn, collectively; the

fice,[a] the divine,[b] the ministrant,[c] who presents the oblation (to the gods), and is the possessor of great wealth.[d]

2. May that AGNI, who is to be celebrated by both ancient and modern sages,[e] conduct the gods hither.

3. Through AGNI the worshipper obtains that

---

letters being arbitrarily changed to *ag*, and *ni*, from the root *ni*, being added. See, also, *Yáska's Nirukta*, 7, 14.

[a] *Agni* is termed the *Purohita*, the priest who superintends family rites, or because he is one of the sacred fires in which oblations are first (*puras*) offered (*hita*).

[b] *Deva*, which, in common use, means a god, is ordinarily explained, in the passages in which it occurs in the *Veda*, as 'the bright, shining, radiant;' being derived from *div*, to shine: or it is also explained, one who abides in the sky or heaven (*dyusthána*). It is, here, also optionally rendered, liberal, donor; the sense of giving being ascribed to the same radical.

[c] *Ṛitwij*, a ministering priest, or, according to some, the *Ṛitwij* who is also the *Hotṛi*,—the term that follows in the text,—the priest who actually presents the oblation, or who invokes or summons the deities to the ceremony, accordingly as the word is derived from *hu*, to sacrifice, or *hve*, to call.

[d] The word is *ratnadhátama*, lit., holder of jewels: but *ratna* is explained, generally, wealth, and, figuratively, signifies the reward of religious rites.

[e] The terms *púrva* and *nútana*, former and recent, applied to *Ṛishis*, or sages, are worthy of remark, as intimating the existence of earlier teachers and older hymns. The old *Ṛishis* are said to be *Bhṛigu*, *Angiras*, and others; perhaps, those who are elsewhere termed *Prajápatis*.—*Vishṇu Puráṇa*, p. 49.

affluence which increases day by day, which is the source of fame, and the multiplier of mankind.

4. AGNI, the unobstructed sacrifice[a] of which thou art, on every side,[b] the protector, assuredly reaches the gods.

5. May AGNI, the presenter of oblations, the attainer of knowledge,[c] he who is true, renowned, and divine, come hither, with the gods.

6. Whatever good thou mayest, AGNI, bestow upon the giver (of the oblation), that, verily, ANGIRAS, shall revert to thee.[d] Varga II.

---

[a] *Adhwaram yajnam.* The first is usually employed as a substantive, meaning, also, sacrifice: it is here used as an adjective, signifying free from injury or interruption,—that is, by *Rákshasas*, evil spirits, always on the alert to vitiate an act of worship.

[b] "On every side" alludes to the fires which, at a sacrifice, should be lighted at the four cardinal points, east, west, south, and north,—termed, severally, the *Áhavaníya*, *Márjáliya*, *Gárhapatya*, and *Agnídhríya*.

[c] *Kavikratu* is here explained to signify one by whom either knowledge or religious acts (*kratu*) have been acquired or performed (*kránta*). The compound is commonly used as a synonym of *Agni*.

[d] That is, the wealth bestowed upon the *Yajamána*—the person by whom, or on whose behalf, the sacrifice is performed,—will enable him to multiply his oblations, by which *Agni*, again, will benefit. Instead of *Agni* repeated, we have, in the second place, *Angiras*, as a synonym, which, in *Manu* and all the *Puráńas*, is the name of a *Rishi* or *Prajápati*, one of the primitive mind-born sons of Brahmá: and the appellation is used, frequently, in the text of the *Veda*, in that sense, as the designation of a *Rishi*, the founder of a family, or of a school. The commentator quotes

7. We approach thee, AGNI, with reverential homage in our thoughts, daily, both morning and evening;

Yáska, for the identity of *Angiras* with *Angára*, a live coal; and a passage from the *Aitareya Bráhmaṅa* is cited, in which it is said, "the coals became the Angirasas" (*ye'ngárá ásanste'ngiraso 'bhavan*). The identification of *Angiras* with *Agni*, in function, though not in person, is the subject of a legend, told, rather confusedly and obscurely, in the *Mahábhárata*, *Vana-parva* (printed edition, Vol. i., p. 712), by *Márkaṅḍeya* to *Yudhishṭhira*, in reply to his question, how it happened, formerly, that *Agni*, having gone to the forest, and his functions having ceased, *Angiras* became *Agni*, and conveyed the oblations to the gods. Connected with this question, he also inquires, how it is that *Agni*, who is one, should become many. *Márkaṅḍeya* therefore relates, that *Agni*, having engaged in penance, and relinquishing his duties, the *Muni Angiras* took upon him his office, and, when he prevailed upon *Agni* to resume it, became his son: his descendants, the *Angirasas*, are, therefore, also the descendants of *Agni*, or so many *Agnis*, or fires. Their enumeration, which follows at some length, shows them to be, for the most part, personifications of light, of luminous bodies, of divisions of time, of celestial phenomena, and fires adapted to peculiar occasions, as the full and change of the moon, or to particular rites, as the *Aswamedha*, *Rájasúya*, the *Páka-yajnas* (or sacrifices with food), obsequial and funeral fires, expiatory fires, and the like. The legend is, possibly, intended to represent the organization of worship with fire,—which, in the first instance, was of a primitive and simple character,—and its appropriation to various occasions, by *Angiras* and his disciples. The *Mahábhárata* is not contented with the first account, but gives a second, in which the first *Agni* is called *Saha*; and he is said to have hidden himself in the ocean, to avoid the approach of *Niyata*, the son of *Bharata*, the fire of the funeral-pile. The text says,

8. Thee, the radiant, the protector of sacrifices, the constant illuminator of truth, increasing in thine own dwelling.[a]

9. AGNI, be unto us easy of access; as is a father to his son: be ever present with us, for our good.

SÚKTA II.

The *Rishi* is MADHUCHCHHANDAS; the metre, *Gáyatri*. Of the nine stanzas of which the Hymn consists, three are addressed to VÁYU, Wind; three, to INDRA and VÁYU, conjointly; and three, to MITRA and VARUṆA.

1. VÁYU, pleasant to behold,[b] approach. These Varga III.

"through fear:" the commentary says, either through fear of being rendered impure by his contact, or being ashamed of his relationship; *Niyata* being his own grandson. The gods coming to look for *Agni*, he designated, as his substitute, *Atharvan*, also called *Angiras*, who, for a time, acted as *Agni*, until the latter was induced to resume his office. The legend is constructed, as the commentary shows, out of *Vaidik* texts: but the details are clumsily and contradictorily put together; indicating, perhaps, their almost obsolete antiquity at the time of the compilation of the *Mahábhárata*.

[a] *Sve dame, sud domo*, the chamber in which fire-worship is performed, and in which the fire increases by the oblations poured upon it. *Dama*, for a home, or house, is peculiar to the *Vedas*.

[b] *Váyu* is invoked in a visible form, as the deity presiding over the wind. It is doubtful if the expressions which, in this and similar instances, intimate personality are to be understood as indicating actual figures or idols: the personification is, probably, only poetical.

libations[a] are prepared for thee. Drink of them; hear our innovation.

2. VÁYU, thy praisers praise thee with holy praises,[b] having poured out the *Soma* juice, and knowing the (fit) season.

3. VÁYU, thy approving speech[c] comes to the giver (of the libation), and to many (others who invite thee) to drink of the *Soma* juice.

4. INDRA and VÁYU, these libations are poured out (for you). Come hither, with food (for us). Verily, the drops (of the *Soma* juice) await you both.

5. INDRA and VÁYU, abiding in the sacrificial rite, you are aware of these libations. Come, both, (then,) quickly, hither.

Varg. IV. 6. VÁYU and INDRA, come to the rite of the

---

[a] These *Somas* are libations of the juice of the *Soma* plant, the acid Asclepias or *Sarcostema viminalis*, which yields to expressure a copious milky juice, of a mild nature and subacid taste.—*Roxburgh*, ii., 32. According to Mr. Stevenson, it is not used, in sacrifices, until it has gone through the process of fermentation, and has become a strong spirituous beverage.—*Introduction to Translation of the Sáma-Veda*. This is warranted by numerous expressions in the following hymns. It is, evidently, the *Hom* of the *Parsees*; although they affirm, that the plant is not to be found in India, and procure it from the mountains of Gilan and Mazenderan, and the neighbourhood of Yezd.

[b] With *ukthas*, also designated *śastras*, hymns of praise, recited, not chanted, or sung.

[c] *Váyu* is supposed to say, I will drink the libation.

sacrificer; for thus, men,[a] will completion be speedily (attained) by the ceremony.

7. I invoke MITRA,[b] of pure vigour, and VARUṆA, the devourer of foes,—the joint accomplishers of the act bestowing water (on the earth).[c]

8. MITRA and VARUṆA, augmenters of water,[d] dispensers of water, you connect this perfect rite with its true (reward).

9. Sapient MITRA and VARUṆA, prosper our sacrifice, and increase our strength. You are born for the benefit of many; you are the refuge of multitudes.

---

[a] *Nará*, dual of *nara*, a man. This term is frequently applied to divine beings: it is usually explained, by the Scholiast, *netri*, leader or guide; but it may be doubted if it does not convey the sense of male or mortal, alluding to the limited existence of the divinities. In this place, it is said to be applicable to *Váyu* and *Indra*; because they are possessed of manly vigour (*paurusheṇa sámarthyenopetau*).

[b] *Mitra*, in its ordinary sense, is a name of the sun; *Varuṇa*, of the regent of the waters: but they are, both, included among the twelve *Ádityas*; and, in another place, *Mitra* is said to be the deity presiding over day; *Varuṇa*, over night: see p. 227, note b.

[c] *Dhiyaṁ ghṛitáchîm sádhantá*. The two first words, in the senses here explained, *dhi*, an act, and *ghṛitáchi*, water-shedding, are peculiar to the *Veda*. As identified with the sun, or as *Ádityas*, *Mitra* and *Varuṇa* are said to cause rain, indirectly, by producing evaporation. The vapours thus raised, becoming condensed in the atmosphere, descend again, in showers.

[d] *Ṛitávṛidhau*. *Ṛita* usually means true or truth; but, in the *Veda*, it imports, also, water and sacrifice.

SÚKTA III.

The *Ṛishi* and metre are the same as in the two preceding Hymns. Of twelve stanzas, three are addressed to the AŚWINS; three, to INDRA; three, to the VIŚWADEVAS; and three, to SARASWATÍ.

Varga V. 1. AŚWINS,[a] cherishers of pious acts, long-armed,[b] accept, with outstretched hands, the sacrificial viands.

2. AŚWINS, abounding in mighty acts, guides (of devotion), endowed with fortitude, listen, with unaverted minds, to our praises.

3. AŚWINS, destroyers of foes,[c] exempt from untruth, leaders in the van of heroes,[d] come to the

---

[a] The *Aświns* are the two sons of the Sun,—begotten during his metamorphosis as a horse (*aśwa*),—endowed with perpetual youth and beauty, and physicians of the gods. They are the heroes of many legends in the *Puráńas*, but of still more in this *Veda*. The enumeration of their wonderful actions is the especial subject of Hymns CXVI. and CXVII.

[b] *Purubhujá*, which may be also rendered, great eaters.

[c] *Dasrá*, destroyers, either of foes or of diseases. The medical character of the *Aświns* is a *Vaidik* tradition, as in a text quoted by *Sáyańa* (*aświnau vai devánám bhishajáviti śrutch*), the two *Aświns*, verily, are the physicians of the gods.—*Veda*.

[d] This is the Scholiast's interpretation of a rather curious compound, *Rudravartaní*. *Rudra*, from the root *rud*, implies weeping; as say the *Taittiríyas*,—Inasmuch as he wept, thence came the property or function of *rudra* (*yad arodít tad rudrasya rudratwam*). This is, also, the *Pauráńik* etymology.—*Vishńu Pur.*, p. 58. The *Vájasaneyis* make the verb causal, "they cause to weep;" therefore they are *rudras* (*yad rodayanti tasmád rudráh*). From these texts *Sáyańa* renders *rudra*, heroes, they who make their

mixed libations sprinkled on the lopped sacred grass.[a]

4. INDRA, of wonderful splendour, come hither. These libations, ever pure, expressed by the fingers (of the priests), are desirous of thee.

5. INDRA, apprehended by the understanding, and appreciated by the wise, approach, and accept the prayers of the priest, as he offers the libation.

6. Fleet INDRA, with the tawny coursers, come hither to the prayers (of the priest), and in this libation accept our (proffered) food.

7. Universal Gods,[b] protectors and supporters of men, bestowers (of rewards), come to the libation of the worshipper. Varga VI.

---

enemies weep. *Vartani* means a road or way,—or here, it is said, the front of the way, the van; and the compound means, they who are in the van of warriors.

[a] *Vriktabarhishah.* The sacred *kuśa* grass (*Poa cynosuroides*), after having had the roots cut off, is spread on the *vedi* or altar; and upon it the libation of *Soma* juice, or oblation of clarified butter, is poured out. In other places, a tuft of it, in a similar position, is supposed to form a fitting seat for the deity or deities invoked to the sacrifice. According to Mr. Stevenson, it is also strown over the floor of the chamber in which the worship is performed.

[b] The *Viśwadevas* are, sometimes, vaguely applied to divinities in general; but they also form a class, whose station and character are imperfectly noticed, but who are entitled, at most religious rites, to share in the solemnity. In this and the two next stanzas, forming a *Tricha*, or triad, to be recited at the worship of the *Viśwadevas*, some of their attributes are particularized, connecting them with the elements.

8. May the swift-moving universal Gods, the shedders of rain, come to the libation; as the solar rays come, diligently, to the days.

9. May the universal Gods, who are exempt from decay, omniscient,[a] devoid of malice, and bearers (of riches), accept the sacrifice.

10. May SARASWATÍ,[b] the purifier, the bestower of food, the recompenser of worship with wealth, be attracted, by our offered viands, to our rite.

11. SARASWATÍ, the inspirer of those who delight in truth, the instructress of the right-minded, has accepted our sacrifice.

12. SARASWATÍ[c] makes manifest, by her acts, a mighty river, and (in her own form,) enlightens all understandings.

---

[a] The original word is uncommon, *ehimáyásah*. The Scholiast explains it by those who have obtained knowledge universally (*sarvato vyáptaprajnáh*). Or it may refer, *Sáyaṇa* states, to a legend, in which the *Viśwadevas* addressed the *Agni Sauchíka*,—who had gone into the water,—saying, *ehi*, come, *má yásìh*, do not go away; from whence they derived the appellation *ehimáyásah*. It is more than probable that the origin and import of the term were forgotten when *Sáyaṇa* wrote.

[b] *Saraswatí* is, here, as elsewhere, the *Vágdevatá*, divinity of speech: other attributes are alluded to in the text; the three stanzas forming a *tricha*, to be repeated at her worship.

[c] *Saraswatí* is here identified with the river so named.

ANUVÁKA II.

SÚKTA I. (IV.)

The *Rishi* and metre continue unchanged: the Hymn is addressed to INDRA.

1. Day by day we invoke the doer of good works, for our protection; as a good milch-cow, for the milking, (is called by the milker). Varga VII.

2. Drinker of the *Soma* juice, come to our (daily) rites, and drink of the libation. The satisfaction of (thee who art) the bestower of riches is, verily, (the cause of) the gift of cattle.[a]

3. We recognize thee in the midst of the right-minded, who are nearest to thee. Come to us; pass us not by, to reveal (thyself to others).[b]

4. Go, worshipper, to the wise and uninjured INDRA,—who bestows the best (of blessings) on thy friends,—and ask him of the (fitness of the) learned (priest who recites his praise).[c]

5. Let our ministers, earnestly performing his

---

[a] That is, if *Indra* be satisfied, he will augment the worshipper's herds. The notion is very elliptically expressed.

[b] Here, again, we have elliptical phraseology. The original is *má no ati khyah*, lit., do not speak beyond us: the complete sense is supplied by the Scholiast.

[c] The injunction is addressed to the *Yajamána*, who is desired to ask if the *Hotri*, or invoker whom he employs, is fit for his duty. The *Hotri* himself is supposed to enjoin this.

worship, exclaim:[a] Depart, ye revilers, from hence and every other place (where he is adored).

Varga VIII. 6. Destroyer of foes, let our enemies say we are prosperous; let men (congratulate us). May we ever abide in the felicity (derived from the favour) of INDRA.

7. Offer to INDRA, the pervader (of every rite of libation), the juice that is present (at the three ceremonies), the grace of the sacrifice, the exhilarator of mankind, the perfecter of the act, the favourite of (that INDRA) who gives happiness (to the offerer).[b]

8. Having drunk, S'ATAKRATU,[c] of this (*Soma* juice), thou becamest the slayer of the VṚITRAS:[d] thou defendest the warrior in battle.

[a] The Scholiast would explain *bruvantu*, "let them say," by let them praise *Indra*; but this does not seem to be necessary. The sense is connected with what follows: let them say *procul este, profani*.

[b] These epithets of the *Soma* juice would be somewhat unintelligible, without the aid of the Scholiast. The perfecter of the acts, *karmáṇi prápnuvantam*, is his rendering of *patayat*, causing to fall; and the last phrase, *mandayatsakham*, the friend of the delighter, he explains as in the text.

[c] *Satakratu*, a name of *Indra*, is explained, by *Sáyaṇa*, he who is connected with a hundred (many) acts, religious rites, *bahukarmayukta*, either as their performer, or their object: or it may be rendered, endowed with great wisdom; *kratu* implying either *karma*, act, or *prajná*, knowledge. In the first sense, the word may be the source of the *Pauráṇik* fiction, that the dignity of *Indra* is attainable by a hundred *Aśwamedhas*.

[d] *Vṛitráṇám*, of the enemies, of whom the *Asura Vṛitra* was the

9. We offer to thee, S'ATAKRATU, the mighty in battle, (sacrificial) food, for the acquirement, INDRA, of riches.

10. Sing unto that INDRA, who is the protector of wealth, the mighty, the accomplisher of good deeds, the friend of the offerer of the libation.

SÚKTA II. (V.)

The deity, *Ṛishi*, and metre, unchanged.

1. Hasten hither, friends, offering praises:[*] sit down, and sing, repeatedly, the praises of INDRA. Varga IX.

2. When the libation is poured forth, respectively praise INDRA, the discomfiter of many enemies, the lord of many blessings.

3. May he be, to us, for the attainment of our objects; may he be, to us, for the acquirement of riches; may he be, to us, for the acquisition of knowledge; may he come to us with food.

4. Sing to that INDRA, whose enemies, in combats, await not his coursers harnessed in his car.

5. These pure *Soma* juices, mixed with curds, are

---

head, according to the Scholiast. We shall hear more of *Vṛitra* hereafter.

[*] *Stomaváhasaḥ*, lit., bearing praises. Rosen translates it *sacra ferentes*; M. Langlois, *vous qui avez un trésor d'hymnes* (*sacrés*). *Sáyaṅa* explains the expression, "presenting, in this rite, *Trivṛit*, *Panchadaśa*, and others," that is, collections of laudatory stanzas in the *Ṛig-Veda*, so denominated.—*Vishṅu Puráṅa*, p. 42.

poured out for the satisfaction of the drinker of the libations.

Varga X. 6. Thou, INDRA, performer of good works, hast suddenly become of augmented vigour, for the sake of drinking the libation, and (maintaining) seniority[a] (among the gods).

7. INDRA, who art the object of praises, may these pervading *Soma* juices enter into thee: may they be propitious for thy (attainment of) superior intelligence.

8. The chants (of the *Sáma*)[b] have magnified thee, S'ATAKRATU; the hymns (of the *Ṛich*) have magnified thee: may our praises magnify thee.

9. May INDRA, the unobstructed protector, enjoy these manifold (sacrificial) viands, in which all manly properties abide.

10. INDRA, who art the object of praises, let not men do injury to our persons. Thou art mighty: keep off violence.

---

[a] *Jyaishṭhyam*, abstract of *jyaishṭha*, elder, oldest; but it may, also, mean best or chiefest.

[b] The Scholiast supplies these particulars, the terms of the text being simply *stomáh* and *ukthá*: the former, he says, are the praises of the singers of the *Sáma* (*Sámagánám stotráṇi*); the latter, the hymns of the reciters of the *Bahṛich* (*Bahṛichánám śastráṇi*). But, of this and other passages where *Sáyaṇa* inserts the designation of other *Vedas*,—the *Sáma* and the *Yajush*,—it is to be observed, that the accuracy of his additions involves the prior existence of those *Vedas*, at least to the hymns of the *Ṛich* in which they are supposed to be alluded to; a conclusion which there is reason to hesitate admitting.

SÚKTA III. (VI.)

The *Rishi* and metre continued. The three first stanzas and the last are addressed to INDRA; the rest, to the MARUTS, or Winds, with, or without, INDRA.

1. The circumstationed (inhabitants of the three worlds)[a] associate with (INDRA), the mighty (Sun), the indestructive (fire), the moving (wind), and the lights that shine in the sky.[b] Varga XI.

2. They (the charioteers,) harness to his car his

---

[a] The text has only *pari tasthushah*, those who are standing around. The *lokatrayavartinah práńinah*, the living beings of the three worlds, is the explanation of the Scholiast.

[b] Of the three first objects the text gives only the epithets *bradhna*, the mighty, to which *Sáyana* adds *Áditya*, the Sun; *arusha*, the non-injuring, to which Fire is supplied; and *charat* the moving, an epithet of Wind. The last phrase is complete,—*rochante rochaná divi*. *Sáyańa's* additions are supported by a *Bráhmańa*, which explains the epithets as equivalent, severally, to *Áditya*, *Agni*, and *Váyu* (*Asau vá, Áditya bradhnah;" "Agnir vá arushah;" "Váyur vai charan*): we may, therefore, admit it. The identification of *Indra* with the three implies, the Scholiast says, his supremacy;—he is *paramaiśvaryayukta*: but the text says they join (*yunjanti*); and it does not appear, exactly, whom; for *Indra* is not named. As the following stanzas show, however, that the hymn is addressed to *Indra*, he may be allowed to keep his place as essentially one with the sun, fire, wind, and the constellations.

two desirable coursers,[a] placed on either hand,[b] bay-coloured, high-spirited, chief-bearing.[c]

3. Mortals, you owe your (daily) birth (to such an INDRA), who, with the rays of the morning, gives sense to the senseless, and, to the formless, form.[d]

4. Thereafter, verily, those who bear names invoked in holy rites, (the MARUTS),[e] having seen the rain about to be engendered), instigated him to resume his embryo condition (in the clouds).

5. Associated with the conveying MARUTS, the traversers of places difficult of access, thou, INDRA, hast discovered the cows hidden in the cave.[f]

---

[a] The horses of *Indra* are named *hari*, usually considered as denoting their colour, green or yellow, or, as Rosen has it, *flavi*. In this same verse, we have them, presently, described as *śoṇa*, crimson, bright bay, or chestnut.

[b] *Vipakshasá*, harnessed on different sides,—*Sáyaṇa* says, of the chariot; we should say, of the pole. But the Hindu *ratha* may not have had a pole.

[c] Literally, men-bearing,—*nṛiváhasá*.

[d] *Indra* is here, again, identified with the sun, whose morning rays may be said to reanimate those who have been dead, in sleep, through the night. There is some difficulty in the construction: for *maryáh*, mortals, is plural, while *ajáyathdh* is the second person singular of the first preterite. *Sáyaṇa* is of opinion that the want of concord is a *Vaidik* license, and that the plural substantive *maryáh* has been put for the singular *maryah*.

[e] The *Maruts* are not named in the text; but the allusions justify the commentator's specification: the winds drive *Indra*, or the firmament, into an aggregation of clouds, in which the rain again collects, as in their womb.

[f] Allusion is here made to a legend, which is frequently ad-

6. The reciters of praises praise the mighty (troop of MARUTS), who are celebrated, and conscious of the power of bestowing wealth, in like manner as they (glorify) the counsellor, (INDRA). Varga XII.

7. May you be seen, MARUTS, accompanied by the undaunted INDRA;[a] (both,) rejoicing, and of equal splendour.

8. This rite is performed in adoration of the powerful INDRA, along with the irreproachable, heavenward-tending, and amiable bands (of the MARUTS).

9. Therefore, circumambient (troop of MARUTS), come hither, whether from the region of the sky, or from the solar sphere;[b] for, in this rite, (the priest) fully recites your praises.

10. We invoke INDRA,—whether he come from

---

verted to, of the *Asuras* named *Paṇis* having stolen the cows of the gods, or, according to some versions, of the *Angirasas*, and hidden them in a cave, where they were discovered by *Indra*, with the help of the bitch *Saramá*. A dialogue between her and the robbers is given, in another place, in which she conciliates them. In other passages, the cows are represented as forcibly recovered by *Indra*, with the help of the *Maruts*.

[a] Allusion, it is said, is here made to a battle between *Indra* and *Vṛitra*. The gods who had come to the aid of the former were driven away by *Vṛitra's* dogs; and *Indra*, to obtain the superiority, summoned the *Maruts* to his assistance.

[b] The region of the winds is, properly, the *dyuloka*, the heaven, or region above the *antariksha*, or sky. Or they may come from a sphere of light further above, or the solar region, *ádityamaṇḍalá*.

this earthly region, or from the heaven above, or from the vast firmament,[a]—that he may give (us) wealth.

Súkta IV. (VII.)

The deity is Indra; the *Ṛishi* and metre, as before.

Varga XIII. 1. The chanters (of the *Sáma*) extol Indra with songs; the reciters of the *Ṛich*, with prayers; (the priests of the *Yajush*), with texts.[b]

---

[a] Either the *prithivíloka* or the *dyuloka*. The text adds *maho rajasah*, which the Scholiast explains the great *antarikshaloka*, the sphere of the firmament, which is, properly, the space between the earth and heaven, corresponding with *vyoman* or *ákáśa*, the sky or atmosphere.—*Manu*, I., 13.

[b] The Scholiast supplies the specification of the several *Vedas*. The first term, *gáthinah*, merely means singers, although he renders it *gíyamánasámayukta udgátárah*, "the *Udgátṛis*, with *Sámas* to be chanted;" an interpretation, he thinks, confirmed by the next term, (songs), *bṛihat*, for *bṛihatá*, "with the *Bṛihat Sáma*." The next phrase, *arkebhir arkinah*, is more akin to *Ṛich*, "Those of the *Ṛig-veda*, with stanzas:" but it is not necessarily confined to that sense; and, as *arka* is a synonym of *mantra*, a prayer, the sense may be, those who pray, or praise, *Indra* with prayers. For the *Adhwaryus*, or priests of the *Yajush*, we have nothing at all in the original; and the term *vánih*, for *vánibhih*, "with texts or words," which occurs, apparently without any grammatical connexion, may be referred either to the singers, or the reciters, of the prayers. It is applied, by the Scholiast, to the texts of the *Yajush*,—apparently, only because he had connected the preceding expressions with the other two *Vedas*. As already remarked, any reference to the *Yajush*, or *Sáma*, in a verse of the *Ṛich*, implies the priority of the two former to the latter.

2. INDRA, the blender of all things, comes, verily, with his steeds that are harnessed at his word,—INDRA, the richly-decorated,[a] the wielder of the thunderbolt.

3. INDRA, to render all things visible, elevated the sun in the sky,[b] and charged the cloud with (abundant) waters.

4. Invincible INDRA, protect us, in battles abounding in spoil, with insuperable defences.

5. We invoke INDRA for great affluence; INDRA, for limited wealth,—(our) ally, and wielder of the thunderbolt against (our) enemies.

6. Shedder of rain, granter of all desires, set open this cloud. Thou art never uncompliant with our (requests). Varga XIV.

7. Whatever excellent praises are given to other divinities, they are (also, the due) of INDRA, the thunderer. I do not know his fitting praise.

8. The shedder of rain, the mighty lord, the always compliant, invests men with his strength; as a bull (defends) a herd of kine.

9. INDRA, who alone rules over men, over riches,

---

[a] So the Scholiast explains the term of the text, *hiraṇyaya*; literally, golden, or made of gold.

[b] The world being enveloped in darkness by *Vṛitra*, *Indra*, in order to remove it, elevated (*á rohayat*, or as the comment says, *sthápitaván*, placed,) the sun in the *dyuloka*, or heaven. The latter part of the passage may also be rendered, he (the sun) animated the mountain (*i. e.*, the world,) with his rays.

and over the five (classes) of the dwellers on earth.[a]

10. We invoke, for you, INDRA, who is everywhere among men. May he be exclusively our own.

ANUVÁKA III.

SÚKTA I. (VIII.)

The deity, *Ṛishi*, and metre, as before.

Varga XV. 1. INDRA, bring, for our protection, riches, most abundant, enjoyable, the source of victory, the humbler of our foes;

2. By which we may repel our enemies, whether (encountering them) hand to hand,[b] or on horseback;[c] ever protected by thee.

3. Defended by thee, INDRA, we possess a ponderous weapon, wherewith we may entirely conquer our opponents.

4. With thee for our ally, INDRA, and (aided by)

---

[a] The text has, over the five men, or classes of men, *pancha kshitínám*. The latter term is explained etymologically, those who are fit for habitations (*nivásárháńám*). The phrase is of not unfrequent recurrence, and is usually said to imply the four castes, *Bráhmańas*, *Kshatriyas*, *Vaiśyas*, and *Śúdras*, and *Nisháda*s,—barbarians, or those who have no caste; intending, possibly, the aboriginal races of India, all in a very low stage of civilisation, like the *Gonds*, *Kolas*, and *Bhils* of the present day.

[b] Literally, by striking with the fist, *mushṭihatyayá*.

[c] "With a horse." The Scholiast explains this and the preceding to intend infantry and cavalry.

missile-hurling heroes, we are able to overcome (our foes) arrayed in hosts.

5. Mighty is INDRA, and supreme. May magnitude ever (belong) to the bearer of the thunderbolt; may his strong (armies) be, ever, vast as the heavens.

6. Whatever men have recourse to INDRA,—in battle, or for the acquirement of offspring,—and the wise who are desirous of understanding, (obtain their desires). Varga XVI.

7. The belly of INDRA, which quaffs the *Soma* juice abundantly, swells, like the ocean, (and is ever) moist, like the ample fluids of the palate.[a]

8. Verily, the words of INDRA to his worshipper are true, manifold, cow-conferring, and to be held in honour: (they are) like a branch (loaded with) ripe (fruit).

9. Verily, INDRA, thy glories are, at all times, the protectors of every such worshipper as I am.

10. Verily, his chanted and recited praises[b] are to be desired and repeated to INDRA, that he may drink the *Soma* juice.

---

[a] The Scholiast expounds the text, *urvír ápo na kákudah*, as rendered above. But *kákuda* may refer to *kakud*, the pinnacle of a mountain; and the phrase might, then, be translated, like the abundant waters (or torrents) from the mountain-tops.

[b] The first is the translation of *stoma*, which the commentary defines *sámasáddhyam stotram*, praise to be accomplished by the *Sáma-Veda*: the second is the rendering of *uktha*, which the same authority describes as the *Riksáddhyam śastram*, the unsung praise to be accomplished by the *Rich*. *Sastram* is explained, by

SÚKTA II. (IX.)

Divinity, *Rishi*, and metre, the same.

Varga XVII. 1. Come, INDRA, and be regaled with all viands and libations, and, thence, mighty in strength, be victorious (over thy foes).

2. The libation being prepared, present the exhilarating and efficacious (draught) to the rejoicing INDRA, the accomplisher of all things.

3. INDRA with the handsome chin,[a] be pleased with these animating praises: do thou, who art to be reverenced by all mankind,[b] (come) to these rites, (with the gods).

Sridhara Swámi, in the scholia on the *Bhágavata Puráńa*, to signify a sacred hymn not sung, *śastram apragítamantrastotram*, the repetition of which is the office of the *Hotri*, *hotuh-karma*; while *stuti* and *stoma* imply the sung or chanted hymn, *sangítam stotram*. M. Burnouf renders *śastra*, *les prières* [*mentales*] *qui sont comme le glaive*; and, in a note in the *Vishńu Puráńa*, I have translated the same expression of the *Bhágavata*, the unuttered incantation (p. 42, n.). But it may be doubted if this is quite correct. The difference between *śastra* and *stoma* seems to be, that one is recited, whether audibly or inaudibly; the other, sung.

[a] *Suśipra*. But *śipra* means either the lower jaw, or the nose; and the compound may equally denote the handsome-nosed.

[b] The epithet *viśwacharshańe* is, literally, "O thou who art all men," or, as *Sáyańa* explains it, *sarvamanushyayukta*, who art joined with all men, which he qualifies as *sarvair yajamánaih pújyah*, to be worshipped by all institutors of sacrifices. It may be doubted if this be all that is intended. Rosen renders it *omnium hominum domine*: M. Langlois has *maître souverain*.

4. I have addressed to thee, INDRA, the showerer (of blessings), the protector (of thy worshippers), praises which have reached thee,[a] and of which thou hast approved.

5. Place before us, INDRA, precious and multiform riches; for enough, and more than enough, are, assuredly, thine.

6. Opulent INDRA, encourage us in this rite for Varga XVIII. the acquirement of wealth; for we are diligent and renowned.

7. Grant us, INDRA, wealth beyond measure or calculation, inexhaustible, the source of cattle, of food, of all life.

8. INDRA, grant us great renown, and wealth acquired in a thousand ways, and those (articles) of food (which are brought from the field,) in carts.[b]

9. We invoke, for the preservation of our property, INDRA, the lord of wealth, the object of sacred verses, the repairer (to the place of sacrifice),[c] praising him with our praises.

10. With libations repeatedly effused, the sacri-

---

[a] The Scholiast makes this, "reached thee in heaven," or *swarga*. It may be questioned if the *Veda* recognizes *swarga* as the heaven of *Indra*.

[b] The original of this hymn, as of many others, is so concise and elliptical as to be unintelligible, without the liberal amplification of the Scholiast. We have, in the text, simply "those car-having viands," *tá rathinír ishah*, meaning, *Sáyańa* says, those articles of food which are conveyed in cars, carts, or waggons, from the site of their production; as rice, barley, and other kinds of grain.

[c] Here, again, we have only *gantáram*, he who goes, that is

ficer glorifies the vast prowess of INDRA, the mighty, the dweller in (an eternal mansion).[a]

SÚKTA III. (X.)

The divinity and *Ṛishi* are the same; the metre is the common *Anushṭubh*.

Varga XIX. 1. The chanters (of the *Sáma*) hymn thee, S'ATAKRATU; the reciters of the *Ṛichas* praise thee, who art worthy of praise; the *Bráhmańas*[b] raise thee aloft, like a bamboo-pole.

---

according to the comment, he who is accustomed to go to the chamber which is appropriated to sacrifices, *yágadeśe gamanaśílam*.

[a] The epithet is *nyokas*, from *ni*, explained *niyata*, fixed, permanent, and *okas*, dwelling.

[b] This stanza is nearly similar to the first stanza of the seventh hymn (see p. 16), and is similarly expounded by the commentator. The first term, *gáyatrińa*, literally, those who employ the *Gáyatrí* metre, is said, by *Sáyańa*, to denote the *Udgátṛi*, the chanter of the hymns of the *Sáma: arkińah* is explained, as before, the reciters of the *Ṛich*, and the same as the *Hotṛi* of a sacrifice. The third term, *brahmáńah*, is explained the *Brahmá* of a sacrifice, or priest so denominated, and the other *Bráhmańas*. The objection to the explanation of the first, as involving the prior recognition of the *Sáma-veda*, has been already noticed. The total disconnection of the term *brahmáńah*, the plural of *brahman*, from any reference to *Bráhmańas*, as bearing a share in religious rites, and as implying only *beter*, utterers of prayer, as proposed by Dr. Roth (*Zeitschrift der Deutschen Morgenländischen Gesellschaft*, Vol. I., p. 60), cannot be admitted without further investigation; although it may be possible that the *Brahmá* of a sacrifice does not necessarily involve the notion of a *Bráhmańa* by caste. Rosen renders the word, *Brahmani*; M. Langlois, *prêtres*. The concluding

2. INDRA, the showerer (of blessings), knows the object (of his worshipper), who has performed many acts of worship (with the *Soma* plant, gathered) on the ridges of the mountain,[a] and (therefore,) comes with the troop (of MARUTS).

3. INDRA, drinker of the *Soma*, having put to thy long-maned, vigorous, and well-conditioned steeds,[b] come nigh, to hear our praises.

4. Come, VASU,[c] (to this our rite): reply to our

---

phrase, *twá . . ud vanśam iva yemire*, "they have raised thee, like a bamboo," is rather obscure. The Scholiast says, they have elevated *Indra*, as tumblers raise a bamboo-pole, on the summit of which they balance themselves; a not uncommon feat in India: or, as *vanśa* means, also, a family, it may be rendered, as ambitious persons raise their family to consequence. Roth's proposed rendering, *Die Betenden schütteln dich auf, . . wie man ein Rohr schüttelt*, "the praying agitate thee up, as one shakes a reed," has no warrant, except from his theory of the purport of *Brahmá*, "irresistible prayer;" as *ud yam* never means to shake, and a bamboo is not a reed, nor is it, when substantial, easily shaken. Rosen has, it is true, *te, . . arundinis instar erigunt:* but he had no preferable equivalent for bamboo. M. Langlois has *comme on élève la hampe d'un drapeau*. *Sáyańa*, no doubt, knew much better than either of the European interpreters, what the expression intended.

[a] The original has only, mounting from ridge to ridge, *yat sánoh sánum áruhat*, which the Scholiast completes by observing that this is said of the *Yajamána*, who goes to the mountain to gather either the *Soma* plant for bruising, or fuel for the fire, or other articles required for the ceremony.

[b] *Kakshyaprá*, lit., filling out their girths.

[c] *Vasu*, here used as a synonym of *Indra*, is explained as the original donor or cause of habitations, from the radical *vas*, to dwell, *nivásaidravyabhúta*.

hymns, answer (to our praises), respond to (our prayers): be propitious, INDRA, to our sacrifice, and (bestow upon us abundant) food.

5. The hymn, the cause of increase, is to be repeated to INDRA, the repeller of many foes; that S'AKRA[a] may speak (with kindness,) to our sons and to our friends.

6. We have recourse to INDRA, for his friendship, for wealth, for perfect might; for he, the powerful INDRA, conferring wealth, is able (to protect us).

Varga XX. 7. INDRA, by thee is food (rendered), everywhere, abundant, easy of attainment, and assuredly perfect. Wielder of the thunderbolt, set open the cow-pastures,[b] and provide (ample) wealth.

8. Heaven and earth are unable to sustain thee, when destroying thine enemies. Thou mayest command the waters of heaven. Send us, liberally, kine.

9. O thou whose ears hear all things, listen, quickly, to my invocation; hold, in thy heart, my praises; keep near to thee this my hymn, as it were (the words of) a friend.

10. We know thee, liberal rainer (of blessings), the hearer of our call in battles: we invoke the thousand-fold profitable protection of thee, the showerer (of bounties).

---

[a] *Sakra* is a common synonym of *Indra*, but is used, if not in this, clearly in the next, stanza, as an epithet, implying 'the powerful,' from *śak*, to be able.

[b] The text is literally rendered; the meaning being, that *Indra*, as the sender of rain, should fertilize the fields, and, by providing abundant pasturage, enable the cattle to yield store of milk.

11. Come quickly, INDRA, son of KUŚIKA:[a] delighted, drink the libation: prolong the life that merits commendation: make me, who am a *Rishi*, abundantly endowed (with possessions).

12. May these our praises be, on all occasions, around thee, deserver of praise; may they augment the power of thee, who art long-lived; and, being agreeable to thee, may they yield delight (to us).

SÚKTA IV. (XI.)

The divinity is, still, INDRA; but the *Rishi* is now styled JETṚI, the son of MADHUCHCHHANDAS: the metre is *Anushṭubh*.

1. All our praises magnify INDRA, expansive as the ocean,[b] the most valiant of warriors who fight in chariots, the lord of food, the protector of the virtuous. Varga XXI.

2. Supported by thy friendship, INDRA, cherisher of strength, we have no fear, but glorify thee, the conqueror, the unconquered.

3. The ancient liberalities of INDRA, his protec-

---

[a] In all the *Paurāṇik* genealogies, the son of *Kuśika* is the sage *Viśvámitra*; and, in order to explain its application to *Indra*, *Sáyaṇa* quotes the legend given in the Index (*Anukramaṇiká*), which states that *Kuśika*, the son of *Ishíratha*, being desirous of a son equal to *Indra*, adopted a life of continence, in requital of which, *Indra* was born as the son of *Gáthi*, the *Gádhi* of the *Puráṇas*.

[b] *Samudravyachasam*, explained *samudravad vyáptavantam*, spreading or pervading like the ocean; a vague mode of indicating the universal diffusion of *Indra* as the firmament.

tions, will not be wanting to him who presents, to the reciters of the hymns, wealth of food and cattle.

4. INDRA was born the destroyer of cities,[a] ever-young, ever-wise, of unbounded strength, the sustainer of all pious acts, the wielder of the thunderbolt, the many-praised.

5. Thou, wielder of the thunderbolt, didst open the cave of BALA,[b] who had there concealed the cattle; and the gods whom he had oppressed no longer feared, when they had obtained thee (for their ally).

6. (Attracted) by thy bounties, I again come, hero, to thee, celebrating (thy liberality), while offering this libation. The performers of the rite approach thee, who art worthy of praise; for they have known thy (munificence).

7. Thou slewest, INDRA, by stratagems, the wily

---

[a] The text has only *purám bhinduḥ*, breaker of cities: the Scholiast adds *asurâṇám*, of the *Asuras*.

[b] *Bala*, according to the Scholiast, was an *Asura*, who stole the cows of the gods, and hid them in a cave: *Indra* surrounded the cave, with his army, and recovered the cattle. In the legend, as cited from the *Anukramaṇiká*, the *Paṇis*,—formerly noticed as the cow-stealers (p. 16, n. f.),—are said to be the soldiers of *Bala*, and the actual thieves and concealers of them in the cave. Rosen conceives some relation to exist between this legend and that of *Cacus*: *Quas fabulas aliquo cognationis vinculo inter se contineri, et ex uno eodemque fonte, quantumvis remoto, derivatas esse, persuasum quidem est mihi.*—*Adnotationes*, p. xxi. But the story is likely to have originated in incidents common to an early and, partly, pastoral stage of society. We have the *Cacus* of the Highlands, and the *Bala* of the *Veda*, in such worthies as Donald Ben Lean.

S'USHṆA:[a] the wise have known of this thy (greatness). Bestow upon them (abundant) food.

8. The reciters of sacred hymns praise, with all their might, INDRA, the ruler of the world, whose bounties are (computed by) thousands, or even more.

ANUVÁKA IV.

SÚKTA I. (XII.)

The deity addressed is AGNI; the *Rishi* is MEDHÁTITHI, the son of KAṆWA; the metre, *Gáyatri*.

1. We select AGNI, the messenger of the gods,[b] their invoker, the possessor of all riches, the perfecter of this rite. Varga XXII.

2. (The offerers of oblations) invoke, with their invocations, AGNI, AGNI, the lord of men,[c] the bearer of offerings, the beloved of many.

3. AGNI, generated[d] (by attrition), bring hither

---

[a] *Shushṇa* is described as an *Asura* slain by *Indra*: but this is, evidently, a metaphorical murder. *Shushṇa* means drier up, exsiccator: *bhútánam śoshaṇahetu*, the cause of the drying or withering of beings, heat or drought,—which *Indra*, as the rain, would put an end to.

[b] The commentator cites the *Taittiríya Bráhmaṇa*, in confirmation of this function; *Uśanas*, the son of *Kavi*, being the messenger of the *Asuras*. *Agnir devánám dúta ásíd; Uśanah kávyo 'suráṇám*.

[c] *Viśpati*; *Viś* being constantly used for *prajá*, progeny, people, men.

[d] The original has only *jajńánah*, 'being born,' that is, being

the gods to the clipped sacred grass. Thou art their invoker for us, and art to be adored.

4. As thou dischargest the duty of messenger, arouse them, desirous of the oblation: sit down, with them, on the sacred grass.

5. Resplendent AGNI, invoked by oblations of clarified butter, consume our adversaries, who are defended by evil spirits.[a]

6. AGNI, the ever-young and wise, the guardian of the dwelling[b] (of the sacrificer), the bearer of offerings, whose mouth is (the vehicle) of oblations, is kindled by AGNI.[c]

Varga XXIII. 7. Praise, in the sacrifice, AGNI, the wise, the observer of truth, the radiant, the remover of disease.

8. Resplendent AGNI, be the protector of that offerer of oblations who worships thee, the messenger of the gods.

9. Be propitious, PÁVAKA,[d] to him who, present-

---

artificially produced by the friction of two pieces of a particular species of wood, that of the *Premna spinosa*, used for the purpose.

[a] *Rakshaswinah*, having or being attended by *Rákshasas*.

[b] *Gṛihapati*. But *pati* is most usually interpreted, by *Sáyaṇa*, *pálaka*, the cherisher or protector. Hence it here characterizes *Agni* as the protector of the house of the *Yajamána*.

[c] That is, the *Áhavaníya* fire, into which the oblation is poured, is lighted by the application of other fire, whether taken from the household fire, or produced by attrition.

[d] A name of fire, or a fire; literally, the purifier.

ing oblations for the gratification of the gods, approaches AGNI.[a]

10. AGNI, the bright, the purifier, bring hither the gods to our sacrifice, to our oblations.

11. Praised with our newest hymn, bestow upon us riches and food, the source of progeny.

12. AGNI, shining with pure radiance, and charged with all the invocations of the gods, be pleased by this our praise.

SÚKTA II. (XIII).

The *Rishi* and the metre are the same; but the Hymn is addressed to a variety of divinities, or deified objects, to which the general name Ápri is applied. The first five stanzas hymn various forms of AGNI; the sixth, the doors of the hall of sacrifice; the seventh, morning and night; the eighth, two divine or deified priests; the ninth, the goddesses IḶÁ, SARASWATÍ, and BHÁRATÍ; the tenth, TWASHṬRI; the eleventh, VANASPATI; and the twelfth, SWÁHÁ. They are, all, considered as identifiable or connected with AGNI.[b]

1. AGNI, who art SUSAMIDDHA,[c] invoker, purifier, bring hither the gods to the offerers of our oblation; and do thou sacrifice. Varga XXIV.

2. Wise (AGNI), who art TANÚNAPÁT,[d] present,

---

[a] This verse is to be repeated, when the worshipper approaches the combined *Áhavaníya* and *Gárhapatya* fires, to offer the oblation.

[b] The *Ápris* are, usually, enumerated as twelve, but, sometimes,—omitting one of the names of fire, *Narásansa*,—only eleven.

[c] *Su*, well, *sam*, completely, and *iddha*, kindled; 'the thoroughly kindled.'

[d] *Tanúnapát*, the devourer of clarified butter (*tanúnapa*); or, according to another etymology, the consumer of its own substance

this day, our well-flavoured sacrifice to the gods, for their food.

3. I invoke the beloved NARÁŚANSA,[a] the sweet-tongued, the offerer of oblations, to this sacrifice.

4. AGNI, (who art) ÍḶITA,[b] bring hither the gods, in an easy-moving chariot; for thou art the invoker instituted by men.

5. Strew, learned priests, the sacred grass,[c] well bound together (in bundles), and sprinkled with clarified butter, the semblance of ambrosia.

6. Let the bright doors,[d] the augmenters of sacrifice, (hitherto) unentered, be set open; for, certainly, to-day is the sacrifice to be made.

Varga XXV. 7. I invoke the lovely night and dawn[e] to sit upon the sacred grass, at this our sacrifice.

(*tanú*) or fuel. *Napát* occurs, in the *Nighaṇṭu*, as a synonym of *tanaya*, son or offspring; but, in this compound, the second member is considered to be either *ad*, who eats, or *pá*, who preserves,—the latter, with *na* prefixed, *napát*, who does not preserve, who destroys.

[a] *Naráśansa*, him whom men (*naráḥ*) praise (*śansanti*).

[b] *Íḷita*, the worshipped; from *íḍ*, to adore, to praise.

[c] *Barhis* is said, here, to be an appellative also of *Agni*. The double meaning pervades the concluding phrase, wherein (in which grass, or in which *Agni*,) is the appearance of ambrosia, *amṛita-darśanam; amṛita* implying either the clarified butter sprinkled on the grass, or the immortal *Agni*. *Amṛitasamánasya ghṛitasya*, or *maraṇarahitasya vá barhirnámakasyágneḥ*.

[d] The doors of the chamber in which the oblation is offered; said to be personifications of *Agni*: *Agnivisheshamúrtayaḥ*.

[e] According to the ordinary import of *nakta* and *ushas*. But they, according to the Scholiast, denote, in this place, two forms of fire, presiding over those seasons,—*tatkálábhimániváhnimúrtidevye*.

8. I call the two eloquent, divine, and sage invokers[a] (of the gods), that they may celebrate this our sacrifice.

9. May the three undecaying goddesses, givers of delight, ILÁ, SARASWATÍ, and MAHÍ,[b] sit down upon the sacred grass.

10. I invoke the chief and multiform TWASHṬṚI:[c] may he be, solely, ours.

11. Present, divine VANASPATI,[d] our oblation to

---

[a] The construction shows that we have two persons, or divinities, here; the Scholiast says, two *Agnis*. The Index has *daivyau hotárau prachetasau*, two divine invokers (*prachetasas*): or the latter word may mean, merely, sages, like the *kavi* of the text.

[b] *Mahí* is said to be a synonym of *Bhárati*, as appears from an analogous passage, where the names occur *Iḍá*, *Saraswatí*, *Bhárati*. These are, also, designated, by the Scholiast, as personifications of *Agni*, *Vahnimúrtayah*: they are, also, called the three personified flames of fire. As goddesses, the first, *Iḍá*, is the earth, the bride of *Vishńu*; *Saraswatí* is, as usual, the goddess of eloquence, and wife of *Brahmá*: the third, synonymous with speech, is called the wife of *Bharata*, one of the *Ádityas*: but these mythological personifications are of a *post-Vaidik* period.

[c] *Twashṭri*, in the popular system, is identified with *Viśwakarma*, the artificer of the gods; and he seems to possess some attributes of that nature in the *Vedas*, being called the fabricator of the original sacrificial vase or ladle. A text of the *Veda* is, also, quoted, which attributes to him the formation of the forms of animals in pairs: *Twashṭá vai paśúnám mithunánám rúpakṛid iti śrutih*. He is, also, one of the twelve *Ádityas*, and here is said to be an *Agni*: *Twashṭrinámakam agnim*.

[d] *Vanaspati*, lord of the woods; usually, a large tree; here, said to be an *Agni*,—as if the fuel and the burning of it were identified.

the gods; and may true knowledge be (the reward) of the giver.

12. Perform the sacrifice conveyed through SWÁHÁ[a] to INDRA, in the house of the worshipper. Therefore I call the gods hither.

SÚKTA III. (XIV.)

The *Ṛishi* and metre are unchanged; but the Hymn is addressed to the VIŚWADEVAS.

Varga XXVI. 1. Come, AGNI, to our adoration, and to our praises, with all these gods, to drink the *Soma* juice; and (do thou) offer sacrifice.

2. The KAŃWAS[b] invoke thee, sapient AGNI, and extol thy deeds. Come, AGNI, with the gods.

3. Sacrifice, (AGNI), to INDRA, VÁYU, BṚIHASPATI, MITRA, AGNI, PÚSHAN, and BHAGA, the ÁDITYAS, and the troop of MARUTS.[c]

---

[a] *Swáhá*, as the exclamation used in pouring the oblation on the fire, may, also, be identified with *Agni*. In the section on the various *Agnis*, in the *Mahábhárata*, *Swáhá* is called the daughter of *Bṛihaspati*, the son of *Angiras*. The *Puráṇas* give her a different origin, and make her the daughter of *Daksha*, and wife of *Agni*.

[b] The *Kaṅwas* properly denote the descendants, or the disciples, of the *Ṛishi Kaṇwa*; but the Scholiast would restrict the term, in this place, to the sense of sages (*medhávinaḥ*), or of officiating priests (*ṛitwijaḥ*).

[c] "Sacrifice, *Agni*, to," are supplied by the commentary; for the verse contains only the proper names in the objective case. Most of these have already occurred. *Mitra*, *Púshan*, and *Bhaga* are forms of the Sun, or *Ádityas*, specified individually, as well as the class of *Ádityas*, or Suns, in the twelve months of the year. Why *Vṛihaspati* or *Bṛihaspati* should be inserted is not explained:

4. For all of you are poured out these juices, satisfying, exhilarating, sweet, falling in drops, or gathered in ladles.

5. The wise priests, desirous of the protection (of the gods), having spread the sacred grass, presenting oblations, and offering ornaments, praise thee.

6. Let the coursers who convey thee, glossy-backed,[a] and harnessed at will, bring the gods to drink the *Soma* juice.

7. AGNI, make those objects of veneration, augmenters of pious acts, (participant of the offering), together with their wives:[b] give them, bright-tongued, to drink of the *Soma* juice. Varga XXVII.

8. Let those objects of veneration and of praise drink, with thy tongue, of the *Soma* juice, at the moment of libation.

9. Let the wise invoker (of the gods) bring hither, from the shining (sphere) of the sun,[c] all the divinities, awaking with the dawn.

10. With all the gods, with INDRA, VÁYU, and

---

the etymology of the name is given from *Páṇini* (VI., I., 157); *bṛihas*, for *bṛihat*, great, divine, a deity; and *pati*, master, or protector, in his character of spiritual preceptor of the gods.

[a] *Ghṛitapṛishṭháh*; their backs shining with, or from, ghee, or clarified butter: the commentary says, with which the horses are fed.

[b] *Patnívatah*, having their wives.

[c] Lit., from the shining of the Sun (*Súryasya rochanát*); equivalent, the Scholiast says, to *Swargalokát*: but *Swarga* and the *Ádityaloka* are, usually, regarded as very different. Perhaps the reading should be *Swarlokát*, from the region of heaven.

the glories of MITRA,[a] drink, AGNI, the sweet *Soma* juice.

11. Thou, AGNI, appointed, by man, as the invoker (of the gods), art present at sacrifices. Do thou present this our oblation.

12. Yoke, divine AGNI, thy fleet and powerful mares, ROHITS,[b] to thy chariot; and, by them, hither bring the gods.

SÚKTA IV. (XV.)

The *Ṛishi* and metre are unchanged; the deity is ṚITU,[c] associated, in each stanza, with some divinity more familiarly known.

Varga XXVIII.

1. INDRA, drink, with ṚITU, the *Soma* juice. Let the satisfying drops enter into thee, and there abide.

2. MARUTS, drink, with ṚITU, from the sacrificial vase: consecrate the rite; for you are bountiful.

3. NESHṬṚI,[d] with thy spouse, commend our sacrifice to the gods: drink, with ṚITU; for thou art possessed of riches.

---

[a] *Mitrasya dhámabhih*, with the rays; or, according to the commentator, with various forms of *Mitra*.

[b] *Tábhih*, with them, in the feminine gender; and, hence, the Scholiast adds *baḍavábhih*, mares. They are termed *Rohits*, which may mean red. The *Nighaṇṭu* defines the term as the name of the horses of *Agni*.

[c] *Ṛitu* is, properly, a season, a sixth of the Hindu year, but is, here, personified as a divinity.

[d] *Neshṭri* is another name of *Twashṭri*, from his having assumed, it is said, upon some occasion, the function of the *Neshṭri*, or priest so denominated, at a sacrifice.

4. AGNI, bring the gods hither; arrange them in three places;[a] decorate them: drink with ṚITU.

5. Drink the *Soma* juice, INDRA, from the precious vase of the *Bráhmaṅa*,[b] after ṚITU, for whom thy friendship is uninterrupted.

6. MITRA and VARUṄA, propitious to pious acts, be present, with ṚITU, at our sacrifice, efficacious, and undisturbed (by foes).

7. (The priests,) desirous of wealth, holding stones[c] in their hands, praise the divine (AGNI,) DRAVIṄODAS,[d] both in the primary and subsidiary sacrifices.[e] Varga XXIX.

---

[a] Either at the three daily ceremonies,—at dawn, midday, and sunset,—or in the three fires lighted at sacrifices, the *Áhavaníya*, *Dákshiṅa*, and *Gárhapatya*.

[b] The text is obscure. *Bráhmaṅád ṛádhasaḥ* is, literally, from Brahmanical wealth: but the latter is explained, a costly or wealthy vessel,—*dhanabhútát pátrát;* and the former, relating to the *Bráhmaṅáchchhansí*,—*Bráhmaṅáchchhansisambaddhát*. The *Bráhmaṅáchchhansí* is one of the sixteen priests employed in sacrifices; corresponding, in the second division of four, to the *Brahmá* in the first: and, perhaps, his function may be to hold some ladle, or vase, in which the offering is presented, or in which the portion not expended is removed; as it is said of him, "the relation is the ladle that has the leavings,"—*tasya sambandhyuchchhishṭaś chamasaḥ*. Rosen renders it, *sacro præcepto congrua ex patera;* M. Langlois, *au vase qui contient l'offrande sainte.*

[c] *Grávahastásaḥ*, having stones in their hands, with which to bruise the *Soma* plant. The *Grávastut* is, also, one of the sixteen priests; but it is, here, used generally.

[d] *Draviṅodas* is either an epithet or an appellative of *Agni*, as the donor (*das*) of wealth, or of strength, *draviṅa*.

[e] In the *adhwara* and in the *yajnas*, the first is said to be the

8. May DRAVIṄODAS give us riches that may be heard of. We ask them for the gods.

9. DRAVIṄODAS desires to drink, with the ṚITUS, from the cup of NESHṬṚI.[a] Hasten, (priests, to the hall of offering); present the oblation, and depart.

10. Since, DRAVIṄODAS, we adore thee, for the fourth time,[b] along with the ṚITUS, therefore be a benefactor unto us.

11. AŚWINS, performers of pious acts, bright with sacrificial fires, accepters, with the ṚITUS, of the sacrifice, drink the sweet draught.

12. Giver of rewards,[c] (AGNI), being identified with the household fire, and partaker, with ṚITU, of the sacrifice, worship the gods, on behalf of their adorer.

SÚKTA V. (XVI.)

The *Rishi* and metre continued: the deity is INDRA.

Varga XXX. 1. INDRA, let thy coursers hither bring thee, bestower of desires, to drink the *Soma* juice: may (the priests), radiant as the sun, (make thee manifest).

---

primary or essential ceremony, *prakṛitirúpa*, such as the *Agnishṭoma*; the second, the modified ceremonies, *vikṛitirúpa*; such as the *Ukthya*, which is, elsewhere, termed an offering with *Soma* juice,—*Somasansthayága*.

[a] Or from the cup of the *Neshṭṛi*, one of the sixteen officiating priests.

[b] That is, *Draviṅodas* has been now celebrated in four stanzas.

[c] The name, in the text, is *Santya*, which is so explained, by the Scholiast, from *san*, to give.

2. Let his coursers convey INDRA, in an easy-moving chariot, hither, where these grains (of parched barley), steeped in clarified butter, are strewn (upon the altar).

3. We invoke INDRA, at the morning rite; we invoke him, at the succeeding sacrifice; we invoke INDRA to drink the *Soma* juice.[a]

4. Come, INDRA, to our libation, with thy long-maned steeds. The libation being poured out, we invoke thee.

5. Do thou accept this our praise, and come to this our sacrifice, for which the libation is prepared: drink, like a thirsty stag.[b]

6. These dripping *Soma* juices are effused upon the sacred grass. Drink them, INDRA, (to recruit thy) vigour. Varga XXXI.

7. May this our excellent hymn, touching thy heart, be grateful to thee; and, thence, drink the effused libation.

8. INDRA, the destroyer of enemies, repairs, assuredly, to every ceremony where the libation is poured out, to drink the *Soma* juice, for (his) exhilaration.

9. Do thou, S'ATAKRATU, accomplish our desire, with (the gift of) cattle and horses. Profoundly meditating, we praise thee.

---

[a] Although not more particularly named, the specification implies the morning, midday, and evening worship.

[b] Like the *gaura*, said to be a sort of deer.

Súkta VI. (XVII.)

Metre and *Ṛishi*, as before; divinities, Indra and Varuńa, conjointly.

Varga XXXII. 1. I seek the protection of the sovereign rulers,[a] Indra and Varuńa. May they, both, favour us accordingly;

2. For you are ever ready, guardians of mankind, to grant protection, on the appeal of a minister such as I am.

3. Satisfy us with wealth, Indra and Varuńa, according to our desires. We desire you ever near us.

4. The mingled (libations) of our pious rites, the mingled (laudations) of our right-minded (priests, are prepared). May we be (included) among the givers of food.[b]

---

[a] *Samrájoh*, of the two emperors; but *rájá* is, in general, equivocally used,—meaning, shining, bright, as well as royal; so that *Sáyańa* explains the term, "possessed of extensive dominion," or "shining very brilliantly." *Indra* may claim the title of *rájá*, as chief of the gods; but it seems to be, in a more especial manner, appropriated to *Varuńa*.

[b] The stanza is rather elliptically and obscurely worded; and the sense of the leading term, *yuráku*, is not very clear: it usually denotes a mixture of curds and ghee. We have, in the text, *yuráku • śachínám; yuráku sumatínám*. The former (*śachínám*) is explained, a mixture of buttermilk, water, and meal, suited for acts of religious worship; the latter, the combination of choice expressions and praises which are the suitable phraseology of the right-minded or pious (*sumatínám*). The final clause is, simply, may we be of (amongst) the givers of food.

5. INDRA is a giver among the givers of thousands: VARUṆA is to be praised among those who are deserving of laudation.

6. Through their protection we enjoy (riches), and heap them up; and, still, there is abundance. Varga XXXIII.

7. I invoke you both, INDRA and VARUṆA, for manifold opulence. Make us victorious (over our enemies).

8. INDRA and VARUṆA, quickly bestow happiness upon us; for our minds are devoted to you both.

9. May the earnest praise which I offer to INDRA and VARUṆA reach you both,—that conjoint praise which you (accepting,) dignify.

ANUVÁKA V.

SÚKTA I. (XVIII.)

The metre and *Rishi* as in the preceding. The first five stanzas are addressed to BRAHMAṆASPATI, associated, in the fourth, with INDRA and SOMA, and, in the fifth, with them and DAKSHIṆÁ: the three next are addressed to SADASASPATI; and the ninth, to the same, or to NARÁŚANSA.

1. BRAHMAṆASPATI,[a] make the offerer of the liba- Varga XXXIV.

---

[a] The Scholiast furnishes us with no account of the station or functions of this divinity. The etymology will justify Dr. Roth's definition of him, as the deity of sacred prayer, or, rather, perhaps, of the text of the *Veda;* but whether he is to be considered as a distinct personification, or as a modified form of one of those already recognized, and, especially, of *Agni*, is doubtful. His giving wealth, healing disease, and promoting nourishment, are properties not peculiar to him; and his being associated with *Indra* and *Soma*, whilst it makes him distinct from them, leaves him

tion illustrious among the gods, like KAKSHÍVAT, the son of UŚIJ.*

2. May he, who is opulent, the healer of disease, the acquirer of riches, the augmenter of nourishment, the prompt (bestower of rewards), be favourable to us.

3. Protect us, BRAHMAŃASPATI, so that no calumnious censure of a malevolent man may reach us.

4. The liberal man whom INDRA, BRAHMAŃASPATI, and SOMA protect never perishes.

Agni as his prototype. His being, in an especial manner, connected with prayer appears more fully in a subsequent passage, Hymn XL. *Agni* is, in an especial degree, the deity of the *Brahman;* and, according to some statements, the *Ṛig-Veda* is supposed to proceed from him; a notion, however, which, according to *Medhátithi*, the commentator on *Manu*, was suggested by its opening with the hymn to *Agni*, *Agnim íḷe*.

* This story is to be found in several of the *Puráńas*, especially the *Matsya* and *Váyu*, as well as in the *Mahábhárata*, Vol. I., p. 154. *Kakshívat* was the son of *Dírghatamas*, by *Uśij*, a female servant of the queen of the *Kalinga Rájá*, whom her husband had desired to submit to the embraces of the sage, in order that he might beget a son. The queen substituted her bondmaid *Uśij*: the sage, cognizant of the deception, sanctified *Uśij*, and begot, by her, a son, named *Kakshívat*, who, through his affiliation by *Kalinga*, was a *Kshattriya*, but, as the son of *Dírghatamas*, was a *Brahman*. He was, also, a *Ṛishi;* as, in another passage, he says of himself, *aham kakshíván Ṛishir asmi*,—I am the *Ṛishi Kakshívat*. The *Taittiríyas* also include him among the holy persons who are qualified to conduct sacrifices and compose hymns. In the *Mahábhárata*, *Dírghatamas* disallows the right of the king, there named *Bali*, to the sons of a *Súdra* female, and claims them as his own.

5. Do thou, BRAHMAṄASPATI, and do you, SOMA, INDRA, and DAKSHIṄÁ,[a] protect that man from sin.

6. I solicit understanding from SADASASPATI,[b] the wonderful, the friend of INDRA, the desirable, the bountiful; Varga XXXV.

7. Without whose aid the sacrifice even of the wise is not perfected: he pervades the association of our thoughts.[c]

8. He rewards the presenter of the oblation: he brings the sacrifice to its conclusion: (through him) our invocation reaches the gods.

9. I have beheld NARÁŚANSA,[d] the most resolute, the most renowned, and radiant as the heavens.

---

[a] *Dakshiṅá* is, properly, the present made to the *Brahmans*,—at the conclusion of any religious rite,—here personified as a female divinity.

[b] Properly, the master or protector (*pati*) of the assembly (*sadas*): it is, here, a name of *Agni*. He is the friend or associate of *Indra*, as, on this occasion, partaking of the same oblations.

[c] *Dhiyám yogam invati*, which may mean, "he pervades the association of our minds," or, "the objects of our pious acts;" as *dhí* means either, as usual, *buddhi*, understanding, or has the *Vaidik* sense of *karma*, act.

[d] This has already occurred, [p. 32] as an appellative of *Agni*, and confirms the application of *Sadasaspati* and *Brahmaṅaspati* to the same divinity. According to *Kátthakya*, it means the personified *yajna*, or sacrifice, at which men (*naráh*) praise (*śansanti*) the gods; according to *Sákapúṅi*, it is, as before (Hymn XIII., v. 3), *Agni*, he who is to be praised of men. The same explanation is quoted from the *Bráhmaṅa*: "I beheld (with the eye of the *Vedas*,) that divinity, *Sadasaspati*, who is to be praised by men, who is also called *Naráśansa*."

SÚKTA II. (XIX.)

The metre and *Rishi* are unchanged; AGNI and the MARUTS are the deities.

VARGA XXXVI. 1. Earnestly art thou invoked to this perfect rite, to drink the *Soma* juice. Come, AGNI, with the MARUTS.

2. Nor god nor man has power over a rite (dedicated) to thee, who art mighty. Come, AGNI, with the MARUTS.

3. Who all are divine,[a] and devoid of malignity, and who know (how to cause the descent) of great waters:[b] come, AGNI, with the MARUTS.

4. Who are fierce, and send down rain,[c] and are unsurpassed in strength: come, AGNI, with the MARUTS.

---

[a] *Deváśah*, explained *dyotamánáh*, shining. By the term 'all' is to be understood the seven troops of the *Maruts*, as by the text *saptagańá vai Marutah*.

[b] Many texts ascribe to the *Maruts*, or winds, a main agency in the fall of rain; as, "*Maruts*, you have risen from the ocean; taking the lead, you have sent down rain,—*Údírayathá, Marutah samudrato: yúyam vrishṭim varshayathá, purishińah*." [V., LV., 5: see Vol. III., p. 335.] *Rajas*, the word used in the text, means water, or light, or the world.—*Nighańṭu*.

[c] Here the word is *arka*: as, according to the *Vájasaneyis*, *Apo vá arkah*. The term is derived from *arch*, to worship, and is explained in two other texts: *So 'rchann acharat, tasyárchata ápo' jáyanta*,—He (*Hirańyagarbha*) proceeded, worshipping, (after creating the solid earth), and, from him, worshipping, the waters were produced; and, again, *Archato vai me kam abhút*,—From me, worshipping, water was. Hence the name *arka* was given to water, or rain.

5. Who are brilliant, of terrific forms, who are possessors of great wealth, and are devourers of the malevolent: come, AGNI, with the MARUTS.

6. Who are divinities abiding in the radiant heaven above the sun:[a] come, AGNI, with the MARUTS. Varga XXXVII.

7. Who scatter the clouds, and agitate the sea (with waves): come, AGNI, with the MARUTS.

8. Who spread (through the firmament), along with the rays (of the sun), and, with their strength, agitate the ocean:[b] come, AGNI, with the MARUTS.

9. I pour out the sweet *Soma* juice, for thy drinking, (as) of old. Come, AGNI, with the MARUTS.

SECOND ADHYÁYA.

ANUVÁKA V. (continued).

SÚKTA III. (XX.)

Metre and *Ṛishi*, as before; addressed to the deified mortals named ṚIBHUS.

1. This hymn, the bestower of riches, has been Varga I.

---

[a] In the heaven (*divi, i.e., dyuloke*): above the sun *nákasyádhi, i.e., súryasyopari*). *Náka*, here explained sun, is, more usually, explained, sky, or heaven.

[b] The influence of the winds upon the sea, alluded to in this and the preceding verse, indicates more familiarity with the ocean than we should have expected from the traditional inland position of the early *Hindus*.

addressed, by the sages, with their own mouths, to the (class of) divinities having birth.[a]

2. They who created, mentally, for INDRA, the horses that are harnessed at his words, have partaken of the sacrifice performed with holy acts.[b]

---

[a] *Devdya janmane*, literally, to the divine or brilliant birth: but the Scholiast explains the latter, *jáyamánáya*, being born, or having birth; and the former, *devasanghdya*, a class of divinities, that is, the *Ṛibhus*, of whom it is only said, that they were pious men, who, through penance, obtained deification,—*manushyáh santas tapasá devatwam práptáh*. Thanks to the learning and industry of M. Nève, of the University of Louvain, we are fully acquainted with the history and character of the *Ṛibhus*, as they appear in different portions of the *Ṛig-veda*.—*Essai sur le Mythe des Ṛibhavas*. Their origin and actions are, also, narrated in the *Níti-manjarí*, as well as in the notes of *Sáyaṅa* on this and other similar passages. The *Ṛibhus* were the three sons of *Sudhanwan*, a descendant (the *Níti-manjarí* says, a son) of *Angiras*, severally named *Ṛibhu*, *Vibhu*, and *Vája*, and styled, collectively, *Ṛibhus*, from the name of the elder. Through their assiduous performance of good works,—*swapas* (*su-apas*),—they obtained divinity, exercised superhuman powers, and became entitled to receive praise and adoration. They are supposed to dwell in the solar sphere; and there is an indistinct identification of them with the rays of the sun: but, whether typical, or not, they prove the admission, at an early date, of the doctrine that men might become divinities.

[b] *Śamíbhir yajnam ásata*. M. Nève renders it: [*ils*] *ont obtenu le sacrifice par leurs œuvres méritoires*; M. Langlois, *ils ont entouré le sacrifice de cérémonies* (*saintes*); Mr. Stevenson, *they pervade our sacrifice by purificatory rites*; Rosen, literally, *ceremoniis sacrificium acceperunt*. That three simple words should admit of this variety of rendering shows the vagueness of some of the *Vaidik* expressions. The sense seems to be, they have pervaded, appro-

3. They constructed, for the NÁSATYAS, a universally-moving and easy car, and a cow yielding milk.[a]

4. The ṚIBHUS, uttering unfailing prayers,[b] endowed with rectitude, and succeeding[c] (in all pious acts), made[d] their (aged) parents young.

5. ṚIBHUS, the exhilarating juices are offered to

---

pervaded, or accepted, the sacrifice offered (which last word is understood), with the usual implements and observances (*śamībhih, ceremoniis*); as *Sáyaṇa*, *grahachamasádinishpádanarúpaih karmabhir, yajnam, asmadíyam ásata* (*vyáptavantah*), they have pervaded (or accepted) our sacrifice, performed with those acts which are executed by the means of tongs, ladles, and other (utensils employed in making oblations). The expression may, perhaps, obscurely intimate the invention of the implements so used, by the *Ṛibhus*; their modification of one of which, at least, is subsequently referred to (v. 6), while other expressions imply mechanical skill.

[a] *Takshan*, for *atakshan*; literally, they chipped, or fabricated. So, in the preceding verse, they carved (*tatakshuh*) *Indra's* horses. There, it is said, they did so mentally (*manasá*); but, in this verse, there is no such qualification; and the meaning of the verb implies mechanical formation. The *Ṛibhus* may have been the first to attempt the bodily representation of these appendages of *Indra* and the *Aświns*.

[b] *Satyamantráh*, having, or repeating, true prayers, *i.e.*, which were certain of obtaining the objects prayed for. There is some variety in the renderings, here, also; but it was scarcely necessary, as the meaning is clear enough.

[c] *Vishṭí*, for *vishṭayah*: according to the Scholiast, *vyáptiyuktáh*, in which *vyápti* means, encountering no opposition in all acts, through the efficacy of their true or infallible *mantras*.

[d] *Akrata*, from *kṛi*, to make, generally; not, as before, *atakshan*, to make mechanically.

you, along with INDRA, attended by the MARUTS, and along with the brilliant ÁDITYAS.[a]

Varga II. 6. The ṚIBHUS have divided into four the new ladle,[b] the work of the divine TWASHṬṚI.

7. May they, moved by our praises, give, to the offerer of the libation, many precious things, and perfect the thrice seven sacrifices.[c]

---

[a] According to *Áswaláyana*, as quoted by *Sáyaṅa*, the libations offered at the third daily (or evening) sacrifice are presented to *Indra*, along with the *Ádityas*, together with *Ṛibhu*, *Vibhu*, and *Vája*, with *Bṛihaspati* and the *Viśwadevas*.

[b] *Twashṭṛi*, in the *Pauráṅik* mythology, is the carpenter or artisan of the gods: so *Sáyaṅa* says, of him, he is a divinity whose duty, with relation to the gods, is carpentry,—*devasambandhí takshaṅavyápárah*. Whether he has *Vaidik* authority of a more decisive description than the allusion of the text does not appear. The same may be said of his calling the *Ṛibhus* the disciples of *Twashṭṛi*,—*Twashṭuh śishyáh Ṛibhavah*. The act ascribed to them, in the text, of making one ladle four, has, probably, rather reference to some innovation in the objects of libation, than to the mere multiplication of the wooden spoons used to pour out the *Soma* juice. The *Níti-manjarí* says, that *Agni*, coming to a sacrifice which the *Ṛibhus* celebrated, became as one of them, and, therefore, they made the ladle fourfold, that each might have his share.

[c] *Trir á sáptáni*. The Scholiast considers that *trih* may be applied to precious things, as meaning best, middling, worst; or to *sáptáni*, seven sacrifices, as classed under three heads. Thus, one class consists of the *Agnyádheya*, seven ceremonies in which clarified butter is offered on fire; one class consists of the *Páka-yajnas*, in which dressed viands are offered to the *Viśwadevas* and others; and one comprehends the *Agnishṭoma* class, in which libations of *Soma* juice are the characteristic offering.

8. Offerers (of sacrifices), they held* (a mortal existence): by their pious acts they obtained a share of sacrifices with the gods.

SÚKTA IV. (XXI.)

Rishi and metre the same: the Hymn is addressed to INDRA and AGNI.

1. I invoke hither INDRA and AGNI, to whom we desire to present our praise. Let them, who are, both, copious drinkers of the *Soma* juice, (accept the libation). Varga III.

2. Praise, men, INDRA and AGNI, in sacrifices; decorate them (with ornaments); and hymn them with hymns.

3. We invoke INDRA and AGNI,—for the benefit of our friend (the institutor of the rite),—drinkers of the *Soma* juice, to drink the libation.

4. We invoke the two who are fierce (to their foes), to attend the rite where the libation is prepared. INDRA and AGNI, come hither.

5. May those two, INDRA and AGNI, who are

---

* *Adhárayanta*, they held, or enjoyed, is all the text gives: what they held is not specified. The Scholiast supplies *práṇán*, vital airs, life: his addition is in harmony with other texts. *Martásaḥ santo amṛitatwam ánaśuḥ*,—Being mortals, they obtained immortality. Their partaking of sacrifices is, also, repeatedly stated: *Saudhanwaná yajniyam bhágam ánaśa*,—By the son of *Sudhanwan* was a sacrificial portion acquired. [See Vol. III., p. 100, note 2.] *Ṛibhavo vai deveshu tapasá somapítham abhyajayan*,—The *Ṛibhus* won, by devotion, the drinking of *Soma* among the gods.

mighty, and guardians of the assembly, render the *Rákshasas* innocuous; and may the devourers (of men) be destitute of progeny.

6. By this unfailing sacrifice be you rendered vigilant, INDRA and AGNI, in the station which affords knowledge (of the consequences of acts); and bestow upon us happiness.

SÚKTA V. (XXII.)

The *Rishi* and metre continue: the Hymn consists of twenty-one stanzas, which are addressed to a variety of divinities, or, four, to the AŚWINS, and four, to SAVITṚI; the next two, to AGNI; the eleventh, to the goddesses, collectively; the twelfth, to the wives of INDRA, VARUŃA, and AGNI; the two next, to Heaven and Earth; the fifteenth, to Earth alone; and the last six, to VISHŃU.

Varga IV. 1. Awaken the AŚWINS, associated for the morning sacrifice. Let them, both, come hither, to drink of this *Soma* juice.

2. We invoke the two AŚWINS, who are, both, divine, the best of charioteers, riding in an excellent car, and attaining heaven.

3. AŚWINS, stir up* the sacrifice with your whip

* *Mimikshatam*, mix intimately the juice of the *Soma*. It is not clear how this is to be done with the whip; allusion to which only intimates, it is said, that the *Aświns* should come quickly. *Tayá*, by that, may, also, mean "with that,"—come with that your whip: or *kaśá*, commonly, a whip, may mean speech; in which case, *madhumati* and *súnritávati*, explained wet and loud, will signify sweet and veracious,—come with such speech, *Aświns*, and taste the libation.

that is wet with the foam (of your horses), and lashing loudly.

4. The abode of the offerer of the libation is not far from you, Aświns, going thither in your car.

5. I invoke Savitri, the golden-handed,[a] to protect me: he will appoint the station of the worshippers.

6. Glorify Savitri, who is no friend to water,[b] for our protection. We desire to celebrate his worship. Varga V.

7. We invoke Savitri, the enlightener of men, the dispenser of various home-ensuring wealth.

8. Sit down, friends. Savitri, verily, is to be praised by us; for he is the giver of riches.

9. Agni, bring hither the loving wives of the gods, and Twashṭṛi, to drink the *Soma* juice.

---

[a] *Savitri* is, ordinarily, a synonym of the Sun. Golden-handed, *hiraṅyapáṅi*, is explained, either he who gives gold to the worshipper, or by a *Vaidik* legend:—At a sacrifice performed by the gods, *Súrya* undertook the office of *Ṛitwij*, but placed himself in the station of the *Brahmá*. The *Adhwaryu* priests, seeing him in that position, gave him the oblation termed *Práśitra*, which, as soon as received by *Súrya*, cut off the hand that had improperly accepted it. The priests who had given the oblation bestowed upon *Súrya* a hand of gold. The legend is narrated in the *Kaushítaki Bráhmaṅa*, it is said; but, there, *Súrya* loses both his hands.

[b] *Apám napátam* might be thought to mean son of the waters; as *napát* is often used, in the *Veda*, in that sense: but the Sun is rather the parent, than the progeny, of the waters; as, *Ádityáj jáyate vṛishṭih*,—Rain is born from the sun. *Napát* is here taken in its literal purport, who does not cherish (*na pálayati*), but dries them up by his heat, *santápena śoshakah*.

10. Youthful AGNI, bring hither, for our protection, the wives (of the gods), HOTRÁ, BHÁRATÍ, VARÚTRÍ, and DHISHAṆÁ.[a]

Varga VI. 11. May the goddesses, whose wings are unclipped,[b] the protectresses of mankind, favour us with protection, and with entire felicity.

12. I invoke hither INDRÁṆÍ, VARUṆÁṆÍ, and AGNÁYÍ, for our welfare, and to drink the *Soma* juice.

13. May the great heaven and the earth be pleased to blend this sacrifice (with their own dews), and fill us with nutriment.

14. The wise taste, through their pious acts, the ghee-resembling waters of these two, (abiding) in the permanent region of the *Gandharvas*.[c]

15. Earth, be thou wide-spreading,[d] free from

---

[a] *Hotrá* is called the wife of *Agni*, or the personified invocation; *Bhárati*, of *Bharata*, one of the *Ádityas*. It is rather doubtful if *Varútri* be a proper name, or an epithet of the following: it is explained by *varaṇíyá*, who is to be chosen or preferred, who is excellent. *Dhishaṇá* is a synonym of *Vách* or *Vágdevi*, the goddess of speech.

[b] *Achchhinnapatráh*. The only explanation given by the Scholiast is, that, the wives of the gods being in the form of birds, no one had cut their wings.

[c] The sphere of the *Gandharvas*, *Yakshas*, and *Apsarasas* is the *antariksha*, the atmosphere, or firmament between heaven and earth, and, so far, considered as the common or connecting station of them both,—*Ákáśe vartamánayoh dyávápṛithivyoh*.

[d] *Syona* has, sometimes, the sense of expanded; sometimes, of pleasant, agreeable. The stanza is repeated, it is said, at the ceremony termed *Mahánámni*, at the same time touching the earth.

thorns, and our abiding place: give us great happiness.

16. May the gods preserve us (from that portion) of the earth whence VISHṆU, (aided) by the seven metres, stepped.[a] Varga VII.

17. VISHṆU traversed this (world): three times he planted his foot;[b] and the whole (world) was collected in the dust of his (footstep).

---

[a] *Vishṅu* is explained, by *Sáyaṅa*, by *Parameśwara*, the supreme ruler, or, in his annotation on the next verse, to mean, he who enters into, or who pervades, the world,—*Vishṅur viśater vá vyaśnoter vá*. *Vi chakrame*, 'stepped,' he explains by *vividhapádakramaṅam kritaván*,—he made the going of various steps. Rosen translates it *transgressus*. According to the *Taittiríyas*, as cited by the Scholiast, the gods, with *Vishṅu* at their head, subdued the invincible earth, using the seven metres of the *Veda* as their instruments. *Sáyaṅa* conceives the text to allude to the *Trivikrama Avatára*, in which *Vishṅu* traversed the three worlds in three steps. The phrase "preserve us from the earth" implies, according to the commentary, the hinderance of the sin of those inhabiting the earth,—*bhúloke vartamánánám pápanivárańam*: but the passage is obscure.

[b] This looks still more like an allusion to the fourth *Avatára*, although no mention is made of king Bali, or the dwarf; and these may have been subsequent grafts upon the original tradition of *Vishṅu's* three paces. Commentators are not agreed upon the meaning of the sentence "thrice he planted his step,"—*tredhá ni dadhe padam*. According to *Śákapúńi*, it was on earth, in the firmament, in heaven; according to *Aurńavábha*, on *Samárohaṅa*, or the eastern mountain, on *Vishṅupada*, the meridian sky, and *Gayaśiras*, the western mountain; thus identifying *Vishṅu* with the Sun, and his three paces, with the rise, culmination, and setting, of that luminary. Allusion is made to the three paces of *Vishṅu*, in

18. VISHṆU, the preserver,[a] the uninjurable, stepped three steps, upholding, thereby, righteous acts.

19. Behold the deeds of VISHṆU, through which (the worshipper) has accomplished (pious) vows. He is the worthy friend of INDRA.

20. The wise ever contemplate that supreme station of VISHṆU;[b] as the eye ranges over the sky.

21. The wise,—ever vigilant, and diligent in praise,—amply glorify that which is the supreme station of VISHṆU.

SÚKTA VI. (XXIII.)

The *Ṛishi* is, still, MEDHÁTITHI, the son of KAṆWA: the metre of the first eighteen stanzas is *Gáyatrí*; in stanza nineteen, *Pura Ushṇih*; in twenty-one, *Pratishṭhá*; and, in the rest, *Anushṭubh*. The Hymn consists of twenty-four stanzas, of which the first is addressed to VÁYU; the two next, to INDRA and VÁYU; then three, to MITRA and VARUṆA; three, to INDRA and the MARUTS; three, to the VIŚWADEVAS; three, to PÚSHAN; seven and a half, to the Waters; and the last verse and a half, to AGNI.

Varga VIII. 1. These sharp and blessing-bearing *Soma* juices

---

the *Vájasaneyi Sanhitá* of the *Yajur-Veda*; and the Scholiast there explains them to imply the presence of *Vishṇu* in the three regions of earth, air, and heaven, in the forms, respectively, of *Agni*, *Váyu*, and *Súrya*,—fire, wind, and the sun. There can be no doubt that the expression was, originally, allegorical, and that it served as the groundwork of the *Pauráṇik* fiction of the *Vámana* or dwarf *Avatára*.

[a] *Gopáh sarvasya jagato rakshakah*, the preserver of all the world, is the explanation of *Sáyaṇa*; thus recognizing *Vishṇu*'s principal and distinguishing attribute.

[b] *Paramam padam*, supreme degree or station. The Scholiast says *Swarga*; but that is very questionable.

are poured out. Come, VÁYU, and drink of them, as presented.

2. We invoke both the divinities abiding in heaven, INDRA and VÁYU, to drink of this *Soma* juice.

3. The wise invoke, for their preservation, INDRA and VÁYU, who are swift as thought, have a thousand eyes,[a] and are protectors of pious acts.

4. We invoke MITRA and VARUŃA, becoming present at the sacrifice, and of pure strength, to drink the *Soma* juice.

5. I invoke MITRA and VARUŃA, who, with true speech, are the encouragers of pious acts, and are lords of true light.[b]

6. May VARUŃA be our especial protector; may MITRA defend us with all defences: may they make us most opulent. Varga IX.

7. We invoke INDRA, attended by the MARUTS,

---

[a] The attribution of a thousand eyes to *Indra*, literally understood, is a *Pauráńik* legend: it is nowhere said of *Váyu*, and, here, is applied to him, it is said, only by the grammatical construction,—*sahasráksháu* being in the dual,— to agree with the two substantives *Indra* and *Váyu*: and it is, probably, stated of *Indra*, or the personified heaven, either to signify its expansiveness, or its being studded with constellations, whence it suggested the legend. In like manner, *manojurá*, swift as thought, although equally in the dual number, is, properly, applicable to *Váyu* only.

[b] *Ritasya jyotishaspatí*. *Mitra* and *Varuńa* are included among the *Ádityas*, or monthly suns, in the *Vaidik* enumeration of the eight sons of *Aditi*. *Srutyantare chádityáḥ putrása aditer ityupakramya mitraś cha varuńaś chetyádikam ámnátam*.

to drink the *Soma* juice. May he, with his associates, be satisfied.

8. Divine MARUTS,—of whom INDRA is the chief, and PÚSHAN,[a] the benefactor,—all hear my invocations!

9. Liberal donors, along with the mighty and associated INDRA, destroy VṚITRA: let not the evil one prevail against us.

10. We invoke all the divine MARUTS, who are fierce, and have the (many-coloured) earth for their mother,[b] to drink the *Soma* juice.

Varga X. 11. Whenever, leaders (of men), you accept an auspicious (offering), then the shout of the MARUTS spreads with exultation, like (that) of conquerors.

12. May the MARUTS, born from the brilliant lightning,[c] everywhere preserve us, and make us happy.

13. Resplendent and (swift) moving PÚSHAN, bring from heaven the (*Soma*) juice, in combination with the variegated sacred grass; as (a man brings back) an animal that was lost.

---

[a] The *Maruts* are styled *Púsharátayah*, of whom *Púshan* is the donor, or benefactor; in what way is not specified.

[b] *Pṛiśnimátarah*,—who have *Pṛiśni* for their mother. According to *Sáyaṅa*, *Pṛiśni* is the many-coloured earth,—*nánávarṅayuktá bhúh*. In the *Nighaṅṭu*, *Pṛiśni* is a synonym of sky, or heaven in general. In some texts, as Rosen shows, it occurs as a name of the Sun.

[c] *Haskárád vidyutah*. The Scholiast explains the latter, variously shining, that is, the *antariksha*, or firmament: but it does not seem necessary to depart from the usual sense of *vidyut*, lightning.

14. The resplendent PÚSHAN has found the royal (*Soma* juice), although concealed, hidden in a secret place,[a] strewed amongst the sacred grass.

15. Verily, he has brought to me, successively, the six[b] (seasons), connected with the drops (of the *Soma* juice); as (a husbandman) repeatedly ploughs (the earth) for barley.

16. Mothers[c] to us who are desirous of sacrificing, the kindred (waters) flow by the paths (of sacrifice), qualifying the milk (of kine) with sweetness. Varga XI.

17. May those waters which are contiguous to the Sun,[d] and those with which the Sun is associated, be propitious to our rite.

18. I invoke the divine waters in which our cattle drink. Offer oblations to the flowing (streams).

19. Ambrosia is in the waters; in the waters are medicinal herbs. Therefore, divine (priests),[e] be prompt in their praise.

---

[a] The phrase is *guhá hitam*, placed in a cave, or in a place difficult of access; or, according to the Scholiast, heaven,—*guhásadṛiśe durgame dyuloke sthitam*.

[b] The text has only *shaṭ*, six: the Scholiast supplies *vasantádín ṛitún*, the seasons,—spring, and the rest.

[c] *Ambayah*, which may mean either mothers, or waters, as in the *Kaushítaki Bráhmaṇa*,—*Ápo vá ambayah*.

[d] So in another text, *Ápah súrye samáhitáh*, the waters are collected in the Sun.

[e] The term is *deváh*, gods: but this were incompatible with the direction to praise the waters. It is, therefore, explained, the *Ṛitwij* and other *Bráhmaṇas*; and the interpretation is defended

20. SOMA has declared to me:[a] "All medicaments, as well as AGNI, the benefactor of the universe, are in the waters." The waters contain all healing herbs.

Varga XII. 21. Waters, bring to perfection all disease-dispelling medicaments, for (the good of) my body, that I may long behold the sun.

22. Waters, take away whatever sin has been (found) in me, whether I have (knowingly) done wrong, or have pronounced imprecations (against holy men), or (have spoken) untruth.

23. I have this day entered into the waters: we have mingled with their essence.[b] AGNI, abiding in the waters, approach, and fill me, thus (bathed), with vigour.

24. AGNI, confer upon me vigour, progeny, and life, so that the gods may know the (sacrifice) of this my (employer), and INDRA, with the *Ṛishis*, may know it.

---

by a text which calls the Brahmans present divinities, *Ete vai devâh pratyakshaṁ yad Bráhmaṅáh*,—These deities, who are perceptibly (present), are the Brahmans.

[a] To *Medhátithi*, the author of the hymn. The presidency of *Soma* over medicinal plants is, generally, attributed to him. The entrance of *Agni* into the water is noticed in many places; as, *So'paḥ právišat*, in the *Taittiríya Bráhmaṇa*. This, however, refers to a legend of *Agni's* hiding himself, through fear. It may allude to the subservience of water, or liquids, to digestion, promoting the internal or digestive heat, or *agni*.

[b] *Rasena samagasmahi*; that is, the Scholiast says, we have become associated with the essence of water, *jalasáreṅa sangatáh smah*.

ANUVÁKA VI.

SÚKTA I. (XXIV.)

This is the first of a series of seven Hymns constituting this section, attributed to SUNAHŚEPA, the son of AJÍGARTA.* The metro is *Trishṭubh*, except in stanzas three, four, and five, in which it is *Gáyatrí*. The first verse is addressed to PRAJÁPATI; the second, to AGNI; the three next, to SAVITṚI, or the last of the three, to BHAGA; the rest, to VARUṆA.

1. Of whom, or of which divinity of the immor- Varga XIII.

* The story of *Śunahśepa*, or, as usually written, *Sunahśepha*, has been, for some time, known to Sanskrit students, through the version of it presented in the *Rámáyaṇa*, b. i., ch. 61, Schlegel; 63, Gorresio. He is, there, called the son of the *Ṛishi Ṛichíka*, and is sold for a hundred cows, by his father, to *Ambarísha*, king of *Ayodhyá*, as a victim for a human sacrifice. On the road, he comes to the lake *Pushkara*, where he sees *Viśwámitra*, and implores his succour, and learns, from him, a prayer, by the repetition of which, at the stake, *Indra* is induced to come and set him free. It is obvious, that this story has been derived from the *Veda*; for *Viśwámitra* teaches him, according to Schlegel's text, two *gáthás*,—according to Gorresio's, a *mantra*: but the latter also states, that he propitiated *Indra* by *Ṛichas*; *mantras* of the *Ṛig-Veda* (*Ṛigbhis tushṭáva devendram*), Vol. I., p. 249. *Manu* also alludes to the story (X., 105), where it is said that *Ajígarta* incurred no guilt by giving up his son to be sacrificed; as it was to preserve himself and family from perishing with hunger. *Kullúka Bhaṭṭa* names the son *Sunahśepha*, and refers, for his authority, to the *Bahwṛicha Bráhmaṇa*. The story is told, in full detail, in the *Aitareya Bráhmaṇa*; but the *Rájá* is named *Hariśchandra*. He has no sons, and worships *Varuṇa*, in order to obtain a son, promising to sacrifice to him his first-born. He has a son, in consequence, named *Rohita*; but, when *Varuṇa* claims his victim, the king delays the sacrifice, under various pretexts, from time to time, until *Rohita*

tals, shall we invoke the auspicious name?* Who

attains adolescence, when his father communicates to him the fate for which he was destined. *Rohita* refuses submission, and spends several years in the forests, away from home. He, at last, meets, there, with *Ajígarta*, a *Ṛishi*, in great distress, and persuades him to part with his second son, *Śunahśepha*, to be substituted for *Rohita*, as an offering to *Varuṅa*. The bargain is concluded; and *Śunahśepha* is about to be sacrificed, when, by the advice of *Viśwámitra*, one of the officiating priests, he appeals to the gods, and is, ultimately, liberated. The *Aitareya Bráhmaṅa* has supplied the commentator with the circumstances which he narrates, as illustrative of the series of hymns in this section. Dr. Rosen doubts if the hymns bear any reference to the intention of sacrificing *Śunahśepha*: but the language of the *Bráhmaṅa* is not to be mistaken; as *Ajígarta* not only ties his son to the stake, but goes to provide himself with a knife, with which to slay him. At the same time, it must be admitted, that the language of the *Súktas* is somewhat equivocal, and leaves the intention of an actual sacrifice open to question. The *Bhágavata* follows the *Aitareya* and *Manu*, in terming *Śunahśepha* the son of *Ajígarta*, and names the *Rájá*, also, *Hariśchandra*. In the *Vishṅu Puráṅa*, he is called the son of *Viśwámitra*, and is termed, also, *Devaráta*, or God-given. But this relates to subsequent occurrences, noticed, in like manner, by the other authorities, in which he becomes the adopted son of *Viśwámitra*, and the eldest of all his sons; such of whom as refused to acknowledge his seniority being cursed to become the founders of various barbarian and outcaste races. *Viśwámitra's* share in the legend may, possibly, intimate his opposition, and that of some of his disciples, to human sacrifices.

* Supposed to be uttered by *Śunahśepa*, when bound to the *yúpa*, or stake, as the *purushapaśu*, the man-animal (or victim), as the *Bhágavata* terms him. "Of whom" (*kasya*) may also be rendered, of *Brahmá*, or *Prajápati*, one of whose names, in the *Veda*, is *Ka*; as, *Ko ha vai náma Prajápatiḥ*.

will give us to the great ADITI,[a] that I may again behold my father and my mother?

2. Let us invoke the auspicious name of AGNI,[b] the first divinity of the immortals, that he may give us to the great ADITI, and that I may behold again my father and my mother.

3. Ever-protecting SAVITṚI,[c] we solicit (our) portion of thee,—who art the lord of affluence,—

4. That wealth which has been retained in thy hands, and is entitled to commendation, as exempt from envy or reproach.

5. We are assiduous in attaining the summit of affluence, through the protection of thee, who art the possessor of wealth.

6. These birds, that are flying (through the air), have not obtained, VARUṆA,[d] thy bodily strength, or thy prowess, nor (are able to endure thy) wrath; Varga XIV.

---

[a] *Aditi*, according to *Sáyaṇa*, here means 'earth.'

[b] A passage from the *Aitareya Bráhmaṇa* is cited, by the Scholiast, stating that *Prajápati* said to him (*Sunahśepa*), "Have recourse to *Agni*, who is the nearest of the gods;" upon which he resorted to *Agni*: *Tam Prajápatir uváchágnir vai devánám nedishṭhas tam evopadháveti; so'gnim upasasára.*

[c] In this and the two following stanzas, application is made to *Savitṛi*, by the advice, it is said, of *Agni*; not, however, it may be remarked, for liberation, but for riches,—a request rather irreconcileable with the supposed predicament in which *Sunahśepa* stands.

[d] *Savitṛi* refers *Sunahśepa*, it is said, to *Varuṇa*. It is not very obvious why any comparison should be instituted between the strength and prowess of *Varuṇa* and of birds.

neither do these waters, that flow unceasingly, nor (do the gales) of wind, surpass thy speed.

7. The regal VARUṆA, of pure vigour, (abiding) in the baseless (firmament), sustains, on high, a heap of light, the rays (of which) are pointed downwards, while their base is above. May they become concentrated in us, as the sources of existence.[a]

8. The regal VARUṆA, verily, made wide the path of the sun,[b]—(by which) to travel on his daily course,—a path to traverse in pathless (space). May he be the repeller of every afflicter of the heart.

9. Thine, O king, are a hundred and a thousand medicaments. May thy favour, comprehensive and profound, be (with us). Keep afar from us NIRṚITI,[c] with unfriendly looks; and liberate us from whatever sin we may have committed.

---

[a] The epithet of *Rájá* is here, as usual, applied to *Varuṅa*; and it may be either radiant or regal: but the latter is, in general, the more suitable. The attributes here assigned to *Varuṅa*, his abiding in the *antariksha*, and his holding a bundle of rays, would rather identify him with the sun, or, at least, refer to him in his character of an *Áditya*. The terms of the original are, however, unusual; and we depend, for their translation, upon the Scholiast: *abudhne*, in the baseless; *múlarahite* he explains *antarikshe*, in the sky; and, for *vanasya stúpam*, he supplies *tejasah*, of radiance, and *sangham*, a heap.

[b] According to the Commentator, the sun's course north and south of the equator is here alluded to. He does not explain what *Varuṅa* has to do with it.

[c] According to *Sáyaṅa*, *Nirṛiti* is the deity of sin, *Pápadevatá*. In the *Nighaṅṭu*, it occurs among the synonyms of earth.

10. These constellations, placed on high, which are visible by night, and go elsewhere by day, are the undisturbed holy acts of VARUṆA; (and, by his command,) the moon moves, resplendent, by night.[a]

11. Praising thee with (devout) prayer, I implore thee for that[b] (life) which the institutor of the sacrifice solicits with oblations. VARUṆA, undisdainful, bestow a thought upon us: much-lauded, take not away our existence. Varga XV.

12. This (thy praise) they repeat to me by night and by day: this knowledge speaks to my heart. May he whom the fettered S'UNAHS'EPA has invoked, may the regal VARUṆA, set us free.

13. S'UNAHS'EPA, seized and bound to the three-footed tree,[c] has invoked the son of ADITI. May the

---

[a] Here, again, we have unusual functions ascribed to *Varuṇa*. The constellations, *rikshâḥ*, may be either, it is said, the seven *Rishis*,—Ursa Major,—or the constellations generally. They and the moon are said to be the pious acts of *Varuṇa* (*Varuṇasya* • *vratáni*): because they shine by his command. Rosen detaches *adabdháni* • *vratáni* by inserting a verb,—*illæsa sunt Varunæ opera*; but *Sáyaṇa* expressly terms the constellations *the acts of Varuṇa*, in the form (or effect) of the appearance, &c., of the asterisms. *Varuṇasya* • • *karmáṇi nakshatradarśanádirúpáṇi*.

[b] The text has only "I ask *that*:" the Scholiast supplies *life*, *tad áyus*. The addition might be disputed; but its propriety is confirmed by the concluding expression, *má na áyuḥ pra moshíḥ*, do not take away our life.

[c] *Trishu drupadeshu*. *Dru*, δρῦς, a tree, is, here, said to mean the sacrificial post, a sort of tripod. Its specification is consistent with the popular legend.

regal VARUŃA, wise and irresistible, liberate him; may he let loose his bonds.

14. VARUŃA, we deprecate thy wrath with prostrations, with sacrifices, with oblations. Averter of misfortune,[a] wise and illustrious, be present amongst us, and mitigate the evils we have committed.

15. VARUŃA, loosen, for me, the upper, the middle, the lower, band.[b] So, son of ADITI, shall we, through faultlessness in thy worship, become freed from sin.

SÚKTA II. (XXV.)

This Hymn is addressed by SUNAHŚEPA to VARUŃA: the metre is *Gáyatrí*.

Varga XVI. 1. Inasmuch as all people commit errors, so do we, divine VARUŃA, daily disfigure thy worship by imperfections.

2. Make us not the objects of death, through thy fatal indignation, through the wrath of thee so displeased.

---

[a] The text has *asura*, which is interpreted *anishṭakshepaśíla*, accustomed to cast off what is undesired,—from the root *as*, to throw. It is an unusual sense of the word: but it would scarcely be decorous to call *Varuńa* an *Asura*.

[b] The text has *ud uttamam • páśam • • adhamam • madhyamam śrathdya*, loosen the upper, lower, and middle, bond; meaning, according to *Sáyańa*, the ligature fastening the head, the feet, and the waist. The result, however, is not loosening from actual bonds, but from those of sin: *anágasah • • syáma*, may we be sinless.

3. We soothe thy mind, VARUṆA, by our praises, for our good; as a charioteer, his weary steed.

4. My tranquil (meditations) revert to the desire of life;[a] as birds hover around their nests.

5. When, for our happiness, shall we bring hither VARUṆA, eminent in strength, the guide (of men), the regarder of many?[b]

6. Partake (MITRA and VARUṆA,) of the common (oblation), being propitious to the giver and celebrator of this pious rite. Varga XVII.

7. He, who knows the path of the birds flying through the air,—he, abiding in the ocean, knows (also,) the course of ships.[c]

8. He, who, accepting the rites (dedicated to him), knows the twelve months and their productions, and that which is supplementarily engendered;[d]

---

[a] *Vasya-ishṭaye. Vasyah*, according to the Scholiast, is equivalent to *vasumataḥ*, precious; that is, *jívanasya*, life, understood.

[b] *Uruchakshasam* is explained *bahúnám drashṭáram*, the beholder of many.

[c] Here we have the usual functions of *Varuṇa* recognized.

[d] *Vedá ya upajáyate*, who knows what is *upa*, additionally, or subordinately, produced. The expression is obscure; but, in connexion with the preceding, *veda máso dwádaśa*, who knows the twelve months, we cannot doubt the correctness of the Scholiast's conclusion, that the thirteenth, the supplementary, or intercalary, month of the Hindu luni-solar year is alluded to; "that thirteenth or additional month which is produced of itself, in connexion with the year,"—*yas trayodaśo'dhikamásaḥ upajáyate samvatsarasamípe*

9. He, who knows the path of the vast, the graceful, and the excellent, wind, and who knows those who reside above;

10. He, VARUŃA, the accepter of holy rites, the doer of good deeds, has sat down, amongst the (divine) progeny,[a] to exercise supreme dominion (over them).

Varga XVIII. 11. Through him the sage beholds all the marvels that have been, or will be, wrought.

12. May that very wise son of ADITI keep us, all our days, in the right path, and prolong our lives.

13. VARUŃA clothes his well-nourished (person), wearing golden armour,[b] whence the (reflected) rays are spread around;—

14. A divine (being), whom enemies dare not to offend, nor the oppressors of mankind, nor the iniquitous, (venture to displease);

15. Who has distributed unlimited food to mankind, and, especially, to us.

---

swayam evodpadyate. The passage is important, as indicating the concurrent use of the lunar and solar years at this period, and the method of adjusting the one to the other.

[a] *Ni shasáda * * pastyásu á.* The commentator explains *pastyásu*, *daivíshu prajásu*, divine progeny; Rosen translates it, *inter homines*; M. Langlois, *au sein de nos demeures*; Dr. Roer, *among his subjects.* The sovereignty of *Varuńa*, *sámrájya*, is distinctly specified.

[b] *Bibhrad drápim hirańyayam*, that is, *suvarńamayam kavacham*, armour or mail made of gold. This looks as if the person of *Varuńa* were represented by an image. The same may be said of the phraseology of v. 18.

16. My thoughts ever turn back to him, who is beheld of many; as the kine return to the pastures. Varga XIX.

17. Let us, together, proclaim that my offering has been prepared, and that you, as if the offerer, accept the valued (oblation).

18. I have seen him whose appearance is grateful to all: I have beheld his chariot upon earth: he has accepted these my praises.

19. Hear, VARUŃA, this my invocation: make us, this day, happy. I have appealed to thee, hoping for protection.

20. Thou, who art possessed of wisdom, shinest over heaven and earth, and all the world. Do thou hear and reply (to my prayers), with (promise of) prosperity.

21. Loose us from the upper bonds, untie the centre and the lower, that we may live.[a]

SÚKTA III. (XXVI).

The supposed author or reciter is ŚUNAHŚEPA, as before; the hymn is addressed to AGNI; the metre is *Gáyatrí*.

1. Lord of sustenance, assume thy vestments (of light),[b] and offer this our sacrifice. Varga XX.

2. (Propitiated) by brilliant strains, do thou,

---

[a] The expressions are, for the most part, the same as in the concluding verse of the preceding hymn; but it ends differently: *jívase*, to live,—that we may live.

[b] The text has only *vastráńi*, clothes; meaning, the Scholiast says, *áchchhádakáni tejáńsi*, investing radiance.

ever-youthful AGNI, selected by us, become our ministrant priest, (invested) with radiance.

3. Thou, AGNI, art, verily, as a loving father to a son, as a kinsman to a kinsman, as a friend to a friend.

4. Let VARUṆA, MITRA, and ARYAMAN[a] sit down upon our sacred grass, as they did at the sacrifice of MANUS.[b]

5. Preceding sacrificer,[c] be pleased with this our sacrifice, and with our friendship, and listen to these thy praises.

Varga XXI. 6. Whatever we offer, in repeated and plentiful oblation, to any other deity is, assuredly, offered to thee.

7. May the lord of men, the sacrificing priest, the gracious, the chosen, be kind to us: may we, possessed of holy fires, be loved of thee.

8. As the brilliant (priests), possessed of holy fires, have taken charge of our oblation, so we, with holy fires, pray to thee.

9. Immortal AGNI, may the praises of mankind be, henceforth, mutually (the sources of happiness) to both, (to ourselves and to thee).

10. AGNI, son of strength,[d] (accept) this sacrifice,

---

[a] *Aryaman* is an *Áditya*, a form of the monthly sun. He is said, also, to preside over twilight.

[b] *Manushah*, of *Manus*, who, the Scholiast says, is the same as *Manu*, the *Prajápati*.

[c] *Púrvyahotṛi*; the *Hotṛi* born before us, according to *Sáyaṇa*.

[d] *Sahaso yaho*; *balasya putrah*, son of strength. The epithet is not unfrequently repeated, and is sometimes applied to *Indra*,

and this our praise, with all thy fires, and grant us (abundant) food.

SÚKTA IV. (XXVII.)

The *Ṛishi*, divinity, and metre, as before, except in the last stanza, in which the metre is *Trishṭubh*, and the VIŚWADEVAS are addressed.

1. (I proceed) to address thee, the sovereign lord of sacrifices, with praises; (for thou scatterest our foes), like a horse, (who brushes off flies with) his tail.[a] Varga XXII.

2. May he, the son of strength, who moves everywhere fleetly, be propitious to us, and shower down (blessings).

3. Do thou, AGNI, who goest everywhere, ever protect us, whether near or afar, from men seeking to do us injury.

4. AGNI, announce, to the gods, this our offering, and these our newest hymns.[b]

5. Procure, for us, the food that is in heaven and mid-air, and grant us the wealth that is on earth.[c]

---

also. As applicable to *Agni*, it is said to allude to the strength required for rubbing the sticks together, so as to generate fire.

[a] The comparison is merely, we praise thee like a horse with a tail. The particulars are supplied by the Scholiast.

[b] *Gáyatram navyánsam*, most new *Gáyatrí* verses; showing the more recent composition of this *Súkta*.

[c] In the supreme, in the middle, and of the end, are the vague expressions of the text: their local appropriation is derived from the commentary.

Varga XXIII. 6. Thou, CHITRABHÁNU,[a] art the distributor of riches; as the waves of a river are parted by interjacent (islets). Thou ever pourest (rewards) upon the giver (of oblations).

7. The mortal whom thou, AGNI, protectest in battle, whom thou incitest to combat, will always command (food).

8. No one will ever be the vanquisher of this thy worshipper, subduer of enemies; for notorious is his prowess.

9. May he, who is worshipped by all men, convey us, with horses, through the battle: may he, (propitiated) by the priests, be the bestower (of bounties).

10. JARÁBODHA,[b] enter into the oblation, for the completion of the sacrifice that benefits all mankind. The worshipper offers agreeable laudation to the terrible (AGNI).[c]

Varga XXIV. 11. May the vast, illimitable, smoke-bannered, resplendent AGNI be pleased with our rite, and grant us food.

12. May AGNI, the lord of men, the invoker and messenger of the gods, the brilliant-rayed, hear

---

[a] A common denominative of *Agni*, he who has wonderful or various lustre. The following simile is very elliptically and obscurely expressed; but such seems to be its purport, according to the explanation of the Scholiast.

[b] He who is awakened (*bodha*) by praise (*jará*).

[c] The text has "to *Rudra*" (*Rudráya*), which the Scholiast explains "to the fierce or cruel *Agni*:" *krúráyágnaye*.

us, with our hymns; as a prince* (listens to the bards).

13. Veneration to the great gods; veneration to the lesser; veneration to the young; veneration to the old!*[b] We worship (all) the gods, as well as we are able. May I not omit the praise of the older divinities.

Súkta V. (XXVIII.)

Sunahśepa is the *Rishi*: the metre of the six first stanzas is *Anushṭubh*; of the three last, *Gáyatrí*. The first four stanzas are addressed to Indra; the two next, to the domestic mortar; the next two, to the mortar and pestle; and the ninth is of a miscellaneous appropriation, either to Harishchandra, (a *Prajápati*), to the *Adhishavana* (or the effused libation), to the *Soma* juice, or to the skin (*charma*) on which it is poured.

1. Indra, as the broad-based stone[c] is raised to express the *Soma* juice, recognize and partake of the effusions of the mortar.   Varga XXV.

2. Indra, (in the rite) in which the two platters,[d]

---

* "As a rich man" (*revān iva*) is the whole of the text. The Commentator suggests all the rest of the comparison.

[b] These distinctions, of older and younger, greater and lesser, gods, are nowhere further explained. *Sunahśepa*, it is said, worships the *Viśwadevas*, by the advice of *Agni*.

[c] The stone, or, rather, here, perhaps, the stone pestle, is that which is used to bruise the *Soma* plants, and so express the juice. The pestle employed in bruising or threshing grain is, usually, of heavy wood.

[d] *Adhishavaṇyá*, two shallow plates or *patera*, for receiving and pouring out the *Soma* juice.

for containing the juice,—as (broad as a woman's) hips,—are employed, recognize and partake of the effusions of the mortar.

3. INDRA, (in the rite) in which the housewife repeats egress from and ingress into (the sacrificial chamber),[a] recognize and partake of the effusions of the mortar.

4. When they bind the churning-staff (with a cord),[b] like reins to restrain (a horse), INDRA, recognize and partake of the effusions of the mortar.

5. If, indeed, O *Mortar*,[c] thou art present in every house, give forth (in this rite,) a lusty sound, like the drum of a victorious host.

Varga XXVI. 6. Lord of the forest,[d] as the wind gently blows before thee, so do thou, O *Mortar*, prepare the *Soma* juice, for the beverage of INDRA.

[a] The Scholiast explains the terms of the text, *aparhyara* and *upachyara*, going in and out of the hall (*śálá*); but it should, perhaps, rather be, moving up and down, with reference to the action of the pestle.

[b] In churning, in India, the stick is moved by a rope passed round the handle of it, and round a post, planted in the ground, as a pivot. The ends of the rope being drawn backwards and forwards, by the hands of the churner, gives the stick a rotatory motion amidst the milk, and thus produces the separation of its component parts.

[c] The mortar is, usually, a heavy wooden vessel, found in every farmer's cottage. According to *Sáyaṇa*, it is the divinities presiding over the mortar and pestle, not the implements themselves, that are addressed.

[d] *Vanaspati*, a large tree, but, in this verse, put, by metonymy, for the mortar, and, in verse 8, for the mortar and pestle. [See p. 33.]

7. Implements of sacrifice, bestowers of food, loud-sounding, sport, like the horses of INDRA champing the grain.

8. Do you two forest lords, of pleasing form, prepare, with agreeable libations, our sweet (*Soma*) juices, for INDRA.

9. Bring the remains of the *Soma* juice upon the platters; sprinkle it upon the blades of *Kuśa* grass; and place the remainder upon the cow-hide.[a]

SÚKTA VI. (XXIX.)

ŚUNAHŚEPA[b] continues to be the reciter: the deity is INDRA; the metre, *Pankti*.

1. Veracious drinker of the *Soma* juice, although Varga XXVII.

---

[a] This verse is addressed, the Scholiast says, to *Hariśchandra*,—either the ministering priest, or a certain divinity so named: no name occurs in the text. It is not very clear what he is to do. Apparently, he is to place what remains, after the libation has been offered, contained in *pateræ* or platters, upon some vessel,—the Scholiast says, upon a cart (*śakaṭasyopari*)—and, having brought it away, cast it upon the *Pavitra*, which is explained, in the comment on the *Yajur-Veda Sanhitá*, to mean two or three blades of *Kuśa* grass, serving as a kind of filter,—typically, if not effectively,—through which the juice falls upon a sheet, or into a bag of leather, made of the skin of the cow (*gos twachi*). According to Mr. Stevenson, the *Soma* juice, after expression, is filtered through a strainer made of goat's hair, and is received in a sort of ewer, the *droṇakalaśa*. Here, however, the directions apply to the *uchchhishṭa*, the remainder, or leavings; such being the term used in the text.

[b] *Śunahśepa* has been directed by the *Viśwadevas*, it is said in the *Bráhmaṇa*, to apply to *Indra*.

we be unworthy, do thou, INDRA, of boundless wealth, enrich us with thousands of excellent cows and horses.

2. Thy benevolence, handsome[a] and mighty lord of food, endures for ever. Therefore, INDRA, of boundless wealth, enrich us with thousands of excellent cows and horses.

3. Cast asleep (the two female messengers of YAMA). Looking at each other, let them sleep, never waking.[b] INDRA, of boundless wealth, enrich us with thousands of excellent cows and horses.

4. May those who are our enemies slumber, and those, O hero, who are our friends, be awake. INDRA, of boundless wealth, enrich us with thousands of excellent cows and horses.

5. INDRA, destroy this ass, (our adversary), praising thee with such discordant speech;[c] and do thou, INDRA, of boundless wealth, enrich us with thousands of excellent cows and horses.

---

[a] *Sipriṇ*, literally, having either a nose or a lower jaw or chin; that is, having a handsome prominent nose or chin.

[b] The text is very elliptical and obscure. It is, literally: "Put to sleep the two reciprocally looking: let them sleep, not being awakened." That two females are intended is inferrible from the epithets being in the dual number and feminine gender; and the Scholiast calls them—upon what authority is not stated—two female messengers of *Yama*: *Yamadútyau*. *Mithúdṛiśá* he explains *mithunatayá yugalarúpeṇa paśyata*, "looking, after the manner of twins, at each other."

[c] *Nurantam papayámuyá*, praising with this speech, that is of the nature of abuse. *Nindárúpayá váchá* is the addition of the

6. Let the (adverse) breeze, with crooked course, alight afar off on the forest. INDRA, of boundless wealth, enrich us with thousands of excellent cows and horses.

7. Destroy every one that reviles us; slay every one that does us injury. INDRA, of boundless wealth, enrich us with thousands of excellent cows and horses.

SÚKTA VII. (XXX.)

The Hymn is ascribed to ŚUNAHŚEPA: of the twenty-two stanzas of which it consists, sixteen are addressed to INDRA; three, to the AŚWINS; and three, to USHAS, or the personified dawn. The metre is *Gáyatrí*, except in verse sixteen, where it is *Trishṭubh*.

1. Let us, who are desirous of food, satisfy this your INDRA, who is mighty and of a hundred sacrifices, with drops (of *Soma* juice); as a well (is filled with water). Varga XXVIII.

2. May he who is (the recipient) of a hundred pure, and of a thousand distilled, (libations) come (to the rite); as water, to low (places).

3. All which (libations), being accumulated for the gratification of the powerful INDRA, are contained in his belly; as water, in the ocean.

4. This libation is (prepared) for thee. Thou approachest it; as a pigeon his pregnant (mate): for, on that account, dost thou accept our prayer.

5. Hero, INDRA, lord of affluence, accepter of

Scholiast, who adds: "Therefore is he called an ass, as braying or uttering harsh sounds intolerable to hear;" *Yathá gardabhah śrotum aśakyam parusham śabdam karoti.*

praise, may genuine prosperity be (the reward of him) who offers thee laudation.

Varga XXIX. 6. Rise up, S'ATAKRATU, for our defence in this conflict. We will talk together in other matters.

7. On every occasion, in every engagement, we invoke, as friends, the most powerful INDRA, for our defence.

8. If he hear our invocation, let him, indeed, come to us, with numerous bounties, and with (abundant) food.

9. I invoke the man (INDRA,) who visits many worshippers, from his ancient dwelling-place,—thee, INDRA, whom my father formerly invoked.

10. We implore thee, as our friend, who art preferred and invoked by all, (to be favourable) to thy worshippers, protector of dwellings.

Varga XXX. 11. Drinker of the *Soma* juice, wielder of the thunderbolt, O friend, (bestow upon) us, thy friends, and drinkers of the *Soma* juice, (abundance of cows) with projecting jaws.*

12. So be it, drinker of the *Soma* juice, wielder of the thunderbolt, our friend, that thou wilt do, through thy favour, whatever we desire.

13. So, INDRA, rejoicing along with us, we may have (abundant food); and cows may be ours, robust, and rich in milk, with which we may be happy.

---

* The expression in the text is *s'iprińínám*, gen. plur. of the feminine *s'iprińí*, having a nose or a jaw. It cannot, therefore, refer to the previous nouns in the gen. plur., *somapávnám* and *sakhínám*, which are masc.; and the Scholiast, therefore, supplies *gavám*, of cows, and adds *samúhah*, a multitude, or herd.

14. O DHṚISHṆU,[a] let some such divinity as thou art, self-presented, promptly bestow, when solicited, (bounties) upon thy praisers; as (they whirl) the axle of the wheels (of a car).[b]

15. Such wealth, S'ATAKRATU, as thy praisers desire, thou bestowest upon them; as the axle (revolves) with the movements (of the waggon).[c]

16. INDRA has ever won riches (from his foes), with his champing, neighing, and snorting (steeds): he, the abounding in acts, the bountiful, has given us, as a gift, a golden chariot.[d] Varga XXXI.

---

[a] The resolute, or firm, or high-spirited,—an appellative of *Indra*.

[b] The verse is, throughout, very elliptical and obscure, and is intelligible only through the liberal additions of the Scholiast. The simile is, literally, like the axle of two cars,—*aksham na chakryoh*, which the commentator renders, *rathasya chakrayoh*, of the two wheels of a car, and adds *prakshipanti*, they cast, or turn over. The phrase seems to have puzzled the translators; Rosen [*Adnotationes*] has *currum velut duabus rotis*; Stevenson, *that blessings may come round to them, with the same certainty that the wheel revolves round the axle*; Dr. Roer, *as a wheel is brought to a chariot*; M. Langlois, *que les autres dieux, * * non moins que toi sensibles à nos louanges, soient pour nous comme l'axe qui soutient et fait tourner les roues du char*. The meaning intended, is, probably, the hope that blessings should follow praise, as the pivot on which they revolve; as the revolutions of the wheels of a car turn upon the axle.

[c] This repetition of the comparison is more obscure than in the preceding stanza. It is like the axle, by the acts,—*aksham na śachībhiḥ*. The Scholiast defines 'the acts' the movements of the car or waggon.

[d] So the *Brāhmaṇa*. By *Indra*, pleased, a golden chariot was

17. AŚWINS, come hither, with viands borne on many steeds. DASRAS, (let our dwelling) be filled with cattle and with gold.

18. DASRAS, your chariot, harnessed for both alike, is imperishable: it travels, AŚWINS, through the air.

19. You have one wheel on the top of the solid (mountain), while the other revolves in the sky.[a]

20. USHAS,[b] who art pleased by praise, what mortal enjoyeth thee, immortal? Whom, mighty one, dost thou affect?

21. Diffusive, many-tinted, brilliant (USHAS), we know not (thy limits), whether they be nigh, or remote.

22. Daughter of heaven,[b] approach, with these viands, and perpetuate our wealth.[c]

---

given to him, that is, to *Sunahśepa*. He, nevertheless, hands him over to the *Aświns*.

[a] There is no explanation of this myth, in the commentary. It may be connected with the *Paurâṇik* notion of the single wheel of the chariot of the sun.—*Vishṇu Puráṇa*, p. 217.

[b] The dawn; daughter of the personified heaven, or its deity, *Dyudevatâyâ duhitá*. Rosen translates the name *Aurora*; but it seems preferable to keep the original denomination; as, except in regard to time, there is nothing in common between the two. In the *Vishṇu Puráṇa*, [but see new edition, Vol. II., p. 249, note •] indeed, *Ushá*, a word of similar derivation as *Ushas*, is called night; and the dawn is *Vyushṭa*. Several passages seem to indicate that *Ushá* or *Ushas* is the time immediately preceding daybreak.

[c] We here take leave of *Sunahśepa*; and, it must be confessed, that, for the greater part, there is, in the hymns ascribed to him, little connexion with the legend narrated in the *Râmâyaṇa* and other authorities.

ANUVÁKA VII.

SÚKTA I. (XXXI.)

This Hymn is addressed to AGNI; *the* Rishi *is* HIRAṆYASTÚPA, *the son of* ANGIRAS. *The eighth, sixteenth, and eighteenth stanzas are in the* Trishṭubh *metre; the rest, in* Jagatí.

1. Thou, AGNI, wast the first ANGIRAS Rishi:[a] a divinity, thou wast the auspicious friend of the deities. In thy rite, the wise, the all-discerning, the bright-weaponed MARUTS were engendered.

2. Thou, AGNI, the first and chiefest ANGIRAS, gracest the worship of the gods;—sapient, manifold,[b] for the benefit of all the world, intelligent, the offspring of two mothers,[c] and reposing in various ways, for the use of man.

3. AGNI, preeminent over the wind,[d] become manifest to the worshipper, in approbation of his worship. Heaven and earth tremble (at thy power).

---

[a] According to Sáyaṇa, he was the first, as being the progenitor of all the Angirasas; they being, according to the Bráhmaṇa, as before quoted, nothing more than the coals or cinders of the sacrificial fire. There is no explanation of the origin assigned, in this verse, to the Maruts.

[b] Vibhu, according to the Scholiast, means "of many kinds;" alluding to the different fires of a sacrifice.

[c] Dwimátá, either of two mothers, i.e., the two sticks, or, the maker of two, i.e., heaven and earth.

[d] Literally, first in, or on, or over, the wind,—prathama anu-váne; alluding, according to the Scholiast, to the text, agnir váyur ádityaḥ, fire, air, sun,—in which Agni precedes Váyu.

Thou hast sustained the burthen, in the rite for which the priest was appointed. Thou, VASU, hast worshipped the venerable (gods).

4. Thou, AGNI, hast announced heaven to MANU:[a] thou hast more than requited PURÚRAVAS,[b] doing homage to thee. When thou art set free by the attrition of thy parents, they bear thee, first, to the east, then, to the west, (of the altar).[c]

5. Thou, AGNI, art the showerer (of desires), the augmenter of the prosperity (of thy worshipper): thou art to be called upon, as the ladle is lifted up. Upon him who fully understands the invocation and makes the oblation,[d] thou, the provider of sustenance, first bestowest light, and, then, upon all men.

Varga XXXIII.

6. AGNI, excellently wise, thou directest the man who follows improper paths, to acts that are fitted to reclaim him;—thou who, in the strife of heroes, (grateful to them) as widely-scattered wealth, destroyest, in the combat, the mighty, by the feeble.

---

[a] It is said that *Agni* explained to *Manu*, that heaven was to be gained by pious works.

[b] The agency of *Purúravas*, the son of *Budha*, the son of *Soma*, in the generation of fire by attrition, and its employment in the form of three sacrificial fires, as told in the *Puráṇas* (*Vishṇu Puráṇa*, p. 397), may be here alluded to: but the phrase is only *sukṛite sukṛittaraḥ*, doing more good to him who did good.

[c] The fire is first applied to kindle the *Áhavaníya* fire, and, then, to the *Gárhapatya*, according to the Scholiast.

[d] He who knows the *áhuti*, with the *vashaṭkṛiti*, or utterance of the word *vashaṭ* at the moment of pouring the butter on the fire.

7. Thou sustainest, Agni, that mortal (who worships thee), in the best immortality, by daily food: thou bestowest on the sage, who is desirous (of creatures) of both kinds of birth,[a] happiness and sustenance.

8. Agni, who art praised, by us, for the sake of wealth, render illustrious the performer of the rite. May we improve the act by a new offspring, (given by thee). Preserve us, heaven and earth, along with the gods.

9. Irreproachable Agni, a vigilant god amongst the gods, (abiding) in the proximity of (thy) parents,[b] and bestowing upon us embodied (progeny), awake us. Be well-disposed to the offerer of the oblation; for thou, auspicious Agni, grantest all riches.

10. Thou, Agni, art well-disposed to us; thou art our protector; thou art the giver of life to us: we are thy kinsmen. Uninjurable Agni, hundreds and thousands of treasures belong to thee, who art the defender of pious acts, and attended by good men.

11. The gods formerly made thee, Agni, the living general of the mortal Nahusha:[c] they made Varga XXXIV.

---

[a] It is not very clear what is meant: the expression is, who is very desirous, or longing, for both births. The Scholiast says, for the acquirement of bipeds and quadrupeds,—*dwipadám chatushpadám lábháya*.

[b] The parents are here said to be heaven and earth.

[c] *Nahusha* was the son of *Ayus*, son of *Purúravas*, who was elevated to heaven, as an *Indra*, until precipitated, thence, for his arrogance. The circumstance alluded to in the text does not appear in the *Pauráńik* narrative.—*Vishńu Puráńa*, p. 413.

IḶÁ the instructress of MANUS, when the son of my father was born.[a]

12. AGNI, who art worthy to be praised, preserve us, who are opulent, with thy bounties, and, also, the persons (of our sons). Thou art the defender of cattle, for the son of my son,[b] who is ever assiduous in thy worship.

13. Thou, four-eyed AGNI,[c] blazest,—as the protector of the worshipper,—who art at hand, for the (security of the) uninterrupted (rite): thou cherish-

---

[a] This circumstance is not related, in the *Puráńas*, of *Ilá*, the daughter of *Vaivaswata Manu*.—*Vishńu Puráńa*, p. 349. Frequent passages in the *Vedas* ascribe to *Iḷá* the first institution of the rules of performing sacrifices. Thus, in the text, she is termed *iḍasni*, which the Scholiast explains *dharmopadeśakartri*, the giver of instruction in duty. The *Taittiríyas* are quoted for the text, "*Iḍá*, the daughter of *Manu*, was the illustrator of sacrifice" (*yajnánukásiní*); and the *Vájasaneyis*, for the passage: "She [*Iḷá*,] said to *Manu*, 'Appoint me, to officiate in sacrifices, principal and supplementary; for by me shalt thou obtain all thy desires'"—*Prayájánuyájánám madhye mám avakalpaya mayá sarván avápsyasi kámán*. M. Burnouf questions if *Iḷá* ever occurs in the sense of daughter of *Manu*, in the *Vedas*, and restricts its meaning to 'earth' or to 'speech.' The passage of the text, *Iḷám akriṇwan manushasya śásaním*, he translates, *les Dieux ont fait d'Iḷa la préceptrice de l'homme*, and considers it equivalent to *les Dieux ont fait de la parole l'institutrice de l'homme*. *Introduction to the Bhágavata Puráńa*, III., pp. LXXXIV.-XCI. We are scarcely yet in possession of materials to come to a safe conclusion on this subject.

[b] We must conclude that this hymn was composed by the author in his old age, as he speaks of his grandson.

[c] Illuminating the four cardinal points.

est, in thy mind, the prayer of thine adorer, who offers the oblation to thee, the harmless, the benevolent.

14. Thou, AGNI, desirest (that the worshipper may acquire) that excellent wealth which is requisite for the many-commended priest: thou art called the well-intentioned protector of the worshipper, who ever needs protection. Thou, who art all-wise, instructest the disciple, and (definest) the points of the horizon.[a]

15. AGNI, thou defendest the man who gives presents (to the priests), on every side, like well-stitched armour.[b] The man who keeps choice viands in his dwelling, and, with them, entertains (his guests), performs the sacrifice of life,[c] and is the likeness of heaven.

---

[a] This is said to allude to a legend in which the gods, intending to offer a sacrifice, were at a loss to determine the cardinal points, until the perplexity was removed by *Agni's* ascertaining the south.

[b] *Varma • syútam*, sewn armour. The *kavacha* was, perhaps, a quilted jacket, such as is still sometimes worn: the Scholiast says, formed with needles, without leaving a fissure.

[c] The expression is rather ambiguous,—*jívayájam yajate*, sacrifices a life-sacrifice. Rosen renders it *vivam hostiam mactat;* but, in this place, it seems, rather, to denote an offering (food and hospitality) to a living being, the *nriyajna*, worship of man, of *Manu*. The expression, however, is not incompatible with the practice of killing a cow for the food of a guest, thence denominated, as M. Langlois remarks, *goghna*, a cow-slayer. The Scholiast sanctions either sense, explaining the phrase either *jívayajana-sahitam yajnam*, a sacrifice with sacrifice of life, or *jívanishpádyam*,

Varga XXXV. 16. AGNI, forgive us this our negligence, this path in which we have gone astray. Thou art to be sought, as the protector and encourager of those who offer suitable libations: thou art the fulfiller (of the end of rites): thou makest thyself visible to[a] mortals.

17. Pure AGNI, who goest about (to receive oblations), go, in thy presence, to the hall of sacrifice, as did MANUS, and ANGIRAS, and YAYÁTI, and others of old.[b] Bring hither the divine personages; seat them on the sacred grass; and offer them grateful (sacrifice).

18. AGNI, do thou thrive through this our prayer, which we make according to our ability, according to our knowledge. Do thou, therefore, lead us to opulence; and endow us with right understanding, securing (abundant) food.

SÚKTA II. (XXXII.)

The *Rishi* and metre are the same: the Hymn is addressed to INDRA.

Varga XXXVI. 1. I declare the former valorous deeds of INDRA,

---

that by which life is to be supported: he also explains *jîrayájam* by *jîváh*, living, priests, who *ijyante dakshináḃhih*, are worshipped by gifts.

[a] *Rishikrit*, becoming present through desire for the offered oblation: the epithet is an unusual one.

[b] In like manner as ancient patriarchs,—such as *Manu*, or *Angiras*,—or former kings, repaired to different places where sacrifices were celebrated. *Yayáti* was one of the sons of *Nahusha*.—*Vishńu Purána*, p. 413.

which the thunderer has achieved: he clove the cloud; he cast the waters down (to earth); he broke (a way) for the torrents of the mountain.[a]

2. He clove the cloud, seeking refuge on the mountain: TWASHṬṚI sharpened his far-whirling bolt: the flowing waters quickly hastened to the ocean; like cows (hastening) to their calves.

3. Impetuous as a bull, he quaffed the *Soma* juice: he drank of the libation at the triple sacrifice.[b] MAGHAVAN took his shaft, the thunderbolt, and, with it, struck the first-born of the clouds.

4. Inasmuch, INDRA, as thou hast divided the

---

[a] In this and subsequent *Súktas*, we have an ample elucidation of the original purport of the legend of *Indra's* slaying *Vṛitra*, converted, by the *Paurániк* writers, into a literal contest between *Indra* and an *Asura*, or chief of the *Asuras*, from what, in the *Vedas*, is, merely, an allegorical narrative of the production of rain. *Vṛitra*, sometimes also named *Ahi*, is nothing more than the accumulation of vapour condensed, or, figuratively, shut up in, or obstructed by, a cloud. *Indra*, with his thunderbolt, or atmospheric or electrical influence, divides the aggregated mass, and vent is given to the rain, which then descends upon the earth, and moistens the fields, or passes off in rivers. The language of the *Richas* is not always sufficiently distinct, and confounds metaphorical and literal representation; but it never approximates to that unqualified strain of personification, which, beginning, apparently, with the *Mahábhárata* (*Vana-parva*, ch. 100; also in other *Parvas*), became the subject of extravagant amplification by the compilers of the *Puráńas*.

[b] At the *Trikadrukas*, the three sacrifices termed *Jyotish*, *Gauh*, and *Ayu*. No further description of them occurs in the commentary.

first-born of the clouds,[a] thou hast destroyed the delusions of the deluders; and, then, engendering the sun, the dawn, the firmament, thou hast not left an enemy (to oppose thee).[b]

5. With his vast destroying thunderbolt, INDRA struck the darkling mutilated VṚITRA. As the trunks of trees are felled by the axe, so lies AHI,[c] prostrate on the earth.

Varga XXXVII. 6. The arrogant VṚITRA, as if unequalled, defied INDRA, the mighty hero, the destroyer of many, the scatterer of foes;—he has not escaped the contact of the fate of (INDRA'S) enemies. The foe of INDRA has crushed the (banks of the) rivers.[d]

7. Having neither hand nor foot, he defied

---

[a] The first-formed cloud.

[b] By scattering the clouds, and dispersing the darkness, *Indra* may be said to be the parent of the sun and daylight; leaving no enemy, that is, nothing to obscure the atmosphere.

[c] We have, here, and in other verses, both names, *Ahi* and *Vṛitra*. They are, both, given as synonyms of *megha*, a cloud, in the *Nighaṇṭu*. The former is derived from *han*, to strike, with *á* prefixed, arbitrarily shortened to *a*: the latter, lit., the encompasser, or concealer, is from *vṛi*, to enclose, or *vṛit*, to be, or to exist, or from *vṛidh*, to increase; a choice of etymologies intimating a vague use of the term. He is said to be *vyaṃsa*, having a part, or, metaphorically, a limb, detached; thus confounding things with persons, as is still more violently done in a following verse, where he is said to have neither hands nor feet.

[d] The text has only *rujánáḥ pipishe*, he has ground the rivers: the Commentator supplies "the banks," which, he says, were broken down by the fall of *Vṛitra*, that is, by the inundation occasioned by the descent of the rain.

Indra, who struck him, with the thunderbolt, upon his mountain-like shoulder, like one emasculated who pretends to virility: then Vṛitra, mutilated of many members, slept.

8. The waters, that delight the minds (of men), flow over him, recumbent on this earth; as a river (bursts through) its broken (banks). Ahi has been prostrated beneath the feet of the waters, which Vṛitra, by his might, had obstructed.

9. The mother of Vṛitra was bending over her son, when Indra struck her nether part with his shaft. So the mother was above, and the son underneath; and Dánu[a] slept (with her son), like a cow with its calf.

10. The waters carry off the nameless body of Vṛitra, tossed into the midst of the never-stopping, never-resting currents. The foe of Indra has slept through a long darkness.

11. The waters, the wives of the destroyer,[b] guarded by Ahi, stood obstructed, like the cows by Pańi: but, by slaying Vṛitra, Indra set open the cave that had confined them. Varga XXXVIII.

12. When the single resplendent Vṛitra returned the blow (which had been inflicted), Indra, by thy thunderbolt, thou becamest (furious), like a

[a] *Dánu* is derived from *dó*, to cut or destroy, or from *Danu*, the wife of *Kaśyapa*, and mother of the *Dánavas* or Titans.

[b] *Dásapatníḥ.* *Dása* is said to be a name of *Vṛitra*, as the destroyer of all things, or all holy acts,—he who *dásayati karmáṇi*.

horse's tail.[a] Thou hast rescued the kine; thou hast won, hero, the *Soma* juice;[b] thou hast let loose the seven rivers to flow.[c]

13. Neither the lightning nor the thunder (discharged by VṚITRA), nor the rain which he showered, nor the thunderbolt, harmed INDRA, when he and AHI contended, and MAGHAVAN triumphed, also, over other (attacks).

14. When fear[d] entered, INDRA, into thy heart, when about to slay AHI, what other destroyer of him

---

[a] We have had this simile before; as a horse lashes his tail, to get rid of the flies.

[b] Alluding, it is said, to a legend of *Indra's* having drunk a libation prepared by *Twashṭṛi*, after the death of his son,—who, according to a *Paurâṇik* legend, was *Triśiras*, also killed by *Indra*,—and to avenge which, *Vṛitra* was created by *Twashṭṛi*.

[c] According to one *Paurâṇik* legend, the Ganges divided, on its descent, into seven streams, termed the *Nalinî*, *Pâvanî*, and *Hlâdinî*, going to the east; the *Chakshu*, *Sîtâ*, and *Sindhu*, to the west; and the *Bhâgirathî*, or Ganges proper, to the south. In one place in the *Mahâbhârata*, the seven rivers are termed *Vaswokasârâ*, *Nalinî*, *Pâvanî*, *Gangâ*, *Sîtâ*, *Sindhu*, and *Jambûnadî*; in another, *Gangâ*, *Yamunâ*, *Plakshagâ*, *Rathasthâ*, *Sarayû*, *Gomatî*, and *Gaṇḍakî*. [See the *Vishṇu Purâṇa*, new edition, Vol. II., pp. 120, 121, and notes.] In a text quoted and commented on by *Yâska*, we have ten rivers, named *Gangâ*, *Yamunâ*, *Saraswatî*, *Sutudrî*, *Parushṇî*, *Asiknî*, *Marudvṛidhâ*, *Vitastâ*, *Arjikîyâ*, and *Sushomâ*. Of these, the *Parushṇî* is identified with the *Irâvatî*; the *Arjikîyâ* with the *Vipâś*; and the *Sushomâ*, with the *Sindhu*. —*Nir.*, III., 26. The original enumeration of seven appears to be that which has given rise to the specifications of the *Purâṇas*.

[d] The Scholiast intimates, that this fear was, the uncertainty whether he should destroy *Vṛitra*, or not; but, in the *Purâṇas*,

didst thou look for, that, alarmed, thou didst traverse ninety and nine streams, like a (swift) hawk?

15. Then INDRA, the wielder of the thunderbolt, became the sovereign of all that is moveable or immoveable, of hornless and horned cattle; and, as he abides the monarch of men, he comprehended all things (within him); as the circumference comprehends the spokes of a wheel.

THIRD ADHYÁYA.

ANUVÁKA VII. (continued).

SÚKTA III. (XXXIII.)

The *Rishi* is, as before, HIRAŃYASTÚPA. INDRA, also, is the divinity: the metre is *Trishṭubh*.

1. Come, let us repair to INDRA,* (to recover our stolen cattle); for he, devoid of malice, exhilarates our minds: thereupon he will bestow upon us perfect knowledge of this wealth, (which consists) of kine. Varga I.

Indra is represented as fearing his enemy's prowess, and hiding himself in a lake. Something like this is, also, intimated in other passages of the text; whence the *Paurúńik* fiction. The *Bráhmańa* and the *Taittiríya* are quoted, as stating that *Indra*, after killing *Vritra*, thinking he had committed a sin, fled to a great distance.

* This is all the text says. The Scholiast adds: "The gods are supposed to say this to one another, when their cows have been carried off."

2. I fly, like a hawk to its cherished nest, to that INDRA who is to be invoked, by his worshippers, in battle; glorifying, with excellent hymns, him who is invincible, and the giver of wealth.

3. The commander of the whole host has bound his quiver (on his back): the lord[a] drives the cattle (to the dwelling) of whom he pleases. Mighty INDRA, bestowing upon us abundant wealth, take not advantage of us, like a dealer.[b]

4. Verily, INDRA, thou hast slain the wealthy barbarian[c] with thine adamantine (bolt);—thou, singly assailing (him), although with auxiliaries (the MARUTS,) at hand.[d] Perceiving the impending manifold destructiveness of thy bow, they, the SANAKAS,[e] the neglecters of sacrifice, perished.

---

[a] *Arya*, here explained *swámin*, master, owner, lord,—meaning *Indra*.

[b] Lit., do not be to us a *paṇi*, a trafficker; such being one sense of the term; from *paṇa*, price, hire. *Indra* is solicited not to make a hard bargain, not to demand too much from his worshippers.

[c] *Vṛitra*, the *Dasyu*, literally, a robber, but, apparently, used in contrast to *Arya*, as if intending the uncivilized tribes of India. He is called wealthy, because, according to the *Vájasaneyis*, he comprehends, within him, all gods, all knowledge, all oblations,—*Vṛitrasyántah sarve deváh sarváś cha vidyáh sarváṇi havínshi chásan*.

[d] So the *Bráhmaṇa*. The *Maruts* who accompanied *Indra* did not attack *Vṛitra*; but they stood nigh, and encouraged the former, saying, "Strike, O Lord; show thyself a hero."

[e] The followers of *Vṛitra* are called by this name, the meaning of which is not very satisfactorily explained by *sanán kúyanti*, they who eulogise benefactors. They are also called, in this and

5. The neglecters of sacrifice, contending with the sacrificers, INDRA, fled, with averted faces. INDRA, fierce, unyielding, lord of steeds, (they disappeared,) when thou didst blow the disregarders of religion from off the heaven, and earth, and sky.

6. (The adherents of VṚITRA) encountered the army of the irreproachable (INDRA): men of holy lives encouraged him.[a] Scattered before him, conscious (of their inferiority), like the emasculated contending with men, they fled by precipitous paths. Varga II.

7. Thou hast destroyed them, INDRA, whether weeping, or laughing, on the furthest verge of the sky; thou hast consumed the robber, (having dragged him) from heaven, and hast received the praises of the worshipper, praising thee and offering libations.

8. Decorated with gold and jewels, they were spreading over the circuit of the earth; but, mighty as they were, they triumphed not over INDRA: he dispersed them with the (rising) sun.[b]

---

the next verse, *ayajwánah*, non-sacrificers, in contrast to the *yajwánah* or sacrificers; here, apparently, also identifying the followers of *Vṛitra* with races who had not adopted, or were hostile to, the ritual of the *Vedas*.

[a] *Kshitayo navagwáh*, men whose practices were commendable. Or the 'men,' it is said, may be the *Angirasas*, engaged in offering libations to *Indra* for nine months, in order to give him courage.

[b] We revert, here, to the allegory. The followers of *Vṛitra* are, here, said to be the shades of night, which are dispersed by the rising of the sun: according to the *Bráhmaṇa*, "Verily, the sun, when he rises in the east, drives away the *Rákshasas*."

9. INDRA, as thou enjoyest both heaven and earth, investing the universe with thy magnitude, thou hast blown away the robber with the prayers which are repeated on behalf of those who do not comprehend them.[a]

10. When the waters descended not upon the ends of the earth, and overspread not that giver of affluence with its productions, then INDRA, the showerer, grasped his bolt, and, with its brightness, milked out the waters from the darkness.

Varga III. 11. The waters flowed, to provide the food of INDRA; but (VṚITRA) increased, in the midst of the navigable (rivers): then INDRA, with his fatal and powerful shaft, slew VṚITRA, whose thoughts were ever turned towards him.

12. INDRA set free (the waters) obstructed by (VṚITRA), when sleeping in the caverns of the earth, and slew the horned dryer up (of the world).[b] Thou,

---

[a] This passage is rather obscure, owing to the vague purport of the preposition *abhi*: *ananyamánán abhi manyamánair brahmabhih*, "with prayers to be understood over those not understanding;" that is, according to the Scholiast, those *yajamánas*, or institutors of sacrifices, who merely repeat the *mantras* without understanding their meaning, are, nevertheless, to be protected by, or are to reap the benefit of, those *mantras*; and with *mantras*, or prayers of this description, *Indra* is to be animated, or empowered to blow away or scatter the followers of *Vṛitra*, clouds and darkness. Rosen renders the expression, *carminibus respirientibus eos, qui hymnorum tuorum sensum vel non perspiciunt*; M. Langlois has (*excité*) *contre ces mécréants par nos chants respectueux*.

[b] *Sṛingiṇam - śushṇam*. The first, literally, having horns, the Scholiast explains "furnished with weapons like the horns of bulls

MAGHAVAN, with equal swiftness and strength, didst kill, with thy thunderbolt, the enemy defying thee to battle.

13. The weapon of INDRA fell upon his adversaries: with his sharp and excellent (shaft) he destroyed their cities: he then reached VṚITRA with his thunderbolt, and, (by) slaying him, exhilarated his mind.

14. Thou, INDRA, hast protected KUTSA, grateful for his praises: thou hast defended the excellent DAŚADYU, engaged in battle: the dust of thy courser's hoofs ascended to heaven: the son of S'WITRÁ (through thy favour,) rose up, to be again upborne by men.[a]

15. Thou hast protected, MAGHAVAN, the excellent son of S'WITRÁ, when combating for his lands, and encouraged, (by thee,) when immersed in water. Do thou inflict sharp pains on those of

---

and buffaloes." *Sushńam*, literally, drying, drying up, is applied to *Vṛitra*, or the cloud, as withholding the moisture necessary for fertility.

[a] *Kutsa* is said to be a *Ṛishi*, founder of a *gotra*, a religious family, or school, and is elsewhere spoken of as the particular friend of *Indra*, or even as his son. He is the reputed author of several hymns. We have a *Purukutsa* in the *Puráńas*; but he was a *Rájá*, the son of *Mándhátṛi*.—*Vishńu Puráńa*, p. 363. [Also see below, especially, Vol. III., p. 205, note 1.] *Daśadyu* is also called a *Ṛishi*; but he appears to have been a warrior: [see VI., XXVI., 4?] no mention of him is found in the *Puráńas*. The same may be said of *Swaitreya*, or *Switrya*, the son of a female termed *Switrá*. *Switrya* is described, in the next stanza, as having hidden himself in a pool of water, through fear of his enemies.

hostile minds, who have long stood (in enmity) against us.

SÚKTA IV. (XXXIV.)

The *Rishi* is the same; the Hymn is addressed to the AŚWINS; the metre is *Jagatí*, except in the ninth and twelfth stanzas, in which it is *Trishṭubh*.

Varga IV. 1. Wise AŚWINS, be present with us thrice to-day.[a] Vast is your vehicle, as well as your munificence: your union is like that of the shining (day) and dewy (night). (Suffer yourselves) to be detained by the learned (priests).

2. Three are the solid (wheels) of your abundance-bearing chariot, as all (the gods) have known (it to be), when attendant on VENÁ, the beloved of SOMA:[b] three are the columns placed (above it) for support;[c] and, in it, thrice do you journey by night, and thrice by day.

[a] We have a variety of changes rung, in this hymn, upon the number 'three.' In this place, allusion, it is said, is made either to the three diurnal sacrifices,—at dawn, mid-day, and sunset,—or to the faculty of all divinities, of being *tripathagáh*, or going equally through the heavens, the firmament, and the earth.

[b] The *Aświns* are said to have filled their *ratha*, or car, with all sorts of good things, when they went to the marriage of *Vená* with *Soma*,—a legend not found in the *Puráńas*.

[c] So the Scholiast explains *skambhásah skabhitása drabhe*, posts standing up from the body of the car, which the riders may lay hold of, if, by its rapid or uneven motion, they should be afraid of falling out.

3. Thrice in one entire day do you repair the faults (of your worshippers). Thrice to-day sprinkle the oblation with sweetness; and thrice, evening and morning, Aświns, grant us strength-bestowing food.

4. Thrice, Aświns, visit our dwelling, and the man who is well-disposed towards us: thrice repair to him who deserves your protection, and instruct us in threefold knowledge: thrice grant us gratifying (rewards): thrice shower upon us food, as (Indra pours down) rain.

5. Aświns, thrice bestow upon us riches: thrice approach the divine rite: thrice preserve our intellects: thrice grant us prosperity; thrice, food. The daughter of the sun has ascended your three-wheeled car.

6. Thrice grant us, Aświns, the medicaments of heaven, and those of earth, and those of the firmament. Give to my son the prosperity of S'anyu.[a] Cherishers of wholesome (herbs), preserve the well-being of the three humours (of the body).[b]

7. Aświns, who are to be thrice worshipped, day by day, repose on the triple (couch of) sacred grass upon the earth, (that forms the altar). Car-borne Varga V.

---

[a] *Sanyu* is said to be the son of *Bṛihaspati*, brought up by the *Aświns*.

[b] The text has only *tridhátu*, the aggregate of three humours, said, by the Scholiast, agreeably to medical writers, to denote wind, bile, and phlegm.

NÁSATYAS,[a] repair, from afar, to the threefold (place of sacrifice);[b] as the vital air, to (living) bodies.

8. Come, AŚWINS, thrice, with the seven mother-streams.[c] The three rivers are ready;[d] the triple oblation is prepared. Rising above the three worlds, you defend the sun in the sky, who is established for both night and day.[e]

9. Where, NÁSATYAS, are the three wheels of your triangular car?[f] Where, the three fastenings and props (of the awning)? When will be the harnessing of the powerful ass,[g] that you may come to the sacrifice?

10. Come, NÁSATYAS, to the sacrifice. The oblation is offered. Drink the juice, with mouths that

---

[a] They in whom there is not (*na*) untruth (*asatya*).

[b] The text has only "to the three:" the Scholiast adds "altars, severally appropriated to oblations of ghee, to animal sacrifices, and to libations of *Soma*,"—*aishṭikapáśukasaumika-rúpá vedih*.

[c] *Gangá* and the other rivers are here considered as the parents of the water which rolls in their streams.

[d] Three sorts of jars, or pitchers, used to contain and pour out the *Soma* juice, at the three daily sacrifices.

[e] Inasmuch as the rising and setting of the sun indicate the arrival of both day and night. In what way the *Aświns* are of service to the luminary does not appear.

[f] The apex of the car is in front, the base is the back part, forming three angles. The text has only *trivṛito rathasya*, which the Scholiast interprets *trisankhyákair aśribhir upetasya rathasya*.

[g] The text has *rásabha*, a synonym of *gardabha*, an ass. According to the *Nighaṇṭu*, there is a pair of them: *Rásabhávaświnoh*, "Two asses are the steeds of the *Aświns*."

relish the sweet savour. Before the dawn, even, SAVITṚI sends, (to bring you) to the rite, your wonderful car,[a] shining with clarified butter.

11. Come, NÁSATYAS, with the thrice eleven divinities:[b] come, AŚWINS, to drink the oblation. Prolong our lives; efface our faults; restrain our enemies; and be ever with us.

12. Borne in your car that traverses the three worlds, bring to us, AŚWINS, present affluence, attended by (male) progeny. I call upon you both, listening to me, for protection. Be to us for vigour in battle.

SÚKTA V. (XXXV.)

The *Ṛishi* is the same: the first and ninth verses are in the *Jagatí* metre; the rest, in the *Trishṭubh*. The divinity of the whole Hymn is SAVITṚI; but, in the first verse, AGNI, MITRA, VARUṆA, and *Night* are included, as subordinate or associated deities.

1. I invoke AGNI first, for protection: I invoke, for protection, MITRA and VARUṆA: I invoke *Night*, Varga VI
who brings rest to the world: I invoke the divine SAVITṚI, for my preservation.

2. Revolving through the darkened firmament,

---

[a] Implying that the *Aświns* are to be worshipped, with this hymn, at dawn.

[b] This is authority for the usual *Paurâṇik* enumeration of thirty-three deities, avowedly resting on *Vaidik* texts. The list is, there, made up of the eight *Vasus*, eleven *Rudras*, twelve *Ádityas*, *Prajápati*, and *Vashaṭkára* (*Vishṇu Puráṇa*, p. 123 and note 27): but the Scholiast intimates a different classification, or the threefold repetition of eleven divinities, agreeably to the text: "Ye eleven deities, who are in heaven,—*Ye deváso divy ekádaśa stha*. [I., CXXXIX., 11: see Vol. II, p. 62.]

arousing mortal and immortal, the divine SAVITṚI travels in his golden chariot, beholding the (several) worlds.

3. The divine SAVITṚI travels by an upward and by a downward path:[a] deserving adoration, he journeys with two white horses: he comes hither, from a distance, removing all sins.

4. The many-rayed adorable SAVITṚI, having power (to disperse) darkness from the world, has mounted his nigh-standing chariot, decorated with many kinds of golden ornaments, and furnished with golden yokes.

5. His white-footed coursers,[b] harnessed to his car with a golden yoke, have manifested light to mankind. Men and all the regions are ever in the presence of the divine SAVITṚI.

6. Three are the spheres: two are in the proximity of SAVITṚI, one leads men to the dwelling of YAMA.[c] The immortal (luminaries)[d] depend

---

[a] That is, ascending from sunrise to the meridian, and then declining.

[b] The horses of *Savitṛi* are here termed *śyâva*, which, properly, signifies 'the brown;' but, in verse three, they have been called 'white:' the present must be, therefore, a proper name, unless the hymner contradicts himself.

[c] The spheres or *lokas* which lie in the immediate path of the sun are said to be heaven and earth: the intermediate *loka*, *antariksha*, or firmament, is described as the road to the realm of *Yama*, the ruler of the dead, by which the *pretâh*, or ghosts, travel. Why this should not be considered equally the course of the sun is not very obvious.

[d] The text has only *amṛitâ*, "the immortals:" the Scholiast

upon SAVITṚI; as a car, upon the pin of the axle. Let him who knows (the greatness of SAVITṚI) declare it.

7. SUPARṆA,[a] (the solar ray), deep-quivering, life-bestowing, well-directed, has illuminated the three regions. Where, now, is SÚRYA? Who knows to what sphere his rays have extended?[b] Varga VII.

8. He has lighted up the eight points of the horizon, the three regions of living beings, the seven rivers. May the golden-eyed SAVITṚI come hither, bestowing upon the offerer of the oblation desirable riches.

9. The golden-handed, all-beholding SAVITṚI travels between the two regions of heaven and earth, dispels diseases, approaches the sun,[c] and overspreads the sky with gloom, alternating radiance.

10. May the golden-handed, life-bestowing, well-guiding, exhilarating, and affluent SAVITṚI be present (at the sacrifice); for the deity, if worshipped

supplies "the moon and constellations," or, in another acceptation, "the rains;" *amṛita* having, for one meaning, water.

[a] *Suparṇa*, the well-winged, is, in the *Nighaṇṭu*, a synonym of *raśmi*, a ray: one of its epithets, *asura*, is here explained life-giving; from *asu*, vital breath, and *ra*, who gives.

[b] This is supposed to be said of the sun before dawn, while he is absent.

[c] *Veti súryam abhi*. The Scholiast endeavours to explain this, by observing, that, although *Savitṛi* and *Súrya* are the same, as regards their divinity, yet they are two different forms, and, therefore, one may go to the other; *yadyapi savitṛisúryayor ekadevatátwam tathápi múrtibhedena gantṛigantavyabhávaḥ*.

in the evening, is at hand, driving away *Rákshasas* and *Yátudhánas*.

11. Thy paths, SAVITṚI, are prepared of old, are free from dust, and well-placed in the firmament. (Coming) by those paths, easy to be traversed, preserve us to-day. Deity, speak to us.

ANUVÁKA VIII.

SÚKTA I. (XXXVI.)

The *Ṛishi* is KAṆWA, son of GHORA: the deity is AGNI, identified, in the thirteenth and fourteenth stanzas, with the *Yúpa*, or sacrificial post. The metre of the odd verses is *Bṛihatí*, having twelve syllables in the third *páda*, or quarter of the stanza: the metre of the even verses is termed *Satobṛihati*, having the first and third *pádas* equal.

Varga VIII.

1. We implore, with sacred hymns, the mighty AGNI,—whom other (*Ṛishis*) also praise,—for the benefit of you, who are many people, worshipping the gods.

2. Men have recourse to AGNI, the augmenter of vigour. Offering oblations, we worship thee. Do thou, liberal giver of food, be well-disposed to us, here, this day, and be our protector.

3. We select thee, AGNI, the messenger and invoker of the gods, who art endowed with all knowledge. The flames of thee, who art mighty and eternal, spread around thy rays, touch the heavens.

4. The deities VARUṆA, MITRA, and ARYAMAN*

---

* *Aryaman* is here explained, he who measures or estimates properly the *aryas*, *aryán mimíte*.

kindle thee, (their) ancient messenger. The man who has offered thee (oblations) obtains, through thee, AGNI, universal wealth.

5. Thou, AGNI, art the giver of delight, the invoker and messenger of the gods,[a] the domestic guardian of mankind. The good and durable actions which the gods perform are, all, aggregated in thee.

6. Youthful and auspicious AGNI, whatever oblation may be presented to thee, do thou, well-disposed towards us, either now or at any other time, convey it to the powerful gods. Varga IX.

7. In this manner the devout adore thee, who art such (as described), bright with thine own radiance. Men, with (seven)[b] ministrant priests,

---

[a] Rosen has *nuntius hominum*, which agrees better with the order of the text, *dúto viśám asi:* but *Sáyańa* connects *viśám* with what, in the original, precedes, *grihapatih*, lord of the dwelling, and explains *dúta* by *devadúta*.

[b] The Scholiast supplies "the seven." According to another text, *sapta hotráh práchir vashaṫkurvanti*, the seven principal priests pour out the oblation. According to Mr. Stevenson, the seven priests or assistants at the *Soma-yága* are:—1. The institutor, or *Yajamána*; 2. The *Hotri*, who repeats the hymns of the *Rich*; 3. The *Udgátri*, who chants the *Sáma*; 4. The *Potri*, who prepares the materials for the oblation; 5. The *Nashtri*, who pours it on the fire; 6. The *Brahmá*, who superintends the whole; and, 7. The *Rakshas*, who guards the door. This enumeration omits one of the principal performers, the *Adhwaryu*, who recites the formulæ of the *Yajush*, and who should, probably, take the place of the *Yajamána*. The others, except the last, are, also, included among the sixteen (see p. 37, note b).

kindle AGNI (with oblations), victorious over their enemies.

8. The destroying (deities, along with thee,) have slain VṚITRA: they have made earth, and heaven, and the firmament, the spacious dwelling-place (of living creatures). May AGNI, possessed of wealth, when invoked, be a benefactor to KAŚWA; like a horse that neighs in a conflict for cattle.[a]

9. Take your seat, AGNI, on the sacred grass; for thou art mighty. Shine forth; for thou art devoted to the gods. Adorable and excellent AGNI, emit the moving and graceful smoke.

10. Bearer of oblations, (thou art he) whom the gods detained for the sake of MANU; whom, giver of wealth, KAŚWA, the host of pious guests,[b] has detained; whom INDRA detained; and whom (now,) some other worshipper has detained.

Varga X. 11. The rays of that AGNI, whom KAŚWA made more brilliant than the sun, preeminently shine: him do these our hymns, him do we, extol.

12. AGNI, giver of food, complete our treasures; for the friendship of the gods is obtainable through thee. Thou art lord over famous viands. Make us happy; for thou art great.

---

[a] *Krandad aśwo gavishṭishu*, like a horse making a noise in wishes for cattle. The Scholiast adds *sangrámeshu*, in battles, having, for their object, the wish to win cattle,—*gavishayechchhdyuktesha*. The relation of the simile to *Agni* is somewhat obscure.

[b] *Medhyátithi*, attended by venerable (*medhya*) guests (*atithi*), is, here, an epithet of *Kaṇwa*, whose son has been before introduced, as *Medhátithi*, the *Ṛishi* of the twelfth and following *Súktas*.

13. Stand up erect, for our protection, like the divine SAVITṚI. Erect, thou art the giver of food, for which we invoke thee with unguents, and priests (offering oblations).[a]

14. Erect, preserve us, by knowledge, from sin: consume every malignant spirit: raise us aloft, that we may pass (through the world); and, that we may live, convey our wealth (of oblations) to the gods.

15. Youthful and most resplendent AGNI, protect us against evil spirits, and from the malevolent (man) who gives no gifts: protect us from noxious (animals), and from those who seek to kill us.

16. AGNI, with the burning rays, destroy entirely our foes, who make no gifts, as (potters' ware,) with a club:[b] let not one who is inimical to us, nor the man who attacks us with sharp weapons, prevail against us. Varga XI.

17. AGNI is solicited for power-conferring (affluence): he has granted prosperity to KAŃWA; he has protected our friends, as well as the (sage who was) the host of the holy, and (every other) worshipper (who has had recourse to him) for riches.

18. We invoke, from afar, along with AGNI, TUR-

[a] *Agni*, as erect, is here said to be identified with the *yúpa* or post to which the victims, at a sacrifice of animals, are bound; and, according to *Áśwaláyana*, this and the next verse are to be recited, on such occasions, at the time of setting up the post.

[b] The text has only *ghaná*, with a club: the Scholiast adds "the pottery," *bháńḍáni*.

VAŚA, YADU, and UGRÁDEVA. Let AGNI, the arrester of the robber, bring hither NAVAVÁSTWA, BṚIHADRATHA, and TURVÍTI.[a]

19. MANU detained thee, AGNI, (to give) light to the various races of mankind. Born for the sake of sacrifice, and satiated with oblations, thou, whom men reverence, hast blazed for KAŃWA.

20. The flames of AGNI are luminous, powerful, fearful, and not to be trusted. Ever, assuredly and entirely, consume the mighty spirits of evil, and all our other adversaries.

SÚKTA II. (XXXVII.)

The *Ṛishi* is KAŃWA; the Hymn is addressed to the MARUTS; the metre is *Gáyatrí*.

Varga XII. 1. Celebrate, KAŃWAS,[b] the aggregate strength of the MARUTS, sportive, without horses,[c] but shining in their car;

---

[a] Nothing more is said, of the persons named in this verse, than that they were *Rájarshis*, royal sages. [See p. 149, and Vols. II., III., IV., *passim*.] *Turvíti* may be another reading of *Turvasu*, who, with *Yadu*, was a son of *Yayáti*, of the lunar race. We have several princes, in the *Puráńas*, of the name of *Bṛihadratha*; but the others are, exclusively, *Vaidik*.

[b] *Kańwas* may mean either the members of the *gotra* (the family, or school) of *Kańwa*, or, simply, sages or priests.

[c] The phrase is *anarváńam*, which the Scholiast explains, *bhrátṛivyarahitam*, literally, without a brother's son, which would be a very unintelligible epithet. *Arvan* is, in its usual acceptation, a horse; and being without horses would not be inapplicable to the *Maruts*, whose chariot is drawn by deer. *Bhrátṛivya* has, for one sense, that of enemy; whence Rosen renders the expression

2. Who, borne by spotted deer, were born self-radiant, with weapons, war-cries,[a] and decorations.

3. I hear the cracking of the whips in their hands, wonderfully inspiring (courage) in the fight.

4. Address the god-given prayer[b] to those who are your strength, the destroyers of foes, the powerful, possessed of brilliant reputation.

5. Praise the sportive and resistless might of the MARUTS, who were born amongst kine,[c] and whose strength has been nourished by (the enjoyment of) the milk.[d]

6. Which is chief leader among you, agita- Varga XIII.

---

of the text, *hostium immunem*, and M. Langlois, *inattaquable*: but it is doubtful if *arvam* can admit of such an interpretation.

[a] *Vásíbhih*, with sounds, or speeches; *i.e.*, according to the Scholiast, with cries terrifying the enemy's army. *Vásí* is a synonym of *vách*, speech, voice, in the *Nighaúṭu*.

[b] *Devattam brahma*, the praise or prayer which recommends the oblation, obtained from the favour or instruction of the gods.

[c] The text has *goshu Márutam*, the tribe of *Maruts* among the cows. Another text is cited, which says the *Maruts* were born of milk, for *Priśni*,—*Priśniyai vai payaso Maruto játáh*.

[d] The passage is brief and obscure,—*jambhe rasasya vávridhe*, which is explained, their vigour, derived from or of the milk, was increased (either) in enjoyment or in the belly,—*gokshírarúpasya sambandhi tat tejo jambhe sukhe udare vá vriddham abhút*. Rosen renders it, *in utero lactis vires augentur*; M. Langlois has *qui règne au milieu des vaches (célestes), et ouvre avec force (leurs mamelles pour en faire couler) le lait*. The cows he considers the clouds; and the milk, the rain: but it is the *śardhas*, the *tejas*, the vigour, or strength, of the *Maruts*, which has been augmented in or by, not exerted upon, the *rasa*, or milk.

tors of heaven and earth, who shake all around, like the top (of a tree)?

7. The householder, in dread of your fierce and violent approach, has planted* a firm (buttress); for the many-ridged mountain is shattered (before you),

8. At whose impetuous approach earth trembles; like an enfeebled monarch, through dread (of his enemies).

9. Stable is their birth-place, (the sky); yet the birds (are able) to issue from (the sphere of) their parent: for your strength is everywhere (divided) between two (regions,—or, heaven and earth).

10. They are the generators of speech: they spread out the waters, in their courses: they urge the lowing (cattle) to enter (the water), up to their knees, (to drink).

Varga XIV 11. They drive, before them, in their course, the long, vast, uninjurable, rain-retaining cloud.

12. MARUTS, as you have vigour, invigorate mankind: give animation to the clouds.

13. Wherever the MARUTS pass, they fill the way with clamour: every one hears their (noise).

14. Come quickly, with your swift (vehicles). The offerings of the KAŚWAS are prepared. Be pleased with them.

15. The offering is prepared for your gratifica-

---

* The text has only *mánusho dadhre*, the man has planted: the Scholiast explains the former, *grihaswámí*, the master of the house, and adds, to the latter, *grihadárḍhyárthaṁ dṛiḍhaṁ stambhaṁ*, a strong post, to give stability to the dwelling.

tion: we are your (worshippers), that we may live all our life.

SÚKTA III. (XXXVIII.)

The Ṛishi, deities, and metre continue the same.

1. MARUTS, who are fond of praise, and for whom the sacred grass is trimmed, when will you take us by both hands, as a father does his son? Varga XV

2. Where, indeed, are you (at present)? When will your arrival take place? Pass from the heaven, not from the earth. Where do they (who worship you) cry (to you,) like cattle?

3. Where, MARUTS, are your new treasures? Where, your valuable (riches)? Where, all your auspicious (gifts)?[a]

4. That you, sons of PṚIŚNI,[b] may become mortals, and your panegyrist, become immortal.

5. Never may your worshipper be indifferent to you,—as a deer (is never indifferent) to pasture,—so that he may not tread the path of YAMA.

6. Let not the most powerful and indestructible NIRṚITI[c] destroy us: let him perish, with our (evil) desires. Varga XVI.

7. In truth, the brilliant and vigorous MARUTS,

---

[a] The expressions of the text, *sumná*, *suritá*, and *saubhagá*, are said to imply, severally, offspring and cattle, jewels and gold, and horses, elephants, and the like.

[b] *Pṛiśnimátarah*, as we have had before (p. 56, note b): but *Pṛiśni* is here explained, by the Scholiast, by *dhenu*, a milch-cow.

[c] He is, here, called a divinity of the *Rákshasa* race (see p. 62, note.) [Also see Vol. III., p. 123, note 2].

cherished by RUDRA,[a] send down rain, without wind, upon the desert.

8. The lightning roars,—like a parent cow that bellows for its calf,—and, hence, the rain is set free by the MARUTS.

9. They spread darkness over the day, by a water-bearing cloud, and, thence, inundate the earth.

10. At the roaring of the MARUTS, every dwelling of earth (shakes), and men, also, tremble.

Varga XVII. 11. MARUTS, with strong hands, come along the beautifully-embanked rivers, with unobstructed progress.

12. May the felloes of your wheels be firm; may your cars and their steeds be steady, and your fingers well-skilled (to hold the reins).

13. Declare, in our presence, (priests,) with voice attuned to praise, BRAHMAŃASPATI,[b] AGNI, and the beautiful MITRA.

14. Utter the verse that is in your mouths; spread it out, like a cloud spreading rain: chant the measured hymn.

15. Glorify the host of MARUTS, brilliant, deserving of praise, entitled to adoration: may they be exalted by this our worship.

---

[a] *Rudriyásah; i.e., Rudrasyeme*, those who are of, or belonging to, *Rudra*; explained, *Rudreńa pálitáh*, cherished or protected by *Rudra*; for the explanation of which, reference is made to the *ákhyánas*, tales or traditions. There is no connexion between *Rudra* and the *Maruts*, in the *Puráńas*.

[b] The lord of the *mantra* (or prayer), or of the sacrificial food.

SÚKTA IV. (XXXIX.)

The *Rishi* and deities are the same: the metre is *Brihati*, in the odd verses; *Satobrihati*, in the even.

1. When, MARUTS, who make (all things) tremble, Varga XVIII.
you direct your awful (vigour) downwards, from afar, as light (descends from heaven), by whose worship, by whose praise, (are you attracted)? To what (place of sacrifice), to whom, indeed, do you repair?

2. Strong be your weapons for driving away (your) foes, firm in resisting them: yours be the strength that merits praise, not (the strength) of a treacherous mortal.

3. Directing MARUTS, when you demolish what is stable, when you scatter what is ponderous, then you make your way through the forest (trees) of earth, and the defiles of the mountains.

4. Destroyers of foes, no adversary of yours is known above the heavens, nor (is any) upon earth. May your collective strength be quickly exerted, sons of RUDRA,* to humble (your enemies).

5. They make the mountains tremble; they drive apart the forest-trees. Go, divine MARUTS, whither you will, with all your progeny, like those intoxicated.

6. You have harnessed the spotted deer to your Varga XIX.
chariot: the red deer, yoked between them, (aids to)

* *Rudrásah*; i.e., *Rudraputráh*, sons of *Rudra*; figuratively, perhaps, as having been protected by him, as intimated in the preceding hymn.

drag the car:[a] the firmament listens for your coming; and men are alarmed.

7. RUDRAS, we have recourse to your assistance, for the sake of our progeny. Come, quickly, to the timid KAŚWA, as you formerly came, for our protection.

8. Should any adversary, instigated by you, or by man, assail us, withhold from him food, and strength, and your assistance.

9. PRACHETASAS,[b] who are to be unreservedly worshipped, uphold (the sacrificer) KAŚWA: come to us, MARUTS, with undivided protective assistances; as the lightnings (bring) the rain.

10. Bounteous givers, you enjoy unimpaired vigour: shakers (of the earth), you possess undiminished strength: MARUTS, let loose your anger, like an arrow, upon the wrathful enemy of the *Rishis*.

---

[a] The spotted deer, *prishatih*, are always specified as the steeds of the *Maruts*. We then have, in the text, *prashṭir vahati rohitah*. *Prashṭi* is said to be a sort of yoke, in the middle of three horses, or other animals, harnessed in a car; but the word stands alone, without any grammatical concord; and it does not appear what is to be done with the yoke. *Rohita*, the Scholiast says, is another kind of deer, the red deer, who, *vahati*, bears or drags the car, *ratham nayati*. The sense may be something like that which is given in the translation; but the construction of the original is obscure, and, apparently, rude and ungrammatical.

[b] Or the appellative may be an epithet only, implying those possessed of superior (*pra*) intellect (*chetas*).

SÚKTA V. (XL.)

The deity is BRAHMAṆASPATI; the Ṛishi is, still, KAṆWA; the metre, the same as in the preceding.

1. Rise up, BRAHMAṆASPATI.[a] Devoted to the gods, we solicit thee. Bounteous MARUTS, be nigh at hand: INDRA, be a partaker of the libation. Varga XX.

2. Man celebrates thee, son of strength,[b] for the wealth abandoned (by the foe). MARUTS, may he who praises you obtain wealth, yielding excellent steeds and eminent vigour.

3. May BRAHMAṆASPATI approach us: may the goddess, speaker of truth,[c] approach us: may the gods (drive away) every adversary, and, present, conduct us to the sacrifice which is beneficial to man, and (abounds) with respectably-presented offerings.

4. He who presents to the ministrant (priest)

---

[a] In a former passage, *Brahmaṇaspati* appeared as a form of *Agni* (p. 41, note); in this hymn, he is associated with the *Maruts*, although *Indra* is, also, separately named.

[b] *Sahasasputra*. Similar epithets, as *sahaso yaho* and *súnuh śavasaḥ*, have been applied to *Agni* (Hymns XXVI., v. 10, and XXVII., v. 2). The Scholiast, however, interprets the compound, in this place, the great or abundant protector of strength,—*balasya bahupálakah*; such being one of the meanings of *putra*, given in the *Nirukta* (*putrah puru trâyate*), where, however, that meaning is only the etymological explanation of *putra*, a son.—*Nirukta*, II., 11.

[c] *Deví sûnṛitá*, the goddess of speech (*Vágdevatá*) in the form of lover of truth (*priyasatyarúpá*), a form of *Saraswati*.

wealth fit to be accepted enjoys inexhaustible abundance: for him we worship IḶÁ,[a] attended by brave warriors, inflicting much injury, receiving none.

5. Verily, BRAHMAṆASPATI proclaims the sacred prayer in which the divinities INDRA, VARUṆA, MITRA, and ARYAMAN have made their abode.[b]

Varga XXI. 6. Let us recite, gods, that felicitous and faultless prayer at sacrifices. If you, leaders, desire (to hear) this prayer, then will all that is to be spoken reach unto you.

7. Who (except BRAHMAṆASPATI,) may approach the man who is devoted to the gods, by whom the

[a] *Manoh putri*, the daughter of *Manu*, and institutrix of sacrifices (see p. 82, note a). Looking upon *Brahmaṅaspati* as the presiding divinity of prayer or sacrifice, allusion to *Iḷá* were not wholly out of place. Why she should be *suvírá*, if that be rightly explained *śobhanair víraír bhaṭair yuktá*, accompanied by excellent heroes, does not appear.

[b] This and the next verse are directed to be recited at the *Agnishṭoma* ceremony, in connexion with prayers addressed to *Indra* and the *Maruts*. Professor Roth cites it in proof of his theory, that *Brahmaṅaspati* is, in an especial manner, the divinity of prayer, which is not incompatible with his being identical with either *Agni* or *Indra*, in the same capacity. He recites, it is said, aloud (*pravadati*) the prayer (*mantram*) which ought to be so recited (*ukthyam*) by the mouth, according to the Scholiast, of the *Hotṛi*; in which *mantra*, *Indra* and the rest abide, or are mystically present. Or, as explained in the commentary on the next stanza, it is the *mantra*, or prayer, that generates or brings them to the presence of the worshipper,—*Indrádisarvadevatápratipádakam mantram*.

clipped sacred grass is spread? The giver of the oblation has proceeded, with the priests, (to the hall of sacrifice); for he has a dwelling (abounding), internally, with precious things.

8. Let BRAHMAṆASPATI concentrate his strength. Associated with the regal (divinities), he slays (the foe): in the time of danger, he maintains his station: armed with the thunderbolt,[a] there is no encourager nor discourager of him in a great battle or a small.

SÚKTA VI. (XLI.)

The *Rishi* is KAṆWA; the three first and the three last stanzas are addressed to VARUṆA, MITRA, and ARYAMAN; the middle three, to the ÁDITYAS:[b] the metre is *Gáyatri*.

1. The man whom the wise VARUṆA, MITRA, and ARYAMAN protect quickly subdues (his foes). Varga XXII.

2. He whom they heap (with riches), as if (collected) by his own arms; the man whom they defend from the malignant; every such man, safe from injury, prospers.

3. The kings (VARUṆA, &c.,) first destroy their strongholds, and then the foes of those (who worship them), and put aside their evil deeds.

[a] This attribute would identify him with *Indra*, in which character he appears throughout this hymn.

[b] In fact, the hymn may be considered as wholly addressed to the *Ádityas*; for the three deities, separately named, are, in one of their characters, *Ádityas*, also; that is, they were the sons of *Aditi*, the wife of *Kaśyapa*, and are representatives of the sun, in as many months of the year.

4. Ádityas, to you, repairing to the sacrifice, the path is easy and free from thorns: no unworthy oblation is here prepared for you.

5. Ádityas, guides, may the sacrifice which you come to by a straight path be, to you, for your gratification.

Varga XXIII. 6. That mortal (whom you favour), exempt from harm, obtains all valuable wealth, and offspring like himself.

7. How, my friends, shall we recite praise (worthy) of the great glory of Mitra, Varuṇa, and Aryaman?

8. I do not denounce to you him who assails or reviles the man devoted to the gods: I rather propitiate you with offered wealth.

9. For he (the worshipper,) loves not, but fears to speak, evil (of any one); as a gamester fears (his adversary) holding the four* (dice), until they are thrown.

---

* The text has only *chaturaś chid dadamánád bibhíyád á nidhátoḥ*, he may fear from one holding four, until the fall. The meaning is supplied by the Scholiast, with the assistance of *Yáska*, *chaturo' kshán dhárayataḥ* * * *kitavát*, from a gambler holding four dice; *Sáyaṇa* says, four *cowri* shells,—*kapardakáḥ*. That is, where two men are playing together, the one who has not the throw of the dice or the shells is in anxious apprehension lest it should be against him.

SÚKTA VII. (XLII.)

Rishi and metre, as before: the deity is PÚSHAN.[a]

1. PÚSHAN, convey us over the road; remove the wicked (obstructer of the way). Son of the cloud, deity, go before us. Varga XXIV.

2. If a wicked (adversary), PÚSHAN, a robber, or one who delights in evil, points out to us (the way we ought not to go), do thou drive him from the road.

3. Drive him far away, apart from the road, the hinderer of our journey, a thief, a deceiver.

---

[a] *Púshan* is, usually, a synonym of the sun; that is, he is one of the twelve *Adityas*. He is described, by the Scholiast, as the presiding deity of the earth,—*prithivyabhimáni devah*: he is, also, the cherisher of the world; from *push*, to nourish. According to the tenour of the hymn, he is the deity presiding especially over roads or journeyings. His being called the son of the cloud is not incompatible with his character of earth personified as a male; as, according to other texts of the *Veda*, the earth was born of the water,—*adbhyah prithivi*; and, again, earth was the essence of the water; *Tad yad apám sára ásit tat samahanyata sá prithivya-bhavat*,—That which was the essence of the waters, that was aggregated, and it became earth. *Púshá* occurs, also, as a feminine noun, in which case it appears to be synonymous with *prithivi*, the earth, as in the text: *Púshádhwanah pátu*, which is explained, *iyam vai púshá*, May this *Púshá* protect the roads; where the gender is denoted by the feminine pronoun *iyam*: and, in another text, *Iyam vai púsheyam hidam sarvam pushyati*,—This is, verily, *Púshá*; for she cherishes this whole world. Throughout the hymn, however, *Púshan* is masculine.

4. Trample, with your feet, upon the mischievous (body) of that evil-minded pilferer of both (what is present and what is absent), whoever he be.

5. Sagacious and handsome PÚSHAN, we solicit of thee that protection wherewith thou hast encouraged the patriarchs.

Varga XXV.

6. Therefore, do thou, who art possessed of all prosperity, and well-equipped with golden weapons, bestow upon us riches that may be liberally distributed.

7. Lead us past our opponents: conduct us by an easy path: know, PÚSHAN, how to protect us on this (journey).*

8. Lead us where there is abundant fodder: let there be no extreme heat by the way: PÚSHAN, know how to protect us on this (journey).

9. Be favourable to us; fill us (with abundance); give us (all good things); sharpen us (with vigour); fill our bellies: PÚSHAN, know how to protect us on this (journey).

10. We do not censure PÚSHAN, but praise him with hymns: we solicit the good-looking (PÚSHAN) for riches.

---

* In this and the two next verses, we have an example of what is not unfrequent, the repetition of a phrase, as a sort of burden or refrain. The expression is, *Púshann iha kratum vidah*,—*Púshan*, know, here, the act or business; that is, on this occasion, or journey, know how to fulfil your function of giving us protection. Rosen renders it, *Púshan! hic sacrificium animadverte*; *kratu* meaning an act of sacrifice, as well as act or action in general.

SÚKTA VIII. (XLIII.)

The *Ṛishi* is the same: the deity is RUDRA;[a] the third stanza is addressed to MITRA and VARUṆA, also; and the last three verses, to SOMA: the metre of the last verse is *Anushṭubh*; of the rest, *Gáyatrí*.

1. When may we repeat a most grateful hymn to the wise, the most bountiful, and mighty RUDRA, who is (cherished) in our hearts? Varga XXVI.

2. By which earth may (be induced to) grant the gifts of RUDRA[b] to our cattle, our people, our cows, and our progeny;

3. By which MITRA, and VARUṆA, and RUDRA, and all the gods, being gratified, may show us (favour).

4. We ask the felicity of S'ANYU[c] from RUDRA,

---

[a] According to the Scholiast, *Rudra* means, "he who makes to weep, who causes all to weep at the end of time;" thus identifying him with the destroying principle, or *S'iva*. But there is nothing, in the hymn, to bear out such an identification: on the contrary, he appears as a beneficent deity, presiding especially over medicinal plants.

[b] *Aditi* is here said to mean the earth, who, it is wished, may so act (*karat*), that *Rudriya* may be obtained. The meaning of *Rudriya*, according to the Scholiast, is, *Rudrasambandhi bheshajam*,—medicament in relation to, or presided over by, *Rudra*, conformably to the text, *Yá te Rudra s'ivá tanúḥ, s'ivá vis'vá ha, bheshají s'ivá, Rudrasya bheshají*,—Whatever are thy auspicious forms, O *Rudra*, they are all auspicious; auspicious are medicaments, the medicaments of *Rudra*.

[c] *Sanyu* is said to be the son of *Bṛihaspati*: nothing more is related of him.

the encourager of hymns, the protector of sacrifices, possessed of medicaments that confer delight;[a]

5. Who is brilliant as SÚRYA, who gratifies like gold, the best of the gods, the provider of habitations;

Varga XXVII. 6. Who bestows easily-obtained happiness on our steeds, our rams, our ewes, our men, our women, and our cows.

7. SOMA, grant us prosperity more than (sufficient for) a hundred men, and much strength-engendering food.

8. Let not the adversaries of SOMA, let not our enemies, harm us: cherish us, INDRA, with (abundant) food.

9. SOMA, who art immortal, and abidest in an excellent dwelling, have regard for thy subjects, when, at their head, in the hall of sacrifice, thou observest them (engaged in) decorating thee.[b]

ANUVÁKA IX.

SÚKTA I. (XLIV.)

PRASKAŃWA, the son of KAŃWA, is the *Rishi*: AGNI is the deity;

---

[a] *Jaláshabheshajam*, he who has medicaments conferring delight; from *ja*, one born, and *lásha*, happiness; an unusual word, except in a compound form, as *abhilásha*, which is of current use. Or it may mean, "sprung from water (*jala*);" all vegetables depending upon water, for their growth.

[b] Apparently, there is some confusion of objects in this place; *Soma*, the moon, being confounded with *Soma*, libation.

but the two first verses are addressed, also, to the Áświns and to Ushas (the dawn): the metre is *Brihati*, in the odd verses; *Satobrihati*, in the even.

1. Agni, who art immortal, and cognizant of all begotten things, bring, from the dawn, to the donor (of the oblation), wealth of many sorts, with an excellent habitation: bring hither, to-day, the gods, awaking with the morning. Varga XXVIII.

2. For thou, Agni, art the accepted messenger of the gods, the bearer of oblations, the vehicle of sacrifices.* Associated with Ushas and the Áświns, bestow upon us abundant and invigorating food.

3. We select, to-day, Agni, the messenger, the giver of dwellings, the beloved of many, the smoke-bannered, the light-shedding, the protector of the worship of the worshipper at the break of day.

4. I praise Agni at the break of day, the best and youngest (of the gods), the guest (of man), the universally-invoked, who is friendly to the man that offers (oblations), who knows all that are born, that he may go (to bring) the other divinities.

5. Agni, immortal sustainer of the universe, bearer of oblations, deserving of adoration, I will praise thee, who art exempt from death, the preserver, the sacrificer.

* *Rathir adhwaráńám.* Rosen renders *rathih*, *auriga*; but Sáyaṇa explains it, *rathasthánīya*, in the place of a chariot; confirmed by other texts; as, *Esha hi devarathah*, He (*Agni*) is, verily, the chariot of the gods, and *Ratho ha vá esha bhútebhyo devebhyo havyam vahati*, Truly, he is the chariot that bears the oblation to the spirits and the gods.

Varga XXIX. 6. Juvenile AGNI, whose flames delight, who art universally invoked, and art praised, (by us,) on behalf of the worshipper, understand (our wishes), and, granting PRASKAŃWA to live a lengthened life, do honour to the divine man.[a]

7. All people kindle thee, AGNI, the sacrificer, the omniscient. Do thou, AGNI, who art invoked by many, quickly bring hither the sapient deities.

8. Object of holy rites,[b] (bring hither,) on the dawn following the night, SAVITṚI, USHAS, the AŚWINS, BHAGA,[c] and AGNI. The KAŃWAS, pouring out libations, kindle the wafter of the burnt-offering.

9. Thou, AGNI, art the protector of the sacrifices of the people, and the messenger (of the gods). Bring hither, to-day, the gods, awaking at dawn, and contemplating the sun, to drink the *Soma* juice.

10. Resplendent AGNI, visible to all, thou hast blazed after many preceding dawns; thou art the protector (of people) in villages; thou art the associate of man placed on the east (of the altar).[d]

Varga XXX. 11. We place thee, AGNI, as MANU's placed thee, who art the implement of sacrifice, the invoker, the ministering priest, very wise, the destroyer (of foes), immortal, the messenger (of the gods).

---

[a] *Namasyá daivyam janam;* that is, the *Ṛishi* of the hymn, *Praskańwa.*

[b] *Swadhwara;* from *su*, good, and *adhwara*, sacrifice; equivalent, according to the Scholiast, to the *Áhavanîya* fire.

[c] *Bhaga* is one of the *Ádityas.*

[d] *Purohita*, which may also mean the domestic priest.

12. When, cherisher of friends, thou art present, as the *Purohita*, at a sacrifice, and dischargest the mission to the gods, then thy flames roar, like the resounding billows of the ocean.

13. AGNI, with sharp ears, hear me. Let MITRA and ARYAMAN, and (other) early-stirring deities, with all the accompanying oblation-bearing gods, sit down at the sacrifice, upon the sacred grass.

14. Let the munificent MARUTS, who have tongues of fire, and are encouragers of sacrifice, hear our praise: let the rite-fulfilling VARUṆA, with the AŚWINS, and with USHAS, drink the *Soma* juice.

SÚKTA II. (XLV.)

The deity and *Ṛishi* are the same, except in the last stanza and the half of the preceding, which include any deified being: the metre is *Anushṭubh*.

1. AGNI, do thou, in this our rite, worship the Varga XXXI.
VASUS, the RUDRAS, the ÁDITYAS, or any other (living) being sprung from MANU, sacrificing well, and sprinkling water.[a]

2. Verily, the discriminating gods are givers of rewards to the offerer (of oblations). Lord of red coursers, propitiated by our praises, bring hither the three and thirty divinities.[b]

---

[a] *Janam, Manujátam*, a man born of *Manu*. *Jana*, according to the Scholiast, here signifies a divine being in connexion with the divinities enumerated,—another man, *devaśarúpa*, of a divine nature or form.

[b] We have had these alluded to on a former occasion (p. 97,

3. AGNI, accomplisher of solemn acts, cognizant of all who are born, hear the invocation of PRASKAŃWA, as thou hast heard those of PRIYAMEDHA, of ATRI, of VIRÚPA, of ANGIRAS.*

4. The performers of great ceremonies, the offerers of acceptable sacrifices, have invoked, for (their protection), AGNI, shining, amidst the solemnities, with pure resplendence.

5. Invoked by oblations, giver of rewards, listen to these praises with which the sons of KAŃWA invoke thee for protection.

Varga XXXII. 6. AGNI, granter of abundant sustenance, who art beloved of many, the sons of men invoke thee, radiant-haired, to bear the oblation (to the gods).

7. The wise have placed thee, AGNI, in (their) sacrifices, as the invoker, the ministrant priest, the

---

note b); but, according to the *Aitareya Bráhmańa*, 2, 18, there are two classes, of thirty-three divinities each, the one consisting of those formerly specified, who are termed, also, *Somapás*, or drinkers of the *Soma* juice, and the other, of eleven *Prayájas* (the same with the *Aprís*, p. 31), eleven *Anuyájas*, and eleven *Upayájas*, who are to be propitiated by oblations of clarified butter, not by libations of *Soma*. They are, evidently, little else than personifications of sacrifices.

* The commentator, on the authority of the *Nirukta*, III., 17, calls these, all, *Ŗishis*. *Atri* and *Angiras* are always enumerated among the *Prajápatis*; *Priyamedha* may be the same as *Priyavrata*, the son of *Swáyambhuva Manu*; and we have a *Virúpa* among the early descendants of *Vaivaswata Manu*, who, as the father of *Ilá*, is the *Manu* of the *Veda*.—*Vishńu Puráńa*, pp. 53 and 359.

donor of vast wealth, the quick-hearing, the far-renowned.

8. The wise (priests), with effused libations of *Soma* juice, have summoned thee, vast and brilliant AGNI, to partake of the (sacrificial food), as they hold the oblation on the part of the individual who presents it.

9. Strength-generated,[a] giver of rewards, provider of dwellings, place here, to-day, upon the sacred grass, the morning-moving deities, or (other) deified being, to drink the *Soma* juice.[b]

10. Worship, with conjoint invocations, AGNI, the present deified being. Bounteous divinities, this is the *Soma* juice: drink it; for it was yesterday expressed.[c]

SÚKTA III. (XLVI.)

The *Rishi*, as before; the deities are the AŚWINS; the metre is *Gáyatri*.

1. The beloved USHAS, until now unseen, scatters Varga XXXIII.

---

[a] Produced by friction, which requires strength to perform effectually.

[b] In this and the next stanza, we have, again, an allusion to some divine or deified person, *daivyam janam*, or to some other divinity, without particularizing him. It may be intended for *Ka* or *Prajápati*, who, with *Agni*, here actually addressed, would make up the thirty-three divinities, with the *Vasus*, *Rudras*, and *Adityas*.

[c] *Tiro-ahnyam* is said to be the appellation of the *Soma* juice so prepared,—from *tiras*, oblique or indirect, and *ahnyam*, diurnal; that juice which is expressed on the preceding day, and offered on the succeeding.

darkness from the sky. Aświns, I greatly praise you,

2. Who are divine, of pleasing appearance, children of the sea,[a] willing dispensers of wealth, and granters of dwellings, (in recompense of) pious acts.

3. Since your chariot proceeds, (drawn) by your steeds, above the glorious heavens, your praises are proclaimed (by us).

4. (Aświns); guides; the sun, (the evaporator) of the waters, the nourisher, the protector and beholder of the (solemn) rite, nourishes (the gods) with our oblation.

5. Násatyas, accepting our praises, partake of the exhilarating *Soma* juice, the animator of your minds.

Varga XXXIV. 6. Aświns, grant us that invigorating food which may satisfy us, having dispelled the gloom (of want).[b]

7. Come, as a ship, to bear us over an ocean of praises: harness, Aświns, your car.

8. Your vessel, vaster than the sky, stops on the sea-shore: your chariot (waits on the land): the

---

[a] *Sindhumátará*. The sun and moon, as the Scholiast states, are said to be born of the sea,—*samudrajau*; and, in the opinion of some, the *Aświns* are the same as the sun and moon, and consequently, are sea-born.

[b] The original has only "disperse the darkness,"—*tamas tiraḥ*. The Scholiast explains the darkness to signify that of poverty,—*dáridryarúpam andhakáram*.

drops (of the *Soma* juice) are expressed for your worship.

9. KAṆWAS, (ask this of the AŚWINS): (How) do the rays (of the sun proceed) from the sky? (How) does the dawn (rise) in the region of the waters? Where do you desire to manifest your own persons?*

10. There was light to irradiate the dawn: the sun (rose) like gold: the fire shone with darkened flames.

11. A fit path was made for the sun to go Varga XXXV.
beyond the boundary (of night): the radiance of the luminary became visible.

12. The worshipper acknowledges whatever boon he receives from the AŚWINS, satiate with the enjoyment of the *Soma* juice.

13. Causers of felicity, co-dwellers with your worshipper, as with MANUS, come hither, to drink of the *Soma* juice, and (accept) our praise.

14. May USHAS follow the lustre of your approach, circumambient AŚWINS; and may you be pleased with the oblations offered by night.

15. AŚWINS, may you both drink (the libation)

* The whole of this stanza is very elliptical and obscure, and largely indebted to the Scholiast. Literally, it would run: "Rays from the sky, *Kaṇwas*, cause of dwelling in the place of the rivers, where do you wish to place own form?" *Sáyaṇa* fills this up, by supposing that the *Kaṇwas* are directed to inquire of the *Aświns* the particulars specified in the translation. Without some such addition, however conjectural it may be, it were impossible to extract any meaning out of such a passage.

and bestow upon us happiness, through your irreproachable protection.

FOURTH ADHYAYA.

ANUVAKA IX. (continued).

SÚKTA IV. (XLVII.)

The *Ṛishi* is PRASKAŚWA: the deities are the AŚWINS: the metre of the odd verses, *Bṛihati*; of the even, *Satobṛihati*.

Varga I. 1. AŚWINS, encouragers of sacrifice, this most sweet *Soma* juice is prepared for you. Drink it of yesterday's expressing, and grant riches to the donor.

2. Come, AŚWINS, with your three-columned, triangular car.* The KAŚWAS repeat your praise at the sacrifice. Graciously hear their invocation.

3. AŚWINS, encouragers of sacrifice, drink this most sweet *Soma* juice: approach, to-day, the giver of the offering, you who are of pleasing aspects, and bearers of wealth.

4. Omniscient AŚWINS, stationed on the thrice-heaped sacred grass, sprinkle the sacrifice with the

---

* *Trivandhureṇa trivṛitâ, rathena*, with a car with three posts, and triangular, is the explanation we have had before. The Scholiast here proposes a somewhat different interpretation, and would render the terms; having three undulating fastenings of timber, and passing, unobstructedly, through the three worlds.

sweet juice. The illustrious KAŃWAS, with effused libations, invoke you.

5. With such desired aids as you protected KAŃWA with, do you, cherishers of pious acts, preserve us: encouragers of sacrifice, drink the *Soma* juice.

6. Good-looking AŚWINS, as you brought, in your car, bearers of wealth, abundance to SUDÁS,[a] so bring to us the riches that many covet, whether from the firmament or the sky beyond. Varga 11.

7. NÁSATYAS, whether you abide far off, or close at hand, come to us, in your well-constructed car, with the rays of the sun.

8. Let your coursers, the grace of the sacrifice, bring you, to be present at our rite. Guides (of men), bestowing food upon the pious and liberal donor (of the offering), sit down on the sacred grass.

9. Come, NÁSATYAS, with your sun-clad chariot,[b] in which you have ever conveyed wealth to the donor (of the offering), to drink of the sweet *Soma* juice.

10. We invoke, with chanted and recited hymns, the very affluent AŚWINS, to be present, for our protection. Have you not ever drunk the *Soma* juice in the favoured dwelling of the KAŃWAS?

---

[a] *Sudás* is called a *Rájá*, the son of *Pijavana*. We have two princes of the name of *Sudása*, in the *Puráńas*: one, in the solar line (*Vishńu Puráńa*, p. 380); the other, in the lunar, the son of *Divodása* (*ibid.*, p. 454).

[b] Literally, sun-skinned,—*súryatwachá*; that is, either surrounded or invested by the sun, or like him in brightness.

SÚKTA V. (XLVIII.)

The *Ṛishi* is the same, but the Hymn is addressed to USHAS, the personified dawn, or Aurora: the metre is the same as in the preceding.

Varga III. 1. USHAS, daughter of heaven, dawn upon us with riches: diffuser of light, dawn upon us with abundant food: bountiful goddess, dawn upon us with wealth (of cattle).

2. Abounding with horses, abounding with kine, bestowers of every sort of wealth,[a] (the divinities of morning) are possessed of much that is necessary for the habitations (of men). USHAS, speak to me kind words: send us the affluence of the wealthy.

3. The divine USHAS has dwelt (in heaven, of old). May she dawn to-day, the excitress of chariots which are harnessed at her coming; as those who are desirous of wealth (send ships) to sea.[b]

4. USHAS, at thy comings wise men turn their minds to benefactions. Of these men the most wise KAŚWA proclaims the fame.

---

[a] These three epithets are, all, in the feminine plural, without a substantive: *aśwávatíh, gomatíh, viśwasuvidah*: the Scholiast supplies, therefore, *ushodevatáh*, the divinities of dawn, as if there were many. Rosen supplies *horæ matutinæ*.

[b] The text is *Samudre na śravasyavah*, Like those desirous of wealth for sea: the commentary supplies "send ships." In the beginning of the stanza, we have only *Uvásoshúh*, which the Scholiast explains, *purá nivásam akarot*, she has made a dwelling, formerly, *i.e.*, *prabhátam kṛitavatí*, she produced the dawn.

5. Ushas, nourishing (all), comes, daily, like a matron, the directress (of household duties), conducting all transient (creatures) to decay. (At her coming) each biped stirs; and she wakes up the birds.

6. She animates the diligent, and sends clients (to their patrons),[a] and, shedder of dews, knows not delay. Bestower of food, at thy rising the soaring birds no longer suspend (their flight). Varga IV.

7. This auspicious Ushas has harnessed (her vehicles) from afar, above the rising of the sun; and she comes gloriously upon man, with a hundred chariots.[b]

8. All living beings adore her, that she may be visible: bringer of good, she lights up the world: the affluent daughter of heaven drives away the malevolent, and disperses the absorbers[c] (of moisture).

9. Shine around, Ushas, with cheering lustre, bringing us, every day, much happiness, and scattering darkness.

10. Inasmuch, bringer of good, as thou dawnest,

---

[a] *Vi* + *srijati* + + *arthinah*, she lets loose askers, solicitors; for they, says *Sáyaṇa*, having risen at early morning, go to the houses of those who are their respective benefactors,—*te'pi* (*yáchakáh*) + *usháhkále samutthága swakiyadátrigrihe gachchhanti.*

[b] Perhaps, "with many rays of light" is what is intended by the many chariots of the dawn.

[c] *Sridhah*, *i.e.*, *soshayitrin*, the driers up. Possibly, the clouds are intended, as taking up the dews of night: but no explanation of the application of the term is given.

the breath and life of all (creatures) rest in thee. Diffuser of light, come to us, with thy spacious car: possessor of wondrous wealth, hear our invocation.

Varga V. 11. Ushas, accept the (sacrificial) food which, of many kinds, exists among the human race, and thereby bring to the ceremony the pious, who, offering oblations, praise thee.

12. Ushas, bring, from the firmament, all the gods, to drink the *Soma* juice; and do thou thyself bestow upon us excellent and invigorating food, along with cattle and horses.

13. May that Ushas, whose bright auspicious rays are visible all around, grant us desirable, agreeable, and easily-attainable riches.

14. Adorable Ushas, whom the ancient sages invoked for protection and for food, do thou, (radiant) with pure light, (pleased) by our offerings, accept our praises.

15. Ushas, since thou hast, to-day, set open the two gates of heaven with light,* grant us a spacious and secure habitation: bestow upon us, goddess, cattle and food.

16. Adorable Ushas, associate us with much and multiform wealth, and with abundant cattle, with all foe-confounding fame, and, giver of sustenance, with food.

* The east and west points of the horizon.

Súkta VI. (XLIX.)

The *Ṛishi* and deity are the same; the metre is *Anushṭubh*.

1. Ushas, come, by auspicious ways, from above Varga VI.
the bright (region of the) firmament: let the purple (kine)[a] bring thee to the dwelling of the offerer of the *Soma* juice.

2. Ushas, in the ample and beautiful chariot in which thou ridest, come, to-day, daughter of heaven, to the pious offerer of the oblation.

3. White-complexioned Ushas, upon thy coming bipeds and quadrupeds (are in motion), and the winged birds flock around, from the boundaries of the sky.

4. Thou, Ushas, dispersing the darkness, illuminest the shining universe with thy rays: such as thou art, the Kaṅwas, desirous of wealth, praise thee with their hymns.

Súkta VII. (L.)

Praskaṅwa is, still, the *Ṛishi*; the deity is Súrya, the sun. The first nine stanzas are in the *Gáyatrí* metre; the last four, in the *Anushṭubh*.

1. His coursers bear on high the divine all- Varga VII.
knowing Sun, that he may be seen by all (the worlds).

2. (At the approach) of the all-illuminating Sun,

---

[a] So the *Nighaṇṭu*,—*aruṇyo gâva ushasâm*, purple cows, the vehicles of the morning.

the constellations[a] depart, with the night, like thieves.

3. His illuminating rays behold men in succession, like blazing fires.

4. Thou, SÚRYA, outstrippest all in speed;[b] thou art visible to all; thou art the source of light;[c] thou shinest throughout the entire firmament.

---

[a] *Nakshatrá*, the stars in general, or the lunar asterisms, which, according to different texts, are considered to be the abodes of the gods, or the visible forms of pious persons after death; as, *Devagrihá vai nakshatráńi*, The constellations are, verily, the dwellings of the gods; and, again, *Yo vá iha yajate 'mum lokam nakshate*, either, He who performs worship here obtains the next world, or, *Sukritám vá etáni jyotínshi yan nakshatráńi*, Those constellations are the luminaries of those who practise religious acts, that is, according to *Sáyańa*, those who, by attending to religious duties in this world, attain *Swarga*, are beheld in the form of constellations,—*iha loke karmánushthíya ye swargam prápnuvanti te nakshatrarúpeńa driśyante*.

[b] *Sáyańa* says, that, according to the *Smriti*, the sun moves 2,202 *yojanas* in half a twinkle of the eye.

[c] *Jyotishkrit*, giving light to all things, even to the moon and the planets, by night: for they, it is said, are of a watery substance, from which the rays of the sun are reflected; in like manner as the rays of the sun, falling upon a mirror placed in the doorway of a chamber, are reflected into the interior, and give it light. *Sáyańa* also explains the whole passage metaphysically, identifying the sun with the supreme spirit, who enables all beings to pass over the ocean of existence, who is beheld by all desirous of final emancipation, who is the author of true or spiritual light, and who renders everything luminous through the light of the mind.

5. Thou risest in the presence of the MARUTS,[a] thou risest in the presence of mankind, and so as to be seen in the presence of the whole (region) of heaven.

6. With that light with which thou, the purifier and defender from evil, lookest upon this creature-bearing world, Varga VIII.

7. Thou traversest the vast ethereal space, measuring days and nights, and contemplating all that have birth.

8. Divine and light-diffusing SÚRYA, thy seven coursers[b] bear thee, bright-haired, in thy car.

9. The Sun has yoked the seven mares[c] that safely draw his chariot, and comes with them self-harnessed.

10. Beholding the up-springing light above the darkness, we approach the divine Sun, among the gods, the excellent light.[d]

---

[a] The text has *pratyañ devánám viśah*, before the men or people of the gods, that is, the *Maruts*, who, in another *Vaidik* text, are so designated: *Maruto vai devánám viśah*.

[b] *Sapta • haritah*, which may, also, mean the seven rays. The seven horses are the days of the week: the seven rays may express the same. They can scarcely be referred to the prismatic rays, although the numerical coincidence is curious.

[c] *Sapta śundhyuvah*, *i.e.*, *aśvastriyah*, mares. They are, also, called *naptyah*, because with them the car does not fall: *yábhir • ratho • na patati*. They were more docile than those of Phaeton's father.

[d] Here, again, we may have an allusion to a spiritual sun. The darkness, it is said, implies sin, and the approach to the sun intimates reunion with supreme spirit; as in other texts, *Agamma*

11. Radiant with benevolent light, rising to-day, and mounting into the highest heaven, do thou, O Sun, remove the sickness of my heart, and the yellowness (of my body).[a]

12. Let us transfer the yellowness (of my body) to the parrots, to the starlings, or to the *Haritála*[b] (tree).

13. This ÁDITYA has risen, with all (his) might,

---

jyotir uttamam, we go to the best light; that is, we become identified with spiritual light,—*sáyujyam gachchhámah*; and, again, he (the worshipper) becomes identical with that which he worships,—*tam yathá yathopásate tad eva bhavati*.

[a] *Hṛidroga* may also mean heart-burn or indigestion; *harimáṇam*, greenness or yellowness, is external change of the colour of the skin, in jaundice or bilious affections. This verse and the two following constitute a *tricha* or triplet, the repetition of which, with due formalities, is considered to be curative of disease. *Súrya*, thus hymned by *Praskaṇwa*, cured him, it is said, of a cutaneous malady, or leprosy, under which he was labouring. Accordingly, *Saunaka* terms the couplets a *mantra*, dedicated to the sun, removing sin, healing disease, an antidote to poison, and the means of obtaining present happiness and final liberation. The especial worship of the sun, in India, at the time of the first incursions of the Mahommedans, attributed to that luminary's having cured *Sámba*, the son of *Kṛishṇa*, of leprosy, is fully related by M. Reinaud, in his interesting *Mémoire sur l' Inde*, and was then, no doubt, of ancient date, originating with the primitive notions of the attributes of *Súrya*, here adverted to. The hymn is, throughout, of an archaic character.

[b] So the Scholiast interprets the *hüridrava* of the text, *haritáladruma*; but there is no tree so called. *Haritála* most usually means yellow orpiment; *háridrava*, a yellow vegetable powder.

destroying my adversary; for I am unable to resist my enemy.[a]

ANUVÁKA X.

SÚKTA I. (LI).

The *Ṛishi* is SAVYA,[b] the son of ANGIRAS: the Hymn is addressed to INDRA: the two last verses are in the *Trishṭubh* metre; the rest, in the *Jagatí*.

1. Animate, with praises, that ram,[c] (INDRA), who is adored by many, who is gratified by hymns, and is an ocean of wealth; whose good deeds spread abroad, for the benefit of mankind, like the rays of light. Worship the powerful and wise INDRA, for the enjoyment of prosperity. Varga IX.

2. The protecting and fostering ṚIBHUS[d] hastened to the presence of INDRA, of graceful motion, and irradiating the firmament,[e] imbued with vigour,

---

[a] The enemy here intended is sickness or disease.

[b] *Angiras*, it is said, having performed worship, to obtain a son who should resemble *Indra*, the deity became his son, under the name of *Savya*.

[c] *Tyam mesham;* referring to a legend in which it is narrated, that *Indra* came, in the form of a ram, to a sacrifice solemnized by *Medhátithi*, and drank the *Soma* juice. Or *mesha* may be rendered "victor over foes."

[d] The *Ṛibhus* are said, here, to mean the *Maruts*, by whom *Indra* was aided and encouraged, when all the gods had deserted him; as in the texts, "All the gods who were thy friends have fled: may there be friendship between the *Maruts* and thee;" and, again, "The *Maruts* did not abandon him."

[e] *Indra*, as *Sakra*, is one of the twelve *Adityas*, or suns.

the humiliator of his enemies, the performer of a hundred pious acts; and by them encouraging words were uttered.[a]

3. Thou hast opened the cloud[b] for the ANGIRASAS; thou hast shown the way to ATRI, who vexes his adversaries by a hundred doors;[c] thou hast granted wealth, with food, to VIMADA:[d] thou art wielding thy thunderbolt in defence of a worshipper engaged in battle.

4. Thou hast opened the receptacle of the waters; thou hast detained, in the mountain, the treasure of the malignant;[e] when thou hadst slain VṚITRA, the destroyer,[f] thou madest the sun visible in the sky.

---

[a] They exclaimed, "Strike; *Bhagavan*, be valiant,"—*Prahara*, *Bhagavo* • *víryaswa*.

[b] The term is *gotra*, explained either a cloud, or a herd of cattle. *Gotrabhid*, as a name of *Indra*, implies, in ordinary language, mountain-breaker,—that is, with the thunderbolt: as applied to cattle, it alludes, it is said, to the recovery of the cows stolen by *Paṇi*. In either case, the act was performed in consequence of the prayers, or for the benefit, of the descendants of *Angiras*.

[c] By a number of means or contrivances,—*yantras*.

[d] *Vimada* is called, in the commentary, a *Maharshi*.

[e] *Parvate dánumad vasu*. "In the mountain" implies the dwelling of *Indra*. *Dánumat* is variously explained, as one doing an injury, hostile or malignant, an enemy; or, one descended from *Danu*, a *Dánava*, an *Asura*: or it may be an epithet of *vasu*, wealth, "fit for liberality;" from *dánu*, giving.

[f] *Vṛitra*, who is *Ahi*; explained, *hantri*, the slayer. From a text cited from the *Yajur-Veda*, *Ahi* appears to be the personification of all the benefits derivable from sacrifice, knowledge,

5. Thou, INDRA, by thy devices, hast humbled the deceivers who presented oblations to their own mouths:[a] propitious to men, thou hast destroyed the cities of PIPRU, and hast well defended ṚIJIŚWAN, in robber-destroying (contests).[b]

6. Thou hast defended KUTSA, in fatal fights with S'USHṆA; thou hast destroyed S'AMBARA, in defence of ATITHIGWA; thou hast trodden, with thy foot, upon the great ARBUDA: from remote times wast thou born, for the destruction of oppressors.[c] Varga X.

7. In thee, INDRA, is all vigour fully concentrated; thy will delights to drink the *Soma* juice: it is known, by us, that the thunderbolt is deposited in thy hands. Cut off all prowess from the foe.

8. Discriminate between the *Áryas* and those

---

fame, food, and prosperity; *Sa yat sarvam etat samabharat tasmád Ahih*,—Inasmuch as he was the same as all that, therefore he was called *Ahi*.

[a] According to the *Kaushítakis*, the *Asuras*, contemning *Agni*, offered oblations to themselves; and the *Vájasaneyis* relate, that, when there was a rivalry between the gods and *Asuras*, the latter arrogantly said, "Let us not offer sacrifice to any one," and, thereupon, made the oblations to their own mouths.

[b] *Pipru* is called an *Asura*; *Ṛijiśwan*, a worshipper whom they oppressed; *dasyuhatyeshu*, in battles killing the *Dasyus*,—robbers or barbarians.

[c] *Sushṇa*, *Sambara*, and *Arbuda* are designated as *Asuras*. *Kutsa* we have had before, as the name of a *Ṛishi*. *Atithigwa* is said to mean the hospitable, and to be also termed *Divodása*; but it does not appear whether he is the same as the *Divodása* of the *Puráṇas*. [See Vol. II., p. 34, note b.]

who are *Dasyus*:[a] restraining those who perform no religious rites, compel them to submit to the performer of sacrifices: be thou, who art powerful, the encourager of the sacrificer. I am desirous of celebrating all thy deeds, in ceremonies that give thee satisfaction.

9. INDRA abides, humbling the neglecters of holy acts, in favour of those who observe them, and punishing those who turn away from his worship, in favour of those who are present (with their praise). VAMRA, while praising him, whether old or adolescent, and spreading through heaven, carried off the accumulated (materials of the sacrifice).[b]

10. If UŚANAS should sharpen thy vigour by his own, then would thy might terrify, by its intensity, both heaven and earth. Friend of man, let the will-harnessed steeds, with the velocity of the wind, convoy thee, replete (with vigour), to (partake of the sacrificial) food.

---

[a] The *Áryas*, as appears from this and the next verse, and as stated by the Scholiast, are those who practise religious rites; while the *Dasyus* are those who do not observe religious ceremonies, and are inimical to those who do; being, probably, the uncivilized tribes of India, yet unsubdued by the followers of the *Vedas*, the *Áryas*, the respectable or civilized race.

[b] The text is, here, obscure,—*Vamro vi jaghána sandihah; Vamra* destroyed the collections. The Scholiast says, that a *Ṛishi* named *Vamra* took advantage of *Indra's* absence from a sacrifice, to carry away the accumulated heap of offerings, the marrow or essence of the earth; *Yad valmíkavapásambháro bharati úrjam eva prithivyáh.*

11. When INDRA is delighted with acceptable hymns, he ascends (his car), drawn by more and more obliquely-curveting coursers: fierce, he extracts the waters, from the passing (cloud), in a torrent, and has overwhelmed the extensive cities of S'USHŃA. Varga XI.

12. Thou mountest thy chariot willingly, INDRA, for the sake of drinking the libations. Such as thou delightest in have been prepared (at the sacrifice of) S'ÁRYÁTA.[a] Be pleased with them, as thou art gratified by the effused *Soma* juices, (at the sacrifices) of others. So dost thou obtain imperishable fame in heaven.

13. Thou hast given, INDRA, the youthful VRICHAYÁ[b] to the aged KAKSHÍVAT, praising thee, and offering libations. Thou, SUKRATU, wast MENÁ, the daughter of VRISHAŃAŚWA.[c] All those thy deeds are to be recited at thy worship.

---

[a] *Sáryáta* was a *Rájarshi*,—according to the Scholiast,—of the race of *Bhrigu*. The *Aitareya Bráhmańa* calls him a prince of the race of *Manu*. The term is a patronymic, implying son or descendant of *Saryáti*, who was the fourth son of the *Manu Vaivaswata*. [See p. 203, note c.] The *Rishi Chyavana* married his daughter; and a solemn sacrifice was held on the occasion, at which *Indra* and the *Aświns* were present. *Chyavana* appropriated to himself the share of the oblation intended for the *Aświns*, at which *Indra* was very angry; and, to appease him, a fresh offering was prepared. The Scholiast quotes this story from the *Kaushítaki Bráhmańa*. It is detailed in the *Bhágavata* and *Padma Puráńas*.

[b] *Vrichayá*, it is said, was given to *Kakshívat*, at the *Rájasúya* ceremony. No notice of her occurs elsewhere.

[c] The *Bráhmańa* is cited for a strange story of *Indra's* having,

14. INDRA has been had recourse to, that he may assist the pious, in their distress. Praise by the PAJRAS[a] is (as stable) as the post of a doorway. INDRA, the giver of riches, who is possessed of horses, cattle, chariots, and wealth,[b] is present.

15. This adoration is offered to the shedder of rain, the self-resplendent, the possessor of true vigour, the mighty. May we be aided, INDRA, in this conflict, by many heroes, and abide in a prosperous (habitation, bestowed) by thee.

SÚKTA II. (LII.)

The *Ṛishi* and divinity are the same: the metre of the thirteenth and fifteenth verses is *Trishṭubh*; of the rest, *Jagati*.

Varga XII. 1. Worship well that ram,[c] who makes heaven known, whom a hundred worshippers at once are assiduous in praising. I implore INDRA, with many prayers, to ascend the car,—which hastens, like a fleet courser, to the sacrifice,—for my protection.

2. When INDRA, who delights in the sacrificial food, had slain the stream-obstructing VṚITRA, and was pouring down the waters, he stood firm, amid the torrents, like a mountain, and, endowed with a

---

himself, become *Mená*, the daughter of *Vrishaṇaśwa*, and having, afterwards, fallen in love with her. The *Mená* of the *Puráṇas* is one of the daughters of the *Pitṛis*, by *Swadhá*, and the wife of *Himavat*, the king of the mountains.

[a] The *Pajras* are said to be the same as the *Angirasas*.

[b] Or it may be rendered "who is desirous of possessing,"—expecting such gifts from the institutor of the ceremony.

[c] See p. 135, note c.

thousand means of protecting (his votaries), increased in vigour.

3. He, who is victorious over his enemies, who is spread through the dewy (firmament), the root of happiness, who is exhilarated by the *Soma* juice,—him I invoke, the most bountiful INDRA, along with learned priests, with a mind disposed to pious adoration; for he is the bestower of abundant food:

4. That INDRA whom, in heaven, the libations sprinkled on the sacred grass replenish, as the kindred rivers, hastening to it, fill the ocean: that INDRA whom the MARUTS, the driers up of moisture, who are unobstructed, and of undistorted forms, attended, as auxiliaries, at the death of VṚITRA.

5. His allies, exhilarated (by libations), preceded him, warring against the withholder of the rain; as rivers rush down declivities. INDRA, animated by the sacrificial food, broke through the defences of BALA, as did TRITA, through the coverings (of the well).*

* The text has only *paridhir iva tritah*; and *tritah* may mean triple or threefold; making the phrase, "as through triple coverings," or defences; whence Rosen has *custodes veluti a tribus partibus constitutos*. M. Langlois is more correct, in considering *Tritah* as a proper name; but it may be doubted if he has authority for rendering it by *Soma*,—*ou la libation qui prend le nom de Trita*,—or for the additional circumstances he narrates. The legend told by the Scholiast, and confirmed by other passages of the text, as well as by the version of the story found in the *Nīti-manjari*, is wholly different. *Ekata*, *Dwita*, and *Trita* were three men produced in water, by *Agni*, for the purpose of removing or rubbing off the reliques of an oblation of clarified butter, the proper func-

Varga XIII. 6. When, INDRA, thou hadst smitten, with thy thunderbolt, the cheek of the wide-extended VṚITRA,

---

tion of the sacred grass, to the three blades of which, placed on the altar, the legend may owe its origin: but this does not appear from the narrative. The Scholiast, following the *Taittirîyas*, says that *Agni* threw the cinders of the burnt-offerings into water, whence successively arose *Ekata*, *Dwita*, and *Trita*, who, it elsewhere appears, were, therefore, called *Aptyas*, or sons of water (*Súkta* CV., v. 9). *Trita*, having, on a subsequent occasion, gone to draw water from a well, fell into it; and the *Asuras* heaped coverings over the mouth of it, to prevent his getting out; but he broke through them with ease. It is to this exploit that *Indra's* breaking through the defences of the *Asura Bala* is compared. The story is somewhat differently related in the *Níti-manjarí*. Three brothers, it is said, *Ekata*, *Dwita*, and *Trita*, were travelling in a desert, and, being distressed by thirst, came to a well, from which the youngest, *Trita*, drew water and gave it to his brothers. In requital, they threw him into the well, in order to appropriate his property, and, having covered the top with a cart-wheel, left him in the well. In this extremity, he prayed to all the gods to extricate him, and, by their favour, he made his escape. *Paridhi*, the term of the text, means a circumference, a circular covering, or lid. Mr. Colebrooke has briefly, but with his usual accuracy, cited this story, in his account of the *Ṛig-Veda* (*As. Researches*, Vol. VIII., p. 388). Dr. Roth conceives *Trita* to be the same as *Traitana*, a name that occurs in a text of the *Ṛich*; and, converting the latter into a deification, he imagines him to be the original of *Thraetona*, the *Zend* form of *Ferîdún*, one of the heroes of the *Sháh-náma*, and of ancient Persian tradition.—*Zeitschrift der D. Morgenländischen Gesellschaft*, Vol. II., p. 216. Professor Lassen seems disposed to adopt this identification.—*Indische Alterthumskunde*, *Additions*. The identity of *Trita* and *Traitana*, however, remains to be established; and the very stanza quoted, by Dr. Roth, as authority for the latter name, is explained, in the *Níti-manjarí*, in a very different sense from that who, having obstructed the waters, reposed in the region above the firmament, thy fame spread afar, thy prowess was renowned.

7. The hymns, INDRA, that glorify thee attain unto thee, as rivulets (flow into) a lake. TWASHṬṚI has augmented thy appropriate vigour: he has sharpened thy bolt with overpowering might.

8. INDRA, performer of holy acts, desirous of going to man, thou, with thy steeds, hast slain VṚITRA, (hast set free) the waters, hast taken, in thy hands, thy thunderbolt of iron, and hast made the sun visible in the sky.

---

which he has given. It is said, that the slaves of *Dirghatamas*, when he was old and blind, became insubordinate, and attempted to destroy him, first, by throwing him into the fire, whence he was saved by the *Aświns*, then, into water, whence he was extricated by the same divinities; upon which, *Traitana*, one of the slaves, wounded him on the head, breast, and arms, and then inflicted like injuries on himself, of which he perished. After these events, the sage recited, in praise of the *Aświns*, the hymn in which the verse occurs:—*Na mâ garan nadyo mâtritamâ, dâsâ yad îm susamubdham avâdhuh; śiro yad asya Traitano vitakshat, swayam dâsa uro ansâvapi gdha*,—"Let not the maternal waters swallow me, since the slaves assailed this decrepit (old man). In like manner as the slave *Traitana* wounded his head, so has he struck it, of himself, and, likewise, his breast and shoulders." [I., CLVIII., 5: see Vol. II., p. 103.] If this interpretation be correct, there can be little relation between *Trita* and *Traitana*, and between the latter and *Ferídún*. The former term has, however, found admission as a numeral, and, apparently, also as a proper name, into the *Zend* books. See M. Burnouf's "*Études sur les Textes Zends*," *Journal Asiatique*, April, 1845: see, also, the word *Trita*, in the Glossary of Benfey's edition of the *Sáma-Veda*.

9. Through fear (of VṚITRA, they, the worshippers,) recited the suitable hymn of the *Bṛihat* (*Sáma*),[a] self-illuminating, strength-bestowing, and ascending to heaven; on which his allies, (the MARUTS), combating for men, (guardians) of heaven, and vivifiers of mankind, animated INDRA (to destroy him).

10. The strong heaven was rent asunder with fear, at the clamour of that AHI, when thou, INDRA, wast inspirited by (drinking) the effused (*Soma* juice), and thy thunderbolt, in its vigour, struck off the head of VṚITRA, the obstructor of heaven and earth.

Varga XIV. 11. Although, INDRA, the earth were of tenfold (its extent), and men multiplied every day, yet, MAGHAVAN, thy prowess would be equally renowned; the exploits achieved by thy might would be spread abroad, with the heavens.

12. Firm-minded INDRA, abiding, (secure,) in thy strength, beyond the limit of the wide-expanded firmament, thou hast framed the earth for our preservation; thou hast been the type of vigour; thou hast encompassed the firmament and the sky, as far as to the heavens.

13. Thou art the type of the extended earth;[b]

---

[a] The text has only *Bṛihat;* the Scholiast adds *Sáma*. An allusion to the *Sáma*, in a verse of the *Ṛich*, would indicate the priority of the former, at least as respects this hymn.

[b] *Bhuvah pratimánam*, the counter-measure of the earth; that is, according to the Scholiast, of similar magnitude and like inconceivable power.

thou art the lord of the vast god-frequented (*Swarga*).[a] Verily, with thy bulk thou fillest all the firmament: of a truth, there is none other such as thou.

14. Thou, INDRA, of whom heaven and earth have not attained the amplitude; of whom the waters of heaven have not reached the limit; of whom, when warring, with excited animation, against the withholder of the rains, (his adversaries have not equalled the prowess);—thou, alone, hast made everything else (than thyself) dependent (upon thee).

15. The MARUTS worshipped thee, in this (encounter). All the gods, in this engagement, imitated thee in exultation, when thou hadst struck the face of VṚITRA with thy angular and fatal (bolt).[b]

SÚKTA III. (LIII.)

The *Rishi* and divinity are the same: the metre of the tenth and eleventh stanzas is *Trishṭubh*; of the rest, *Jagatí*.

1. We ever offer fitting praise to the mighty INDRA, in the dwelling of the worshipper, by which he (the deity) has quickly acquired riches; as (a thief) hastily carries (off the property) of the sleeping. Praise ill-expressed is not valued among the munificent. Varga XV.

2. Thou, INDRA, art the giver of horses, of cattle,

[a] *Rishwavírasya brihatah patih*, lord or protector of the great (region), in which are the pleasant (*rishwa*) gods (*víra*).

[b] The text has only *bhrishṭimatá vadhena*,—with the killer (or weapon) that has angles. According to the *Aitareya Bráhmaṇa*, the *vajra*, or thunderbolt, of *Indra* has eight angles, or, perhaps, blades; *ashṭáśrir vai vajrah*.

of barley, the master and protector of wealth, the foremost in liberality, (the being) of many days: thou disappointest not desires (addressed to thee): thou art a friend to our friends. Such an INDRA we praise.

3. Wise and resplendent INDRA, the achiever of great deeds, the riches that are spread around are known to be thine: having collected them, victor (over thy enemies), bring them to us: disappoint not the expectation of the worshipper who trusts in thee.

4. Propitiated by these offerings, by these libations, dispel poverty with cattle and horses. May we, subduing our adversary, and relieved from enemies by INDRA, (pleased) by our libations, enjoy, together, abundant food.

5. INDRA, may we become possessed of riches and of food; and, with energies agreeable to many, and shining around, may we prosper, through thy divine favour, the source of prowess, of cattle, and of horses.

Varga XVI. 6. Those who were thy allies (the MARUTS,) brought thee joy. Protector of the pious, those libations and oblations (that were offered thee, on slaying VṚITRA), yielded thee delight, when thou, unimpeded by foes, didst destroy the ten thousand obstacles* opposed to him who praised thee and offered thee oblations.

---

* *Daśa vṛitráṇi* • • • *sahasráṇi. Vṛitráṇi* is interpreted by *áváraṇáni*, covers, concealments, obstructions.

7. Humiliator (of adversaries), thou goest from battle to battle, and destroyest, by thy might, city after city. With thy foe-prostrating associate, (the thunderbolt), thou, INDRA, didst slay, afar off, the deceiver named NAMUCHI.[a]

8. Thou hast slain KARANJA and PARṆAYA with thy bright gleaming spear, in the cause of ATITHIGWA. Unaided, thou didst demolish the hundred cities of VANGṚIDA, when besieged by ṚIJIŚWAN.[b]

9. Thou, renowned INDRA, overthrewest, by thy not-to-be-overtaken chariot-wheel, the twenty kings of men, who had come against SUŚRAVAS, unaided, and their sixty thousand and ninety and nine followers.[c]

10. Thou, INDRA, hast preserved SUŚRAVAS, by thy succour; TÚRVAYÁṆA, by thy assistance. Thou hast made KUTSA, ATITHIGWA, and ÁYU[d] subject to the mighty, though youthful, SUŚRAVAS.

11. Protected by the gods, we remain, INDRA, at the close of the sacrifice, thy most fortunate friends.

---

[a] *Namuchi* is termed an *Asura*. He appears, in the *Purâṇas*, as a *Dánava*, or descendant of *Danu*.

[b] The first two are the names of *Asuras*. *Atithigwa* we have had before: *Vangrida* is called an *Asura*; and *Ṛijiśwan*, a *Rájá*. We have no further particulars; nor do they appear in the *Purâṇas*. [See Vol. III., pp. 148, 481.]

[c] Here, again, we derive no aid from the *Bháshya*. The legend is not *Paurâṇik*; and, though we have a *Suśravas* among the *Prajápatis* in the *Váyu Purâṇa*, he does not appear as a king.

[d] *Áyus*, the son of *Purúravas*, may be intended; but the name, here, is *Áyu*, without the final sibilant.

We praise thee, as enjoying, through thee, excellent offspring and a long and prosperous life.

SÚKTA IV. (LIV.)

The deity and *Rishi* are the same: the metre of the sixth, eighth, ninth, and eleventh stanzas is *Trishṭubh*; of the other seven, *Jagatí*.

Varga XVII. 1. Urge us not, MAGHAVAN, to this iniquity, to these iniquitous conflicts; for the limit of thy strength is not to be surpassed. Thou hast shouted, and hast made the waters of the rivers roar. How (is it possible) that the earth should not be filled with terror?

2. Offer adoration to the wise and powerful S'AKRA. Glorifying the listening INDRA, praise him who purifies both heaven and earth by his irresistible might, who is the sender of showers, and, by his bounty, gratifies our desires.

3. Offer exhilarating praises to the great and illustrious INDRA, of whom, undaunted, the steady mind is concentrated in its own firmness; for he, who is of great renown, the giver of rain, the repeller of enemies, who is obeyed by his steeds, the showerer (of bounties), is hastening hither.

4. Thou hast shaken the summit of the spacious heaven; thou hast slain S'AMBARA, by thy resolute self; thou hast hurled, with exulting and determined mind, the sharp and bright-rayed thunderbolt against assembled *Asuras*.

5. Since thou, loud-shouting, hast poured the rain upon the brow of the breathing (wind), and

(on the head) of the maturing and absorbing (sun), who shall prevent thee from doing, to-day, (as thou wilt), endowed with an unaltered and resolute mind?

6. Thou hast protected NARYA, TURVAŚA, YADU, and TURVÍTI, of the race of VAYYA.[a] Thou hast protected their chariots and horses,[b] in the unavoidable engagement: thou hast demolished the ninety-nine cities (of S'AMBARA).[c] Varga XVIII.

7. That eminent person, the cherisher of the pious, (the institutor of the ceremony), promotes his own prosperity, who, while offering oblations to INDRA, pronounces his praise; or who, along with the offerings he presents, recites hymns (in honour of him). For him the bounteous INDRA causes the clouds to rain from heaven.

8. Unequalled is his might; unequalled is his wisdom. May these drinkers of the *Soma* juice become equal to him, by the pious act; for they, INDRA, who present to thee oblations augment thy vast strength and thy manly vigour.

9. These copious *Soma* juices, expressed with stones, and contained in ladles, are prepared for

---

[a] Of these names, *Turvaśa* may be the *Turvasu* of the *Purâṇas*, one of the sons of *Yayáti*, as another, *Yadu*, is named. *Narya* and *Turvíti* are unknown: the latter appears hereafter, as a *Ṛishi*. See *Súkta* LXI., v. 11, [Also see p. 104, note a, and p. 291, note e.]

[b] *Ratham, etaśam*. The latter is a synonym of *aśwa*, in the *Nighaṇṭu*: but both words may, also, be regarded as the names of two *Ṛishis*. [See p. 329, note c.]

[c] The commentary supplies this appellation.

thee; they are the beverage of INDRA. Quaff them; satiate thine appetite with them; and, then, fix thy mind on the wealth that is to be given (to us).

10. The darkness obstructed the current of the waters; the cloud was within the belly of VṚITRA: but INDRA precipitated all the waters which the obstructor had concealed, in succession, down to the hollows (of the earth).

11. Bestow upon us, INDRA, increasing reputation; (bestow upon us) great, augmenting, and foe-subduing strength; preserve us in affluence; cherish those who are wise; and supply us with wealth from which proceed excellent progeny and food.

SÚKTA V. (LV.)

Deity and *Ṛishi*, as before; the metre, *Jagatí*.

Varga XIX. 1. The amplitude of INDRA was vaster than the (space of) heaven: earth was not comparable to him, in bulk; formidable and most mighty, he has been, ever, the afflicter (of the enemies of) those men (who worship him); he whets his thunderbolt, for sharpness, as a bull, (his horns).

2. The firmament-abiding INDRA grasps the wide-spread waters with his comprehensive faculties,* as the ocean (receives the rivers): he rushes, (impetuous,) as a bull, to drink of the *Soma* juice; he, the warrior, ever covets praise for his prowess.

* *Gṛibháyati* • *varimabhiḥ*,—he grasps, with his powers of comprehending or collecting, *samvaraṇaiḥ*: or, it may be, by his vastness, *urutwaiḥ*.

3. Thou, INDRA, hast not (struck) the cloud for (thine own) enjoyment; thou rulest over those who are possessed of great wealth. That divinity is known, by us, to surpass all others in strength: the haughty (INDRA) takes precedence of all gods, on account of his exploits.

4. He, verily, is glorified by adoring (sages) in the forest; he proclaims his beautiful vigour amongst men; he is the granter of their wishes (to those who solicit him); he is the encourager of those who desire to worship (him), when the wealthy offerer of oblations, enjoying his protection, recites his praise.

5. INDRA, the warrior, engages in many great conflicts, for (the good of) man, with overwhelming prowess. When he hurls his fatal shaft, every one immediately has faith in the resplendent INDRA.

6. Ambitious of renown, destroying the well-built dwellings of the *Asuras*, expanding like the earth, and setting the (heavenly) luminaries free from concealment,* he, the performer of good deeds, enables the waters to flow, for the benefit of his worshippers. Varga XX.

7. Drinker of the *Soma* juice, may thy mind incline to grant our desires: hearer of praises, let thy coursers be present (at our sacrifice). Thy charioteers are skilful in restraining (thy steeds); nor, INDRA,

* The sun and the constellations were obscured by the same cloud which detained the aggregated waters.

can crafty (enemies), bearing arms, prevail against thee.

8. Thou holdest, in thy hands, unexhausted wealth: thou, renowned (INDRA), hast irresistible strength in thy body: thy limbs are invested with (glorious) exploits; as wells[a] (are surrounded by those who come for water): in thy members, INDRA, are many exploits.

SÚKTA VI. (LVI.)

Deity, *Ṛishi*, and metre, as in the preceding.

Varga XXI. 1. Voracious (INDRA) has risen up,—(as ardently) as a horse (approaches) a mare,—to partake of the copious libations (contained) in the (sacrificial) ladles. Having stayed his well-horsed, golden, and splendid chariot, he plies himself, capable of heroic (actions, with the beverage).

2. His adorers, bearing oblations, are thronging round (him); as (merchants) covetous of gain crowd the ocean, (in vessels,) on a voyage. Ascend quickly, with a hymn to the powerful INDRA, the protector of the solemn sacrifice; as women (climb) a mountain.[b]

3. He is quick in action, and mighty; his faultless and destructive prowess shines in manly (conflict), —like the peak of a mountain (afar),—with which,

---

[a] "Like wells" is the whole of the simile, in the usual elliptical style of the text: the amplification is from the commentary.

[b] The Scholiast here, also, ekes out the scantiness of the text,—as women climb a hill, to gather flowers.

clothed in iron (armour),[a] he, the suppressor of the malignant, when exhilarated (by the *Soma* juice), cast the wily S'USHṆA into prison and into bonds.

4. Divine strength waits—like the sun upon the dawn—upon that INDRA who is made more powerful, for protection, by thee, (his worshipper), who, with resolute vigour, resists the gloom, and inflicts severe castigation upon his enemies, making them cry aloud (with pain).

5. When thou, destroying INDRA, didst distribute the (previously) hidden life-sustaining, undecaying waters through the different quarters of the heaven, then, animated (by the *Soma* juice), thou didst engage in battle, and, with exulting (prowess), slowest VṚITRA, and didst send down an ocean of waters.

6. Thou, mighty INDRA, sendest down, from heaven, by thy power, upon the realms of earth, the (world)-sustaining rain. Exhilarated (by the *Soma* juice), thou hast expelled the waters (from the clouds), and hast crushed VṚITRA by a solid rock.[b]

SÚKTA VII. (LVII.)

Deity, *Ṛishi*, and metre, unchanged.

1. I offer especial praise to the most bountiful, Varga XXII.

[a] *Ayasah*, consisting of iron; that is, according to the Scholiast, whose body is defended by armour of iron; showing the use of coats of mail, at this period, and intimating, also, a representation of the person of *Indra*, as an image, or idol.

[b] *Samayá pátshyá*. The latter may be either, with a stone or a spear; but the adjective *samá*, whole, entire, seems to require the former.

the excellent, the opulent, the verily powerful and stately INDRA, whose irresistible impetuosity is like (the rush) of waters down a precipice, and by whom widely-diffused wealth is laid open (to his worshippers), to sustain (their) strength.

2. All the world, INDRA, was intent upon thy worship; the oblations of the sacrificer (flowed), like water (falling) to a depth; for the fatal golden thunderbolt of INDRA, when hurling it (against the foe), did not sleep upon the mountain.*

3. Beautiful USHAS, now present the oblation, in this rite, to the formidable, praise-deserving INDRA, whose all-sustaining, celebrated, and characteristic radiance has impelled him hither and thither, (in quest) of (sacrificial) food; as (a charioteer drives) his horses (in various directions).

4. Much-lauded and most opulent INDRA, we are they who, relying (on thy favour), approach thee. Accepter of praise, no other than thou receives our commendations. Do thou be pleased (with our address); as the earth (cherishes) her creatures.

5. Great is thy prowess, INDRA. We are thine. Satisfy, MAGHAVAN, the desires of this thy worshipper. The vast heaven has acknowledged thy might: this earth has been bowed down through thy vigour.

6. Thou, thunderer, hast shattered, with thy bolt, the broad and massive cloud into fragments, and

* Or against the side of *Vritra*; that is, it did not stop, until it had performed its office.

hast sent down the waters that were confined in it, to flow (at will). Verily, thou alone possessest all power.

ANUVÁKA XI.

SÚKTA I. (LVIII.)

The deity is AGNI: the *Ṛishi*, NODHAS, the son of GOTAMA: the metre of the first five verses is *Jagatí*; of the last four, *Trishṭubh*.

1. The strength-generated, immortal AGNI quickly issues forth, when he is the invoker of the gods and the messenger (of the worshipper). (Then, proceeding) by suitable paths, he has made the firmament, and worships (the deities), in the sacrifice, with oblations.[a] Varga XXIII.

2. Undecaying AGNI, combining his food[b] (with his flame), and devouring it quickly, ascends the dry wood. The blaze of the consuming (element) spreads like a (fleet) courser, and roars like a roaring (cloud) in the height of heaven.

3. The immortal and resplendent AGNI, the bearer of oblations, honoured[c] by the RUDRAS and the VASUS, the invoker of the gods, who presides

---

[a] The firmament existed, but in darkness, until fire, identified with light, rendered it visible; so that *Agni* may be said to have made or created it—*vi mame*, or *nirmamé*.

[b] The text has *adma*, food, or what may be eaten: but the Scholiast explains it, *triṇagulmaddikam*, straw and twigs; in contrast to *atasa*, which presently occurs, and which he explains by *káshṭha*, wood or timber.

[c] The term is *purohitah*, explained *puraskṛitah*, which may also imply, placed in front of, preceding.

over oblations, and is the distributor of riches, praised by his worshippers, and admired like a chariot amongst mankind, accepts the oblations that are successively presented.

4. Excited by the wind, and roaring loudly, AGNI penetrates easily, with his flames and diffusive (intensity), among the timber. When, undecaying and fiercely-blazing AGNI, thou rushest rapidly, like a bull amongst the forest trees, thy path is blackened.

5. The flame-weaponed and breeze-excited AGNI, assailing the unexhaled moisture (of the trees) with all his strength, in a volume of fire, rushes triumphant (against all things), in the forest, like a bull; and all, whether stationary or moveable, are afraid of him, as he flies along.

Varga XXIV. 6. The BHṚIGUS, amongst men, for the sake of a divine birth,* cherished thee, like a precious treasure, AGNI, who sacrificest for men, who art the invoker (of the gods), the (welcome) guest at sacrifices, and who art to be valued like an affectionate friend.

7. I worship, with oblations, that AGNI, whom the seven invoking priests invite, as the invoker of the gods; who is most worthy of worship at sacrifices, and who is the donor of all riches: I solicit of him wealth.

8. Son of strength, favourably-shining AGNI, grant to thy worshippers, on this occasion, uninterrupted felicity. Offspring of food, preserve him who praises thee from sin, with guards of iron.

---

* *Divyáya janmane*, for the sake of being born as gods.

9. Variously-shining AGNI, be a shelter to him who praises thee: be prosperity, MAGHAVAN,[a] to the wealthy (offerers of oblations): protect, AGNI, thy worshipper from sin. May AGNI, who is rich with righteous acts, come (to us) quickly in the morning.

SÚKTA II. (LIX.)

The Rishi is NODHAS; the deity, AGNI, in the form of VAIŚWÁNARA;[b] the metre is Trishṭubh.

1. Whatever other fires there may be, they are but ramifications, AGNI, of thee: but they all rejoice, being immortal, in thee. Thou, VAIŚWÁNARA, art the navel of men, and supportest them, like a deep-planted column.[c] Varga XXV.

2. AGNI, the head of heaven, the navel of earth, became the ruler over both earth and heaven. All the gods engendered thee, VAIŚWÁNARA, in the form of light, for the venerable sage.[d]

---

[a] This is a very unusual appellative of *Agni*, and is a common synonym of *Indra;* although, in its proper sense of a possessor of riches, it may be applied to either.

[b] *Vaiśwánara;* from *viśwa*, all, and *nara*, a man; a fire common to all mankind; or, as here indicated, the fire or natural heat of the stomach, which is a principal element of digestion.

[c] That is, as a pillar or post, fixed firmly in the ground, supports the main beam or roof of a house.

[d] This is the first verse of a *Tricha*, to be recited at a ceremony observed on the day of the equinox. *Agni* is said to be the head of heaven, as the principal element, and the navel of earth, as its main source of support. The term *áryáya* may apply either to

3. Treasures were deposited in the AGNI VAIŚWÁNARA, like the permanent rays (of light) in the sun. Thou art the sovereign of all the treasures that exist in the mountains, in the herbs, in the waters, or amongst men.

4. Heaven and earth expanded, as it were, for their son.[a] The experienced sacrificer recites, like a bard,[b] many ancient and copious praises addressed to the graceful-moving, truly vigorous, and all-guiding VAIŚWÁNARA.

5. VAIŚWÁNARA, who knowest all that are born, thy magnitude has exceeded that of the spacious heaven: thou art the monarch of MANU-descended men; thou hast regained, for the gods, in battle, the wealth (carried off by the *Asuras*).[c]

6. I extol the greatness of that showerer of rain whom men celebrate as the slayer of VṚITRA. The AGNI VAIŚWÁNARA slew the stealer (of the waters), and sent them down (upon earth), and clove the (obstructing) cloud.[d]

Manu, as the institutor of the first sacrifice, or to the *yajamána*, the institutor of the present rite.

[a] The Scholiast supports this affiliation by citing another text; but that does not apply particularly to any form of *Agni*, but to himself: *Ubhá pitará mahayann ajáyatágnir dyáváprithiví*,—Both parents, heaven and earth, expanding, *Agni* was born.

[b] The text has *manushya* only, "like a man;" that is, according to the Scholiast, a *bandi*, a panegyrist, or bard, who recites the praises of a prince or great man, for largess.

[c] This clause is from the Scholiast.

[d] We have *Vaiśwánara* here evidently identified with *Indra*;

7. VAIŚWÁNARA, by his magnitude, is all men,[a] and is to be worshipped, as the diffuser of manifold light, in offerings of nutritious viands.[b] AGNI, the

an identification not inconsistent with *Vaidik* theogony, which resolves all the divinities into three,—Fire, Air, and the Sun, and those three, again, into one, or the Sun (*Nirukta*, VII., 4). But the Scholiast says, we are to understand *Vaiśwánara*, in this verse, as the *Agni* of the firmament, the *vaidyuta*, the lightning or electric fire. The firmament, or middle region, is, properly, that of *Váyu*, the Wind, or of *Indra*; the inferior region, or earth, is the proper sphere of *Agni*; and that of the upper region, or heaven, of the Sun. The Scholiast cites a passage from the *Nirukta*, VII., 21, in which it is discussed who *Vaiśwánara* is, and two opinions are compared,—one, which places him in the middle region, and identifies him with *Indra* or *Váyu*, or both, in which character he sends rain, an office that the terrestrial *Agni* cannot discharge; and another, which identifies him with *Súrya*, or the Sun, in the upper sphere. Both are, however, considered, by the Scholiast, to be untenable, chiefly from the etymologies of the name, which make *Vaiśwánara* an *Agni*, the fire—as above stated —of the middle region, or lightning; from which, when fallen to earth, the terrestrial fire is born, and from which, also, the rain is indirectly generated, the burnt-offering ascending to the sun; and it is, in consequence, from the sun that rain descends: *Vaiśwánara* is, therefore, an *Agni*. According to *Pauráṇik* astronomy, *Vaiśwánara* is the central path of the sun; in mythology, he occurs as one of the *Dánavas*. The cloud is termed, in the text, *Śambara*, who is, elsewhere, called an *Asura*.

[a] *Viśwakṛishṭi*, literally rendered, all men: the Scholiast says, of whom all men are same nature,—*swabhútáḥ*.

[b] *Bharadwájeshu*,—in sacrifices which present food in the shape of nutritious (*pushṭikara*) oblations of clarified butter (*havis*). Or it may mean, who is to be worshipped by the *Rishis* termed *Bharadwájas*, or of the *gotra*, or race, of *Bharadwája*.

speaker of truth, praises, with many commendations, PURUŚÍTHA, the son of S'ATAVANI.[a]

SÚKTA III. (LX.)

The *Ṛishi* is the same; the deity is AGNI; the metre, *Trishṭubh*.

Varga XXVI. 1. MÁTARIŚWAN brought, as a friend, to BHṚIGU,[b] the celebrated VAHNI, the illuminator of sacrifices, the careful protector (of his votaries), the swift-moving messenger (of the gods), the offspring of two parents,[c] (to be to him), as it were, a precious treasure.

2. Both (gods and men)[d] are the worshippers of

---

[a] These are *Vaidik* names. *Satavani* is so called, as the offerer of a hundred, *i.e.*, numerous, sacrifices: his son has the patronymic *Sátavaneya*.

[b] The wind brought *Agni* to the sage *Bhṛigu*, as a friend (*ráti*): some translate it 'a son,' as in the text, *rátim Bhṛigúṇám*,—the son of the *Bhṛigus*. The more modern Sanskrit confirms the first sense; as, although it has lost the original simple term, it preserves it in the compound *aráti*, an enemy, one not (*a*) a friend (*ráti*), an unfriend.

[c] As before; either of heaven and earth, or of the two pieces of wood.

[d] The text has only *ubhayásah*, "both," which the Scholiast explains, either gods and men, or the ministering priests and their employer,—the *yajamána*. The same authority would repeat the phrase "gods and men," as the sense of the text *Uśijo ye cha martáh*; explaining the first by *kámayamáná deváh*,—those who are to be wished for,—the gods. He also proposes, as an alternative for *uśijah*, *medhávinah*, wise, or the priests, and, for mortals, the *yajamánas*.

this ruler,—those who are to be desired (the gods), and those who are mortal, bearing oblations: for this venerable invoker (of the gods), the lord of men, and distributor (of desired benefits), was placed, by the officiating priests, (upon the altar), before the sun was in the sky.[a]

3. May our newest celebration[b] come before that AGNI, who is sweet-tongued, and is to be engendered in the heart;[c] whom men, the descendants of MANUS, sacrificing and presenting oblations to him, beget, in the time of battle.[d]

4. AGNI, the desirable, the purifying, the giver of dwellings, the excellent, the invoker (of the gods), has been placed (upon the altar), among men. May he be inimical (to our foes), the protector of (our) dwellings, and the guardian of the treasures in (this) mansion.

5. We, born of the race of GOTAMA, praise thee, AGNI, with acceptable (hymns), as the lord of riches; rubbing thee, the bearer of oblations, as (a rider rubs down) a horse.[e] May he who has acquired

---

[a] The priests conduct the *Yajamána* to the place where the fire has been prepared, before the break of day, by the *Adhwaryu*.

[b] *Navyasí* . . *sukírtiḥ*; as if the hymn were of very recent composition.

[c] *Agni*, it is said, is engendered of air: but that air is the vital air, or breath; and *Agni*, therefore, is said to be produced in the heart, or in the interior of the human body.

[d] In order to make burnt-offerings, to secure success.

[e] The text has only rubbing, or, rather, sweeping, thee, as a horse; that is, according to the Scholiast, brushing the place of

wealth by sacred rites come hither, quickly, in the morning.

SÚKTA IV. (LXI.)

The deity is INDRA; the *Ṛishi* and metre are the same as in the preceding.

Varga XXVII. 1. I offer adoration to that powerful, rapid, mighty, praise-meriting, and unobstructed INDRA,—adoration that is acceptable, and oblations that are grateful, as food (to a hungry man).

2. I offer (oblations, acceptable as) food, (to the hungry,) to that INDRA: I raise (to him) exclamations that may be of efficacy in discomfiting (my foes). Others (also,) worship INDRA, the ancient lord, in heart, in mind, and in understanding.

3. I offer, with my mouth, a loud exclamation, with powerful and pure words of praise, to exalt him who is the type (of all,) the giver (of good things), the great, the wise.

4. I prepare praises for him, as a carpenter constructs a car, (that the driver) may, thence, (obtain) food,*—praises well-deserved, to him who is entitled

---

the fire for the burnt-offering,—the altar, perhaps,—in like manner as persons about to mount a horse rub, with their hands, the part where they are to sit; one inference from which is, that the early Hindus had no saddles.

* *Ratham na tashṭeva tatsináya*. *Sina*, according to the *Nirukta*, is a synonym of food (*Nirukta*, V., 5): *tat* implies the owner of the car, "for his food."

to commendation, and excellent oblations to the wise INDRA.

5. To propitiate that INDRA, for the sake of food, I combine praise with utterance,[a] as (a man harnesses) a horse (to a car), in order to celebrate the heroic, munificent, and food-conferring INDRA, the destroyer of the cities (of the *Asuras*).

6. For that INDRA, verily, TWASHṬṚI sharpened the well-acting, sure-aimed thunderbolt, for the battle, with which fatal (weapon) the foe-subduing and mighty sovereign severed the limbs of VṚITRA. Varga XXVIII.

7. Quickly quaffing the libations, and devouring the grateful viands (presented) at the three (daily) sacrifices which are dedicated to the creator (of the world),[b] he, the pervader of the universe,[c] stole the ripe (treasures of the *Asuras*): the vanquisher (of his foes), the hurler of the thunderbolt, encountering, pierced the cloud.[d]

---

[a] *Arkam juhwá*. The latter is defined, the instrument of invocation, the organ of speech: the former means, as usual, hymn, or praise in metre.

[b] He may be so termed, as everything in the world proceeds from rain.

[c] The term of the text is *Vishńu*, applied to *Indra*, as the pervader of all the world,—*sarvasya jagato vyápakah*.

[d] *Varáha*, one of the synonyms of *megha*, cloud, in the *Nighańṭu*. Or it may mean sacrifice, from *vara*, a boon, and *aha*, a day. In reference to this purport, a different explanation of the text is given, which is somewhat obscure. *Vishńu*, it is said, means the personified sacrifice (*yajna*), in which character he stole, or attracted, the accumulated wealth of the *Asuras;* after which

8. To that INDRA the women, the wives of the gods,[a] addressed their hymns, on the destruction of AHI. He encompasses the extensive heaven and earth. They two do not surpass thy vastness.

9. His magnitude, verily, exceeds that of the heaven, and earth, and sky. INDRA, self-irradiating in his dwelling, equal to every exploit, engaged with no unworthy foe, and, skilled in conflict, calls to battle.[b]

10. INDRA, by his vigour, cut to pieces, with his thunderbolt, VṚITRA, the absorber (of moisture), and set free the preserving waters, like cows (recovered from thieves); and, consentient (to the wishes) of the giver of the oblation, (grants him) food.

---

he remained concealed behind seven difficult passes, or the days of initiatory preparation for the rite. *Indra*, having crossed the seven defiles, or gone through the seven days of initiation, pierced, or penetrated to, or accomplished, the sacrifice. This explanation is supported by a citation from the *Taittiríya*, which is still more obscure: This *Vardha*, the stealer of what is beautiful,(?) cherishes, beyond the seven hills, the wealth of the *Asuras*; he (*Indra*), having taken up the tufts of the sacred grass, and pierced the seven hills, slew him.—*Varáho 'yam vámamoshah saptánám giríṇám parastád vittam vedyam asuráńám bibhartíti; sa darbha-pinjúlam uddhritya, sapta girín bhittwá, tam ahann iti cha.*

[a] The wives of the gods are the personified *Gáyatrí*, and other metres of the *Vedas*: according to the Scholiast, the term *gnáh*; preceding *devapatníh*, usually means females, or women, whose nature, the Scholiast says, is locomotive,—*gamanaswabhádráh*.

[b] The Scholiast says, he calls *the clouds* to battle; for by the mutual collision of the clouds rain is engendered.

11. Through his power, the rivers sport; since he Varga XXIX.
has opened (a way for them,) by his thunderbolt. Establishing his supremacy, and granting a (recompense) to the giver (of the oblation), he, the swift-moving, provided a resting-place for TURVÍTI.[a]

12. INDRA, who art the quick-moving and strength-endowed lord (of all), hurl thy thunderbolt against this VṚITRA, and sever his joints,—as (butchers cut up) a cow,[b]—that the rains may issue from him, and the waters flow (over the earth).

13. Proclaim, with new hymns, the former exploits of that quick-moving INDRA, when, wielding his weapons in battle, he encounters and destroys his enemies.

14. Through fear of him, the stable mountains (are still); and, through dread of his appearance, heaven and earth tremble. May NODHAS, praising, repeatedly, the preserving power of that beloved INDRA, be speedily (blessed) with vigour.

15. To him has that praise been offered which he, sole (victor over his foes), and lord of manifold

---

[a] The name of a *Ṛishi*, who, the Scholiast adds, had been immersed in water: *Indra* brought him to dry land.

[b] The text has, cut in pieces the limbs of *Vṛitra*, as of a cow, (*gor na*): the commentator supplies the rest,—as worldly men, the carvers of flesh, divide, here and there, the limbs of animals. The expression is remarkable, although it may not be quite clear what is meant by the term used by *Sáyaṇa*, *vikartáraḥ*, cutters-up, or carvers. Perhaps the word should be *vikretáraḥ*, venders of meat, butchers. At any rate, it proves that no horror was attached to the notion of a joint of beef, in ancient days, among the Hindus.

wealth, prefers (to receive) from those (who praise him). INDRA has defended the pious sacrificer ETAŚA, when contending with SÚRYA, the son of SWAŚWA.*

16. INDRA, harnesser of steeds, the descendants of GOTAMA have offered, to thee, prayers of efficacy, to secure thy presence. Bestow upon them every sort of affluence. May he who has acquired wealth by pious acts come hither, quickly, in the morning.

FIFTH ADHYÁYA.

ANUVÁKA XI. (continued).

SÚKTA V. (LXII.)

The *Ṛishi* is NODHAS, and deity, INDRA, as in the last; the metre, *Trishṭubh.*

Varga 1. 1. We meditate, like ANGIRAS, an acceptable address to that powerful and praise-deserving INDRA, who is to be adored, by his worshippers, (with prayers) of efficacy, to bring him to the ceremony. Let us repeat a prayer to the celebrated leader of all.

---

* The legend relates, that a king named *Swaśwa*, or the lord of good (*su*) horses (*aśwa*), being desirous of a son, worshipped *Súrya*, who, himself, was born as the son of the king. At a subsequent period, in some dispute between him and the *Ṛishi Etaśa*, *Indra* took part with the latter.

2. Do you, priests, offer, to the vast and most powerful INDRA, earnest veneration, a chant fit to be sung aloud;[a] for, through him, our forefathers, the ANGIRASAS, worshipping him, and knowing the footmarks, recovered (the stolen) cattle.

3. When the search was set on foot by INDRA and the ANGIRASAS, SARAMÁ secured food for her young.[b] Then BṚIHASPATI[c] slew the devourer, and rescued the kine; and the gods, with the cattle, proclaimed their joy aloud.

4. Powerful INDRA, who art to be gratified with a laudatory and well-accented hymn by the seven priests, whether engaged for nine months, or for ten,[d]

---

[a] The expression is *ángúshyam* + *Sáma*, a *Sáma* fit to be recited aloud,—*ághoshyayogyam*: such as the *Rathantaras*, and other prayers, which are usually considered portions of the *Sáma Veda*. But the commentator understands *Sáma*, in this place, to mean, singing or chanting of the *Richas*:—*Ṛikshu yad gánam tasya sámetyákhyá*.

[b] When *Indra* desired the bitch *Saramá* to go in search of the stolen cattle, she consented to do so, only on condition that the milk of the cows should be given to her young ones, which *Indra* promised.

[c] *Bṛihaspati* is here used as a synonym of *Indra*, the protector or master (*pati*) of the great ones (*bṛihatám*),—the gods.

[d] *Sáyaṇa* identifies the priests (*vipras*) with the *Angirasas*, who, he says, are of two orders,—those who conduct sacrifices for nine months, and those who conduct them for ten. He cites the *Nirukta*, for the confirmation of this (XI., 19): but the meaning of *Yáska's* interpretation of the word *navagwá* is doubtful, as *navagati* may mean, 'that one whose course or condition is new,' better than 'for nine.' Another explanation which he suggests,—*nava-*

and desirous of (safe) protection, thou hast terrified, by thy voice, the divisible fructifying cloud.[a]

5. Destroyer of foes, praised by the ANGIRASAS, thou hast scattered the darkness with the dawn and with the rays of the sun: thou hast made straight the elevations of the earth: thou hast strengthened the foundations of the ethereal region.

Varga II. 6. The deeds of that graceful INDRA are most admirable: his exploits are most glorious, in that he has replenished the four rivers[b] of sweet water, spread over the surface of the earth.

7. He, who is not to be attained by violence,[c] but (is easily propitiated) by those who praise him with

---

sitagati,—is still less intelligible, for *navanita* usually means fresh butter. The seven priests are said to be *Medhátithi* and other *Ṛishis* of the race of *Angiras*.

[a] *Adrim* • *phaligam* • *valam*. The last is here explained, cloud; the first, that which is to be divided by the thunderbolt; and the second, that which yields fruit, or causes grain to grow by its rain. Or the three words may be considered as substantives; *adri* implying, as usual, a mountain; *phaliga*, a cloud; and *vala*, an *Asura*; all of whom were terrified by *Indra's* voice or thunder.

[b] No specification of these four is given, beyond their being the *Ganges* and others.

[c] The term *ayásya* has perplexed the Scholiast. It may be derived from *yása*, effort,—that which is not attainable by effort; that is, according to one interpretation, not to be overcome in battle: whence Rosen has rendered it by *invictus*. It is contrasted, apparently, with what follows, and which requires the insertion of *suśaddhya*,—easily to be reached, or influenced, by praises, and the like. Other etymologies are suggested; but they are still less satisfactory.

sacred hymns, parted twofold the eternal and united (spheres of heaven and earth). The graceful INDRA cherished the heaven and earth, like the sun in the august and most excellent sky.

8. (Night and dawn), of various complexion, repeatedly born, but ever-youthful, have traversed, in their revolutions, alternately, from a remote period, earth and heaven,—night, with her dark, dawn, with her luminous, limbs.

9. The son of strength, assiduous in good works, diligent in pious acts, retains his ancient friendship (for his votary). Thou, (INDRA,) providest, within the yet immature cows, whether black or red, the mature and glossy milk.

10. From a remote time the contiguous, unshifting, and unwearied fingers practise, with (all) their energies, many thousand acts of devotion (towards INDRA);[a] and, like the wives (of the gods), the protecting sisters[b] worship him who is without shame.

---

[a] This seems to intimate, that the fingers were employed in the performance of what is, at present, termed *mudrá*, certain intertwinings and gesticulations accompanying prayer: the commentary understands it as merely their employment in acts of worship or homage. That the practice is not altogether modern appears from the paintings of the *Ajenta* caves, several of which are, evidently, performing the finger-gesticulations.

[b] *Patníh swasárah* may mean only the protecting or propitiatory and moving epithets of *avaníh*, fingers. *Janayo na* is the expression for 'like wives;' *i.e.*, says *Sáyana*, *devánám*,—of the gods.

Varga III. 11. Beautiful INDRA, who art to be praised with holy hymns, the pious who are desirous of holy rites, those who are anxious for riches, and those who are wise, repair to thee, with veneration. Powerful INDRA, their minds adhere to thee, as affectionate wives to a loving husband.

12. Beautiful INDRA, the riches that have long since been held in thy hands have suffered neither loss nor diminution. Thou, INDRA, art illustrious, addicted to good works, and resolute. Enrich us, thou who art diligent in action, by thy acts.

13. Mighty INDRA, NODHAS, the son of GOTAMA, has composed, for us, this new hymn, (addressed) to thee, who hast been for ever, who harnessest thy coursers (to thy car), and art the sure guide (of all). May he who has acquired wealth by pious acts come hither, quickly, in the morning.

SÚKTA VI. (LXIII.)

Rishi, deity, and metre, as before.

Varga IV. 1. INDRA, thou art the mighty one who, becoming manifest in (the hour of) alarm, didst sustain, by thy energies, heaven and earth.* Then, through fear of thee, all creatures, and the moun-

* The term explained, by the Scholiast, *balaih*, by forces, or strength, is, in the text, *sushmaih*, the driers up, that is, it is said, of enemies. Of the circumstance alluded to we have no other explanation than that *Indra* became manifest, and sustained earth and heaven, when they were filled with fear of an *Asura*. Perhaps *Vritra* is intended: but the passage is obscure.

tains, and all other vast and solid things, trembled, like the (tremulous) rays of the sun.

2. When, INDRA, thou harnessest thy variously-moving horses, thy praiser places thy thunderbolt in thy hands, wherewith, accomplisher of undesired acts,[a] thou assailest thine enemies, and, glorified by many, destroyest their numerous cities.

3. Thou, INDRA, the best of all beings, the assailer and humiliator (of thy foes), the chief of the ṚIBHUS,[b] the friend of man, the subduer of enemies, didst aid the young and illustrious KUTSA,[c] and slewest S'USHṆA,[c] in the deadly and close-fought fight.

4. Thou, verily, didst animate him to (acquire) such (renown) as that which, sender of rain and wielder of the thunderbolt, thou (didst acquire), when thou slewest VṚITRA, and when, munificent hero, who easily conquerest (thy foes), thou didst put to flight the *Dasyus*[d] in battle.

---

[a] *Arihāryatakratu*. Rosen has *desideratas res faciens*; but the Scholiast has *aprepsitakarman*, that is, he does actions undesired by his foes.

[b] So the Scholiast explains *Ṛibhukshá*,—*Ṛibhúṇám adhipatih*: or it may mean, he who abides in the *Ṛibhus*,—*teshu kṛitanirdeśah*: but he understands *Ṛibhu*, here, to mean a wise man, a sage (*medhávin*).

[c] These names have occurred before, in the same relation (see p. 137).

[d] The *Dasyus* are described as the enemies of *Kutsa*,—*Kutsasyopakshayitárah*. Agreeably to the apparent sense of *Dasyu*,—barbarian, or one not Hindu,—*Kutsa* would be a prince who bore an active part in the subjugation of the original tribes of India.

5. Do thou, INDRA, who art unwilling to harm any resolute (mortal),[a] set open all the quarters (of the horizon) to the horses of us who praise thee, (when we are exposed) to the aversion (of our enemies); and, wielder of the thunderbolt, demolish our foes, as with a club.

Varga V. 6. Men invoke thee, such as thou art, in the thick-thronged and wealth-bestowing conflict. May this thy succour, powerful INDRA, ever be granted, in war, worthy to be enjoyed (by warriors) in battle.

7. INDRA, wielder of the thunderbolt, warring on behalf of PURUKUTSA,[b] thou didst overturn the seven cities; thou didst cut off, for SUDÁS, the wealth of ANHU, as if (it had been a tuft) of sacred grass, and didst give it to him, O king, ever satiating thee (with oblations).

8. Increase, divine INDRA, for us, throughout the earth, abundant food,—(that it may be as plentiful) as water,—by which, hero, thou bestowest upon us (existence), as thou causest water to flow on every side.

9. Praises have been offered to thee, INDRA, by

---

[a] Even although hostile to him. That is, *Indra* is, in himself, indifferent to those who are opposed to him, and, if he undertakes their destruction, it is not on his own behalf, but in defence of his friends and worshippers, as in the case of *Kutsa*, alluded to in the preceding stanza.

[b] *Purukutsa* is called a *Ṛishi; Sudás*, a king (see p. 127); and *Anhu*, an *Asura:* but no further information is given in the comment.

the sons of GOTAMA: (they have been) uttered, with reverence, (to thee), borne (hither) by thy steeds. Grant us various sorts of food. May he who has acquired wealth by pious acts come hither, quickly, in the morning.

SÚKTA VII. (LXIV.)

The *Rishi* is the same; the deities are the MARUTS, collectively; the metre is *Jagatí*, except in the last verse, in which it is *Trishṭubh*.

1. Offer, NODHAS, earnest praise to the company of the MARUTS, the senders of rain and ripeners of fruit, deserving of adoration. Composed, and with folded hands, I utter the praises conceived in my mind, which are efficacious in sacred rites, (and flow readily) as the waters. Varga VI.

2. They were born, handsome and vigorous, from the sky, the sons of RUDRA,[a] the conquerors of their foes, pure from sin, and purifying (all), radiant as suns, powerful as evil spirits,[b] diffusers of rain-drops, and of fearful forms.

---

[a] *Rudrasya maryáh*; literally, the mortals, or men, of *Rudra*. But the Scholiast observes, the *Maruts* are immortal; and the term must, therefore, imply sons, agreeably to another text, *Á te pitar Marutám sumnam etu*,—May he obtain thy favour, father of the *Maruts*; [II., XXXIII., 1: see Vol. II., p. 289] or, as in stanza twelve, where the *Maruts* are called, collectively, *Rudrasya súnuh*,—the son of *Rudra*.

[b] *Satwáno na*. *Satwánah* is explained, *Parameśwarasya bhúta-gaṇáh*,—the troop of demons attendant on *Parameśwara* or *Śiva*.

3. Youthful RUDRAS, and undecaying, destructive of those who do not worship (the gods), of unobstructed progress, and immoveable as mountains, they are desirous of granting (the wishes of the worshipper), and, by their strength, agitate all substances, whether of heaven or of earth.

4. They decorate their persons with various ornaments; they have placed, for elegance, brilliant (garlands) on their breasts; lances are borne upon their shoulders, and, with them and their own strength, have they been born, leaders, from the sky.

5. Enriching their worshipper, agitating the clouds, devourers of foes, they create the winds and lightnings by their power. The circumambient and agitating MARUTS milk heavenly udders, and sprinkle the earth with the water.

Varga VII. 6. The munificent MARUTS scatter the nutritious waters, as priests, at sacrifices, the clarified butter. As grooms lead forth a horse, they bring forth, for its rain, the fleet-moving cloud, and milk it, thundering and unexhausted.

7. Vast, possessed of knowledge, bright-shining, like mountains in stability, and quick in motion, you, like elephants, break down the forests, when you put vigour into your ruddy (mares).

8. The most wise MARUTS roar like lions: the all-knowing are graceful as the spotted deer, destroying (their foes), delighting (their worshippers): of deadly strength in their anger, they come, with

their antelopes,[a] and their arms, (to defend the sacrificer) against interruption.

9. MARUTS, who are distinguished in troops, who are benevolent to men, who are heroes, and whose strength is deadly in your anger, you make heaven and earth resound (at your coming); your (glory) sits in the seat-furnished chariots, conspicuous as (a beautiful) form, or as the lovely lightning.

10. The MARUTS, who are all-knowing, co-dwellers with wealth, combined with strength, loud-sounding, repellers of foes, of infinite prowess, whose weapon (of offence) is INDRA, and who are leaders (of men), hold, in their hands, the shaft.

11. Augmenters of rain, they drive, with golden wheels, the clouds asunder; as elephants[b] (in a herd, break down the trees in their way). They are honoured with sacrifices, visitants of the hall of offering, spontaneous assailers (of their foes), subverters of what are stable, immoveable themselves, and wearers of shining weapons. Varga VIII.

12. We invoke, with praise, the foe-destroying, all-purifying, water-shedding, all-surveying band of MARUTS, the offspring of RUDRA. (Priests), to

[a] *Prishatibhih*, with the spotted deer, which are the *vâhanas*, or steeds, of the *Maruts*.

[b] *Apathyo na*; literally, "like that which is produced, or occurs, on the road," leaving a wide range for explanation. *Sáyaṇa*, therefore, proposes another meaning: "like a chariot which drives over and crushes sticks and straws on the way."

obtain prosperity, have recourse to the dust-raising and powerful band of MARUTS, receiving libations from sacred vessels,[a] and showering down (benefits).

13. The man whom, MARUTS, you defend, with your protection, quickly surpasses all men in strength: with his horses, he acquires food, and, with his men, riches: he performs the required worship; and he prospers.

14. MARUTS, grant to your wealthy (worshippers, a son),[b] eminent for good works, invincible in battle, illustrious, the annihilator (of his adversaries), the seizer of wealth, the deserver of praise, and all-discerning. May we cherish such a son, and such a grandson, for a hundred winters.

15. Grant us, MARUTS, durable riches, attended by posterity, and mortifying to our enemies,—(riches) reckoned by hundreds and thousands, and ever-increasing. May they who have acquired wealth by pious acts come hither, quickly, in the morning.

---

[a] *Ṛijīshinam*, which Rosen renders *hoste vincentem*, and M. Langlois, *victorieuse:* but the commentary offers no such signification. The *Maruts*, it is said, are worshipped at the third or evening ceremonial, according to the text. *Ṛijīsham abhishunwanti*,—"They (the priests) pour the *Soma* juice into the vessel." *Ṛijīsham*, in its ordinary sense, is a frying-pan; but here it may mean any sacrificial vessel.

[b] *Putra*, son, is supplied by the comment: the concluding phrases authorise the addition.

ANUVÁKA XII.

SÚKTA I. (LXV.)

The deity is AGNI; the *Rishi*, PARÁSARA, son of SAKTI, the son of VASISHTHA; the metre is termed *Dwipadá Virát*.[a]

1. The firm and placid divinities followed thee, Varga IX.
AGNI, by thy foot-marks, when hiding in the hollow (of the waters),[b] like a thief (who has stolen) an animal,—thee, claiming oblations, and bearing them to the gods. All the deities who are entitled to worship sit down near to thee.

2. The gods followed the traces of the fugitive: the search spread everywhere, and earth became like heaven: the waters swelled, (to conceal him), who was much enlarged by praise, and was manifested, as it were, in the womb in the waters, the source of sacrificial food.[c]

3. AGNI is grateful as nourishment, vast as the earth, productive (of vegetable food), as a mountain,

---

[a] Each stanza is divided into half; and each two *padas* are considered as forming a complete stanza: hence this hymn and the five following are said to be *dasarcha*, or to have ten stanzas each; whilst, in fact, they have only five.

[b] *Guhá chatantam*. The first term, usually, 'a cave,' is said to apply either to the depth of the waters, or to the hollow of the *Aswattha* tree, in both of which *Agni* hid himself for a season.

[c] A fish revealed to the gods where *Agni* had hidden; as, according to the *Taittiríyas*, "He, concealing himself, entered into the waters: the gods wished for a messenger to him: a fish discovered him,"—*Sa nilíyata, so 'pah právisat: tam deváh praisham aichchhan: tam matsyah prábravít*.

delightful as water: he is like a horse urged to a charge in battle, and like flowing waters.[a] Who can arrest him?

4. He is the kind kinsman of the waters, like a brother to his sisters: he consumes the forest, as a *Rájá* (destroys) his enemies: when excited by the wind, he traverses the woods, and shears the hairs of the earth.[b]

5. He breathes amidst the waters, like a sitting swan: awakened at the dawn, he restores, by his operations, consciousness to men: he is a creator, like SOMA:[c] born from the waters, (where he lurked,) like an animal with coiled-up limbs, he became enlarged; and his light (spread) afar.

---

[a] The epithets are, in the text, attached to the objects of comparison, although equally applicable to *Agni*: thus, he is *pushṭir na raṇwá*,—like grateful nourishment; *kshitir na prithwí*,—like the vast earth; &c. Several of the comparisons admit of various interpretations; as the first may signify the increase of desired fruits or rewards, as the consequence of sacrifices with fire: in no case does it import the *frugum maturitas* of Rosen.

[b] The fruit, flowers, grasses, shrubs, and the like, termed, in the text, *romá prithivyáh*.

[c] *Somo na vedháh*; in like manner as *Soma* creates or causes useful plants to grow, so *Agni* creates, or extracts from them, their nutritive faculty. The *Agni* here alluded to is the fire of digestion, the heat of the stomach: *Agnir annádo 'nnapatih*,—*Agni* is the eater and sovereign of food; and, in the *Vájasaneyi Yajush*, we have *Etávad vá idam annam chaivánnádaś cha Soma evánnam Agnir annádah*,—Inasmuch as there is food and feeder, so *Soma* is the food, and the feeder is *Agni*.

SÚKTA II. (LXVI.)

Deity, *Rishi*, and metre, the same.

1. AGNI, who is like wondrous wealth, like the all-surveying Sun, like vital breath, like a well-conducted son, like a rider-bearing steed, like a milk-yielding cow, who is pure and radiant, consumes the forests. Varga X.

2. Like a secure mansion, he protects property: he (nourishes people), like barley: he is the conqueror of (hostile) men: he is like a *Rishi*, the praiser (of the gods), eminent amongst (devout) persons. As a spirited horse (goes to battle), he repairs, delighted, to the hall of sacrifice. May he bestow upon us food.

3. AGNI, of unattainable brightness, is like a vigilant sacrificer:[a] he is an ornament to all (in the sacrificial chamber), like a woman in a dwelling. When he shines, with wonderful lustre, he is like the white (sun), or like a golden chariot amongst men, resplendent in battle.

4. He terrifies (his adversaries), like an army sent (against an enemy), or like the bright-pointed shaft of an archer. AGNI, as YAMA, is all that is born; as YAMA, all that will be born.[b]

---

[a] As the performer of a sacrifice takes care that nothing vitiates the rite, so *Agni* defends it from interruption by *Rákshasas*.

[b] *Yamo ha játo, yamo janitwam*, is the phraseology of the text, and is somewhat obscure. According to the Scholiast, *yama*, here, has its etymological purport only, "he who gives the desired object

He is the lover of maidens,[a] the husband of wives.[b]

5. Let us approach that blazing AGNI with animal and vegetable offerings,[c] as cows hasten to their stalls. He has tossed about his flames (in every direction), like running streams of water: the rays commingle (with the radiance) visible in the sky.

---

to the worshippers,"—*yachchhati dadáti stotṛibhyah kámán*, in which sense it is a synonym of *Agni*,—*yamo'gnir uchyate*. Or it may be applied to him as one of the twins (*yama*), from the simultaneous birth of *Indra* and *Agni*, according to *Yáska*. *Játa* is said to imply all existing beings; *janitwa*, those that will exist: both are identical with *Agni*, as *Yama*, from the dependence of all existence, past, present, or future, upon worship with fire.

[a] Because they cease to be maidens, when the offering to fire, the essential part of the nuptial ceremony, is completed.

[b] The wife bearing a chief part in oblations to fire. Or a legend is alluded to, of *Soma*, who, having obtained—it does not appear how—a maiden, gave her to the *Gandharva Viśwávasu*: he transferred her to *Agni*, who gave her to a mortal husband, and bestowed upon her wealth and offspring. The whole of this stanza is similarly commented upon in the *Nirukta*, X., 21.

[c] So the Commentator explains the terms *charáthá* and *vasatyá*, invocations prompted by minds purified by offerings of moveable things, that is, animals; or of immoveable things, as rice, and the like: *tatprabhavair hṛidayádibhih sádhyáhutih*; or, *paśuprabhava-hṛidayádisádhanayáhutyá*.

SÚKTA III. (LXVII.)

The same deity, *Ṛishi*, and metre, continued.

1. Born in the woods, the friend of man, AGNI protects his worshipper, as a *Rájá* favours an able man. Kind as a defender, prosperous as a performer of (good) works, may he, the invoker of the gods, the bearer of oblations,[a] be propitious. Varga XI.

2. Holding, in his hand, all (sacrificial) wealth, and hiding in the hollows (of the waters), he filled the gods with alarm. The leaders, (the gods), the upholders of acts, then recognize AGNI, when they have recited the prayers conceived in the heart.

3. Like the unborn (sun), he sustains the earth and the firmament, and props up the heaven with true prayers.[b] AGNI, in whom is all sustenance, cherish the places that are grateful to animals; repair (to the spots) where there is no pasturage.[c]

---

[a] *Havyaváh*, here used generally, is, properly, the bearer of oblations to the gods; the *Veda* recognizing, besides the usual fires, three *Agnis*: *Havyaváh* or *Havyaváhana*, that which conveys offerings to the gods; *Kavyaváh*, which conveys them to the *Pitṛis*, or *Manes*; and *Saharakshas*, that which receives those offered to the *Rákshasas*.

[b] According to the *Taittiríyas*, the gods, alarmed at the obliquity of the region of the sun, and fearing that it might fall, propped it up with the metres of the *Veda*,—an act here attributed to *Agni*.

[c] *Guhá guham gah*. Rosen has *de specu in specum procedas*; but *guhá* here means, apparently, any arid or rugged tract unfit

4. He who knows AGNI, hidden in the hollows; he who approaches him, as the maintainer of truth; those who, performing worship, repeat his praises; to them, assuredly, he promises affluence.

5. The wise, (first) honouring AGNI, as they do a dwelling,[a] worship him who implants their (peculiar) virtues in herbs, as progeny in their parents, and who, the source of knowledge and of all sustenance, (abides) in the domicile of the waters.

SÚKTA IV. (LXVIII.)

The *Ṛishi*, &c., unchanged.

Varga XII. 1. The bearer (of the oblations), (AGNI), mixing them (with other ingredients), ascends to heaven, and clothes all things, moveable and immoveable,[b] and the nights themselves, (with light), radiant amongst the gods, and, in himself alone, comprehending the virtues of all these (substances).[c]

2. When, divine AGNI, thou art born, living,

---

for pasture, or, as the commentary says, *sanchárdyogyasthánam*, —a place unfit for grazing, and which *Agni* may, therefore, scorch up with impunity.

[a] In building a house, worship is first offered to the edifice; and it is then put to use. So, *Agni* is to be first adored, and then employed in any sacrificial rites.

[b] That is, the world, made up of moveable and immoveable things.

[c] Or it may be rendered, he alone surpasses the glories (*mahitwá*) of all these gods; as Rosen has it, *excellit deus deorum magnitudine*.

from the dry wood, (by attrition), then all (thy worshippers) perform the sacred ceremony, and obtain, verily, true divinity, by praising thee, who art immortal, with hymns that reach thee.

3. Praises are addressed to him who has repaired (to the solemnity); oblations (are offered) to him who has gone (to the sacrifice); in him is all sustenance; (and to him) have all (devout persons) performed (the customary) rites. Do thou, AGNI, knowing (the thoughts of the worshipper), grant riches to him who presents to thee oblations, or who wishes (to be able to present them).

4. Thou hast abided with the descendants of MANU,* as the invoker (of the gods): thou art, indeed, the lord of their possessions. They have desired (of thee) procreative vigour in their bodies; and, associated with their own excellent offspring, they contemplate (all things), undisturbed.

5. Hastening to obey the commands of AGNI, like sons (obedient to the orders) of a father, they celebrate his worship. Abounding in food, AGNI sets open, before them, treasures that are the doors of sacrifice; and he who delights in the sacrificial chamber has studded the sky with constellations.

SÚKTA V. (LXIX.)

The same as the preceding.

1. White-shining (AGNI), like the (sun), the extinguisher of the dawn, is the illuminator (of all), Varga XIII.

* With mankind.

and fills united (heaven and earth with light), like the lustre of the radiant (sun). Thou, as soon as manifested, hast pervaded all the world with devout acts, being (both) the father and son of the gods.[a]

2. The wise, the humble, and discriminating AGNI is the giver of flavour to food; as the udder of cows (gives sweetness to the milk). Invited (to the ceremony), he sits in the sacrificial chamber, diffusing happiness, like a benevolent man, amongst mankind.

3. He diffuses happiness in a dwelling, like a son (newly) born; he overcomes (opposing) men, like an animated charger. Whatever (divine) beings I may, along with other men, invoke (to the ceremony), thou, AGNI, assumest all (their) celestial natures.[b]

4. Never may (malignant spirits) interrupt those rites in which thou hast given the (hope of) reward to the persons (who celebrate them); for, should (such spirits) disturb thy worship, then, assisted by

---

[a] *Devánám pitá putraḥ san.* The passage is also explained, the protector, either of the gods, or of the priests (*ritwijám*), and their messenger, that is, at their command, like a son: but the expressions are, probably, to be used in their literal sense, with a metaphorical application. *Agni*, as the bearer of oblations, may be said to give paternal support to the gods; whilst he is their son, as the presenter, to them, of sacrificial offerings.

[b] *I.e., tattaddevatárúpo bhavati,*—he becomes of the form, or nature, of that deity; as in the text *Twam Agne Varuṇo jáyase, yat twam Mitro bhavasi, &c.,*—Thou art born as *Varuṇa*, thou becomest *Mitra*. [V. III., 1: see Vol. III., p. 237.]

followers like thyself,[a] thou puttest the intruders to flight.

5. May Agni, who is possessed of manifold light, like the extinguisher of the dawn,[b] the granter of dwellings, and of cognizable form, consider (the desires of) this (his worshipper). (His rays), spontaneously bearing the oblation, open the doors (of the sacrificial chamber), and, all, spread through the visible heaven.

Súkta VI. (LXX.)

Rishi, &c. as before.

1. We solicit abundant (food). Agni, who is to be approached by meditation, and shines with pure light, pervades all holy rites, knowing well the acts that are addressed to the deities, and (those which regulate) the birth of the human race. Varga XIV.

2. (They offer oblations) on the mountain, or in the mansion, to that Agni, who is within the waters, within woods,[c] and within all moveable and immoveable things, immortal, and performing pious acts, like a benevolent (prince) among his people.

---

[a] *Samánair nṛibhiḥ*,—with equal leaders, or men; that is, with the *Maruts*.

[b] This phrase is, here, as well as in the first verse, *usho na járaḥ*: the latter being explained by *jaráyitṛi*, the causer of decay. The sun obliterates the dawn by his superior radiance.

[c] He is the *garbha*, the embryo, the internal germ of heat and life, in the waters, &c., all which depend, for existence, upon natural or artificial warmth.

3. AGNI, the lord of night,* grants riches to (the worshipper) who adores him with sacred hymns. AGNI, who art omniscient, and knowest the origin of gods and men, protect all these (beings dwelling) upon earth.

4. AGNI, whom many variously-tinted (mornings) and nights increase, whom, invested with truth, all moveable and immoveable things augment, has been propitiated, and is kindly seated at the holy rite, as the invoker (of the gods), and rendering all (pious) acts (productive) of reward.

5. AGNI, confer excellence upon our valued cattle; and may all men bring us acceptable tribute. Offering, in many places, sacrifices to thee, men receive riches from thee, as (sons) from an aged father.

6. (May AGNI), who is like one who succeeds (in his undertakings), and acquires (what he wishes for), who is like a warrior casting a dart, and resembles a fearful adversary, who is brilliant in combats, (be, to us, a friend).

---

* *Kshapávat*,—having, or possessing, the night, as then especially bright and illuminating; as the text, *Ágneyí vai rátrih*,—Night is characterized by *Agni*. So, also, in one of the mantras of the *Agnyádheya* ceremony, we have, *Agnir jyotir, jyotir Agnih swáhá* (*Vájasaneya Sanhitá*, p. 64). Or the term may be rendered, also, "capable of destroying" (the *Rákshasas*).

SÚKTA VII. (LXXI.)

The deity and *Ṛishi* are the same; but the metre is *Trishṭubh*.

1. The contiguous fingers, loving the affectionate AGNI, as wives love their own husbands, please him (with offered oblations), and honour him, who is entitled to honour, (with gesticulations), as the rays of light (are assiduous in the service) of the dawn, which is (at first,) dark, (then,) glimmering, and (finally,) radiant. Varga XV.

2. Our forefathers, the ANGIRASAS, by their praises (of AGNI), terrified the strong and daring devourer, (PAŚI), by the sound. They made, for us, a path to the vast heaven, and obtained accessible day, the ensign of day,[a] (ÁDITYA), and the cows (that had been stolen).

3. They secured him, (AGNI, in the sacrificial chamber); they made his worship the source of wealth;[b] whence opulent votaries preserve his fires, and practise his rights. Free from all (other) desire, assiduous in his adoration, and sustaining gods and men by their offerings, they come into his presence.[c]

---

[a] *Ketu*, the indicator or causer of day being known; that is, according to the Scholiast, *Áditya*, the Sun.

[b] *Aryah*, explained *dhanasya swáminah*. It does not appear why Rosen renders it *matrone*.

[c] This and the preceding stanza are corroborative of the share borne, by the *Angirasas*, in the organisation, if not in the origination, of the worship of Fire.

4. When the diffusive vital air[a] excites AGNI, he becomes bright and manifest[b] in every mansion; and the institutor of the rite, imitating BHṚIGU, prevails on him to perform the function of messenger; as a prince who has become a friend sends an ambassador to his more powerful (conqueror).[c]

5. When (the worshipper) offers an oblation to his great and illustrious protector, the grasping (*Rakshas*), recognizing thee, AGNI, retires: but AGNI, the archer, sends after him a blazing arrow from his dreadful bow; and the god bestows light upon his own daughter, (the dawn).

Varga XVI. 6. When (the worshipper) kindles thee in his

---

[a] *Mátariśwan* is a common name of *Váyu*, or Wind; but it is here said to mean the principal vital air (*mukhyapráńa*), divided (*vihṛita*) into the five airs so denominated, as in a dialogue between them, cited by the Scholiast: "To them said the *Arishṭa* breath, 'Be not astonished; for I, having made myself five-fold, and having arrested the arrow, sustain (life).'"

[b] *Jenya*, from *jana*, to be born; or it may be derived from *ji*, to conquer, and be rendered 'victorious;' as, according to the *Taittiríyas*, "the gods and *Asuras* were once engaged in combat: the former, being alarmed, entered into fire: therefore, they call *Agni* all the gods, who, having made him their shield, overcame the *Asuras*." So, in the *Aitareya Bráhmańa*, "the gods, having awoke *Agni*, and placed him before them, at the morning sacrifice, repulsed, with him in their van, the *Asuras* and *Rákshasas*, at the morning rite."

[c] This expresses a notion still current amongst the nations of the East, that the mission of an envoy to a foreign prince is an acknowledgment of the latter's superiority.

own dwelling, and presents an oblation to thee, daily desiring it, do thou, AGNI, augmented in two ways, (as middling, and as best), increase his means of sustenance. May he whom thou sendest with his car to battle return with wealth.

7. All (sacrificial) viands concentrate in AGNI, as the seven great rivers flow into the ocean.[a] Our food is not partaken of by our kinsmen:[b] therefore, do thou, who knowest (all things), make our desires known to the gods.

8. May that (digestive) faculty (of AGNI) which regards food be imparted to the devout and illustrious protector of priests, as the source of virile vigour;[c] and may AGNI be born, as (his) robust, irreproachable, youthful, and intelligent son, and instigate him (to acts of worship).

9. The Sun, who traverses, alone, the path of heaven, with the speed of thought, is, at once, lord of all treasures: the two kings, MITRA and VARUṆA, with bounteous hands, are the guardians of the precious ambrosia of our cattle.

10. Dissolve not, AGNI, our ancestral friendship; for thou art cognizant of the past, as well as of the present. In like manner as light (speeds over) the

---

[a] See note c, p. 88.

[b] That is, we have not any to spare for others.

[c] That is, the vigour derived from the digestive *agni*. Or *retas* may be rendered 'water;' when the passage will mean, "may fire and water, or heat and moisture, be spread through the earth, for the generation of corn."

sky, so decay impairs (my body). Think of me, before that source of destruction (prevails).[a]

SÚKTA VIII. (LXXII.)

Ṛishi, &c., as before.

Varga XVII. 1. AGNI, holding, in his hands, many good things for men, appropriates the prayers addressed to the eternal creator.[b] AGNI is the lord of riches, quickly bestowing (on those who praise him) all golden (gifts).

2. All the immortals, and the unbewildered (MARUTS), wishing for him who was (dear) to us as a son, and was everywhere around, discovered him not. Oppressed with fatigue, wandering on foot, and cognizant of his acts, they stopped at the last beautiful (hiding)-place of AGNI.

3. Inasmuch, AGNI, as the pure (MARUTS) worshipped thee, (equally) pure, with clarified butter, for three years, therefore they acquired names worthy (to be repeated) at sacrifices, and, being regenerated, obtained celestial bodies.[c]

---

[a] Which is tantamount to asking *Agni* to grant immortality,—*amṛitatwam prayachchheti yávat.*

[b] *I.e, Swátmábhimukham karoti*,—he makes them present, or applicable, to himself. The creator is named *Vedhas*,—usually a name of *Brahmá*,—and is, here, associated with *śaśwata*, the eternal. This looks as if a first cause were recognized, distinct from *Agni* and the elemental deities, although, in a figurative sense, they are identified with it.

[c] The next has only *śuchayah*, the pure: the Scholiast sup-

4. Those who are to be worshipped, (the gods), inquiring, between the expansive heaven and earth, (for AGNI), recited (hymns) dedicated to RUDRA.[a] The troop of mortal[b] (MARUTS), with (INDRA), the sharer of half the oblation,[c] knowing where AGNI was hiding, found him in his excellent retreat.

5. The gods, discovering thee, sat down, and, with their wives, paid reverential adoration to thee,

---

plies *Maruts*, for whom, it is said, seven platters are placed at the *Agnichayana* ceremony: and they are severally invoked by the appellations *Idṛiś*, *Anyádṛiś*, *Tádṛiś*, *Pratidṛiś*, *Mitah*, *Sammitah*, and others. In consequence of this participation, with *Agni*, of sacrificial offerings, they exchanged their perishable, for immortal, bodies, and obtained heaven. The *Maruts* are, therefore, like the *Ribhus*,—deified mortals.

[a] The allusion to *Agni*'s hiding himself, occurring previously,—also in verse two,—has already been explained in p. 3, note d. But we have, here, some further curious identifications, from which it appears that *Rudra* is *Agni*. The hymns of the gods are addressed to *Agni*, and are, therefore, termed *Rudriyá*; for *Rudra* is *Agni*, *Rudro'gnih*. The legend which is cited, in explanation, from the *Taittiríya* branch of the *Yajush*, relates, that, during a battle between the gods and *Asuras*, *Agni* carried off the wealth which the former had concealed. Detecting the theft, the gods pursued the thief, and forcibly recovered their treasure. *Agni* wept (*arodít*) at the loss, and was, thence, called *Rudra*.

[b] The text has only *martah*, 'the mortal:' the Scholiast supplies *Marudgaṇah*.

[c] Here, also, we have only the epithet *aṅsadhítá*, 'the half-sharer,' from *aṅsa*, a half; to which, according to the *Taittiríya* school, *Indra* is entitled, at all sacrifices: the other half goes to all the gods:—*Sarve devá eko'rdhah. Indra eka evápare'rdhah.*

upon their knees.[a] Secure, on beholding their friend, of being protected, thy friends, the gods, abandoned the rest of their bodies in sacrifice.[b]

Varga XVIII. 6. (Devout men), competent to offer sacrifices, have known the thrice seven mystic rites comprised in thee,[c] and, with them, worshipped thee. Do thou, therefore, with like affection, protect their cattle. and all that (belongs to them), moveable or stationary.

7. AGNI, who art cognizant of all things to be known, ever provide, for the subsistence of men, grief-alleviating (food). So shalt thou be the diligent bearer of oblations, and messenger of the gods, knowing the paths between (earth and heaven), by which they travel.

8. The seven pure rivers that flow from heaven (are directed, AGNI, by thee: by thee the priests),

---

[a] *Abhijnu*; or it may be applied to *Agni* kneeling before them.

[b] So the text *Devá vai yajnam atanwata*,—The gods, verily, constituted the sacrifice. But the expression is, still, obscure, and refers to some legend, probably, which has not been preserved.

[c] *Guhyáni* * * *padá*,—secret or mysterious steps, by which heaven is to be obtained; meaning the ceremonies of the *Vedas*. These are arranged in three classes, each consisting of seven, or: the *Pákayajnas*, those in which food of some kind is offered, as in the *Aupásana*, *Homa*, *Vaiswadeva*, &c.; the *Haviryajnas*, those in which clarified butter is presented, as at the *Agnyádheya*, *Darśa*, *Púrńamása*, and others; and the *Somayajnas*, the principal part of which is the libation of the *Soma* juice, as the *Agnishtoma*, *Atyagnishtoma*, &c. All these are comprised in *Agni*, because they cannot be celebrated without fire.

skilled in sacrifices, knew the doors of the (cave where) the treasure (their cattle,) was concealed: for thee SARAMÁ discovered the abundant milk of the kine, with which man, the progeny of MANUS, still is nourished.[a]

9. Thou hast been fed, (AGNI, with oblations), ever since the ÁDITYAS, devising a road to immortality, instituted all (the sacred rites) that secured them from falling,[b] and mother earth, ADITI, strove,

---

[a] These circumstances are stated, in the text, absolutely, without any reference to the instrument, or agent. The Scholiast supplies "*Agni*, by thee, &c.;" but the completion of the ellipse is consistent with prevailing notions. The sun, nourished by burnt-offerings, is enabled to send down the rain which supplies the rivers; the *Angirasas* recovered their cattle, when carried off by *Bala*, through the knowledge obtained by holy sacrifices; and *Indra* sent *Saramá* on the search, when propitiated by oblations with fire. Hence, *Agni* may be considered as the prime mover in the incidents.

[b] It may be doubted if either of the former translators has given a correct version of this passage. Rosen has *Qui cunctas luce destitutas per noctes stant*: M. Langlois has *Qui s'élèvent*, * * *assurant la marche de (l'astre) voyageur*. The text has *ye viśwá swapatyáni*, interpreted, by *Sáyańa*, *śobhanány apatanahetubhútáni*—those which were the prosperous causes of not falling; that is to say, certain sacred acts, which secured, to the *Ádityas*, their station in heaven; or, that immortality the way to which they had made or devised. This interpretation is based upon a *Taittiríya* text: "The *Ádityas*, desirous of heaven (*suvarga*, or *swarga*), said, 'Let us go down to the earth:' they beheld, there, that (*shattrinśadrátra*) rite of thirty-six nights: they secured it, and sacrificed with it." It is to this, and a similar rite of fourteen nights, connected with the

with her magnitude, to uphold (the world), along with her mighty sons.

10. (The offerers of oblations) have placed, in this (AGNI), the graceful honours (of the ceremony), and the two portions of clarified butter that are the two eyes* (of the sacrifice). Then the immortals come from heaven; and thy bright flames, AGNI, spread in all directions, like rushing rivers; and the gods perceive it, (and rejoice).

SÚKTA IX. (LXXIII.)

The Ṛishi, deity, and metre, are the same.

Varga XIX. 1. AGNI, like patrimonial wealth, is the giver of food: he is a director, like the instructions of one learned in scripture: he rests in the sacrificial chamber, like a welcome guest; and, like an officiating priest, he brings prosperity on the house of the worshipper.

---

ayanas, or 'comings,' of the *Ádityas*, that allusion is made. Some reference to solar revolutions may be intended; although it is not obvious what can be meant, as no such movement is effected by thirty-six nights or days; and the Scholiast terms them *karmáṇi*, 'acts or ceremonies.' *Á tasthuḥ* is also explained, they made or instituted. *Á* • • *swapatyáni tasthuḥ* means, according to him, *chaturdaśarátrashaṭtriṇśadrátrádityánám ayanádíni karmáṇi* • • *kṛitavantaḥ*,—they made the rites, or acts, which were the *ayanas* and others, of the *Ádityas*, (and which were for) thirty-six or fourteen nights.

* An expression found, also, in another text: or there are, as it were, two eyes of a sacrifice, which are the two portions of the clarified butter.

2. He, who is like the divine Sun, who knows the truth (of things), preserves, by his actions, (his votaries), in all encounters. Like nature,[a] he is unchangeable, and, like soul,[b] is the source of happiness. He is ever to be cherished.

3. He, who, like the divine (Sun), is the supporter of the universe, abides on earth, like a prince, (surrounded by) faithful friends. In his presence men sit down, like sons in the dwelling of a parent; and (in purity, he resembles) an irreproachable and beloved wife.

4. Such as thou art, AGNI, men preserve thee, constantly kindled, in their dwellings, in secure places, and offer, upon thee, abundant (sacrificial) food. Do thou, in whom is all existence, be the bearer of riches, (for our advantage).

5. May thy opulent worshippers, AGNI, obtain (abundant) food: may the learned, (who praise thee) and offer thee (oblations), acquire long life: may we gain, in battles, booty from our foes,—presenting their portion to the gods, for (the acquisition of) renown.

6. The cows, loving (AGNI, who has come to the hall of sacrifice), sharing his splendour, have brought, Varga XX.

---

[a] *Amati*, the term of the text, is explained *rúpa* or *swarúpa*, peculiar form or nature. As this is, essentially, the same in all the modifications of earth, or any other element, so *Agni* is one and the same in all the sacrifices performed with fire.

[b] As soul is the seat and source of all happiness, so *Agni*, as the chief agent of sacrifice, is the main cause of felicity, both here and hereafter.

with full udders, (their milk,) to be drunk. The rivers, soliciting his good will, have flowed from a distance, in the vicinity of the mountain.

7. (The gods), who are entitled to worship, soliciting thy good will, have entrusted to thee, resplendent AGNI, the (sacrificial) food; and, (for the due observance of sacred rites), they have made the night and morning of different colours,—or black and purple.

8. May we, mortals, whom thou hast directed (to the performance of sacrifices), for the sake of riches, become opulent. Filling heaven and earth, and the firmament, (with thy radiance), thou protectest the whole world, like a (sheltering) shade.*

9. Defended, AGNI, by thee, may we destroy the horses (of our enemies), by (our) horses; their men, by (our) men; their sons, by (our) sons: and may our sons, learned, and inheritors of ancestral wealth, live for a hundred winters.

10. May these our praises, sapient AGNI, be grateful to thee, both in mind and heart. May we be competent to detain thy well-supporting wealth,—offering, upon thee, their share of the (sacrificial) food to the gods.

---

* As anything affording shade keeps off the heat of the sun, so *Agni* guards the world against affliction.

ANUVÁKA XIII.

SÚKTA I. (LXXIV.)

The deity is AGNI; the *Ṛishi*, GOTAMA, son of RAHÚGAṆA; the metre, *Gáyatrí*.

1. Hastening to the sacrifice, let us repeat a prayer to AGNI, who hears us from afar; Varga XXI.

2. Who, existing of old, has preserved wealth, for the sacrificer, when malevolent men are assembled together.

3. Let men praise AGNI, as soon as generated, the slayer of VṚITRA,* and the winner of booty in many a battle.

4. (The sacrificer), in whose house thou art the messenger of the gods, whose offering thou conveyest for their food, and whose sacrifice thou renderest acceptable,

5. Him, ANGIRAS, son of strength, men call fortunate in his sacrifice, his deity, his oblations.

6. Bring hither, radiant AGNI, the gods, to (receive) our praise, and our oblations for their food. Varga XXII.

7. Whenever thou goest, AGNI, on a mission of the gods, the neighing of the horses of thy (swift-) moving chariot, however audible, is not heard.

8. He who was formerly subject to a superior, having been protected, AGNI, by thee, now stands in thy presence, as an offerer (of oblations), without bashfulness, and supplied with food.

---

* *Vṛitra* may be here understood, an enemy in general; or, *Agni* may be identified with *Indra*.

9. Verily, divine AGNI, thou art desirous of bestowing, upon the offerer of oblations) to the gods, ample (wealth), brilliant and giving vigour.

SÚKTA II. (LXXV.)

Rishi, deity, and metre, as before.

Varga XXIII. 1. Attend to our most earnest address, propitiatory of the gods, accepting our oblations in thy mouth.

2. And then, most wise AGNI, chief of the ANGIRASAS, may we address (to thee) an acceptable and gratifying prayer.

3. Who, AGNI, amongst men, is thy kinsman? Who is worthy to offer thee sacrifice? Who, indeed, art thou? And where dost thou abide?

4. Worship, for us, MITRA and VARUṆA; worship, for us, all the gods; (celebrate) a great sacrifice; be present in thine own dwelling.

SÚKTA III. (LXXVI.)

Rishi and deity as before: the metre is *Trishṭubh*.

Varga XXIV. 1. What approximation of the mind, AGNI, to thee can be accomplished for our good? What can a hundred encomiums (effect)? Who, by sacrifices, has obtained thy might? With what intent may we offer thee (oblations)?[a]

[a] That is, it is not possible to offer sacrifice, praise, or prayer, that shall be worthy of *Agni*.

2. Come, AGNI, hither: invoker (of the gods), sit down:[a] be our preceder; for thou art irresistible. May the all-expansive heaven and earth defend thee, that thou mayest worship the gods to their great satisfaction.

3. Utterly consume all the *Rákshasas*, AGNI; and be the protector of our sacrifices against interruption. Bring hither the guardian of the *Soma* juice, (INDRA),[b] with his steeds, that we may show hospitality to the giver of good.

4. I invoke (thee), who art the conveyer (of oblations), with thy flames, with a hymn productive of progeny (to the worshipper). Sit down here, with the gods; and do thou, who art deserving of worship, discharge the office of *Hotṛi*, or of *Potṛi*, and awaken us, thou who art the depositary and generator of riches.

5. As, at the sacrifice of the holy MANUS, thou, a sage amongst sages, didst worship the gods with oblations, so, also, AGNI, veracious invoker of the gods, do thou to-day (present the oblations) with an exhilarating ladle.

SÚKTA IV. (LXXVII.)

Ṛishi, &c. as before.

1. What (oblations) may we offer to AGNI? Varga XXV.

---

[a] In the chamber where burnt-offerings are presented.

[b] *Somapati*, which is a rather unusual appellative of *Indra*. The latter name is not in the text; but the deity is indicated by *haribhyám*, his two steeds.

What praise is addressed to the luminous (AGNI), that is agreeable to the gods,—that AGNI who is immortal, and observant of truth, who is the invoker of the gods, the performer of sacrifices, and who, (present) amongst men, conveys oblations to the deities?

2. Bring hither, with praises, him who is most constant in sacrifices, observant of truth, and the invoker (of the gods); for AGNI, when he repairs to the gods, on the part of man, knows those (who are to be worshipped), and worships them with reverence.[a]

3. For he is the performer of rites; he is the destroyer and reviver (of all things);[b] and, like a friend, he is the donor of unattained wealth. All men reverencing the gods, and approaching the well-looking AGNI, repeat his name first, in holy rites.

4. May AGNI, who is the chief director of sacrifices, and the destroyer of enemies, accept our praise and worship, with oblations; and may those who are affluent with great wealth, who are endowed with strength, and by whom the sacrificial food has been prepared, be desirous to offer adoration.

---

[a] The expression of the text is *manasá*, 'with the mind;' but the Scholiast reads *namasá*, 'with reverence,' asserting that the letters *n* and *m* are transposed.

[b] The words are *marya* and *sádhu*: the Commentator explains the first, the killer or extirpator of all; and the latter, the producer.

5. Thus has AGNI, the celebrator of sacrifices, and by whom all things are known, been hymned by the pious descendants of GOTAMA. To them has he given the bright *Soma* juice to drink, along with the sacrificial food; and, gratified by our devotion, he obtains nutriment (for himself).

SÚKTA V. (LXXVIII.)

The *Rishi* and deity are the same: the metre is *Gáyatrí*.

1. Knower and beholder of all that exists, GOTAMA[a] celebrates thee, AGNI, with praise: we praise thee, repeatedly, with commendatory (hymns).[b] Varga XXVI.

2. To thee, that (AGNI) whom GOTAMA, desirous of riches, worships with praise, we offer adoration, with commendatory (hymns).

3. We invoke thee, such as thou art, the giver of abundant food, in like manner as did ANGIRAS: we praise thee, repeatedly, with commendatory (hymns).

4. We praise thee, repeatedly, with commendatory (hymns), who art the destroyer of VṚITRA, and who puttest the *Dasyus* to flight.

5. The descendants of RAHÚGAṆA have recited sweet speeches to AGNI: we praise him, repeatedly, with commendatory (hymns).

---

[a] The word is *Gotamáh*, in the plural; whence Rosen renders it *Gotamidæ*. The Scholiast limits it to the sense of the singular, asserting that the plural is used honorifically only.

[b] *Mantras* is supplied by the commentator: the text has only *dyumnaih*, 'with bright,' or those manifesting *Agni's* worth.

SÚKTA VI. (LXXIX.)

The *Rishi* is the same, GOTAMA: the hymn consists of four *Trichas*, or triads: the deity of the first is the AGNI of the middle region, the ethereal or electric fire, or lightning; the deity of the other triads is AGNI, in his general character: the metre of the first of them is *Trishṭubh*; of the second, *Ushṇih*; and, of the last two, *Gáyatrí*.

Varga XXVII. 1. The golden-haired AGNI is the agitator of the clouds, when the rain is poured forth, and, moving with the swiftness of the wind, shines with a bright radiance. The mornings know not (of the showers),[a] like honest[b] (people), who, provided with food, are intent upon their own labours.

2. Thy falling (rays), accompanied by the moving (MARUTS), strike against (the cloud): the black shedder of rain has roared: when this is done, (the shower) comes, with delightful and smiling (drops), the rain descends, the clouds thunder.

3. When this (the lightning, AGNI,) nourishes the world with the milk of the rain, and conducts it, by the most direct ways,[c] to (the enjoyment of)

---

[a] *Agni*, in his manifestation of lightning, takes part in the production of rain, by piercing the clouds. The dawn is not concerned in the operation; but this is said, not to depreciate the excellence of *Ushas*, but to enhance that of *Agni*.

[b] *Satyáh*, true, sincere: there is no substantive; but *prajáh*, people, or progeny, is supplied by the commentary. Rosen substitutes *mulieres*, *satyáh* being feminine: but so also is *prajáh*.

[c] Or uses,—as drinking, washing, bathing, and the like.

water, then MITRA, ARYAMAN, VARUṆA, and the circumambient (troop of MARUTS), pierce through the (investing) membrane, into the womb of the cloud.

4. AGNI, son of strength, lord of food and of cattle, give us abundant sustenance, thou who knowest all that exists.

5. He, the blazing AGNI, who is wise, and the granter of dwellings, is to be praised by our hymns. O thou whose mouth (glows) with many (flames),[a] shine (propitiously, so) that food-providing wealth may be ours!

6. Shining AGNI, drive off (all disturbers of the rite), either by thyself, or (thy servants), whether by day or by night: sharp-visaged AGNI, destroy the *Rakshasas* entirely.

7. AGNI, who, in all rites, art to be praised, guard us with thy protection, (propitiated) by the recitation of the metrical hymn.[b] Varga XXVIII.

8. Grant us, AGNI, riches that dispel poverty, that are desirable (to all), and cannot be taken (from us), in all encounters (with our foes).

9. Grant us, AGNI, for our livelihood, wealth,

---

[a] *Purváníka;* from *puru,* many, and *aníka,* face or mouth: flames are understood, agreeably to a common name of *Agni, Jwálájihwa,* flame-tongued. Rosen has, evidently, read the *mukha* of the commentary, *sukha,* and explains *purváníka, multis gaudiis fruens.*

[b] *Gáyatra;* either a portion of the *Sáma,* so termed, or the *Gáyatrí* metre, according to the Scholiast.

with sound understanding, conferring happiness, and sustaining (us) through life.

10. GOTAMA, desirous of wealth, offers, to the sharp-flaming AGNI, pure prayers and praises.

11. May he, AGNI, who annoys us, whether nigh or afar, perish; and do thou be, to us, (propitious) for our advancement.

12. The thousand-eyed,[a] all-beholding AGNI drives away the *Rakshasas*; and, (praised, by us,) with holy hymns, he (the invoker of the gods,) celebrates their praise.

SÚKTA VII. (LXXX.)

The *Ṛishi* is GOTAMA, as before; but the deity is INDRA: the metre is *Pankti*.

Varga XXIX. 1. Mighty wielder of the thunderbolt, when the priest[b] had thus exalted thee (by praise), and the exhilarating *Soma* juice (had been drunk), thou didst expel, by thy vigour, AHI from the earth, manifesting thine own sovereignty.[c]

2. That exceedingly exhilarating *Soma* juice,

---

[a] The literal rendering of the epithet of the text, *Sahasráksha*, which identifies *Agni* with *Indra*; but *Sáyaṇa* interprets it, having countless flames,—*asankhyátajwála*.

[b] The *Brahmá*, which the Scholiast interprets *Bráhmaṇa*.

[c] The burden of this and of all the other stanzas of this hymn is *archann anu swarájyam*. The first term usually implies worshipping, honouring; but the Commentator gives, as its equivalent, *prakaṭayan*: *swasya swámitwam prakaṭayan*,—making manifest his own mastership or supremacy.

which was brought by the hawk,[a] (from heaven), when poured forth, has exhilarated thee, so that, in thy vigour, thunderer, thou hast struck VṚITRA from the sky, manifesting thine own sovereignty.

3. Hasten, assail, subdue. Thy thunderbolt cannot fail: thy vigour, INDRA, destroys men. Slay VṚITRA, win the waters, manifesting thine own sovereignty.

4. Thou hast struck VṚITRA from off the earth, and from heaven. (Now) let loose the wind-bound, life-sustaining rain, manifesting thine own sovereignty.

5. Indignant INDRA, encountering him, has struck, with his bolt, the jaw of the trembling VṚITRA, setting the waters free to flow, and manifesting his own sovereignty.

6. INDRA has struck him, on the temple, with his hundred-edged thunderbolt, and, exulting, wishes to provide means of sustenance for his friends, manifesting his own sovereignty. Varga XXI.

7. Cloud-borne INDRA, wielder of the thunderbolt, verily, thy prowess is undisputed; since thou, with (superior) craft, hast slain that deceptive deer,[b] manifesting thine own sovereignty.

8. Thy thunderbolts were scattered widely over

---

[a] *Syenábhṛita*, as Rosen translates it, *accipitre delatus*. The Scholiast says, it was brought from heaven by the *Gáyatrí*, having the wings of a hawk.

[b] The commentary says *Vṛitra* had assumed the form of a deer; but nothing further relating to this incident occurs.

ninety and nine rivers:[a] great is thy prowess. Strength is deposited in thy arms, manifesting thine own sovereignty.

9. A thousand[a] mortals worshipped him, together; twenty[b] have hymned (his praise); a hundred (sages) repeatedly glorify him. So, INDRA, is the oblation lifted up, manifesting thine own sovereignty.

10. INDRA overcame, by his strength, the strength of VṚITRA: great is his manhood, wherewith, having slain VṚITRA, he let loose the waters, manifesting his own sovereignty.

Varga XXXI. 11. This heaven and earth trembled, thunderer, at thy wrath, when, attended by the MARUTS, thou slewest VṚITRA by thy prowess, manifesting thine own sovereignty.

12. VṚITRA deterred not INDRA by his trembling, or his clamour: the many-edged iron thunderbolt fell upon him, (INDRA) manifesting his own sovereignty.

13. When thou (INDRA,) didst encounter, with thy bolt, VṚITRA and the thunderbolt (which he hurled), then, INDRA, the strength of thee, determined to slay AHI, was displayed in the heavens, manifesting thine own sovereignty.

14. At thy shout, wielder of the thunderbolt, all

---

[a] Put for any indefinite number.

[b] The sixteen priests employed at a sacrifice, the *Yajamána* and his wife, and two functionaries entitled the *Sadasya* and *Samitri*, directors, probably, of the ceremonies of the assembly, not of the worship.

things, moveable or immoveable, trembled: even Twashṭri shook with fear, Indra, at thy wrath, manifesting thine own sovereignty.

15. We know not, of a certainty, the all-pervading Indra. Who (does know him, abiding) afar off,[a] in his strength? For in him have the gods concentrated riches, and worship, and power, manifesting his own sovereignty.

16. In like manner as of old, so, in whatever act of worship Atharvan, or father Manus, or Dadhyach[b] engaged, their oblations and their hymns were, all, congregated in that Indra, manifesting his own sovereignty.

SIXTH ADHYAYA.

ANUVÁKA XIII. (continued).

Súkta VIII. (LXXXI.)

The *Rishi*, deity, and metre, as before.

1. Indra, the slayer of Vṛitra, has been augmented, in strength and satisfaction, by (the adorn- Varga I.

---

[a] The expression is very elliptical, *ko viryá parah;* being, literally, who—with vigour—afar. The Scholiast completes the sentence as in the text.

[b] *Manushpitá*; *Manus* being the progenitor of all mankind. *Dadhyach*, or *Dadhichi*, is a well-known *Rishi*, the son of *Atharvan*, of whom mention, subsequently, more than once, recurs.

tion of) men.[a] We invoke him in great conflicts, as well as in little. May he defend us in battles.

2. For thou, hero, INDRA, art a host: thou art the giver of much booty: thou art the exalter of the humble: thou bestowest (riches) on the worshipper who offers thee oblations; for abundant is thy wealth.

3. When battles arise, wealth devolves on the victor. Yoke thy horses, humblers of the pride (of the foe), that thou mayest destroy one, and enrich another.[b] Place us, INDRA, in affluence.

4. Mighty through sacrifice, formidable (to foes), partaking of the sacrificial food, INDRA has augmented his strength. Pleasing in appearance, having a handsome chin, and possessing (bright) coursers, he grasps the iron thunderbolt in his contiguous hands, for (our) prosperity.

5. He has filled the space of earth and the fir-

---

[a] The Scholiast explains this,—"a deity, acquiring vigour by praise, increases;" that is, becomes more powerful and mighty. The notion is clear enough; but, although 'increases' is the literal rendering of *pravardhate*, it expresses its purport but incompletely.

[b] We have a legend, in illustration of this passage: *Gotama*, the son of *Rahúgaṇa*, was the *purohita* of the *Kuru* and *Srinjaya* princes, and, in an engagement with other kings, propitiated *Indra* by this hymn, who, in consequence, gave the victory to the former. Rosen puts the phrase interrogatively: *Quemnam occisurus es? quemnam opulentiæ dabis?* But the Scholiast explains *kam*, whom, by *kanchit*, any one, some one: that is, *Indra* gives the victory to whomsoever he is pleased with.

mament, (with his glory); he has fixed the constellations in the sky. No one has been, ever, born, or will be born, INDRA, like to thee: thou hast sustained the universe.

6. May INDRA, the protector, who returns to the giver (of oblations) the food that is fit for mortals, bestow (such food) on us. Distribute thy wealth, which is abundant, so that I may obtain (a portion) of thy riches. Varga II.

7. The upright performer of (pious) acts is the donor of herds of cattle to us, when receiving frequent enjoyment (from our libations). Take up, INDRA, with both hands, many hundred (sorts) of treasure: sharpen (our intellects): bring us wealth.

8. Enjoy, along with us, O hero, the suffused libation, for (the increase of our) strength and wealth. We know thee (to be) the possessor of vast riches, and address to thee our desires. Be, therefore, our protector.

9. These, thy creatures, INDRA, cherish (the oblation) that may be partaken of by all. Thou, lord of all, knowest what are the riches of those men who make no offerings. Bring their wealth to us.

SÚKTA IX. (LXXXII.)

The deity and *Rishi* are the same; the metre is *Pankti*, except in the last stanza, where it is *Jagatí*.

1. Approach, MAGHAVAN, and listen to our praises: be not different (from what thou hast Varga III.

hitherto been).[a] Since thou hast inspired us with true speech, thou art solicited with it. Therefore, quickly yoke thy horses.

2. (Thy worshippers) have eaten the food which thou hadst given, and have rejoiced, and have trembled through their precious (bodies): self-illuminated sages have glorified thee with commendable thoughts. Therefore, INDRA, quickly yoke thy horses.

3. We praise thee, MAGHAVAN, who lookest benignly (upon all). Thus praised by us, repair, (in thy car), filled with treasure, to those who desire thy presence. INDRA, quickly yoke thy horses.

4. May he ascend that chariot which rains (blessings), and grants cattle, and which provides the vessel filled with the mixture of *Soma* juice and grain.[b] Quickly, INDRA, yoke thy horses.

5. Performer of many (holy) acts, let thy steeds be harnessed on the right and on the left; and, when exhilarated by the (sacrificial) food, repair, in thy

---

[a] The text is merely *mátathá iva*,—(be) not, as it were, non-such; that is, according to *Sáyaṇa*, be not the contrary of that propitious divinity which thou hast always been to us. The rest of the stanza is equally obscure: "Since thou makest us possessed of true speech (*súnṛitávatah*), therefore thou art asked (*ád arthayása it*, *i.e.*, *arthayasa eva*)," that is, to accept our praises. In this hymn, also, we have a burden repeated at the close of each stanza.

[b] *Pátram háriyojanam*, a plate or patera filled with *hariyojana*; the appellation of a mixture of fried barley, or other grain, and *Soma* juice.

chariot, to thy beloved wife. Quickly, INDRA, yoke thy horses.

6. I harness thy long-maned steeds with (sacred) prayers. Depart; take the reins in your hands. The effused and exciting juices have exhilarated thee, wielder of the thunderbolt. Thus filled with nutriment, rejoice, with thy spouse.

SÚKTA X. (LXXXIII.)

Rishi and deity as before; the metre is Jagatí.

1. The man who is well-protected, INDRA, by thy cares, (and dwells) in a mansion where there are horses, is the first who goes to (that where there are) cows. Enrich him with abundant riches; as the unconscious rivers[a] flow, in all directions, to the ocean. Varga IV.

2. In like manner as the bright waters flow to the sacrificial ladle, so they (the gods,) look down (upon it); as the diffusive light (descends to earth). The gods convey it, desirous of being presented to them, by progressive (movements, to the altar), and are impatient to enjoy it, filled with the oblation; as bridegrooms (long for their brides).[b]

---

[a] *Apo vichetasah*. The epithet is explained, by the Scholiast, the sources of excellent knowledge,'—*vitishtajnánahetubhútáh;* and Rosen renders it, accordingly, *sapientiam conferentes*: but it seems preferable to understand the prefix *vi* in its sense of privation; for it is not very intelligible how the waters should confer, or even possess, intelligence.

[b] In this stanza, as usual in the more elaborate metres, we

3. Thou hast associated, INDRA, words of sacred praise with both (the grain and butter of oblation), placed together in ladles, and jointly presented to thee; so that (the sacrificer), undisturbed, remains (engaged) in thy worship, and is prosperous: for, to the sacrificer, pouring out oblations (to thee), auspicious power is granted.

4. The ANGIRASAS first prepared (for INDRA,) the sacrificial food, and then, with kindled fire, (worshipped him) with a most holy rite: they, the institutors (of the ceremony), acquired all the wealth of PAṆI, comprising horses, and cows, and (other) animals.

5. ATHARVAN first, by sacrifices, discovered the path (of the stolen cattle): then the bright sun, the cherisher of pious acts, was born.* ATHARVAN re-

---

encounter strained collocations, and elliptical and obscure allusions, imperfectly transformed into something intelligible, by the additions of the Scholiast. Thus, *avaḥ paśyanti*, 'they look down,' is rendered special by adding *devāḥ*, 'the gods,' who look down, it is said, upon the sacrificial ladle, *hotriyam*, well-pleased to behold it filled with the intended libation. The text, again, has only "as diffused light:" the comment adds, "descends on earth." In the next phrase, we have, "the gods lead that which is pleased, by the libation, and wishes for them, either by progressive movements, or in an eastern direction (*práchaiḥ*), as bridegrooms delight." What is so led? And whither? The ladle, *chamasa*, the altar, *vedi*, as well as the bride or maiden, *kanyaká*, are filled up by the comment. The same character of brevity and obscurity pervades the entire hymn.

* *Ajani*. But it may mean, as the Scholiast says, "the sun

gained the cattle; KÁVYA (UŚANAS) was associated with him.[a] Let us worship the immortal (INDRA), who was born to restrain (the *Asuras*).[b]

6. Whether the holy grass be cut (for the rite) that brings down blessings;[c] whether the priest repeat the (sacred) verse, in the brilliant (sacrifice); whether the stone (that expresses the *Soma* juice) sound like the priest who repeats the hymn; on all those occasions, INDRA rejoices.

SÚKTA XI. (LXXXIV.)

The deity and the *Rishi* are the same; but the metre is diversified. The first six stanzas are in the *Anushṭubh* measure; the three next, in *Ushṇih*; the three next, in *Pankti*; the three next, in *Gáyatrí*; and the next three, in the *Trishṭubh*: the nineteenth verse is in the *Bṛihatí*; and the twentieth, in the *Satobṛihatí* metre.

1. The *Soma* juice has been expressed, INDRA, Varga V.

---

appeared, in order to light the way to the cave where the cows were hidden."

[a] With *Indra*, according to the comment, which also identifies *Kávya* with *Uśanas*; and the latter, with *Bhṛigu*: *Káryaḥ Kaveḥ putra Uśaná Bhṛiguḥ*; meaning, however, perhaps, only that *Uśanas* was of the family of *Bhṛigu*.—*Vishṇu Puráṇa*, p. 82, n. 1. [See the new edition, Vol. I., p. 152, and, particularly, a note at p. 200.]

[b] The text has only *yamasya játam*: the comment explains the former, *asuráṇám niyamanártham*.

[c] *Swapatyáya*. Resolving this into *su* and *apatya*, Rosen renders it, *egregiam prolem conferentis causa*; and M. Langlois has *jaloux d'obtenir une heureuse postérité, (le chef de famille)*. *Sáyaṇa* understands it differently, and explains it by *śobhanápatanahetubhútáya*,—for the sake of the descent, or coming down, of what is good.

for thee: potent humbler (of thy foes), approach. May vigour fill thee (by the potation); as the sun fills the firmament with his rays.

2. May his horses bear INDRA, who is of irresistible prowess, to the praises and sacrifices of sages and of men.

3. Slayer of VṚITRA, ascend thy chariot; for thy horses have been yoked by prayer. May the stone (that bruises the *Soma*) attract, by its sound, thy mind towards us.

4. Drink, INDRA, this excellent, immortal, exhilarating libation, the drops of which pellucid (beverage) flow towards thee, in the chamber of sacrifice.

5. Offer worship, quickly, to INDRA; recite hymns (in his praise): let the effused drops exhilarate him: pay adoration to his superior strength.

Varga VI. 6. When, INDRA, thou harnessest thy horses, there is no one a better charioteer than thou: no one is equal to thee in strength: no one, although well-horsed, has overtaken thee.

7. He who alone bestows wealth upon the man who offers him oblations is the undisputed sovereign, INDRA. Ho![*]

8. When will he trample, with his foot, upon the man who offers no oblations, as if upon a coiled-up

---

* This verse and the two following end with the unconnected term *anga*, which the Scholiast interprets 'quick:' but it is, more usually, an interjection of calling. So Rosen has *Ohe!* M. Langlois, *Oh viens!*

snake?[a] When will INDRA listen to our praises? Ho!

9. INDRA grants formidable strength to him who worships him, having libations prepared. Ho!

10. The white cows drink of the sweet *Soma* juice, thus poured forth, and, associated with the bountiful INDRA, for the sake of beauty, rejoice: abiding (in their stalls), they are expectant of his sovereignty.[b]

11. Desirous of his contact, those brindled cows dilute the *Soma* juice with their milk: the milch kine that are loved of Indra direct his destructive thunderbolt against his foes, abiding (in their stalls), expectant of his sovereignty. Varga VII.

12. These intelligent kine reverence his prowess with the adoration (of their milk); they celebrate his many exploits,—as an example to later (adversaries),—abiding (in their stalls), expectant of his sovereignty.

---

[a] The text has *kshumpa*, explained *ahichchhatraka*, properly, a thorny plant, but apparently intended, by the Scholiast, for a snake coiled up, or one sleeping in a ring, which is, therefore, killed without difficulty: *maṅḍalákáreṅa śayánam kaś chid anáyásena hanti*. Rosen prefers the usual sense, *pede fruticem velut, contere*t.

[b] This, which constitutes the burden of the triad, is rather obscure. The text is *vaswír anu swarájyam*, literally, dwelling after, or according to, his own dominion. *Sáyaṅa* does not make it more intelligible. "Those cows," he says, "who, by giving milk, are the means of providing habitation (*nivásakáriṅyah*), remain looking to the kingdom of him, or *Indra*." So Rosen has *domicilium procurantes, quæ ipsius dominium respicientes adstant*.

13. INDRA, with the bones of DADHYACH, slew ninety times nine VṚITRAS.*

14. Wishing for the horse's head hidden in the mountains, he found it at S'ARYAṆÁVAT.

15. The (solar rays) found, on this occasion, the

---

* *Dadhyach*, also named *Dadhícha* and *Dadhíchi*, is a well-known sage in *Pauráṇik* legend, of whom it is said that his bones formed the thunderbolt of *Indra*. The story seems to have varied from the original *Vaidik* fiction, as we shall have subsequent occasion to notice (*Súkta* CXVI.). In this place the story told by the Scholiast also somewhat differs. He relates, that, while *Dadhyach*, the son of *Atharvan*, lived, the *Asuras* were intimidated and tranquillized by his appearance; but, when he had gone to *Swarga*, they overspread the whole earth. *Indra*, inquiring what had become of him, and whether nothing of him had been left behind, was told, that the horse's head with which he had, at one time, taught the *Madhuvidyá* to the *Aświns*, was somewhere in existence, but no one knew where. Search was made for it, and it was found in the lake *Saryaṇávat*, on the skirts of *Kurukshetra*; and, with the bones of the skull, *Indra* slew the *Asuras*, or, as otherwise explained, foiled the nine times ninety (or eight hundred and ten) stratagems or devices of the *Asuras* or *Vṛitras*. The Scholiast accounts for the number by saying, that, in the beginning, the *Ásurí máyá*, or demoniac illusion, was practised, in the three worlds, for three periods in each,—past, present, and future,—whence it was ninefold: each being exerted with three *śaktis*, or energies, made the number twenty-seven: each of these, again, being modified by the three *guṇas*, they become eighty-one; and the scene of their display extending to each of the ten regions of space, the total reaches the nine times ninety of the text, or eight hundred and ten. This seems to be pure invention, without any rational or allegorical meaning.

light of TWASHṬṚI, verily, concealed in the mansion of the moving moon.[a]

16. Who yokes, to-day, to the pole of the car (of INDRA) his vigorous and radiant steeds, whose fury is unbearable, in whose mouths are arrows, who trample on the hearts (of enemies), who give happiness (to friends)? (The sacrificer) who praises their (performance of their) duties obtains (long) life.[b] Varga VIII.

---

[a] The text has only "they found;" the Scholiast, following *Yáska* (*Nir.*, IV., 25), supplies *Ádityasya raśmayah*, the rays of the sun. *Twashṭṛi* is here used for the sun, being one of the *Ádityas*; or, according to the Scholiast, for *Indra*, to whom the hymn is addressed, and who is, also, one of the *Ádityas*. The purport of the stanza is, apparently, the obscure expression of an astronomical fact,—known to the authors of the *Vedas*,—that the moon shone only through reflecting the light of the sun. So it is said, "the rays of the sun are reflected back in the bright watery orb of the moon;" and, again, "the solar radiance, concealed by the night, enters into the moon, and thus dispels darkness by night, as well as by day." According to the *Nirukta*, II., 6, it is one ray of the sun (that named *Sushumńa*,) which lights up the moon; and it is with respect to that that its light is derived from the sun. The *Puráńas* have adopted the doctrine of the *Vedas*.—*Vishńu Puráńa*, p. 236.

[b] Another interpretation may be assigned to this verse, which turns upon rendering *kah* by *Prajápati*, instead of *who*, and *gáh* by *words of the Veda*, instead of *horses*: making "*Prajápati* combines, to-day, with the burden of the sacrifice the sacred words that are effective, brilliant, essential, emitted from the mouth, animating the heart, and productive of happiness: the worshipper who fulfils the object of such prayers obtains life."

17. Who goes forth, (through dread of foes, when INDRA is at hand)? Who is harmed (by his enemies)? Who is terrified? Who is aware that INDRA is present? Who, that he is nigh?[a] What need is there that any one should importune INDRA for his son, his elephant, his property, his person, or his people?

18. Who praises the (sacrificial) fire, (lighted for INDRA)? Or worships him with the oblation of clarified butter, presented in the ladle, according to the constant seasons?[b] To whom do the gods quickly bring (the wealth) that has been called for? What sacrificer, engaged in offering oblations, and favoured by the gods, thoroughly knows INDRA?

19. Powerful INDRA, be present, and be favourable to the mortal (who adores thee). There is no other giver of felicity, MAGHAVAN, than thou. Hence, INDRA, I recite thy praise.

20. Granter of dwellings, let not thy treasury, let not thy benefits,[c] ever be detrimental to us. Friend of mankind, bring to us, who are acquainted with prayers, all sorts of riches.

---

[a] That is, we know it very well, and are, therefore, secure in his presence, at this ceremony. Or *kah* may again be explained by *Prajápati*, with the sense of the stanza modified accordingly.

[b] *Ṛitubhir dhruvebhih*; in which, *ṛitu* may have its ordinary sense of 'season.' Or the passage may mean, 'presented by the divinities called *Ṛitus*, who preside over sacrifices,' as in the text *Ṛitavo vai prayájáh*,—The *Ṛitus* are the chief sacrifices, *i.e.*, *prayájadevatáh*, the deities presiding over them.

[c] *Útayah*, benefits, assistances: but it may be read *dhútayah*, shakers, agitators, *i.e.*, the *Maruts*, or Winds.

ANUVÁKA XIV.

SÚKTA I. (LXXXV).

The deities are the MARUTS; the *Rishi*, GOTAMA: the metre of the fifth and twelfth verses is *Trishtubh*; of the rest, *Jagati*.

1. The MARUTS, who are going forth, decorate themselves like females: they are gliders (through the air), the sons of RUDRA, and the doers of good works, by which they promote the welfare of earth and heaven. Heroes, who grind (the solid rocks), they delight in sacrifices. Varga IX.

2. They, inaugurated by the gods,[a] have attained majesty: the sons of RUDRA have established their dwelling above the sky: glorifying him (INDRA,) who merits to be glorified, they have inspired him with vigour: the sons of PRIŚNI have acquired dominion:

3. When the sons of earth[b] embellish themselves with ornaments, they shine resplendent, in their persons, with (brilliant) decorations: they keep aloof every adversary: the waters follow their path.[c]

4. They, who are worthily worshipped, shine with

---

[a] *Ukshitásah*, wetted, sprinkled with holy water by the gods,—*devair abhishiktáh*.

[b] Here they are called *gomátarah*, having, for their mother, the cow; that is, the earth, under that type,—equivalent to *Priśni* in the preceding stanza.

[c] That is, rain follows the wind.

various weapons: incapable of being overthrown, they are the overthrowers (of mountains). MARUTS, swift as thought, entrusted with the duty of sending rain, yoke the spotted deer to your cars.

5. When, MARUTS, urging on the cloud, for the sake of (providing) food, you have yoked the deer to your chariots, the drops fall from the radiant* (sun), and moisten the earth, like a hide, with water.

6. Let your quick-paced, smooth-gliding coursers bear you (hither); and, moving swiftly, come, with your hands (filled with good things). Sit, MARUTS, upon the broad seat of sacred grass, and regale yourselves with the sweet sacrificial food.

Varga X. 7. Confiding in their own strength, they have increased in (power): they have attained heaven by their greatness, and have made (for themselves,) a spacious abode. May they, for whom VISHṆU defends (the sacrifice) that bestows all desires and confers delight, come, (quickly,) like birds, and sit down upon the pleasant and sacred grass.

8. Like heroes, like combatants, like men anxious for food, the swift-moving (MARUTS) have engaged in battles. All beings fear the MARUTS, who are the leaders (of the rain), and awful of aspect, like princes.

9. INDRA wields the well-made, golden, many-

---

* *Arusha* is the term of the text,—'the radiant,' which may apply either to the sun or to the *Agni* of lightning; either being, in like manner, the source of rain.

bladed thunderbolt, which the skilful TWASHṬṚI[a] has framed for him, that he may achieve great exploits in war. He has slain VṚITRA, and sent forth an ocean of water.

10. By their power, they bore the well aloft, and clove asunder the mountain that obstructed their path. The munificent MARUTS, blowing upon their pipe,[b] have conferred, when exhilarated by the *Soma* juice, desirable (gifts upon the sacrificer).

11. They brought the crooked well to the place (where the *Muni* was), and sprinkled the water upon the thirsty GOTAMA.[c] The variously-radiant (MARUTS) come to his succour, gratifying the desire of the sage with life-sustaining (waters).

12. Whatever blessings (are diffused) through the three worlds, and are in your gift, do you bestow upon the donor (of the oblation), who addresses you with praise. Bestow them, also, MARUTS, upon us; and grant us, bestowers of all good, riches, whence springs prosperity.

---

[a] *Twashṭṛi* here reverts to his usual office of artisan of the gods.

[b] *Dhamanto váṇam.* The Scholiast explains *váṇam* to be a lute, a *víṇá* with a hundred strings; a sort of Æolian harp, perhaps. *Dhamanto*, 'blowing,' would better apply to a pipe, a wind-instrument.

[c] In this and the next stanza, allusion is made to a legend in which it is related, that the *Ṛishi Gotama*, being thirsty, prayed to the *Maruts* for relief, who, thereupon, brought a well, from a distance, to his hermitage. This exploit is subsequently (*Súkta* CXVI.) related of the *Aświns.*

SÚKTA II. (LXXXVI.)

Ṛishi and deities, the same; the metre is *Gáyatrí*.

Varga XI. 1. The man in whose mansion, resplendent MARUTS, descending from the sky, you drink (the libation) is provided with most able protectors.

2. MARUTS, bearers of oblations, hear the invocation of the praises of the worshipper with or (without) sacrifices.[a]

3. And may he for whom ministrant priests have sharpened[b] the sapient (troop of the MARUTS) walk among pastures crowded with cattle.

4. The libation is poured out for the hero (-band), at the sacrifice, on the appointed days; and the hymn is repeated; and their joy (is excited).

5. May the MARUTS, victorious over all men, hear (the praises) of this (their worshipper); and may (abundant) food be obtained by him who praises them.

Varga XII. 6. Enjoying the protection of you who behold all things, we have offered you, MARUTS, (oblations,) for many years.

7. MARUTS, who are to be especially worshipped, may the man whose offering you accept be ever prosperous.

8. Possessors of true vigour, be cognizant of the

---

[a] The expression is *yajnair vá*, 'with sacrifices, or:' the 'without' is supplied by the Scholiast.

[b] *Atakshata*, have sharpened, *i. e.*, have excited, or animated, by their offerings.

wishes of him who praises you, and toils in your service, desirous of (your favour).

9. Possessors of true vigour, you have displayed your might, with the lustre (of which) you have destroyed the *Rakshasas*.

10. Dissipate the concealing darkness: drive away every devouring (foe): show us the light we long for.

SÚKTA III. (LXXXVII.)

Ṛishi and deities as before; metre, *Jagatí*.

1. Annihilators (of adversaries), endowed with great strength, loud-shouting, unbending, inseparable[a] partakers of the evening oblation,[b] constantly worshipped, and leaders (of the clouds), (the MARUTS), by their personal[c] decorations, are conspicuous (in the sky), like certain rays of the sun. Varga XIII.

---

[a] Always associated in troops.

[b] The term is *ṛijíshiṇah*, which is not very clearly explained. *Ṛijísha*, in ordinary use, means a frying-pan; but here the Scholiast seems to consider it as a synonym of *Soma*; the *Maruts* being thus named, because they are entitled, at the third daily ceremonial, or the evening worship, to a share of the effusion of the *ṛijísha*,—*ṛijíshasyábhishavát*. Or the term may signify, he adds, 'the acquirers or receivers of the juices,'—*prárjayitáro rasánám*; from *arj*, to acquire. Rosen has *lance sacrifico culti*; M. Langlois, *amis de nos offrandes*.

[c] *Stṛibhih*, covering, or clothing; from *stṛi*, to cover; an epithet of *anjibhih*, ornaments: *swaśaríracyáchchhádakair* • • *ábharaṇaih*,—with ornaments covering their own persons. As the word is separated from the substantive, however, by the inter-

2. When, MARUTS, flying, like birds, along a certain path (of the sky), you collect the moving passing (clouds), in the nearest portions (of the firmament), then, coming into collision with your cars, they pour forth (the waters). Therefore do you shower upon your worshipper the honey-coloured rain.[a]

3. When they assemble (the clouds), for the good work, earth trembles at their impetuous movements, like a wife (whose husband is away): sportive, capricious, armed with bright weapons, and agitating (the solid rocks), they manifest their inherent might.

4. The troop of MARUTS is self-moving, deer-borne, ever young, lords of this (earth), and invested with vigour. You, who are sincere liberators from debt,[b] irreproachable, and shedders of rain, are the protectors of this our rite.

5. We declare, by our birth from our ancient sire, that the tongue (of praise) accompanies the manifesting (invocation of the MARUTS), at the libations

---

vening simile, "like some rays" (*ke chid usrá iva*), it has been understood in a different sense by former translators. Thus, Rosen has *ornamentis dignoscuntur, rari lucis radii velut qui stellis effunduntur*; and M. Langlois, (*les Marouts*) *brillent sous leurs parures, comme les nuages sous les feux des étoiles*: but *stṛibhiḥ* cannot have any relation to *stars*.

[a] *Madhuvarṇam*, 'having the colour of honey;' or, according to the commentator, being equally pure or pellucid (*swachchha*.

[b] By making their worshippers wealthy.

of the *Soma*; for, inasmuch as they stood by, encouraging INDRA in the conflict, they have acquired names that are to be recited at sacrifices.

6. Combining with the solar rays, they have willingly poured down (rain), for the welfare (of mankind), and, hymned by the priests, have been pleased partakers of the (sacrificial food). Addressed with praises, moving swiftly, and exempt from fear, they have become possessed of a station agreeable and suitable to the MARUTS.

SÚKTA IV. (LXXXVIII.)

Ṛishi and deity, as before: the metre of the first and last stanzas, *Prastárapankti*; of the fifth, *Viráḍrúpá*; and, of the rest, *Trishṭubh*.

1. Come, MARUTS,* with your brilliant, light-moving, well-weaponed, steed-harnessed, chariots. Doers of good deeds, descend, like birds, (and bring us) abundant food. Varga XIV.

2. To what glorifier (of the gods) do they repair,

* The Scholiast here proposes various etymologies of the name *Marut*, some of which are borrowed from *Yáska*, *Nir.*, XI., 13. They *sound* (*ruvanti*, from *ru*), having attained mid-heaven (*mitam*); or, They *sound* without measure (*amitam*); or, They *shine* (from *ruch*), in the clouds *made* (*mitam*) by themselves; or, They *hasten* (*dravanti*) in the sky. All the minor divinities that people the mid-air are said, in the *Vedas*, to be styled *Maruts*: as in the text, "All females whose station is the middle heaven, the all-pervading masculine *Váyu*, and all the troops (of demigods), are *Maruts*." *Sáyaṇa* also cites the *Paurāṇik* tradition of the birth of the forty-nine *Maruts*, in seven troops, as the sons of *Kaśyapa* (*Vishṇu Puráṇa*, p. 152).

with their ruddy, tawny, car-bearing horses, for his advantage? Bright as burnished (gold), and armed with the thunderbolt, they furrow the earth with their chariot-wheels.

3. MARUTS, the threatening (weapons) are upon your persons, (able to win) dominion: (to you) they raise lofty sacrifices, like (tall) trees. Well-born MARUTS, for you do wealthy worshippers enrich the stone (that grinds the *Soma* plant).

4. Fortunate days have befallen you, (sons of GOTAMA), when thirsty, and have given lustre to the rite for which water was essential. The sons of GOTAMA, (offering) oblations with sacred hymns, have raised aloft the well (provided) for their dwelling.[a]

5. This hymn is known to be the same as that which GOTAMA recited, MARUTS, in your (praise), when he beheld you seated in your chariots with golden wheels, armed with iron weapons, hurrying hither and thither, and destroying your mightiest foes.

6. This is that praise, MARUTS, which, suited (to your merits), glorifies every one of you. The speech of the priest has now glorified you, without difficulty, with sacred verses, since (you have placed) food in our hands.

---

[a] See note c, p. 221.

SÚKTA V. (LXXXIX.)

The *Rishi*, as before, GOTAMA; but the hymn is addressed to the VIŚWADEVAS. The metre of the first five stanzas, and of the seventh, is *Jagatí*; of the sixth, *Virátsthána*; and, of the last three, *Trishṭubh*.

1. May auspicious works, unmolested, unimpeded, and subversive (of foes), come to us from every quarter. May the gods, turning not away from us, but granting us protection day by day, be ever with us, for our advancement. Varga XV.

2. May the benevolent favour of the gods (be ours): may the bounty of the gods, ever approving of the upright, light upon us: may we obtain the friendship of the gods; and may the gods extend our days to longevity.

3. We invoke them with an ancient text,[a]—BHAGA, MITRA, ADITI, DAKSHA, ASRIDH, ARYAMAN, VARUŃA, SOMA, the AŚWINS: and may the gracious SARASWATÍ grant us happiness.[b]

---

[a] *Púrvayá nividá*. *Nivid* is a synonym of *vách*, speech, or a text,—here said to be a text of the *Veda*.

[b] Most of these, here included amongst the *Viśwadevas*, have occurred before. But the Scholiast here also explains their functions:—*Bhaga* and *Mitra* are *Ádityas*; and the latter is, especially, the lord of day, as by the text *Maitram vá ahah*,—The day is dependent on *Mitra*. *Aditi* is the mother of the gods; *Daksha* is called a *Prajápati*, *able* to make the world: or, he is the creator (*Hiraṅyagarbha*), diffused among breathing or living creatures, as breath, or life; as by the text *Práńo vai Dakshah*,—*Daksha*, verily, is breath. *Asridh*, from *sridh*, to dry up; un-

4. May the wind waft to us the grateful medicament:[a] may mother earth, may father heaven, (convey) it (to us):[b] may the stones that express the *Soma* juice, and are productive of pleasure, (bring) it (to us). Áświns, who are to be meditated upon, hear (our application).

5. We invoke that lord of living beings, that protector of things immoveable, Indra, who is to be propitiated by pious rites, for our protection. As Púshan has ever been our defender, for the increase of our riches, so may he (continue) the unmolested guardian of our welfare.

---

drying, unchanging; that is, the class of *Maruts*. *Aryaman* is the sun, as by the text *Asau vá áditya' ryamá*,—He, the sun, is *Aryaman*. *Varuṇa* is named from *vṛi*, to surround, encompassing the wicked with his bonds: he is, also, the lord of night, as by the text *Váruṇí rátrih*,—The night is dependent on *Varuṇa*. *Soma* is twofold; the plant so called on earth, and the moon, as a divinity in heaven. The *Aświns* are so termed, either from having horses (*aśwavantau*); or from pervading all things, the one, with moisture, the other, with light, according to *Yáska*, who also states the question: Who were they? which is thus answered: According to some, they are heaven and earth; to others, day and night; according to others, the sun and moon; and, according to the traditionists (*aitihásika*), they were two virtuous princes.—*Nirukta*, XII., 1.

[a] *Bheshajam*; that medicament which the *Aświns*, as the physicians of the gods, are qualified to bestow. No other specification is given.

[b] Earth is so termed, as producing all things necessary for life; and heaven, as sending rain, and, therefore, indirectly nourishing all things.

6. May INDRA, who listens to much praise, guard our welfare: may PÚSHAN, who knows all things, guard our welfare: may TÁRKSHYA,[a] with unblemished weapons, guard our welfare. Varga XVI.

7. May the MARUTS, whose coursers are spotted deer, who are the sons of PṚIŚNI, gracefully-moving, frequenters of sacrifices, (seated) on the tongue of AGNI,[b] regarders (of all), and radiant as the sun,—may all the gods,—come hither for our preservation.

8. Let us hear, gods, with our ears, what is good: objects of sacrifice, let us see, with our eyes, what is good: let us, engaged in your praises, enjoy, with firm limb and (sound) bodies, the term of life granted by the gods.[c]

---

[a] *Tárkshya* is a patronymic, implying son of *Tṛiksha*, and, according to the Scholiast, *Garuḍman*. He is termed, in the text, *Arishṭanemi*,—he who has unharmed or irresistible (*arishṭa*) weapons (*nemi*): or the latter may imply, as usual, the circumference of a wheel,—whose chariot-wheel is unimpeded. But *Arishṭanemi* occurs, in the *Váyu Puráṇa*, as the name of a *Prajápati*, so that the passage might mean *Arishṭanemi*, the son of *Tṛiksha*, which, according to some authorities, is a name of the patriarch *Kaśyapa*: the same make *Tárkshya* a synonym of *Aruṇa*, the personified dawn. It is doubtful if we have any reference to the vehicle of *Vishṇu*, *Garuḍa*.

[b] This may be predicated of all the deities; as they receive oblations through the mouth of *Agni*.

[c] *Devahitam;* whence it may be rendered, as the Scholiast proposes, in the singular; understanding, by *deva*, *Prajápati*, either a patriarch or *Brahmá*. The Commentator says, the limit of human life is 116 or 120 years; but the next stanza specifies a century.

9. Since a hundred years were appointed (for the life of man), interpose not, gods, in the midst of our passing existence, by inflicting infirmity on our bodies, so that our sons become our sires.[a]

10. ADITI[b] is heaven; ADITI is the firmament; ADITI is mother, father, and son; ADITI is all the gods; ADITI is the five classes of men;[c] ADITI is generation and birth.[d]

SÚKTA VI. (XC.)

The *Ṛishi* and deities are the same; the metre is *Gáyatrí*, except in the last stanza, where it is *Anushṭubh*.

Varga XVII. 1. May VARUṆA and the wise MITRA lead us, by straight paths, (to our desires),—and ARYAMAN,[e] rejoicing with the gods.

---

[a] That is, let us not become so feeble and infirm as to be, as it were, infants, and to require the paternal care of our own sons.

[b] *Aditi*, literally meaning the independent or the indivisible, may, here, signify either the earth or the mother of the gods, according to the Scholiast. According to *Yáska*, the hymn declares the might of *Aditi*,—*Aditer vibhútim áchashṭe* (*Nir.*, IV., 23); or, as *Sáyaṇa*, "*Aditi* is hymned as the same with the universe."

[c] As before noticed, the five orders of men are said to be the four castes and the outcastes. It is also interpreted, five classes of beings, or, Gods, Men, *Gandharvas* (including *Apsarasas*), Serpents, and *Pitṛis*; or, as it occurs in the *Nirukta*, III., 7, *Gandharvas*, *Pitṛis*, Gods, *Asuras*, and *Rakshasas*.

[d] *Játa* is the actual birth of beings; *janitwa*, the faculty of being born, generation. Rosen renders the terms, *natum* and *nasciturum*.

[e] *Aryaman* is said to be the sun, in his function of separating day from night.

2. For they are the distributors of wealth (over the world), and, never heedless, discharge their functions every day.

3. May they, who are immortal, bestow, upon us mortals, happiness, annihilating our foes.

4. May the adorable INDRA, the MARUTS, PÚSHAN, and BHAGA, so direct our paths, (that they may lead) to the attainment of good gifts.

5. PÚSHAN, VISHŃU,[a] MARUTS,[b] make our rites restorative of our cattle; make us prosperous.

6. The winds bring sweet (rewards) to the sacrificer; the rivers bring sweet (waters). May the herbs yield sweetness to us. Varga XVIII.

7. May night and morn be sweet; may the region of the earth be full of sweetness; may the protecting heaven be sweet to us.

8. May VANASPATI be possessed of sweetness towards us; may the sun be imbued with sweetness; may the cattle be sweet to us.

9. May MITRA be propitious to us; may VARUŃA, may ARYAMAN, be propitious to us; may INDRA and BṚIHASPATI be propitious to us; may the wide-stepping VISHŃU be propitious to us.

---

[a] *Vishńu* is said to mean the pervader, or pervading deity.

[b] The term of the text is *swayáśah*, which is explained, by the Scholiast, the troop of *Maruts*, from their going with horses (*aświh*).

SÚKTA VII. (XCI.)

The *Ṛishi* is, still, GOTAMA; the deity is SOMA: from the fifth to the sixteenth stanza, the metre is *Gáyatrí*; the seventeenth, *Ushńih*; the rest, *Trishṭubh*.

Varga XIX. 1. Thou, SOMA, art thoroughly apprehended by our understanding; thou leadest us along a straight path. By thy guidance, INDRA, our righteous fathers obtained wealth amongst the gods.

2. Thou, SOMA, art the doer of good by holy acts; thou art powerful, by thine energies, and knowest all things; thou art the showerer (of benefits), by thy bounties, and (art great,) by thy greatness: thou, the guide of men, hast been well nourished by sacrificial offerings.

3. Thy acts are (like those) of the royal VARUŃA:*

---

* *Rájnah* • *te Varuńasya*. The Scholiast would seem to argue that *Varuńa* here means that which is enclosed in a cloth, or the *Soma* plant that has been purchased for a sacrifice,—*yágárthám dhṛitah krito vastreńávṛitah Somo Varuńah*, chiefly because *Soma* is the king of the Brahmans; as by the text of the *Veda*, *Somo 'smákam Bráhmańánám rájá*,—Soma is the king of us Brahmans; and *Somarájáno Bráhmańáh*,—The Brahmans have Soma for king. But, in that sense, the moon, not the plant, is usually understood by *Soma*; and there does not appear any reason for understanding the term *Varuńa* in any other than its usual acceptation. The title of *rájá*, we have already seen, is, not unfrequently, assigned to him, although, as the following stanzas show, it was equally given to *Soma*.

thy glory, SOMA, is great and profound: thou art the purifier (of all), like the beloved MITRA: thou art the augmenter of all, like ARYAMAN.

4. Endowed with all the glories (that are displayed) by thee in heaven, on earth, in the mountains, in the plants, in the waters, do thou, illustrious[a] SOMA, well-disposed towards us, and devoid of anger, accept our oblations.

5. Thou, SOMA, art the protector, the sovereign of the pious,[b] or even the slayer of VṚITRA; thou art holy sacrifice.[c]

6. Thou, SOMA, fond of praise, the lord of plants, art life to us. If thou wilt, we shall not die. Varga XX.

7. Thou bestowest, SOMA, upon him who worships thee, whether old or young, wealth, that he may enjoy, and live.

8. Defend us, royal SOMA, from every one seeking to harm us. The friend of one like thee can never perish.

9. SOMA, be our protector with those assistances which are sources of happiness to the donor (of oblations).

10. Accepting this our sacrifice, and this our

---

[a] Or royal (*rájan*) *Soma*.

[b] *Satpatis twam rájota*. *Sat* may be explained, also, according to the Scholiast, by Brahman, making the sentence, "the protector, or lord (*pati*), or the king (*rájá*), of the Brahmans."

[c] *Soma* may be considered as identifiable with sacrifice, from the essential part it performs in it (*tadrúpo bhavati, sádhyatwád yajnánám*).

praise, approach, SOMA, and be, to us, as the augmenter of our rite.

Varga XXI. 11. Acquainted with hymns, we elevate thee with praises. Do thou, who art benignant, approach.

12. Be, unto us, SOMA, the bestower of wealth, the remover of disease, the cognizant of riches, the augmenter of nutriment, an excellent friend.

13. SOMA, dwell happy in our hearts, like cattle in fresh pastures, like men in their own abodes.

14. The experienced sage commends the mortal who, through affection, divine SOMA, praises thee.

15. Protect us, SOMA, from calumny; preserve us from sin: pleased with our service, be our friend.

Varga XXII. 16. Increase, SOMA. May vigour come to thee from every side. Be diligent in the supply of food (to us).

17. Exulting SOMA, increase with all twining plants: be, to us, a friend. Well-supplied with food, we may prosper.

18. May the milky juices flow around thee: may sacrificial offerings and vigour be concentrated in the destroyer of foes; and, being fully nourished, do thou provide, SOMA, excellent viands in heaven, for our immortality.

19. Whichever of thy glories (men) worship with oblations, may our sacrifice be invested with them all. Come to our mansions, SOMA, who art the bestower of wealth,' the transporter (over difficulties), attended by valiant heroes, the non-destroyer of progeny.

20. To him who presents (offerings) SOMA gives a milch-cow, a swift horse, and a son who is able in affairs, skilful in domestic concerns, assiduous in worship, eminent in society, and who is an honour to his father.

21. We rejoice, SOMA, contemplating thee, invincible in battle, triumphant amongst hosts, the granter of heaven, the giver of rain, the preserver of strength, born amidst sacrifices, occupying a brilliant dwelling, renowned, and victorious. Varga XXIII.

22. Thou, SOMA, hast generated all these herbs, the water, and the kine; thou hast spread out the spacious firmament; thou hast scattered darkness with light.

23. Divine and potent SOMA, bestow, upon us, with thy brilliant mind, a portion of wealth: may no (adversary) annoy thee. Thou art supreme over the valour of (any) two (mutual) opponents. Defend us (from our enemies,) in battle.[a]

SÚKTA VIII. (XCII.)

The *Ṛishi* is GOTAMA: the deity is USHAS (the Dawn), except in the last triad, which is addressed to the AŚWINS: the metre of the first four verses is *Jagatí*; of the last six, *Ushṇih*; of the rest, *Trishṭubh*.

1. These divinities of the morning[b] have spread Varga XXIV.

---

[a] There is, evidently, great confusion, in this hymn, between *Soma*, the moon, and *Soma*, the acid Asclepias. Few passages indicate the former distinctly, except, perhaps, verse twenty-two, which alludes to the function of scattering darkness by light.

[b] We have the term *Ushasah*, in the plural, intending, according

light (over the world): they make manifest the light in the eastern portion of the firmament, brightening all things, like warriors burnishing their weapons: the radiant and progressing mothers[a] (of the earth), they travel daily, (on their course).

2. Their purple rays have readily shot upwards; they have yoked the easily-yoked and ruddy kine (to their car); the deities of the dawn have restored, as of yore, the consciousness (of sentient creatures), and, bright-rayed, have attended upon the glorious sun.

3. The female leaders (of the morning) illuminate,[b] with their inherent radiance, the remotest parts (of the heaven), with a simultaneous effort,—like warriors[c] (with their shining arms, in the van of battle),—bringing every kind of food to the performer of good works, to the bountiful, and to the worshipper who presents libations.

4. Ushas cuts off the accumulated (glooms); as

---

to the Commentator, the divinities that preside over the morning: but, according to *Yáska*, the plural is used honorifically only, for the singular personification.—*Nirukta*, XII., 7.

[a] Or *mátṛi* may mean simply maker, author; authors of light,—*bhása nirmátryah.*—*Nirukta*, XII., 7.

[b] *Archanti*; literally, worship,—that is, the heavens: but the term is used for spreading over, or extending.

[c] The text has only "like warriors." The Scholiast explains the comparison: "As they spread, with bright arms, along the front of the array, so the rays of the dawn spread along the sky, before the coming of the sun."

a barber (cuts off the hair):[a] she bares her bosom; as a cow yields her udder (to the milker): and, as cattle hasten to their pastures, she speeds to the east, and, shedding light upon all the world, dissipates the darkness.

5. Her brilliant light is first seen towards (the east): it spreads and disperses the thick darkness. She anoints her beauty; as the priests anoint the sacrificial food in sacrifices. The daughter of the sky[b] awaits the glorious sun.

6. We have crossed over the boundary of darkness. Varga XXV.
Ushas restores the consciousness (of living beings). Bright-shining, she smiles, like a flatterer, to obtain favour, and, lovely in all her radiance, she has swallowed, for our delight, the darkness.

7. The brilliant daughter of the sky, the exciter of pleasant voices,[c] is praised by the descendants of Gotama. Ushas, grant us food, associated with progeny and dependants, and distinguished by horses and cattle.

8. May I obtain, Ushas, that ample wealth which confers fame, posterity, troops of slaves, and

---

[a] *Nṛitúr iva*, "like a barber," is the phrase of the text. Or *nritú* may mean a dancing-girl, when the translation will be, "*Ushas* displays graces, like a dancing-girl" (*peśáṃsi vapate*); the former meaning either darkness or elegance, the latter, either to cut off, or to possess. There is no point of similitude expressed in Rosen's version: *Tenebras dissipat Aurora, saltatrix veluti*.

[b] *Divah duhitá*, the daughter of heaven, or the sky.

[c] With the appearance of dawn, the cries of various animals and birds, and the voices of men, are again heard.

is characterized by horses,—which thou, who aboundest in riches, and art the giver of food, displayest, (when gratified) by hymns and holy sacrifices.

9. The divine (USHAS), having lighted up the whole world, spreads, expanding with her radiance, towards the west, arousing all living creatures to their labours. She hears the speech of all endowed with thought.

10. The divine and ancient USHAS, born again and again, and bright with unchanging hues, wastes away the life of a mortal, like the wife of a hunter cutting up and dividing the birds.[a]

Varga XXVI. 11. She has been seen illuminating the boundaries of the sky, and driving into disappearance the spontaneously-retiring (night).[b] Wearing away the ages of the human race, she shines with light, like the bride of the Sun.[c]

12. The affluent and adorable USHAS has sent her rays abroad,—as (a cowherd drives) the cattle (to pasture),—and spreads, expansive, like flowing water.

---

[a] Like a *swaghní*; literally, the wife of a dog-killer, but explained, *vyádhastrí*, as in the text.

[b] *Swasáram* is the only term in the text, explained, *swayam eva sarantím*,—going of her own accord. The Scholiast adds *night*: otherwise, we might have understood it in its usual sense of 'sister,'—making night the sister of morning.

[c] *Yoshá járasya*. *Jára*, meaning the causer of the decay, or disappearance, of night, is explained by *Súrya*, the Sun.

She is beheld associated with the rays of the sun, unimpeding sacred ceremonies.[a]

13. Ushas, possessor of food, bring us that various wealth by which we may sustain sons and grandsons.

14. Luminous Ushas, possessor of cows and horses, true of speech, dawn here, to-day, upon this (ceremony), that is to bring us wealth.

15. Possessor of food, Ushas, yoke, indeed, to-day, your purple steeds, and bring to us all good things.

16. Aświns, destroyers of foes, turn, with favourable intentions, your chariot towards our abode, which contains cattle and gold. Varga XXVII.

17. Aświns, who have sent adorable light from heaven[b] to man, bring us strength.

18. May the steeds, awakened at dawn, bring hither, to drink the *Soma* juice, the divine Aświns, —who are the givers of happiness, the destroyers of foes,—seated in a golden chariot.

[a] *Aminati daivyáni vratáni*, not injuring, that is, favouring, divine rites, or offerings to the gods, which are to be performed by daylight, or after dawn; as by the text, *Na rátrau na sáyam asti devayá ajushtam*,—Sacrifice is not acceptable to the gods at night, or in the evening.

[b] As before observed, the *Aświns* are, sometimes, identified with the sun and moon.

SÚKTA IX. (XCIII.)

The *Ṛishi* is GOTAMA: the deities are AGNI and SOMA: the metre of the three first stanzas is *Anushṭubh*: of three, beginning with the ninth, *Gáyatri*; of the eighth, *Jagati* or *Trishṭubh*; and, of the rest, *Trishṭubh*.

Varga XXVIII. 1. AGNI and SOMA, showerers (of desires), favourably hear this my invocation, graciously accept my hymns, and bestow felicity on the donor (of the oblation).

2. AGNI and SOMA, grant, to him who addresses this prayer to you both, store of cattle with sound strength, and good horses.

3. AGNI and SOMA, may he who offers you the oblation of clarified butter enjoy sound strength, with progeny, through all his life.

4. AGNI and SOMA, that prowess of yours, by which you have carried off the cows that were the food of PAṆI, is (well-) known to us. You have slain the offspring of BṚISAYA[a]; and you have acquired the one luminary (the sun[b]), for the benefit of the many.

---

[a] *Brisayasya śeshah*. The latter is a synonym of *apatya*, offspring.—*Nirukta*, III., 2. *Brisaya* is said to be a synonym of *Twashṭṛi*, here styled an *Asura*. The offspring of *Twashṭṛi* is *Vṛitra*; and the agency of *Agni* and *Soma* in his death is explained by identifying them with the two vital airs *Práṇa* and *Apána*, the separation of which from *Vṛitra* was the approximate cause of his death.

[b] By the destruction of *Vṛitra*, the enveloping cloud, or gathered darkness, the sun was enabled to appear in the sky.

5. You two, AGNI and SOMA, acting together, have sustained these constellations in the sky: you have liberated the rivers that had been defiled, from the notorious imputation.[a]

6. AGNI and SOMA, the wind brought one of you from heaven; a hawk carried off the other, by force, from the summit of the mountain:[b] growing vast by praise, you have made the world wide, for (the performance of) sacrifice.

7. AGNI and SOMA, partake of the proffered oblation; be gracious to us: showerers (of desires), be pleased: prosperous and diligent protectors, be propitious; and grant, to the sacrificer, health and exemption from ill. Varga XXIX.

8. AGNI and SOMA, protect his sacrifice, and defend him from ill, who, with a mind devoted to

[a] The imputation, or charge, of Brahmanicide was incurred by *Indra*, it is said, in killing *Vṛitra*, who was a Brahman, but which guilt he transferred to rivers, women, and trees. This looks rather like a *Pauráṅik* legend. One of a more *Vaidik* character is, also, given: the rivers were defiled by the dead body of *Vṛitra*, which had fallen into them; their waters were, consequently, unfit to bear any part in sacred rites, until they were purified by *Agni* and *Soma*, that is, by oblations to fire, and libations of *Soma* juice.

[b] The legend relates that *Váyu* brought *Agni* from heaven, at the desire of *Bhṛigu*, when performing a sacrifice; *Soma* was brought from *Swarga*, on the top of Mount *Meru*, by *Gáyatri*, in the shape of a hawk. These are, clearly, allegorical allusions to the early use of fire and the *Soma* plant in religious ceremonies.

the gods, worships you with clarified butter and oblations: grant to the man engaged (in devotion,) extreme felicity.

9. Agni and Soma, endowed with the like wealth, and invoked by a common invocation, share our praises; for you have (ever) been the chief of the gods.*

10. Agni and Soma, give ample (recompence) to him who presents to you both this clarified butter.

11. Agni and Soma, be pleased with these our oblations, and come to us, together.

12. Agni and Soma, cherish our horses; and may our cows, affording (milk that yields butter for) oblations, be well nourished. Give to us, who are affluent, strength (to perform) religious rites; and make our sacrifice productive of wealth.

ANUVÁKA XV.

Súkta I. (XCIV.)

The *Ṛishi* is Kutsa, the son of Angiras: the deity is Agni, associated, in three parts of the eighth stanza, with the gods in general, and, in the latter half of the last, with different divinities: the metre of the two last stanzas is *Trishṭubh*; of the rest, *Jagatí*.

Varga XXX. 1. To him who is worthy of praise, and all-

* The term is simply *devatrá*, explained *deveshu praśastah*. Another text is quoted, which states that *Agni* and *Soma* are they who are the two kings of the gods (*rájánau vá etau devánám yad agníshomau*.)

knowing, we construct, with our minds, this hymn, as (a workman makes) a car. Happy is our understanding, when engaged in his adoration. Let us not suffer injury, AGNI, through thy friendship.[a]

2. He for whom thou sacrificest accomplishes (his objects), abides free from aggression, and enjoys (wealth, the source of) strength: he prospers; and poverty never approaches him. Let us not suffer injury, AGNI, through thy friendship.

3. May we be able to kindle thee. Perfect the rite; for, through thee, the gods partake of the offered oblations. Bring hither the ÁDITYAS;[b] for we love them. Let us not suffer injury, AGNI, through thy friendship.

4. We bring fuel, we offer oblations, reminding thee of the successive seasons (of worship). Do thou thoroughly complete the rite, in order to prolong our lives. Let us not suffer injury, AGNI, through thy friendship.

5. His genial (flames), the preservers of mankind, spread around; and both bipeds and quadrupeds are enlivened by his rays. Shining with various lustre, and illuminating (the world by night), thou art superior to the dawn. Let us not, AGNI, suffer injury, through thy friendship.

---

[a] This last clause is the burden of all the stanzas except the concluding two: *Sakhye má rishámá vayam tava*,—May we not be injured in, or by, thy friendship; that is, according to the Scholiast, Do thou preserve us.

[b] The sons of *Aditi*, that is, all the gods.

Varga XXXI. 6. Thou art the sacrificing or the invoking priest; thou art the principal (presenter of the offering), the director (of the ceremonies), their performer, or, by birth, the family-priest.[a] Thus conversant with all the priestly functions, thou performest perfectly the rite. Let us not, AGNI, suffer injury through thy friendship.

7. Thou art of graceful form, and alike on every side, and, although remote, shinest as if nigh. Thou seest, divine AGNI, beyond the darkness of night. Let us not, AGNI, suffer injury through thy friendship.

8. Gods,[b] let the chariot of the offerer of the libation be foremost:[c] let our denunciations overwhelm the wicked: understand and fulfil my words. Let us not suffer injury, AGNI, through thy friendship.

9. Overcome, with your fatal (weapons), the wicked and the impious, all who are enemies,

---

[a] *Agni* is here identified with the chief of the sixteen priests engaged at solemn sacrifices. He is the *Adhwaryu*, usually called the reciter of the *Yajush*,—here defined, by the Scholiast, as the presenter of the offerings: he is the *Hotṛi*, or invoking priest: he is the *Praśástṛi*, or the *Maitrávaruṇa*, whose duty it is to direct the other priests what to do, and when to perform their functions: he is the *Potṛi*, or priest so termed, and the family or hereditary *Purohita*: or *Purohita* may be the same as the *Brahmá* of a ceremony,—being, to men, what *Bṛihaspati* is to the gods.

[b] *Devdh*. All the gods are here considered to be but portions or members of *Agni*.

[c] *Púrva*, before. The Scholiast explains this by *mukhya*, principal: otherwise, it might be thought that we had, here, an allusion to chariot-races.

whether distant or near; and then provide an easy (path) for the sacrificer who praises thee. Let us not, AGNI, suffer injury through thy friendship.

10. When thou hast yoked the bright red horses, swift as the wind, to thy car, thy roar is like that of a bull; and thou enwrappest the forest-trees with a banner of smoke. Let us not, AGNI, suffer injury through thy friendship.

11. At thy roaring even the birds are terrified: Varga XXXII.
when thy flames, consuming the grass, have spread in all directions, (the wood) is easy of access to thee, and to thy chariots. Let us not, AGNI, suffer injury through thy friendship.

12. May this (thy adorer) enjoy the support of MITRA and of VARUṆA. Wonderful is the fury of the MARUTS. (Dwellers in the region) below (the heavens),* encourage us; and may their minds again (be gracious) to us. Let us not suffer injury, AGNI, through thy friendship.

13. Thou, brilliant (AGNI), art the especial friend of the gods; thou, who art graceful in the sacrifice, art the confirmer of all riches. May we be present in thy most spacious chamber of sacrifice. Let us not, AGNI, suffer injury through thy friendship.

14. Pleasant is it to thee, when thou art lighted in thine own abode, and, propitiated by libations, art praised (by the priests). Then, much delighted, thou givest rewards and riches to the worshipper. Let us not, AGNI, suffer injury through thy friendship.

---

* Below *Swargaloka*, or in the *antariksha*, or firmament.

15 (Fortunate is the worshipper) to whom, (assiduous) in all pious works, thou, possessor of riches, indivisible AGNI, grantest exemption from sin,—whom thou associatest with auspicious strength. May he be (enriched), by thee, with wealth that comprehends progeny.

16. Do thou, divine AGNI, who knowest what is good fortune, on this occasion prolong our existence; and may MITRA, VARUṆA, ADITI, ocean, earth, and heaven, preserve it to us.[a]

SEVENTH ADHYÁYA.

ANUVÁKA XV. (continued).

SÚKTA II. (XCV.)

The deity is AGNI, having the attributes of the dawn, or the AGNI entitled to a share of the morning oblation, or the pure or simple AGNI: the *Ṛishi* is KUTSA; the metre, *Trishṭubh*.

Varga I. 1. Two periods, of different complexions,[b] revolve,

---

[a] This verse terminates the following hymns, with two exceptions, as far as the hundred and first *Súkta*. *Mitra*, *Varuṇa*, and *Aditi* have been before noticed. By *Sindhu* is to be understood the divinity presiding over, or identified with, flowing water; and it may mean either the sea, or flowing streams collectively, or the river Indus. *Prithivî* and *Div* are the personified earth and heaven. These are requested to *honour*, meaning, to preserve, or perpetuate, whatever blessing has been asked for (*tat* * * *mámahantam*); from *mah*, to venerate or worship: *tat*, *that*, refers, here, to *áyus*, or life.

[b] *Virúpe*, of various nature, or, here, complexions; black and

for their own purposes; and each, in succession, severally nourishes a son. In one, HARI is the receiver of oblations; in the other, the brilliant AGNI is beheld.

2. The vigilant and youthful Ten beget, through the wind, this embryo AGNI,* inherent (in all be-

---

white, or night and day. Day is said to be the mother of fire, which is then, as it were, in an embryo state, and is not fully manifested, or born, until it is dark. So the sun is in the womb of night, and is born, or shines, in the morning. *Hari*, or the sun, being manifested in the morning, is then to be worshipped; *Agni*, shining at night, is to be worshipped in the evening,—*tasmád Agnaye sáyam húyate Súryáya prátah*, which is rather at variance with the preliminary statement, that the *Agni* of the hymn is the one entitled to a share of the morning oblation (*Ushasi prátahkále havirbhágyo 'gnir asti sa devatá*): therefore, it is said, the *Agni* is that endowed with the properties of dawn: or it may be the simple, discrete *Agni* (*aushasaguna-viśishto 'gnih śuddho 'gnir vá devatá*). We must, therefore, consider *Agni* to be treated as identical with *Hari*, or the sun, as well as referred to in his own personification.

* This stanza is somewhat differently interpreted. The *Ten* are said, by the Scholiast, to be, in one acceptation, the ten regions of space, which generate the electrical fire, or lightning, as an embryo in the clouds, through the agency of the winds; as in the text: "Wind is the cause of fire; fire, of wind" (*Agner hi váyuh káranam, váyor agnih*). The term, in the text, for wind, or its agency, is *tvashtuh*, which is here said to mean 'brilliant,'—from "the brilliant central proximity of wind" (*díptánmadhyamád váyoh sakáśát*). Rosen connects *tvashtuh* with *garbham*, and renders them, *fulminatoris parentem*. He also follows the explanation of the Ten, which applies it to the ten

ings,)[a] sharp-visaged, universally renowned, shining among men. Him they conduct (to every dwelling).

3. They contemplate three places of his birth,—one in the ocean, one in the heaven, one in the firmament; and, dividing the seasons of the year, for the benefit of earthly creatures, he formed, in regular succession, the eastern quarter.[b]

4. Which of you discerns the hidden[c] AGNI? A son, he begets his mothers by oblations.[d] The germ of many (waters), he issues from the ocean,[e] mighty and wise, the recipient of oblations.

---

fingers, which generate *Agni* through the air of attrition, as an embryo in the sticks. *Sáyaṇa* gives both interpretations.

[a] *Vibhṛitram*, deposited in all creatures; that is, in the capacity of the digestive faculty, which is referred to the action of natural heat.

[b] As submarine fire, *Agni* is born in the ocean; as the sun, in heaven; and, as lightning, in the firmament. In his character of the sun, he may be said to be the distributor of time and space,—regulating the seasons, and indicating the points of the horizon.

[c] Latent heat; the natural heat extant in the waters, in the woods, and in all fixed and moveable things, although not perceptible to sense.

[d] *Agni*, in the form of lightning, may be considered as the son of the waters collected in the clouds; and those waters he is said to generate by the oblations which he conveys: as, in the *Smṛiti*, it is said,—"Oblations offered in fire ascend to the sun: rain is produced from the sun; corn, from rain; and thence spring mankind."

[e] *Agni* is thought to rise, in the morning, in the shape of the sun from out of the ocean,—*upasthát samudrát* • • *nirgachchhati*.

5. Appearing amongst them (the waters), the bright-shining (AGNI) increases, rising above the flanks of the waving waters,[a] spreading his own renown. Both (heaven and earth) are alarmed, as the radiant AGNI is born; and, approaching the lion,[b] they pay him honour.

6. Both the auspicious ones[c] (day and night,) wait upon him, like two female attendants; as lowing kine (follow their calves), by the paths (that they have gone). He has been the lord of might among the mighty, whom (the priests), on the right (of the altar), anoint. Varga 11.

7. Like the sun, he stretches forth his arms; and the formidable AGNI, decorating both heaven and earth (with brightness), labours (in his duties). He draws up, from everything, the essential (moisture), and clothes (the earth) with new vestments, (derived) from his maternal (rains).

8. Associated, in the firmament, with the moving waters, he assumes an excellent and lustrous form; and the wise sustainer (of all things) sweeps over

---

[a] Above, on the side, or tip, of the crooked waters,—*dru jihmánám . . upasthe*. *Agni*, here, is the lightning, which appears on the skirts of the unevénly-disposed, or undulating, rain falling from the clouds.

[b] *Sinham* the Scholiast considers as applicable to *Agni*, to imply his ability to suffer or be overcome,—*sahanaśílam*, *abhibhavanaśílam*. There does not seem to be any objection to the metaphorical use of the literal meaning of the word, 'a lion.'

[c] *Both* may, also, intimate heaven and earth; or the two pieces of wood rubbed together to produce flame.

the source[a] (of the rains, with his radiance), whence a concentration of light is spread abroad by the sportive deity.

9. The vast and victorious radiance of thee, the mighty one, pervades the firmament. AGNI, who hast been kindled by us, preserve us with all thy undiminished and protecting glories.

10. He causes the waters to flow, in a torrent, through the sky; and, with those pure waves, he inundates the earth. He gathers all (articles of) food in the stomach, and, for that purpose, sojourns in the new-sprung parents[b] (of the grain).

11. AGNI, who art the purifier, growing with the fuel we have supplied, blaze, for the sake of (securing) food to us who are possessed of wealth; and may MITRA, VARUṆA, ADITI, ocean, earth, and heaven, preserve it to us.

SÚKTA III. (XCVI.)

The *Ṛishi* and metre are as before; the deity is AGNI, but either in his general character, or as *Draviṅodá*.

Varga III. 1. Engendered by force, AGNI, verily, appropriates, as soon as born, the offerings of the sages:

---

[a] *Budhna* is the term, in this and in the next verse, for the *antariksha*, or firmament, as the root, or source, of the rains.

[b] The text has merely *navâsu prasûshu*,—in the new parents, or mothers; that is, in the *oshadhis*, the annuals, or the cerealia, which ripen after the rains, and bear food, being impregnated by the terrestrial *Agni*.

the waters and voice make him their friend ;[a] and the gods retain him, as the giver of (sacrificial) wealth.[b]

2. (Propitiated) by the primitive laudatory hymn of Áyu, he created the progeny of the Manus,[c] and pervades, with his all-investing splendour, the heavens and the firmament. The gods retain Agni, as the giver of (sacrificial) wealth.

3. Approaching him, let all men adore Agni, the chief[d] (of the gods), the accomplisher of sacrifices, who is gratified by oblations, and propitiated by praises, the offspring of food, the sustainer of (all men), the giver of continual gifts. The gods retain Agni, as the giver of (sacrificial) wealth.

4. May Agni, the dweller in the firmament, the nourisher with abundant benefits, the bestower of *Swarga*, the protector of mankind, the progenitor of heaven and earth, instruct my sons in the right way. The gods retain Agni, as the giver of (sacrificial) wealth.

---

[a] The *Agni* alluded to is the ethereal or electric fire, combined, at its production, with rain and with sound.

[b] As the conveyer of oblations, the term is *draviṅodá*, the giver of wealth; but the wealth is that of sacrifice, or abundance of clarified butter.

[c] *Áyu* is said, by the Scholiast, to be another name of *Manu*. What is intended by the progeny of the *Manus* is not very obvious; but it appears to intend simply mankind. The Scholiast says, being hymned by *Manu*, he created all the offspring of *Manu* (*Manuná stutah san mánavíh sarváh prajá ajanayat*).

[d] The term is *prathama*,—the first, which the Commentator interprets by *mukhya*, chief.

5. The night and the day, mutually effacing each other's complexion, give nourishment, combined together, to one infant,* who, radiant, shines between earth and heaven. The gods retain AGNI, as the giver of sacrificial wealth.

Varga IV. 6. The source of opulence, the bestower of riches, the director of the sacrifice, the accomplisher of the desires (of the man) who has recourse to him,—him the gods, preserving their immortality, retain, as the giver of (sacrificial) wealth.

7. The gods retain AGNI,—as the giver of (sacrificial) wealth,—who now is, and heretofore has been, the abode of riches, the receptacle of all that has been, and all that will be, born, and the preserver of all (that) exists, (as well as of all) that are coming into existence.

8. May DRAVIŚODÁ grant us (a portion) of moveable wealth; may DRAVIŚODÁ grant us (a portion) of that which is stationary; may DRAVIŚODÁ give us food, attended by progeny; may DRAVIŚODÁ bestow upon us long life.

9. Thus, AGNI, who art the purifier, growing with the fuel (we have supplied), blaze, for the sake of securing food to us who are possessed of wealth; and may MITRA, VARUŃA, ADITI, ocean, earth, heaven, preserve it to us.

---

* *Agni*, whom they nourish with the oblations offered during their continuance.

SÚKTA IV. (XCVII.)

The Ṛishi is the same; the deity, AGNI, as pure fire, or that of which purity is the attribute; the metre is *Gáyatrí*.

1. May our sin, AGNI, be repented of.[a] Manifest riches to us. May our sin be repented of. Varga V.

2. We worship thee, for pleasant fields, for good roads, and for riches. May our sin be repented of.

3. (In like manner as, among these thy worshippers, KUTSA) is the pre-eminent panegyrist, so are our encomiasts (of thee) the most distinguished. May our sin be repented of.

4. Inasmuch as thy worshippers (are blessed with descendants), so may we (by repeating thy praise,) obtain posterity.[b] May our sin be repented of.

5. Since the victorious flames of AGNI penetrate universally, may our sin be repented of.

---

[a] *Apa naḥ śośuchad agham.* *Śośuchat* is from *śuch*, to sorrow, in the intensative form, and the *Vaidik* imperative, or *leṭ*, with *apa* prefixed, although locally detached. The commentator proposes two interpretations: "Let our sin pass away from us, and light upon our adversaries;" or, "Let our sin, affected by grief, perish." Rosen renders it, *nostrum expietur scelus.*

[b] *Pra • • jáyemahi • • vayam;* from *jan*, to be born:—May we be born successively, in the persons of our posterity. Rosen has *vincamus tuo auxilio;* but this is, evidently, an oversight, from confounding the radical with *ji—jaye*, conquering. M. Langlois follows his rendering, with some additions:—*O Agni! si ces chefs de famille, si nous-mêmes nous nous avançons avec respect, puissions-nous obtenir la victoire!*

6. Thou, whose countenance is turned to all sides, art our defender. May our sin be repented of.

7. Do thou, whose countenance is turned to all sides, send off our adversaries, as if in a ship, (to the opposite shore). May our sin be repented of.

8. Do thou convey us, in a ship, across the sea, for our welfare. May our sin be repented of.

SÚKTA V. (XCVIII.)

The *Ṛishi*, as before; the deity is either VAIŚWÁNARA, or the pure (*śuddha*) AGNI; the metre is *Trishṭubh*.

Varga VI. 1. May we continue in the favour of VAIŚWÁNARA;[a] for, verily, he is the august sovereign of all beings. As soon as generated from this (wood), he surveys the universe; he accompanies the rising sun.[b]

2. AGNI, who is present[c] in the sky, and present upon earth, and who, present, has pervaded all herbs,—may the AGNI VAIŚWÁNARA, who is present

---

[a] *Vaiśwánara* implies either he who rules over all (*viśwa*) men (*nara*), or who conducts them (*nara*) to another region,—either to heaven, through oblations, or, possibly, to future life, through the funeral fire.

[b] Either as the combined heat with solar radiance; or, it is said, that, at the rising of the sun, in proportion as the solar rays descend to earth, so the rays of the terrestrial fire ascend, and mix with them.

[c] *Pṛishṭa*, explained by *saṃspṛishṭa*, in contact with, or *nihita*, placed, or present, in the sky. *Agni* is in contact with, or present in, the sun; on earth, in sacred and domestic fire; and, in herbs, or annuals, as the cause of their coming to maturity.

in vigour, guard us, night and day, against our enemies.

3. VAIŚWÁNARA, may this (thy adoration be attended) by real (fruit): may precious treasures wait upon us:[a] and may MITRA, VARUṆA, ADITI, ocean, earth, and heaven, preserve them to us.

SÚKTA VI. (XCIX.)

The *Ṛishi* is KAŚYAPA, the son of MARÍCHI; and the Hymn, consisting of a single stanza, in the *Trishṭubh* metre, is addressed to AGNI, as JÁTAVEDAS.[b]

1. We offer oblations of *Soma* to JÁTAVEDAS. May he consume the wealth of those who feel enmity against us: may he transport us over all difficulties. May AGNI convey us, as in a boat over a river, across all wickedness. Varga VII.

SÚKTA VII. (C.)

The deity is INDRA; the *Ṛishis* are the VÁRSHÁGIRAS,—or five sons of VṚISHÁGIRA,[c] a *Rájá*,—who were *Rájarshis*, or regal sages, severally named in the seventeenth stanza; the metre is *Trishṭubh*.

1. May he, who is the showerer of desires; who Varga VIII.

---

[a] Rosen has *divitiæ nos opulentas sequuntor*; but the *maghavánah* of the text cannot be the accusative plural, which would be either *maghavatah* or *maghonah*. It is the adjective of the word immediately preceding, *ráyah*, 'riches,' here said to mean wealth in family, or sons, grandsons, &c.

[b] There is nothing remarkable in this *Súkta*, except its brevity, it consisting of a single stanza.

[c] We have no mention of *Vṛisbágir* and his sons in the *Puráṇas*.

is co-dweller with (all) energies, the supreme ruler over the vast heaven and earth, the sender of water, and to be invoked in battles;—may INDRA, associated with the MARUTS, be our protection.

2. May he, whose course, like that of the sun, is not to be overtaken; who, in every battle, is the slayer of his foes, the witherer (of opponents); who, with his swift-moving friends, (the winds), is the most bountiful (of givers);—may INDRA, associated with the MARUTS, be our protection.

3. May he, whose rays, powerful and unattainable, issue forth, like those of the sun, milking (the clouds); he, who is victorious over his adversaries, triumphant by his manly energies;—may INDRA, associated with the MARUTS, be our protection.

4. He is the swiftest among the swift,* most bountiful amongst the bountiful, a friend with friends, venerable among those who claim veneration, and preeminent among those deserving of praise. May INDRA, associated with the MARUTS, be our protection.

5. Mighty with the RUDRAS, as if with his sons; victorious in battle over his enemies; and sending down, with his co-dwellers, (the waters, which are productive of) food,—INDRA, associated with the MARUTS, be our protection.

---

* *Angirobhir angirastamah*, "the most *Angiras* of *Angirasas*," which might be thought to refer to the *Ṛishis* so named: but the Commentator derives it from *ang*, to go, and explains *angirasah* by *gantárah*, goers; 'those who go swiftly.'

6. May he, the represser of (hostile) wrath, the author of war, the protector of the good, the invoked of many, share, with our people, on this day, the (light of the) sun.[a] May INDRA, associated with the MARUTS, be our protection. Varga IX.

7. Him his allies, the MARUTS, animate in battle; him men regard as the preserver of their property: he alone presides over every act of worship. May INDRA, associated with the MARUTS, be our protection.

8. To him, a leader (to victory), his worshippers apply, in contests of strength, for protection and for wealth; as he grants them the light (of conquest), in the bewildering darkness (of battle).[b] May INDRA, associated with the MARUTS, be our protection.

9. With his left hand he restrains the malignant; with his right, he receives the (sacrificial) offerings: he is the giver of riches, (when propitiated) by one who celebrates his praise. May INDRA, associated with the MARUTS, be our protection.

10. He, along with his attendants, is a bene-

---

[a] The *Várshágiras* are supposed to address this prayer to *Indra*, that they might have daylight, in which to attack their enemies, and to recover the cattle that had been carried away by them, or that the light may be withheld from their opponents.

[b] The expression *jyotish*, 'light,' and *chittamasi*, 'in the darkness of thought,' may, also, be applied more literally, and express the hope that *Indra* will give the light of knowledge to darkness of understanding.

factor: he is quickly recognized by all men, to-day, through his chariots: by his manly energies he is victor over unruly (adversaries). May INDRA, associated with the MARUTS, be our protection.

Varga X. 11. Invoked by many, he goes to battle, with his kinsmen, or with (followers) not of his kindred: he secures the (triumph) of those who trust in him, and of their sons and grandsons. May INDRA, associated with the MARUTS, be our protection.

12. He is the wielder of the thunderbolt, the slayer of robbers, fearful and fierce, knowing many things, much eulogized, and mighty, and, like the *Soma* juice, inspiring the five classes of beings with vigour. May INDRA, associated with the MARUTS, be our protection.

13. His thunderbolt draws cries (from his enemies); he is the sender of good waters, brilliant as (the luminary) of heaven, the thunderer, the promoter of beneficent acts: upon him do donations and riches attend. May INDRA, associated with the MARUTS, be our protection.

14. May he, of whom the excellent measure (of all things), through strength,* eternally and everywhere cherishes heaven and earth, propitiated by our acts, convey us beyond (evil). May INDRA, associated with the MARUTS, be our protection.

15. Nor gods, nor men, nor waters, have reached

---

* *Swasá sadnam*, the distributor of all things, through his power. Or it may mean, that he is the prototype of everything endued with vigour.

the limit of the strength of that beneficent (divinity);[a] for he surpasses both earth and heaven by his foe-consuming (might). May INDRA, associated with the MARUTS, be our protection.

16. The red and black coursers,—long-limbed, well-caparisoned, and celestial, and harnessed, well-pleased, to the yoke of the chariot in which the showerer of benefits is conveyed, for the enrichment of ṚIJRÁŚWA,—are recognized amongst human hosts.[b] Varga XI.

17. INDRA, showerer (of benefits), the VÁRSHÁGIRAS,—ṚIJRÁŚWA, and his companions, AMBARÍSHA, SAHADEVA, BHAYAMÁNA, and SURÁDHAS,—address to thee this propitiatory praise.

18. INDRA, who is invoked by many, attended by the moving (MARUTS), having attacked the *Dasyus* and the *S'imyus*,[c] slew them with his thunderbolt: the thunderer then divided the fields with his white-complexioned friends,[d] and rescued the sun, and set free the water.

---

[a] The text has *na yasya devá devatá*. The latter is said to be put for *devasya*, a *Vaidik* license, and is explained, "endowed with the properties of giving, &c." : (*dánádiguṇayuktasya*).

[b] *Náhushíshu vikshu*. *Nahusha* is explained by 'man;' whence the derivative will mean manly, or human: *viś* also imports 'man;' whence Rosen renders the phrase, *inter humanas gentes*. The Scholiast interprets *vikshu* by *senálakshaṇásuprajásu*, "people designated as an army."

[c] The commentary explains these, 'enemies' and *Rákshasas*; but they, more probably, designate races not yet subjected by the Vaidik Hindus, or Arians.

[d] *Sakhibhih świtnyebhih*. These, according to the Scholiast,

19. May INDRA be, daily, our vindicator; and may we, with undiverted course, enjoy (abundant) food; and may MITRA, VARUŃA, ADITI, ocean, earth, and heaven, preserve it to us.

SÚKTA VIII. (CI.)

The *Ṛishi* is KUTSA, the son of ANGIRAS; the deity, INDRA: the metre of the first seven stanzas is *Jagatí*; of the last four, *Trishṭubh*.

Varga XII. 1. Offer adoration, with oblations, to him who is delighted (with praise); who, with ṚIJIŚWAN, destroyed the pregnant wives of KṚISHŃA.[a] Desirous of protection, we invoke, to become our friend, him, who is the showerer (of benefits), who holds the thunderbolt in his right hand, attended by the MARUTS.

2. We invoke, to be our friend, INDRA, who is attended by the MARUTS; him who, with increasing wrath, slew the mutilated VṚITRA, and S'AMBARA,

---

are the winds, or *Maruts;* but why they should have a share of the enemy's country, (*śatrúńám bhúmim*), seems doubtful. Allusion is, more probably, intended to earthly friends, or worshippers, of *Indra*, who were white (*świtnya*) in comparison with the darker tribes of the conquered country.

[a] *Ṛijiśwan* is said to be a king, the friend of *Indra: Kṛishńa*, to be an *Asura*, who was slain, together with his wives, that none of his posterity might survive. [See Vol. II., p. 35, note b, and Vol. III., p. 148, note 7.] *Kṛishńa, the black*, may be another name for *Vṛitra*, the black cloud; or we may have, here, another allusion to the dark-complexioned aborigines.

and the unrighteous PIPRU,[a] and who extirpated the unabsorbable S'USHṄA.[b]

3. We invoke, to become our friend, INDRA, who is attended by the MARUTS; whose great power (pervades) heaven and earth; in whose service VARUṄA and SÚRYA are steadfast; and whose command the rivers obey.

4. Who is the lord over all horses and cattle; who is independent; who, propitiated by praise, is constant in every act; and who is the slayer of the obstinate abstainer from libations: we invoke, to become our friend, INDRA, attended by the MARUTS.

5. Who is the lord of all moving and breathing creatures; who, first, recovered the (stolen) kine, for the *Brahman;*[c] and who slew the humbled *Dasyus:* we invoke, to become our friend, INDRA, attended by the MARUTS.

6. Who is to be invoked by the brave and by the timid, by the vanquished and by victors, and whom all beings place before them, (in their rites):

---

[a] *Sambara* and *Pipru* are, both, termed *Asuras*. The latter is also styled *avrata*, not performing, or opposing, *vratas*, or religious rites.

[b] *Sushṅam ashusham*, the dryer up; who is without being dried up, who cannot be absorbed.

[c] *Brahmaṅe*, that is, for *Angiras*, or the *Angirasas*, who, according to the Scholiast, were of the Brahmanical caste. Several passages concur in stating the cows to have been stolen from the *Angirasas*; and *Angiras* cannot be identified with *Brahmá*. The term used, therefore, very probably denotes a *Brahman*: so Rosen has *Brahmani* * vaccas tribuit.

we invoke, to become our friend, INDRA, attended by the MARUTS.

Varga XIII. 7. The radiant INDRA proceeds (along the firmament), with the manifestation of the RUDRAS:* through the RUDRAS, speech spreads with more expansive celerity, and praise glorifies the renowned INDRA: him, attended by the MARUTS, we invoke, to become our friend.

8. Attended by the winds, giver of true wealth, whether thou mayest be pleased (to dwell) in a stately mansion, or in a lowly dwelling, come to our sacrifice. Desirous of thy presence, we offer thee oblations.

9. Desirous of thee, INDRA, who art possessed of excellent strength, we pour forth, to thee, libations: desirous of thee, who art obtained by prayer, we offer thee oblations. Therefore, do thou, who art possessed of horses, sit down, with pleasure, upon the sacred grass, attended by the MARUTS, at this sacrifice.

---

* *Indra* is here said to be radiant, through identity with the sun; and the *Rudras*, to be the same as the *Maruts*, in their character of vital airs, or *prâńâh*: as it is said, in another text, "When shining, he rises, having taken the vital airs of all creatures" (*Yo 'sau tapann udeti sa sarveshâm bhûtânâm prâńân âdâyodeti*). Hence, also, the subservience of the *Rudras* to the expansion of voice, or speech. Another application of the etymological sense of *Rudra* is here given by *Sâyańa*; he deriving it, as elsewhere, from the causal of *rud*, to weep. When the vital airs depart from the body, they cause the kindred of the deceased to weep: hence they are called *Rudras*.

10. Rejoice, INDRA, with the steeds who are of thy nature: open thy jaws; set wide thy throat, (to drink the *Soma* juice): let thy horses bring thee, who hast a handsome chin, (hither); and, benignant towards us, be pleased by our oblations.

11. Protected by that destroyer (of foes) who is united, in praise, with the MARUTS, we may receive sustenance from INDRA: and may MITRA, VARUṆA, ADITI, ocean, earth, and heaven, preserve it to us.

SÚKTA IX. (CII.)

The *Rishi* and deity, as in the last: the metre of the first ten stanzas is *Jagati*; of the last, *Trishṭubh*.

1. I address to thee, who art mighty, this excellent hymn; because thy understanding has been gratified by my praise. The gods have successively delighted that victorious INDRA with the power (of praise), for the sake of prosperity and wealth. Varga XIV.

2. The seven rivers display his glory: heaven, and earth, and sky display his visible form. The sun and moon, INDRA, perform their revolutions, that we may see, and have faith in what we see.

3. MAGHAVAN, despatch thy chariot, to bring us wealth,—that victorious car which, INDRA, who art much praised, by us, in time of war, we rejoice to behold in battle. Do thou, MAGHAVAN, grant happiness to those who are devoted to thee.

4. May we, having thee for our ally, overcome our adversaries in every encounter. Defend our

portion; render riches easily attained by us; enfeeble, MAGHAVAN, the vigour of our enemies.

5. Many are the men who call upon thee for thy protection. Mount thy car, to bring wealth to us; for thy mind, INDRA, is composed, and resolved on victory.

Varga XV. 6. Thy arms are the winners of cattle; thy wisdom is unbounded; thou art most excellent, the granter of a hundred aids in every rite. The author of war, INDRA is uncontrolled; the type of strength: wherefore, men who are desirous of wealth invoke him in various ways.

7. The food, MAGHAVAN, (which is to be given, by thee,) to men, may be more than sufficient for a hundred, or for more, even, than a thousand. Great praise has glorified thee, who art without limit, whereupon thou destroyest thy enemies.

8. Strong as a twice-twisted rope, thou art the type of strength: protector of men, thou art more than able to sustain the three spheres, the three luminaries,[a] and all this world of beings, INDRA, who hast, from birth, ever been without a rival.

9. We invoke thee, INDRA, the first among the gods. Thou hast been the victor in battles. May INDRA put foremost, in the battle, this our chariot, which is efficient, impetuous, and the uprooter (of all impediments).[b]

---

[a] The three fires; or, the sun in heaven, lightning in mid-air, and fire (sacred or domestic,) on earth.

[b] Or the epithets may be applied to *putra*, a son, understood,

10. Thou conquerest, and withholdest not the booty. In trifling, or in serious, conflicts, we sharpen thee, fierce MAGHAVAN, for our defence. Do thou, therefore, inspirit us, in our defiances.

11. May INDRA daily be our vindicator; and may we, with undiverted course, enjoy abundant food: and may MITRA, VARUṆA, ADITI, ocean, earth, and heaven, preserve it to us.

SÚKTA X. (CIII.)

The *Ṛishi* and deity, as before; the metre, *Trishṭubh.*

1. The sages have formerly been possessed of this thy supreme power, INDRA, as if it were present with them,[a]—one light of whom shines upon the earth; the other, in heaven: and both are in combination with each other;[b] as banner (mingles with banner,) in battle. Varga XVI.

2. He upholds, and has spread out, the earth. Having struck (the clouds), he has extricated the

---

—may *Indra* give us (a son), an offerer of praises, all-wise, and the subduer of foes, and (give us), also, a chariot foremost in battle.

[a] The term is *parâchaiḥ*, which is rather equivocal. Rosen renders the phrase,—*tuo robore* » *contra ipsorum inimicos directo*; but it, rather, means the contrary,—inverse, averted (*parâchîna*, *parâṅmukha*). But the other sense proposed by the Scholiast seems preferable.—*abhimukham eva*, as if present.

[b] The sun and fire are equally, it is said, the lustre of *Indra*. In the day, fire is combined (*samprichyate*) with the sun; in the night, the sun is combined with fire.

waters. He has slain AHI; he has pierced RAUHIṆA; he has destroyed, by his prowess, the mutilated (VṚITRA).[a]

3. Armed with the thunderbolt, and confident in his strength, he has gone on destroying the cities of the *Dasyus*. Thunderer, acknowledging (the praises of thy worshipper), cast, for his sake, thy shaft against the *Dasyu*, and augment the strength and glory of the *Árya*.[b]

4. MAGHAVAN, possessing a name[c] that is to be glorified, offers, to him who celebrates it, these (revolving) ages of man.[d] The thunderer, the scatterer (of his foes), sallying forth, to destroy the *Dasyus*, has obtained a name (renowned for victorious) prowess.

---

[a] *Ahi* and *Vṛitra* have, on former occasions, been considered as synonyms: here they are distinct, but mean, most probably, only differently formed clouds. *Rauhiṇa*, termed an *Asura*, is, in all likelihood, something of the same sort,—a purple, or red, cloud.

[b] We have, here, the *Dasyu* and *Árya* placed in opposition; the one, as the worshipper, the other, as the enemy of the worshipper. *Dásíḥ*, as the adjective to *puraḥ*, cities, is explained 'of, or belonging to, the *Dasyus*.' The mention of cities indicates a people not wholly barbarous, although the term may designate villages or hamlets.

[c] *Náma bibhrat*. The Scholiast interprets *náma*, strength, "that which is the bender or prostrator of foes;" from *nam*, to bow down. But it does not seem necessary to adopt any other than the usual sense.

[d] *Mánushá yugáni*, 'these mortal *yugas*': the *Kṛita*, *Tretá*, *&c.*, according to the Scholiast, which *Indra* successively evolves, in the character of the sun.

5. Behold this, the vast and extensive (might of INDRA): have confidence in his prowess. He has recovered the cattle; he has recovered the horses, the plants, the waters, the woods.

6. We offer the *Soma* libation to him who is the performer of many exploits, the best (of the gods), the showerer (of benefits), the possessor of true strength, the hero who, holding respect for wealth, takes it from him who performs no sacrifice,—like a foot-pad (from a traveller),—and proceeds (to give it) to the sacrificer. Varga XVII.

7. Thou didst perform, INDRA, a glorious deed, when thou didst awaken the sleeping AHI with thy thunderbolt. Then the wives (of the gods), the MARUTS, and all the gods, imitated thy exultation.

8. Inasmuch, INDRA, as thou hast slain S'USHŃA, PIPRU, KUYAVA, and VṚITRA, and destroyed the cities of S'AMBARA, therefore may MITRA, VARUŃA, ADITI, ocean, earth, and heaven, grant us that (which we desire).

SÚKTA XI. (CIV.)

The *Rishi*, deity, and metre, as before.

1. The altar has been raised, INDRA, for thy seat: hasten to sit upon it,—as a neighing horse (hastens to his stable),—slackening the reins, and letting thy coursers free, who, at the season of sacrifice,* bear thee, night and day. Varga XVIII.

* We have only 'for the season of sacrifice,' *prapitwe*,—for *prápte*,—literally, 'arrived;' synonymous, in the *Nirukta*, III., 20,

2. Those persons have come to INDRA, (to solicit) his protection. May he quickly direct them on the way. May the gods repress the wrath of the destroyer, and bring to our solemnity the obviator of evil.

3. (The *Asura*),[a] knowing the wealth of others, carries it off, of himself. Present in the water, he carries off, of himself, the foam. The two wives of KUYAVA bathe with the water: may they be drowned in the depths of the S'IPHÁ river.

4. The abiding-place of the vagrant[b] (KUYAVA) was concealed (in the midst) of the water. The hero increases, with the waters formerly (carried off), and is renowned (throughout the world). The ANJASÍ, KULIŚÍ, and VÍRAPATNÍ[c] rivers, pleasing him with their substance, sustain him with their waters.

5. Since the track that leads to the dwelling of the *Dasyu*[d] has been seen by us,—as a cow knows the way to her stall,—therefore do thou, MAGHAVAN, (defend us) from his repeated violence: do not thou cast us away, as a libertine throws away wealth.

---

with adverbs signifying proximity,—near, nigh, at hand. The Scholiast supplies *yágakále prápte*, the time of sacrifice being arrived.

[a] Presently named *K'uyava*. His exploits are obscurely alluded to; and the river *S'iphá* is not elsewhere found.

[b] *Aya* is said, by the Scholiast, to be an appellative of *K'uyava*; from *ay*, to go,—one going about to do mischief to others.

[c] Neither of these is found in the *Pauráńik* lists.

[d] Of *K'uyava*, according to the commentary; intending, possibly, by him, one of the chiefs of the barbarians.

6. Excite, in us, INDRA, veneration for the sun, Varga XIX.
for the waters, and for those who are worthy of the praise of living beings, as exempt from sin. Injure not our offspring, while yet in the womb; for our trust is in thy mighty power.

7. Hence, INDRA, I meditate on thee: on this (thy power) has our trust been placed. Showerer (of benefits), direct us to great wealth: consign us not, thou who art invoked by many, to a destitute dwelling: give, INDRA, food and drink to the hungry.

8. Harm us not, INDRA; abandon us not; deprive us not of the enjoyments that are dear to us. Injure not, affluent S'AKRA, our unborn offspring; harm not those who are capable (only of crawling) on their knees.

9. Come into our presence. They have called thee, fond of the *Soma* juice: it is prepared: drink of it, for thine exhilaration. Vast of limb, distend thy stomach; and, when invoked, hear us, as a father (listens to the words of his sons).

SÚKTA XII. (CV.)

The Hymn is addressed to the VIŚWADEVAS, by TRITA, or by KUTSA, on his behalf; the metre is *Pankti*, except in the eighth verse, where it is *Maháběrihati Yavamadhyá*, and in the last, where it is *Trishṭubh*.

1. The graceful-moving moon[a] speeds along the Varga XX.

---

[a] *Chandramáh* . . *suparńah*. The latter the Scholiast explains, *śobhanapatana*, the well, or elegantly, going. Or it may mean,

middle region in the sky: bright golden rays (my eyes,) behold not your abiding-place.[a] Heaven and earth, be conscious of this (my affliction).[b]

2. Those who seek for wealth obtain it: a wife enjoys (the presence of) her husband, and, from their union, progeny is engendered. Heaven and earth, be conscious of this (my affliction).

3. Never, gods, may this (my ancestry), abiding above, in heaven, be excluded (from it);[c] never may we be in want (of a son), the cause of joy (to his progenitors), entitled to libations of the *Soma* juice. Heaven and earth, be conscious of this (my affliction).

"connected with the ray of the sun called *Susperṇa*," the combination with which gives the moon its light.

[a] This refers to the supposed position of *Trita*, at the bottom of the well, which, being covered over, shuts out from him all visible objects: see the story of *Trita*, Hymn LII., note *e*, p. 141.

[b] The text has only "heaven and earth, know of this of me" (*vittam me asya rodasî*); that is, according to *Sâyaṇa*, either "be aware of this my affliction," or "attend to this my hymn."

[c] By failure of posterity, such as *Trita* anticipates for himself; as by a text quoted: "By a son, a man conquers the worlds: there is no world (*loka*) for one who has no son." It may be observed, of this reference, that, although the Scholiast cites the *Veda*,—*iti śrutaḥ*,—the passage occurs in the *Aitareya Bráhmaṇa*. It may, possibly, be found in the text of a hymn; but it is, also, possible that *Sâyaṇa* includes the *Bráhmaṇa* under the designation *Śruti*; in which case we must receive his citations, generally, with reserve; for the *Bráhmaṇa* is *not* the *Śruti*, as applicable to the original *Vaidik* text, although it is so regarded by all the native interpreters of the *Vedas*. (See Introduction, pp. ix., &c.)

4. I implore the first (of the gods),[a] the object of sacrifice, that he will become my messenger, and narrate (my condition to the other deities). Where, AGNI, is thy former benevolence? What new being now possesses it? Heaven and earth, be conscious of this (my affliction).

5. Gods, who are present in the three worlds, who abide in the light of the sun, where, now, is your truth? Where, your untruth? Where, the ancient invocation (that I have addressed) to you? Heaven and earth, be conscious of (my affliction).

6. Where, deities, is your observance of the truth? Where, the (benignant) regard of VARUṆA? Where is the path of the mighty ARYAMAN,[b] (so that) we may overcome the malevolent? Heaven and earth, be conscious of this (my affliction). Varga XXI.

7. I am he, Gods, who formerly recited (your praise), when the libation was poured out. Yet sorrows assail me, like a wolf (that falls upon) a thirsty deer. Heaven and earth, be conscious of this (my affliction).

8. The ribs (of the well close) round me, like the rival wives (of one husband): cares consume me, S'ATAKRATU,—although thy worshipper,—as a rat

---

[a] According to the (*Aitareya*) *Bráhmaṇa*, *Agnir vai devánám avamah*; which the Scholiast explains, the first-produced of all the gods; as, by another text, *Agnir mukham prathamo devatánám*,—*Agni* is the mouth, the first, of the deities.

[b] *Varuṇa* is here explained to mean the 'obstructor of evil,' as what is undesired (*anishṭanivárakah*); *Aryaman*, the restrainer of enemies (*arínám niyantá*).

(gnaws a weaver's) threads.[a] Heaven and earth, be conscious of this (my affliction).

9. Those which are the seven rays (of the sun), in them is my navel expanded.[b] TRITA, the son of the waters,[c] knows that (it is so); and he praises them for his extrication (from the well). Heaven and earth, be conscious of this (my affliction).

10. May the five shedders[d] (of benefits), who

---

[a] Which, according to the Scholiast, have been steeped in rice-water, to render them more tenacious, and which are, therefore, palatable to rats. Or it may be rendered, "as a rat gnaws, or licks, its tail, having just dipped it in oil, or grease." The practice of thickening threads with starch we have noticed by *Manu*, where the law requires that the cloth returned shall be heavier than the thread given, on this account (VIII., 397).

[b] It is not very clear what is intended by the term *nábhi*. Rosen renders it domicile: *Hi qui septem solis radii sunt, inter illos meum domicilium collocatum est.* But it is not so explained in the commentary; and the ordinary sense of *nábhi* is navel, in which the Scholiast seems to understand it; identifying the solar rays with the seven vital airs abiding in the ruling spirit (*teshu súryaraśmishwadhyátmam saptaprúńarúpeńa vartamáneshu*); alluding, perhaps, though obscurely, to the mystic practice of contemplating the umbilical region, as the seat of the soul.

[c] *Áptya*, explained *apám putrah*, son of the waters. But it may be doubted if it can properly bear such an interpretation; for, as admitted by the Scholiast, such a patronymic from *apa* would be, properly, *ápya*; and the insertion of the *t* is an anomaly.

[d] They are said to be *Indra*, *Varuńa*, *Agni*, *Aryaman*, and *Savitri*, or, according to other texts, Fire, Wind, the Sun, the Moon, and the Lightning: for these, according to the *Sátyáyana Bráhmańa*, are, all, luminous, in their respective spheres; or, fire,

abide in the centre of the expanded heavens, having together conveyed my prayers quickly to the gods, (speedily) return. Heaven and earth, be conscious of this (my affliction).

11. The rays of the sun abide in the surrounding centre of heaven: they drive back the wolf, crossing the great waters, from the path.[a] Heaven and earth be conscious of this (my affliction). Varga XXII.

12. That new praiseworthy and commended (vigour)[b] is seated in you, ye gods, (by which) the rivers urge on the waters, and the sun diffuses his constant (light). Heaven and earth, be conscious of this (my affliction).

13. Worthy of praise, AGNI, is that thy relationship (with the gods). Do thou, who art most wise, seated at our (solemnity), worship (the gods), as (at the sacrifice of) MANUS.

---

upon earth, wind, in the firmament, the sun, in heaven, the moon, in the planetary region, and lightning, in the clouds. The *Taittiriyas* substitute, for lightning, the *nakshatras*, or asterisms, shining in the *Swarloka*.

[a] Alluding, it is said, to a story of a wolf, who was about to swim across a river, to devour *Trita*, but was deterred by the brightness of the solar rays. According to *Yáska*, as quoted by *Sáyaṇa*, he interprets *vṛika*, the moon, and *apaḥ*, the firmament, and renders the passage: "The rays of the sun prevent the moon from appearing, or being visible, in the firmament."

[b] *Bala*, 'strength,' is said, by the Commentator, to be understood, —of which *ukthya*, praiseworthy, is an epithet. Rosen takes *ukthya* for the substantive, in its not unusual sense of 'hymn,' and translates the text: *Nova hæc cantilena dicata est vobis, dii!*

14. May that wise and liberal AGNI, a sage amongst the gods, seated at our rite, as at the sacrifice of MANUS, be the invoker of the deities, and offer them oblations. Heaven and earth, be conscious of this (my affliction).

15. VARUṆA performs the rite of preservation.[a] We desire him, as the guide of our way: (to him the repeater of praise) addresses praise, with his (whole) heart. May he, who is entitled to laudation, become our true (support). Heaven and earth, be conscious of this (my affliction).

Varga XXIII. 16. The sun, who is, avowedly, made the path in heaven,[b] is not to be disregarded, gods, by you;[c] but you, mortals, regard him not. Heaven and earth, be conscious of this (my affliction).

17. TRITA, fallen into the well, invokes the gods, for succour. BṚIHASPATI, who liberates many from sin, heard (the supplication). Heaven and earth, be conscious of this (my affliction).

18. Once, a tawny wolf beheld me faring on my

---

[a] *Brahmá kriṅoti Varuṅah.* The first is here explained, *rakshaṅarúpam karma,* "the act which is of the nature of preserving."

[b] *Asau yah panthá ádityo divi pravácyam kritah.* One meaning of *panthúh* is given as an epithet of *áditya,* the sun, as *satatagámí,* the ever-going: but the more usual sense is a road, a path; and this interpretation is borne out by texts which represent the sun as the road to heaven; as *Súryadwáreṅa te virajáh prayánti,*—Those who are free from soil go by the gate of the sun.

[c] For the gods depend, for existence, indirectly upon the sun, who regulates the seasons at which sacrifices are offered.

way, and, having seen me, rushed upon me, (rearing); as a carpenter* whose back aches (with stooping stands erect from his work).

19. By this recitation may we, becoming possessed of INDRA, and strong with multiplied progeny, overcome our foes in battle; and may MITRA, VARUṆA, ADITI, ocean, earth, and heaven, be gracious to us, in this (request).

ANUVÁKA XVI.

SÚKTA I. (CVI.)

The *Ṛishi* is KUTSA, or it may be TRITA: the Hymn is addressed to the VIŚWADEVAS: the metre is *Jagatí*, except in the last verse, in which it is *Trishṭubh*.

1. We invoke, for our preservation, INDRA, MITRA, VARUṆA, AGNI, the might of the MARUTS, and ADITI. May they, who are bountiful, and bestowers of dwellings, extricate us from all sin, as a chariot from a defile. Varga XXIV.

2. Sons of ADITI, come, with all (your hosts), to battle. Be, to us, the cause of happiness in combats;

---

* The meaning of the comparison is not very clear, and is only rendered intelligible by the additions of the commentary. The wolf, like the carpenter, was *ūrdhwábhimukha* (standing in presence erect). The passage admits of a totally different rendering, by interpreting *vṛika*, the moon, and uniting *má sakṛit*, *me once*, into *másakṛit*, month-maker. He, the moon, it is said, having contemplated the constellations going along the path of the sky, became united with one of them; paying, therefore, no attention to *Trita* in the well.

and may they, who are bountiful, and bestowers of dwellings, extricate us from all sin, as a chariot from a defile.

3. May the *Pitṛis*,[a] who are easily to be praised, protect us; and may the two divinities, heaven and earth, the promoters of sacrifices, and of whom the gods are the progeny, protect us; and may they, who are bountiful, and the givers of dwellings, extricate us from sin, as a chariot from a defile.

4. Exciting him who is the praised of men and the giver of food, (to be present) at this rite, we solicit, (also,) with our praises, him who is the purifier, and destroyer of heroes.[b] May they, who are bountiful, and the givers of food, extricate us from sin, as a chariot from a defile.

5. BṚIHASPATI, always confer happiness upon us. We solicit that faculty of both (alleviating pain and obviating peril), implanted in thee by MANU.[c] May they, who are bountiful, and the givers of dwellings, extricate us from all sins, as a chariot from a defile.

6. KUTSA,[d] the *Ṛishi*, thrown into a well, has

---

[a] The *Agnishwáttas* and others.—See *Manu*, III., 195.

[b] In the first clause, it is said, *Agni* is alluded to; in the second, *Púshan* is named: but the term is explained, by the Scholiast, *poshakam devam,—nutrientem deum.*

[c] *S'am yor yat te Manur hitam,*—the good, or blessing, of those two (things, or properties,) which was placed in them by *Manu*. The two are explained, in the commentary, as in the translated text.

[d] *Kutsa* here identifies himself, apparently, with *Trita*.

invoked, to his succour, INDRA, the slayer of enemies, the encourager of good works.* May they, who are bountiful, and the givers of dwellings, extricate us from all sin, as a chariot from a defile.

7. May the goddess ADITI, with the gods, protect us; and may the radiant guardian, (the sun), be vigilant for our protection; and may they, who are bountiful, and the givers of dwellings, extricate us from all sin, as a chariot from a defile.

SÚKTA II. (CVII.)

The *Rishi* is KUTSA; the deities, the VIŚWADEVAS; the metre, *Trishtubh*.

1. May our sacrifice give satisfaction to the gods. Varga XXV.
ÁDITYAS, be gracious; and may your good intentions be directed towards us, so as to be an abundant source of affluence to the poor.

2. May the gods, who are to be lauded by the hymns of the ANGIRASAS, come hither, for our protection: may INDRA, with his treasures; the MARUTS, with the vital airs; and ADITI, with the ÁDITYAS; (come, and) give us felicity.

3. May INDRA, may VARUŃA, may AGNI, may ARYAMAN, may SAVITRI, bestow upon us that food (which we solicit); and may MITRA, VARUŃA, ADITI, ocean, earth, and heaven, preserve it (to us).

---

* *Śachîpati;* which might be rendered 'the husband of *Śachî*.' But the more usual sense of *śachî*, in the *Veda*, is *karma*, act, or rite; and it is so rendered, in this place, by the Commentator.

SÚKTA III. (CVIII.)

The *Ṛishi* is, still, KUTSA, who addresses INDRA and AGNI; the metre is *Trishṭubh*.

Varga XXVI. 1. INDRA and AGNI, sitting together, in your car, —that wonderful car which illuminates all beings, —approach, and drink of the effused *Soma* juice.

2. Vast as is the whole universe in expanse, and profound in depth, such, INDRA and AGNI, may this *Soma* be, for your beverage,—sufficient for your desires.

3. You have made your associated names renowned, since, slayers of VṚITRA, you have been allied (for his death). The showerers of benefits, INDRA and AGNI, are the two seated together (on the altar). Receive (your portion) of the libation.

4. The fires being kindled, the two (priests stand by),* sprinkling the clarified butter from the ladles, —which they raise,—and spreading the sacred grass (upon the altar). Therefore, INDRA and AGNI, come before us, for our gratification, (attracted) by stimulating *Soma* juices sprinkled all around.

5. Whatever heroic exploits you have achieved, whatever forms (you have created), whatever benefits (you have poured down), whatever ancient and fortunate friendships (you have contracted, come, with them all), and drink of the effused *Soma* juice.

* We have merely, in the text, the epithets in the dual number: the Commentator supplies the *Adhwaryu* and his assistant priest.

6. Come, and witness the sincere faith with which, selecting you two, I first promised (you the libation). Drink of the effused libation; for the *Soma* juice is prepared by the priests. Varga XXVII.

7. If, adorable INDRA and AGNI, you have ever been delighted (with libations,) in your own dwelling, in that of a Brahman, or in that of a prince,[a] then, showerers of benefits, come hither, from wherever you may be, and drink of the effused libation.

8. If, INDRA and AGNI, you are amongst men who are inoffensive, malevolent, or tyrannical, or those who live (to fulfil the duties of life), or those who receive the fruits (of good deeds),[b] then,

---

[a] *Yad Brahmaṇi Rájani vá.* The first is explained, a Brahman who is a different institutor of a sacrifice (*Bráhmaṇo'nyasmin yajamánas*); the second, by *Kshatriya*, a man of the second, or military, caste.

[b] The terms thus rendered, in conformity to the explanations of the Scholiast, would seem, rather, to be intended for proper names,—the names of tribes or families well known in the *Puráṇas*, —being, severally, *Yadus, Turvasas, Druhyus, Anus* and *Púrus*, descendants of the five sons of *Yayáti*, similarly named. (*Mahábh.*, I., 138.) Here, however, *Yadu* is explained by *ahinsaka*, non-injurious; *Turvasa*, by *hinsaka*, injurious; *Druhyu*, by *upadrava-chchhu*, tyrannical; *Anu*, by *práṇair yuktah*, having breath, or life, wherewith to acquire knowledge and perform religious acts; and *Púru*, by *kámaih púrayitavyah*, to be filled full of the objects of desire. The meanings may be supported by the etymology of the words; but the interpretation seems to be a needless refinement.

showerers of benefits, come hither, from wherever you may be, and drink of the effused libation.

9. Whether, INDRA and AGNI, you are in the lower, the central, or the upper, region of the world, showerers of benefits, come hither, from wherever you may be, and drink of the effused libation.

10. Whether, INDRA and AGNI, you are in the upper, central, or lower, region of the world, come, showerers of benefits, hither, from wherever you may be, and drink of the effused libation.

11. Whether, INDRA and AGNI, you are in heaven, or upon earth, in the mountains, in the herbs, or in the waters, showerers of benefits, come hither, from wherever you may be, and drink of the effused libation.

12. Although, INDRA and AGNI, in the midst of the sky, on the rising of the sun, you may be exhilarated by your own splendour, yet, showerers of benefits, come hither, from wherever you may be, and drink of the effused libation.

13. Thus, INDRA and AGNI, drinking deep of the libation, grant to us all (kinds of) wealth: and may MITRA, VARUŃA, and ADITI, ocean, earth, and heaven, preserve it to us.

SÚKTA IV. (CIX.)

Ṛishi, deities, and metre, as in the last.

Varga XXVIII. 1. INDRA and AGNI, desirous of wealth, I consider you, in my mind, as kinsmen and relations.

The clear understanding you have given me (is given) by no one else; and, (so gifted), I have composed this hymn to you, intimating my wish for sustenance.

2. I have heard, INDRA and AGNI, that you are more munificent givers than an unworthy bridegroom,[a] or the brother of a bride.[b] Therefore, as

---

[a] *Vijámátṛi.* The prefix *vi* indicates, according to the Scholiast, a son-in-law (*jámátṛi*) who is not possessed of the qualifications required by the *Vedas*, and who is, therefore, obliged to conciliate his father-in-law by liberal gifts; which is, in fact, paying for, or buying, his wife; as in the interpretation of this stanza, by *Yáska*, it is said (*Nirukta*, VI., 9), that the *vijámátṛi* is the *asusamápta*, the unfulfilled, or unaccomplished, bridegroom, which implies, according to some, that he is the husband of a purchased bride (*krítápati*). This recognition, in the *Veda*, of the act of receiving money from the bridegroom is at variance with the general tenour of the law of marriage, as laid down by *Manu*, which condemns the acceptance of anything, by the father of a maiden, beyond a complimentary present, and censures the receipt of money, as equivalent to a sale: "Let no father who knows the law receive a gratuity, however small, for giving his daughter in marriage; since the man who, through avarice, takes a gratuity for that purpose is a seller of his offspring." (*Laws of Manu*, III., 51.) And, again: "A bribe, whether large or small, is an actual sale of the daughter;" although a bull and cow might be given at a marriage of saintly persons or *Ṛishis*. (*Ibid.*, 53.) We have, here, therefore, an indication of a different condition of the laws of marriage.

[b] The *syála*, the brother of the maiden, who makes her gifts through affection. The word is derived, by *Yáska*, from *sya*, a winnowing-basket, and *lá*, for *lájá*, fried grains, which are scattered, at the marriage ceremony, by the bride's brother.

I offer you a libation, I address you, INDRA and AGNI, with a new hymn.

3. Never may we cut off the long line (of posterity). Thus soliciting and asking for descendants endowed with the vigour of their progenitors, the (worshippers), begetting children, praise INDRA and AGNI, for their happiness; and they two, destroyers of foes, are nigh, (to hear this adoration).

4. The sacred prayer,[a] desiring your presence, offers to you both, INDRA and AGNI, for your exhilaration, the *Soma* libation. Do you two, who have horses, handsome arms, and graceful hands, come quickly, and mix (the libation) with sweetness in the waters.

5. I have heard, (when you were present) at the division of the treasure (among the worshippers), that you two, INDRA and AGNI, were most vigorous in the destruction of VṚITRA. Beholders of all things, seated at this sacrifice, upon the sacred grass, be exhilarated, (by drinking of the effused libation).

Varga XXIX. 6. Attending to the summons, at the time of battle, you surpass all men (in magnitude): you are vaster than the earth, than the sky, than the rivers, than the mountains: you exceed all other existent things.

7. Bring wealth, thunderers, and give it to us: protect us, INDRA and AGNI, by your deeds. May those rays of the sun,[b] by which our forefathers

---

[a] *Devî dhishaṇá*, divine speech,—*mantrarúpá*, in the form of prayer.

[b] By the rays of the sun, in this place, it is said, are intended

have attained, together,[a] a heavenly region, shine also upon us.

8. INDRA and AGNI, wielders of the thunderbolt, overturners of cities, grant us wealth; defend us in battles: and may MITRA, VARUṆA, ADITI, ocean, earth, and heaven, be propitious to this (our prayer).

SÚKTA V. (CX.)

This Hymn is addressed to the ṚIBHUS: the *Ṛishi* is KUTSA: the eighth and ninth stanzas are in the *Trishṭubh*; the rest, in the *Jagatí* metre.

1. ṚIBHUS, the rite formerly celebrated by me is again repeated; and the melodious hymn is recited in your praise. In this ceremony, the *Soma* juice is sufficient for all the gods. Drink of it, to your utmost content, when offered on the fire. Varga XXX.

2. When, ṚIBHUS, you, who were amongst my ancestors, yet immature (in wisdom), but desirous of enjoying (the *Soma* libations), retired to the forest, to perform (penance), then, sons of SUDHANWAN,[b]

---

the radiance of *Indra* and *Agni*, as identical with the sun. By praising the latter, therefore, *Indra* and *Agni* are praised also.

[a] *Sapitwam* is explained, *sahaprâptavyam sthânam*, a place to be obtained together; that is, according to the Commentator, the world of *Brahmá*, to which the pious proceed by the path of light, &c.—(*archirâdimârgeṇa* • *Brahmalokam upâsakâ gachchhanti*).

[b] *Sudhanwan*, the father of the *Ṛibhus*, was a descendant of *Angiras*; so is *Kutsa*: therefore, they are related; although, as *Kutsa* is the son of *Angiras*, it seems not very consistent to call them

through the plenitude of your completed (devotions), you came to the (sacrificial) hall of the worshipper, SAVITṚI.

3. Then SAVITṚI bestowed upon you immortality, when you came to him,—who is not to be concealed,[a]—and represented (your desire) to partake of the libations; and that ladle for the sacrificial viands, which the *Asura*[b] had formed single, you made fourfold.

4. Associated with the priests, and quickly performing the holy rites, they, being yet mortals, acquired immortality; and the sons of SUDHANWAN, the ṚIBHUS, brilliant as the sun, became connected with the ceremonies (appropriated to the different seasons) of the year.

5. Lauded by the bystanders, the ṚIBHUS, with a sharp weapon, meted out the single sacrificial ladle,—like a field (measured by a rod),—soliciting the best (libations), and desiring (to participate of) sacrificial food amongst the gods.

Varga XXXI. 6. To the leaders (of the sacrifice),[c] dwelling in

---

his kinsmen of a former period (*práncháh*, or *púrvakálínáh*). Rosen calls them *sapientes*: but this is an evident inadvertence; as the epithet is *apákáh*, unripe; *aparipakwajnánáh*, immature in wisdom.

[a] In the preceding verse, *Savitṛi*, derived from *sú*, to offer oblations, might mean merely the presenter of oblations; but here we have, evidently, the sun alluded to.

[b] *Twashṭṛi*; as in a former passage.—See p. 48, note *b*.

[c] *Nṛibhyah*, *i.e.*, *yajnasya netṛibhyah*; as in the text *Ṛibhavo hi yajnasya netárah*,—"The *Ṛibhus* are the leaders of the sacrifice;" on which account they obtained immortality. Or the term may

the firmament, we present, as with a ladle, the appointed clarified butter, and praise, with knowledge, those Ṛibhus, who, having equalled the velocity of the protector (of the universe,—the sun),[a] ascended to the region of heaven, through (the offerings) of (sacrificial) food.

7. The most excellent Ṛibhu is, in strength, our defender; Ṛibhu, through gifts of food and of wealth, is our asylum. May he bestow them upon us, gods, through your protection. May we, upon a favourable occasion, overcome the hosts of those who offer no libations.

8. Ṛibhus, you covered the cow with a hide, and reunited the mother with the calf:[b] sons of Sudhanwan, leaders (of sacrifice), through your good works, you rendered your aged parents young.[c]

9. Indra, associated with the Ṛibhus, supply us, in the distribution of viands, with food,[d] and consent to bestow upon us wonderful riches: and may

---

be connected with *antarikshasya*, which precedes, in the text, and may mean, as Rosen has it, to the chiefs of the firmament (*aeris regibus*).

[a] A text of the *Veda* identifies the *Ṛibhus* with the solar rays (*Ádityaraśmayo'pyṛibhava uchyante*). The *Ṛibhus* are, indeed, said to be the rays of the sun.

[b] A story is related, that a *Ṛishi*, whose cow had died, leaving a calf, prayed to the *Ṛibhus* for assistance, on which they formed a living cow, and covered it with the skin of the dead one, from which the calf imagined it to be its own mother.

[c] See p. 47.

[d] *Vájebhir no vájasátávavíḍḍhi* may be also rendered, "protect us, in battle, with your horses."

MITRA, VARUŃA, ADITI, ocean, earth, and heaven, preserve them for us.

SÚKTA VI. (CXI.)

The *Ṛishi* and deities are the same: the metre of the fifth verse is *Trishṭubh*; of the rest, *Jagatí*.

VARGA XXXII. 1. The ṚIBHUS, possessed of skill in their work, constructed (for the AŚWINS,) a well-built car: they framed the vigorous horses bearing INDRA; they gave youthful existence to their parents; they gave, to the calf, its accompanying mother.[a]

2. Prepare fully, for our sacrifice, resplendent[b] sacrificial food, and, for our rite, and for our strength, such nutriment as may be the cause of excellent progeny; so that we may live (surrounded) by vigorous descendants. Such wealth do you confer upon us, for our benefit.

3. ṚIBHUS, conductors (of sacrifice), bestow ample sustenance upon us, upon our chariots, upon our horses. Let every one daily acknowledge our victorious wealth; and may we triumph, in battle, over our foes, whether strangers or kinsmen.

4. I invoke the mighty[c] INDRA, for protection;

---

[a] See the preceding Hymn; also, Hymn xx., p. 45.

[b] *Ṛibhumat*; explained, having much light: for, according to the *Nirukta* etymology, *ṛibhu* means 'much light,' from *uru* much, and *bhá*, to shine.

[c] *Ṛibhukshaṇam Indram* might be '*Indra*, who is *Ṛibhukshan*,' of which *Ṛibhukshaṇam* is the accusative. In the following expressions, *Ṛibhún* and *váján*, plural accusatives, we are to understand,

and the Ṛibhus, Vájas, and Maruts, to drink the *Soma* juice; also, both Mitra, Varuṇa, and the Aświns: and may they direct us to opulence, to holy rites, and to victory.

5. May Ṛibhu supply us with wealth for war; may Vája, victorious in battle, protect us; and may Mitra, Varuṇa, Aditi, ocean, earth, and heaven, be propitious to this (our prayer).

Súkta VII. (CXII.)

The *Ṛishi* is Kutsa: the first quarter-stanza is addressed to the Earth and Sky; the second, to Agni; the rest of the Hymn, to the Aświns. The metre of the twenty-fourth and twenty-fifth stanzas is *Trishṭubh*; of the rest, *Jagatí*.

1. I praise Heaven and Earth, for preliminary meditation, (prior to the coming of the Aświns): I praise the hot and bright-shining Agni, upon their approach, (as preparatory) to their worship. With those appliances with which you sound the conch-shell, in battle, for your share (in the booty),—with those aids,[a] Aświns, come, willingly, hither. Varga XXXIII.

2. Earnest and exclusive adorers stand, Aświns, round your car, (to benefit) by your bounty; as (disciples listen) to the words (of a teacher), for

---

according to the Commentator, the three sons of *Sudhanwan*,—*Ṛibhu*, *Vibhu*, and *Vája*.

[a] *Útibhiḥ*, instr. plur. of *úti*, help, aid, assistance, protection. It is rather an awkward term to render into English with the sense of plurality, although not without precedent.

instruction. With those aids with which you defend the pious who are engaged in acts of worship, come, Aświns, willingly, hither.

3. By the vigour infused from celestial nectar, you are able, leaders (of sacrifice), to rule over those beings (who people the three worlds). With those aids by which you gave (milk) to the barren cow,[a] come, Aświns, willingly, hither.

4. With those aids by which the circumambient (wind), endowed with the vigour of his son,[b] the measurer of the two worlds (of heaven and earth),[c] and swiftest of the swift, beautifies (all things), and by which (Kakshívat) became learned in the three kinds of sacrifice;[d]—with them come, Aświns, willingly, hither.

---

[a] Alluding, according to the commentary, to the cow of a *Rishi* named *Śayu*, to which, although barren, the *Aświns*, at his entreaty, gave abundance of milk. [See p. 313; also, Vol. IV., *passim*.]

[b] *Agni* is said to be the son of *Váyu*; as by the text *Váyor Agnih*, either as generated, in the character of digestive warmth, by the vital airs, or as having been excited into flame, by the wind, at the time of creation.

[c] *Dwimátṛi* may be applied to the wind, in conjunction with *Agni*, as the respective occupants of the earth and the firmament; the former being the region of *Agni*, the latter, of *Váyu*. Or it may be rendered, as in former instances, 'the son of two mothers;' or the two sticks used for attrition, and, thence, be applicable to *Agni*.

[d] Or *trimantu*, acquainted with the *pákayajnas*, or offerings of food; the *haviryajnas*, or oblations of clarified butter; and the *somayajnas*, or libations of *Soma* juice. In this sense, *trimantu*

5. With those aids by which you raised up, from the water, REBHA, who had been cast, bound, (into a well), and also VANDANA (similarly circumstanced), to behold the sky; by which you protected KAŃWA, when longing to see the light;[a]—with them, AŚWINS, come, willingly, hither.

6. With those aids by which you rescued ANTAKA,[b] (when cast) into a deep (pool), and about to be destroyed; by which, inflicting no distress, you preserved BHUJYU;[c] and by which you relieved KARKANDHU and VAYYA;[d]—with them, AŚWINS, come, willingly, hither. Varga XXXIV.

is synonymous, apparently, with *Kakshîvat*, whose name is supplied by the Scholiast.

[a] *Rebha* and *Vandana* are said to have been *Rishis* who were cast into wells by the *Asuras*. According to the *Nîti-manjarî*, they brought this upon themselves, by maintaining a friendly intercourse with the *Asuras*. *Kańwa* is said, also, to have been thrown, by them, into darkness. In these, and similar instances subsequently noticed, we may, possibly, have allusions to the dangers undergone, by some of the first teachers of Hinduism, among the people whom they sought to civilize.

[b] *Antaka* is called a *Rájarshi*, whom the *Asuras* threw into a pond, or a well.

[c] Of *Bhujyu*, the son of the *Rájá Tugra*, we shall hear again, rather more in detail. The tradition is remarkable. *Bhujyu* had embarked on a maritime expedition against the enemies of his father, but encountered a storm, in which his vessel was lost; he was saved, and brought back to his father, by the intervention of the *Aświns*.

[d] These are said to be *Asuras* whom the *Aświns* extricated from misfortunes: but, for the latter, see p. 149.

7. With those aids by which you enriched S'UCHANTI,[a] and gave him a handsome habitation, and rendered the scorching heat pleasurable to ATRI;[b] and by which you preserved PRIŚNIGU and PURUKUTSA;[c]—with them, AŚWINS, come, willingly, hither.

8. Showerers (of benefits), with those aids by which you enabled (the lame) PARÁVṚIJ (to walk), the blind (ṚIJRÁŚWA) to see, and (the cripple) S'ROṆA to go;[d] and by which you set free the quail,[e] when seized (by a wolf);—with those aids, AŚWINS, come, willingly, hither.

9. With those aids by which you caused the sweet stream to flow; by which you, who are exempt from decay, gratified VASISHṬHA; and by which

---

[a] No account is given of this person.

[b] *Atri*, the patriarch, was thrown, it is said, by the *Asuras*, into a cave with a hundred doors, at all of which fires of chaff were kindled: they were extinguished, with cold water, by the *Aświns*. Or, according to *Yáska*, *Atri* is, here, a name of *Agni*,—the eater (*atri*) of clarified butter,—but whose appetite, or intensity, being checked by the heat of the sun in the hot weather, was renovated by the rain sent down by the *Aświns*.

[c] We have no particulars of these, except that *Priśnigu* is so named from his possessing brindled cows (*priśnayo* • *gávo yasya*).

[d] *Parávṛij* is called a *Ṛishi*; so are *Ṛijráśwa* and *Sroṇa*. The first is named without an epithet, in the text; instead of the second (see p. 259), we have *prándha*, the totally blind; and *Sroṇa* is not called a cripple, but is said to have been made to walk. The Scholiast supplies the details. [But see Vol. II., p. 242, note b.]

[e] *Vartiká* the commentary calls a bird like a sparrow: the ordinary sense is 'quail.'

you protected KUTSA, S'RUTARYA, and NARYA;[a]—with them, AŚWINS, come, willingly, hither.

10. With those aids by which you enabled the opulent VIŚPALÁ, when she was unable to move, to go to the battle rich in a thousand spoils; and by which you protected the devout VAŚA, the son of AŚWA;[b]—with them, AŚWINS, come, willingly, hither.

11. With those aids by which, beauteous donors, the cloud (was made to) shed its sweet (water), for the sake of the merchant DÍRGHAŚRAVAS, the son of UŚIJ; and by which you protected the devout KAKSHÍVAT;[c]—with them, AŚWINS, come, willingly, hither. Varga XXXV.

12. With those aids by which you filled the (dry) river-bed with water; by which you drove the chariot, without horses, to victory; and by which TRIŚOKA[d] recovered his (stolen) cattle;—with them, AŚWINS, come, willingly, hither.

---

[a] *Vasishṭha* is well known; but in what manner he was assisted by the *Aświns* does not appear. Of the three others named in the text, it is only said that they were *Ṛishis*.

[b] The story of *Viśpalá* is subsequently more fully alluded to. She was the wife of *Khela*, the son of *Agastya*. *Vaśa* and *Aświa* are called *Ṛishis*.

[c] *Dírghaśravas* was the son of *Dírghatamas*, and, therefore, a *Ṛishi*. But, in a time of famine, he followed trade, to obtain a livelihood: hence he is termed a *vaṇik*, a merchant. As the son of *Uśij*, he should be the same as *Kakshívat* (see p. 42, note a); but the text treats them, apparently, as distinct.

[d] *Triśoka* is called a *Ṛishi*, the son of *Kaṇwa*. These holy persons were much exposed, apparently, to cattle-stealing.

13. With those aids by which you encompassed the sun, when afar off, (to extricate him from eclipse); by which you defended MANDHÁTṚI, in (the discharge of) his sovereign functions;[a] and by which you protected the sage BHARADWÁJA;[b]—with them, AŚWINS, come, willingly, hither.

14. With those aids by which you defended the mighty and hospitable DIVODÁSA, (when, having undertaken) the death of S'AMBARA, he hid himself in the water, (through fear of the *Asuras*);[c] by which you protected TRASADASYU,[d] in war;—with them, AŚWINS, come, willingly, hither.

15. With those aids by which you preserved VAMRA, praised by all around him, when drinking (the dews of the earth); by which you protected KALI, when he had taken a wife, and PṚITHI, when

---

[a] *Mandhátṛi* is called a *Ṛishi*; but a *Rájarshi*, a royal sage, is intended; as *Mándhátṛi* is a celebrated prince of the solar dynasty (*Vishńu Puráńa*, p. 363). His regal character is, also, evident from his office (*kshaitrapatyeshu*), the derivative of *kshetrapati*, the lord, either of fields or of the earth.

[b] Here we have, also, a name well known in *Pauráńik* tradition. (*Vishńu Puráńa*, p. 449, and note 15). He is termed, in the text, *vipra*, usually intending a Brahman, but here explained, *medhávin*, wise.

[c] *Divodása* is a king well known in the *Pauráńik* traditions (*Vishńu Puráńa*, p. 407). But no notice there occurs of his war with the *Asura Sambara*, whom we have elsewhere seen destroyed by *Indra* (p. 148), in defence, it is also said (p. 137), of this prince, or, as he is there named, *Atithigwa*, the cherisher of guests (*atithi*), which is here employed as an epithet.

[d] The son of *Purukutsa*, according to the Scholiast, concurring, in this respect, with the *Vishńu Puráńa*, p. 371. [And see Vol. III., p. 205, note 1, also p. 272; and Vol. IV., p. 63.]

he had lost his horse;[a]—with them, AŚWINS, come, willingly, hither.

16. With those aids, leaders (of sacrifices), which you afforded to S'AYU, to ATRI, and, formerly, to MANU, anxious (to show them) the way to (escape from evil); with those by which you shot arrows (upon the foes) of SYÚMARAŚMI;[b]—with them, AŚWINS, willingly come hither. Varga XXXVI.

17. With those aids by which PAṬHARVAN[c] shone with strength of form in battle, like a blazing fire piled up (with fuel); by which you defended S'ARYÁTA in war;—with them, AŚWINS, come, willingly, hither.

---

[a] *Vamra* is called a *Rishi*, the son of *Vikhanas*. The text calls him *vipipána*, drinking much and variously, which the Scholiast explains, drinking, especially earthly moisture, or dew, *párthivam rasam*. (See p. 138.) Of *Kali*, no more is said than that he was a *Rishi*; nor of *Prithi*, than that he was a *Rájarshi*.

[b] The second and third names have occurred before. The first is called a *Rishi*. The text has only, "You wished them to go" (*gátum ishathuh*): the Scholiast adds, "out of evil or danger." *Manu* is here called a *Rájarshi*, whom the *Aświns* extricated from want, by teaching him the art of sowing the seeds of barley and other grains. *Syúmaraśmi* is styled a *Rishi*.

[c] *Patharvan* is merely called a *Rájarshi*. *Saryáta* is, probably, intended for *Saryáti*, the fourth son of *Vaivaswata Manu* (*Vishńu Puráńa*, pp. 354, 358); and the same prince is, no doubt, meant, in a former passage (see p. 139), by *Sáryáta*, which may be an epithet of *yajna*, sacrifice, understood,—the sacrifice of *Saryáti*,—rather than a patronymic, although there rendered as a proper name, upon the authority of *Sáyańa*. "Of the race of *Bhrigu*" applies, also, to *Chyavana*, not to *Saryáti*. [But see Vol. III., p. 81.]

18. ANGIRAS, (praise the AŚWINS). AŚWINS, with those aids by which, with (gratified) minds, you delight (in praise), and thence preceded the gods to the cavern, to recover the stolen cattle;[a] by which you sustained the heroic MANU with food;[b]—with them, AŚWINS, come, willingly, hither.

19. With those aids by which you gave a wife to VIMADA;[c] by which you recovered the ruddy kine; by which you conferred excellent wealth upon SUDÁS;[d]—with them, AŚWINS, come, willingly, hither.

20. With those aids by which you are bestowers of happiness upon the donor (of oblations); by which you have protected BHUJYU and ADHRIGU; and by which you have granted delighting and nourishing (food) to ṚITASTUBH;[e]—with them, AŚWINS, come, willingly, hither.

---

[a] We have here attributed to the *Aświns* a similar feat as that usually ascribed to *Indra*.

[b] By making him aware, according to the commentary, of the grain hidden in the earth, or teaching him, in fact, agriculture.

[c] The *Aświns* were the means, it is said, of obtaining the daughter of *Purumitra* as a wife for the *Ṛishi Vimada*.

[d] The name of a king, the son of *Pijavana* (p. 127). [Also see Vol. III., p. 50, note 2,—where correct "*Piyavana*"; and Vol. IV., p. 62.] Both names are unknown in the *Puráńas*,—although we have more than one *Sudása*,—but they are sprung from other princes. (*Vishńu Puráńa*, pp. 380, 455.) A prince named *Paiyavana*, or son of *Piyavana*, is noticed by *Manu*, VIII., 110.

[e] *Bhujyu* has been named before (p. 289, note c). *Adhrigu* is called a sacrificer, or immolator, along with *Chápa*, of the gods; as by the text: *Adhrigus Chápas cha ubhau devánám śamitárau*. *Ṛitastubh* is called a *Ṛishi*. [See Vol. IV., p. 264.]

21. With those aids by which you defended Kṛiśánu, in battle;[a] with which you succoured the horse of the young Purukutsa[b] in speed; and by which you deliver the pleasant honey to the bees;—with them, Aświns, come, willingly, hither. Varga XXXVII.

22. With those aids by which you succoured the worshipper contending in war for cattle; by which you assist him in the acquisition of houses and wealth; by which you preserve his chariots and horses;—with them, Aświns, come, willingly, hither.

23. With those aids by which you, who are worshipped in many rites,[c] protected Kutsa, the son of Arjuna, as well as Turvíti, Dabhíti, Dhwasanti, and Purushanti;[d]—with them, Aświns, come, willingly, hither.

24. Aświns, sanctify our words with works: showerers (of benefits), subduers of foes, (invigorate)

---

[a] *Kṛiśánu* is enumerated, by the *Taittiríyas*, amongst a class called *somapálas*, venders or providers,—apparently, of the *Soma* plants; as by the text: *Hastaruhastakṛiśánavah, te vah somakrayaṇáh*. The term occurs also amongst the synonyms of *Agni*. [Also see Vol. III., p. 174.]

[b] *Purukutsa*, in the *Puráṇas*, is the son of *Mándhátṛi*, and husband of *Narmadá*, the river (*Vishṇu Puráṇa*, p. 371). The text has only "of the young:" the comment supplies *Purukutsa*. [See Vol. III., p. 205, note 1.]

[c] *Śatakratu*, the usual epithet of *Indra*, 'he to whom many rites are addressed,' or 'by whom many acts are performed,' is here applied to the *Aświns*.

[d] *Kutsa* and *Turvíti* have occurred before, although the affiliation of the former is new. Of the other names no account is given, except that *Purushanti* is that of a *Ṛishi*.

our understanding, (for the sacred study). We invoke you both, in the last watch of the night,[a] for our preservation. Be to us for increase in the provision of food.

25. Cherish us, Aświns, always, by night or day, with undiminished blessings: and may Mitra, Varuńa, Aditi, ocean, earth, and heaven, be favourable to this (our prayer).

EIGHTH ADHYAYA.

ANUVÁKA XVI. (continued).

Súkta VIII. (CXIII.)

The Hymn is addressed to Ushas (the Dawn), and, in the second half of the first stanza, also to *Night*. The *Ṛishi* is Kutsa; the metre, *Trishṭubh*.

Varga I. 1. This most excellent luminary of all luminaries has arrived: the wonderful and diffusive manifester (of all things) has been born. In like manner as night is the offspring of the sun, so she becomes the birth-place of the dawn.[b]

---

[a] *Adyútye*, 'in the absence of light;' that is, in the last watch of the night, or that preceding the dawn, at which time, according to *Áśwaláyana*, as quoted by *Sáyańa*, the *Áświns* are especially to be worshipped.

[b] That is, when the sun sets, the night comes on; or it is generated by the setting of the sun, and may, figuratively, be termed his offspring; and, in like manner, as the precursor, night may be termed the parent, or womb, of the dawn.

2. The white-shining dawn, the parent of the sun,[a] has arrived: dark night has sought her own abode. Both allied to the same (sun), immortal, succeeding to each other, and mutually effacing each other's complexion, they traverse the heavens.

3. The path of the sisters is unending: they travel it alternately, guided by the radiant (sun). Combined in purpose, though of different forms, night and dawn, giving birth (to all things), obstruct not each other; neither do they stand still.

4. Brilliant guide of the speakers of truth,[b] the many-tinted dawn is recognized by us: she has opened our doors: having illuminated the world, she has made our riches manifest. USHAS gives back all the regions (that had been swallowed up by night).

5. The opulent (dawn) arouses to exertion the man bowed down in sleep,—one man, to enjoyments; another, to devotion; another, to (the acquirement of) wealth. She has enabled those who were almost sightless to see distinctly. The expansive USHAS has given back all the regions. Varga II.

6. The dawn rouses one man, to acquire wealth; another, to earn food; another, to achieve greatness; another, to sacrifices; another, to his own (pursuits); another, to activity; and lights all men to their

---

[a] A like conceit to that of the preceding verse: the dawn precedes, and, therefore, figuratively bears, or is the parent of, the sun.

[b] Upon the appearance of the dawn, the animals and birds utter their *true*, or *natural*, cries.

various means of maintaining life. USHAS has given back all the regions.

7. The daughter of heaven, young, white-robed, the mistress of all earthly treasure, is beheld dissipating the darkness. Auspicious USHAS, shine upon us, to-day, in this (hall of sacrifice).

8. Following the path of the mornings that have passed, and first of the endless mornings that are to come, USHAS, the disperser of darkness, arouses living beings, and awakens every one (that lay) as dead.

9. USHAS, inasmuch as thou hast caused the sacred fire to be kindled,[a] inasmuch as thou hast lighted the world with the light of the sun, inasmuch as thou hast wakened men to perform sacrifice, thou hast done good service to the gods.

10. For how long a period is it that the dawns have risen? For how long a period will they rise? Still desirous to bring us light, USHAS pursues the functions of those that have gone before, and, shining brightly, proceeds with the others (that are to follow).

Varga III. 11. Those mortals who beheld the pristine USHAS dawning have passed away: to us she is now visible; and they approach who may behold her in after-times.

12. The beings hostile (to acts of devotion) now withdraw;[b] for she is the protectress of sacred rites,

---

[a] Fires for burnt-offerings being properly lighted at the dawn.

[b] *Rákshasas* and other malignant spirits vanish, with the dawn.

who is manifested for their performance; she is the giver of happiness, the awakener of pleasant voices, the enjoyer of felicity, and provider of food for the gods. Most excellent USHAS, dawn, to-day, on this (sacrificial hall).

13. The divine USHAS dawned continually, in former times: the source of wealth, she still rises on this (world). So will she give light hereafter, through future days; for, exempt from decay, or death, she goes on in her splendour.

14. The divine USHAS lights up, with her beams, the quarters of the heavens: she has thrown off her gloomy form, and, awaking (those who sleep), comes in her car drawn by purple steeds.

15. Bringing, with her, life-sustaining blessings, and giving consciousness (to the unconscious), she imparts (to the world) her wonderful radiance. The similitude of the numerous dawns that have gone by, the first of the brilliant (dawns that are to come), USHAS has to-day appeared.

16. Arise! Inspiring life revives; darkness has departed; light approaches. USHAS has opened the road for the sun to travel. Let us repair to where they distribute food. Varga IV.

17. The offerer of praise, the recitor of praise, celebrating the brilliant USHASAS, repeats the well-connected words (of the *Veda*). Possessor of affluence, dawn, to-day, upon him who praiseth thee; bestow upon us food, whence progeny may be obtained.

18. May he who has offered the libation obtain-

upon the conclusion of his praises, (enunciated), like the wind, (with speed,—the favour of) those USHASAS who are givers of horses, and of cattle, and of progeny, and who shed light upon the mortal presenting to them (offerings).

19. Mother of the gods,[a] rival of ADITI, illuminator of the sacrifice, mighty USHAS, shine forth: approving of our prayer, dawn upon us. Do thou, who art cherished by all, make us eminent among the people.

20. Whatever valuable wealth the USHASAS convey is beneficial to the sacrificer and to the praiser. May MITRA, VARUṆA, ADITI, ocean, earth, and heaven, be favourable to this (our prayer).

SÚKTA IX. (CXIV.)

The deity is RUDRA; the *Rishi*, KUTSA. The tenth and eleventh verses are in the *Trishṭubh* metre; the rest, in the *Jagatí*.

Varga V. 1. We offer these praises to the mighty RUDRA,[b]

---

[a] The gods are awakened at dawn, by the worship they then receive; and, hence, the dawn may be said, figuratively, to be their parent (*mátá devánám*); and, in that character, she is the enemy, or rival, of *Aditi*, who is their mother.

[b] We have a repetition, here, of the usual etymologies of *Rudra*, with some additions: He causes all to weep (*rodayati*) at the end of the world; or *rut* may signify 'pain,'—the pain of living, which he drives away (*drávayati*); or *rut* may mean 'word,' or 'text,' or the *Upanishads* of the *Vedas*, by which he is approached, or propitiated (*dráyate*); or *rut* may mean 'holy or divine speech,' or 'wisdom,' which he confers (*ráti*) upon his worshippers; or

with the braided hair,[a] the destroyer of heroes,[b] in order that health may be enjoyed by bipeds and quadrupeds, and that all beings in this village may be (well-) nourished, and exempt from disease.

2. Be gracious to us, RUDRA. Grant us happiness; for we worship the destroyer of heroes with oblations. And, by thy directions, RUDRA, may we obtain that freedom from disease, and exemption from dangers, which our progenitor, MANU, bestowed upon us, (having obtained them from the gods).

3. RUDRA, showerer (of benefits), may we obtain, through our worship of the gods, the favour of thee, who art the destroyer of heroes. Come to our posterity, purposing to promote their happiness, while we, having our sons in safety, offer thee oblations.

4. We invoke, for our preservation, the illustrious

---

rut may mean 'darkness,' that which invests or obstructs (*ruṇaddhi*) all things, and which he dissipates (*driṇáti*). Or, again, it is said, that, while the gods were engaged in battle with the *Asuras*, *Rudra*, identified with *Agni*, came and stole their treasure: after conquering the enemy, the gods searched for the stolen wealth, and recovered it from the thief, who wept (*arudat*); and *Agni* was, thence, called *Rudra*.

[a] *Kapardine*, from *kaparda*, of which one meaning is, the *jaṭá*, or braided hair, of *Śiva*, whence the Scholiast gives, as its equivalent, *jaṭiláya*. This looks very like a recognition of *Śiva* in the person of *Rudra*. It is not easy to suggest any other interpretation, unless the term be an interpolation.

[b] *Kshayad víráya*, in whom heroes (*víráḥ*) perish (*vinaśyanti*). Or it may mean, of whom the imperial (*kshayantaḥ práptaiśwaryáḥ*) heroes (that is, the *Maruts*) are the sons. The epithet is repeated in the following verses.

RUDRA, the accomplisher of sacrifices,[a] the tortuous,[b] the wise. May he remove far from us his celestial wrath; for we earnestly solicit his favour.

5. We invoke, from heaven, with reverence, him who has excellent food,[c] who is radiant, and has braided hair, who is brilliant, and is to be ascertained (by sacred study), holding, in his hands, excellent medicaments. May he grant us health, defensive armour, and a (secure) dwelling.

Varga VI. 6. This praise, the sweetest of the sweet, and cause of increase (to the reciter), is addressed to RUDRA, the father of the MARUTS.[d] Immortal

---

[a] *Yajnasádhanam*, i.e., *sádhayitáram*, he who makes the sacrifice well-desired, or perfect (*svishṭam*, or *su ishṭam*.)

[b] *Vanku*, he who goes crookedly. What is meant by this is not explained.

[c] The phrase is *varáha*, literally, a boar; and one who has a hard body, like a boar's, may be intended. But the Scholiast prefers considering it as an abbreviation of *varáhára*, from *vara*, good, and *áhára*, food.

[d] The paternity of *Rudra*, with respect to the *Maruts*, is thus accounted for by the Scholiast: "After their birth from *Diti*, under the circumstances told in the *Puráńas* (*Vishńu Puráńa*, p. 152), they were beheld in deep affliction by *Siva* and *Párvatí*, as they were passing sportively along. The latter said to the former: 'If you love me, transform these lumps of flesh into boys.' *Maheśa* accordingly made them boys, of like form, like age, and similarly accoutred, and gave them to *Párvatí*, as her sons, whence they are called the sons of *Rudra*." The *Níti-manjarí* adds other legends; one, that *Párvatí*, hearing the lamentations of *Diti*, entreated *Siva* to give the shapeless births forms, telling them not to weep (*má rodíh*); another, that he actually begot

RUDRA, grant us food sufficient for mortals, and bestow happiness on me, my son, and my grandson.

7. Injure not, RUDRA, those, amongst us, who are old, or young, who are capable of begetting, or who are begotten, nor a father, nor a mother; nor afflict our precious persons.

8. Harm us not, RUDRA, in our sons, or grandsons, or other male descendants, nor in our cattle, nor in our horses. Inflamed with anger, kill not our valiant men; for we, presenting clarified butter, perpetually invoke thee.

9. I restore to thee the praises (derived from thee); as a shepherd (returns his sheep to their owner). Father of the MARUTS, bestow happiness upon me. Thy auspicious benignity is the cause of successive delight: therefore, we especially solicit thy protection.

10. Destroyer of heroes, may thy cow-killing or man-slaying (weapon) be far away; and let the felicity granted by thee be ours. Favour us! Speak, brilliant hero, in our behalf; and grant us, thou who art mighty over the two (realms of heaven and earth), prosperity.

11. Desirous of protection, we have said: Reverence be to him. May RUDRA, with the MARUTS,

---

them, in the form of a bull, on *Pṛithivî*, the Earth, as a cow. These stories are, evidently, fictions of a much later era than that of the *Vedas*,—being borrowed, if not fabricated, from the *Tantras*,—and may be set aside, without hesitation, as utterly failing to explain the meaning of those passages in the *Vedas*, which call the *Maruts* the sons of *Rudra*.

hear our invocation: and may MITRA, VARUṆA, ADITI, ocean, earth, and heaven, be favourable to this (our prayer).

SÚKTA X. (CXV.)

KUTSA is the *Ṛishi*; the deity is SÚRYA; the metre, *Trishṭubh*.

Varga VII. 1. The wonderful host of rays has risen; the eye of MITRA, VARUṆA, and AGNI;[a] the sun, the soul of all that moves or is immoveable,[b] has filled (with his glory,) the heaven, the earth, and the firmament.

2. The sun follows the divine and brilliant USHAS,—as a man (follows a young and elegant) woman,—at which season pious men perform (the ceremonies established for) ages,[c] worshipping the auspicious (sun), for the sake of good (reward).

---

[a] Or *chakshus* may mean 'the enlightener.' *Mitra*, *Varuṅa*, and *Agni* are said to be typical of the world,—or of the seasons, perhaps, over which they preside.

[b] *Átmá jagatah*, 'the soul of the world;' from his pervading and animating all things. Or *jagatah* may be rendered 'of what is moveable:' it is followed by *tasthushah*, 'of that which is fixed.' The sun is the cause of all effects, whether moveable or immoveable,—(*sa hi sarvasya sthávarajangamátmakasya káryavargasya káraṅam*).

[c] *Yugáni*, which may also be rendered 'yokes for ploughs;' for, at this season (dawn), men, seeking to propitiate the gods by the profit which agriculture yields, equip their ploughs, or engage in the labours of the field.

3. The auspicious, swift horses of the sun, well-limbed, road-traversing, who merit to be pleased with praise, reverenced by us, have ascended to the summit of the sky, and quickly circumambulate earth and heaven.

4. Such is the divinity, such is the majesty, of the sun, that, when he has set, he has withdrawn (into himself) the diffused (light which had been shed) upon the unfinished task.[a] When he has unyoked his coursers from his car, then night extends the veiling darkness over all.

5. The sun, in the sight of MITRA and VARUṆA,[b] displays his form (of brightness) in the middle of the heavens; and his rays[c] extend, on one hand, his infinite and brilliant power, or, on the other, (by their departure), bring on the blackness of night.

6. This day, gods, with the rising of the sun, deliver us from heinous sin: and may MITRA, VARUṆA, ADITI, ocean, earth, and heaven, be favourable to this (our prayer).

---

[a] *Madhyá kartor vitatam*, "spread in the middle of the affair;" that is, the cultivator, or artisan, desists from his labour, although unfinished, upon the setting of the sun.

[b] *Mitra* and *Varuṇa* are used, according to the commentary, by metonymy, for the world.

[c] *Haritah*, which may mean, also, his horses.

ANUVÁKA XVII.

SÚKTA I. (CXVI.)

The deities are the Aświns; the *Rishi* is Kakshívat; the metre is *Trishtubh*.

Varga VIII. 1. In like manner as a worshipper strews the sacred grass for the Násatyas, so do I urge on their laudations,—as the wind drives on the clouds,—they who gave a bride to the youthful Vimada,[a] and bore her away in their car, outstripping the rival host.

2. Násatyas, borne by strong and rapid (steeds), and (urged) by the encouragements of the gods, the ass[b] of you, thus instigated, overcame a thousand (enemies), in conflict, in the war grateful to Yama.

3. Tugra,[c] verily, Aświns, sent (his son,) Bhujyu

---

[a] See p. 294. The story told by the Scholiast is, that *Vimada*, having won his bride at a *swayamvara*, or 'choice of a husband by a princess,' was stopped, on his way home, by his unsuccessful competitors, when the *Aświns* came to his succour, and placed the bride in their chariot, repulsed the assailants, and carried the damsel to the residence of the prince.

[b] An ass (*rásabha*) given by *Prajápati*. The chariot of the *Aświns* is drawn by two asses (*rásabhávaświnoh*)—*Nighaṇṭu*, I., 14. Or it may mean "one going swiftly;" and the rest of the passage, "obtained precedence, for the *Aświns*, over other gods in the oblation, through his mastering the stanzas declared by *Prajápati*."

[c] See p. 289. *Tugra*, it is said, was a great friend of the *Aświns*. Being much annoyed by enemies residing in a different island,

to sea; as a dying man parts with his riches. But you brought him back in vessels of your own, floating over the ocean, and keeping out the waters.

4. Three nights and three days, NÁSATYAS, have you conveyed BHUJYU, in three rapid, revolving cars, having a hundred wheels, and drawn by six horses,[a] along the dry bed of the ocean, to the shore of the sea.

5. This exploit you achieved, AŚWINS, in the ocean, where there is nothing to give support, nothing to rest upon, nothing to cling to,—that you brought BHUJYU, sailing in a hundred-oared ship,[b] to his father's house.

6. AŚWINS, the white horse you gave to PEDU— whose horses were indestructible,—was ever, to him, success. That, your precious gift, is always to be celebrated: the horse of PEDU, the scatterer (of enemies), is always to be invoked.[c] Varga IX.

---

he sent his son *Bhujyu* against them, with an army, on board ship. After sailing some distance, the vessel foundered in a gale. *Bhujyu* applied to the *Aświns*, who brought him and his troops back, in their own ships, in three days' time, as appears from this and the two following stanzas.

[a] This is a rather unintelligible account of a sea-voyage, although the words of the text do not admit of any other rendering.

[b] *Śatáritrám návam*, a ship with a hundred, that is, with many, oars. This stanza is consistent with the first of the triad.

[c] *Pedu*, it is said, was a certain *Rájarshi*, who worshipped the *Aświns*: they, therefore, gave him a white horse, through the possession of which he was always victorious over his enemies. [See Vol. IV., p. 154.]

7. You gave, leaders (of sacrifice), to KAKSHÍVAT, of the race of PAJRA,[a] various knowledge: you filled, from the hoof of your vigorous steed, as if from a cask, a hundred jars of wine.[b]

8. You quenched, with cold (water), the blazing flames (that encompassed ATRI), and supplied him with food-supported strength: you extricated him, AŚWINS, from the dark (cavern) into which he had been thrown headlong, and restored him to every kind of welfare.[c]

9. NÁSATYAS, you raised up the well, and made the base, which had been turned upwards, the curved mouth, so that the water issued, for the beverage of the thirsty GOTAMA, the offerer.[d]

10. NÁSATYAS, you stripped off, from the aged CHYAVÁNA, his entire skin, as if it had been a coat of mail;[e] you reversed, DASRAS, the life of the sage

---

[a] *Pajras* is another name for *Angirasas*, in which race *Kakshívat* was born.

[b] No account of the occasion of this miracle is given.

[c] See p. 290, note b.

[d] This has been elsewhere related of the *Maruts* (p. 221). The manner in which the well was presented to *Gotama* is somewhat obscurely described. [See Vols. III. and IV., *passim*.]

[e] The restoration of the ascetic *Chyavana* to youth and beauty is related in several *Puráńas;* following, probably, the *Mahábhárata, Vana-parva,* (Vol. I., p. 577). He is there called the son of *Bhṛigu*, and was engaged in penance, near the *Narmadá* river, until the white ants constructed their nests round his body, and left only his eyes visible. *Sukanyá*, the daughter of King *Saryáti*, having come to the place, and seeing two bright spots in what

who was without kindred, and constituted him the husband of many maidens.

11. NÁSATYAS, leaders, glorious was that exploit of yours, one to be celebrated, to be adored, to be desired by us, when, becoming aware (of the circumstance), you extricated VANDANA, (hidden,) like a concealed treasure, from the (well) that was visible (to travellers).* Varga X.

12. I proclaim, leaders (of sacrifice), for the sake of acquiring wealth, that inimitable deed which you performed,—as the thunder (announces) rain,—when, provided, by you, with the head of a horse,

---

seemed to be an ant-hill, pierced them with a stick. The sage visited the offence upon *Saryáti* and his attendants, and was appeased only by the promise of the king to give him his daughter in marriage. Subsequently, the *Aświns*, coming to his hermitage, compassionated *Sukanyá's* union with so old and ugly a husband as *Chyavana*, and, having made trial of her fidelity, bestowed on the sage a similar condition of youth and beauty to their own. This story does not seem to be the same, however, as that of the text, in which no allusion occurs to *Sukanyá*, and the transformation of *Chyavana* precedes his matrimonial connexion. He is termed *jahita*, in the text,—properly, 'abandoned;' that is, according to the Scholiast, by sons, and others *(putrádibhiḥ parityaktaḥ)*: but it may denote, perhaps, merely his solitary condition as an ascetic. In return for their friendly office, *Chyavana* compelled *Indra* to assent to the *Aświns'* receiving, at sacrifices, a share of the *Soma* libation, which is not noticed in the text.

* See p. 289. For 'well' we have only *darśatát*, in the text,—that which was to be seen by thirsty travellers, according to the commentary.

DADHYACH, the son of ATHARVAN,[a] taught you the mystic science.

13. The intelligent (VADHRIMATÍ)[b] invoked you, NÁSATYAS, who are the accomplishers (of desires), and the protectors of many, with a sacred hymn: her prayer was heard,—like (the instructions of) a teacher;—and you, AŚWINS, gave, to the wife of an impotent husband, HIRAŃYAHASTA, her son.

14. NÁSATYAS, leaders, you liberated the quail from the mouth of the dog[c] that had seized her;

---

[a] We have, here, rather obscure allusions to a legend which was, probably, afterwards modified by the *Puráńas*, in which the name also occurs as *Dadhicha* (see, also, p. 216). In the *Mahábhárata*, *Vana-parva*, (Vol. I., p. 554), it is merely related, that the gods, being oppressed by the *Kálakeya Asuras*, solicited, from the sage *Dadhicha*, his bones, which he gave them, and from which *Twashṭṛi* fabricated the thunderbolt with which *Indra* slew *Vṛitra* and routed the *Asuras*. The legend of the text differs from this. *Indra*, having taught the sciences called *pravargyavidyá* and *madhuvidyá* to *Dadhyach*, threatened that he would cut off his head, if ever he taught them to any one else. The *Aświns* prevailed upon him, nevertheless, to teach them the prohibited knowledge, and, to evade *Indra's* threat, took off the head of the sage, replacing it by that of a horse. *Indra*, apprised of *Dadhyach's* breach of faith, struck off his equine head with the thunderbolt; on which the *Aświns* restored to him his own. The *pravargyavidyá* is said to imply certain verses of the *Ṛik*, *Yajur*, and *Sáma Vedas*; and the *madhuvidyá*, the *Bráhmańa*.

[b] *Vadhrimatí* was the wife of a certain *Rájarshi* who was impotent. The *Aświns*, propitiated by her prayers, gave her a son.

[c] *Vṛika*, more usually, 'a wolf,' but here said to be synonymous

and you, who are benefactors of many, have granted, to the sage who praises you, to behold (true wisdom).

15. The foot of (VIŚPALÁ, the wife of) KHELA was cut off, like the wing of a bird, in an engagement by night. Immediately you gave her an iron leg, that she might walk; the hidden treasure (of the enemy being the object of the conflict.)[a]

16. When his father caused ṚIJRÁŚWA[b]—as he was giving, to a she-wolf,[c] a hundred sheep cut up in pieces,—to become blind, you, DASRAS, physicians (of the gods), gave him eyes, (that had been) unable to find their way, with which he might see. Varga XI.

17. The daughter of the Sun[d] ascended your car,

---

with *śwan*, 'a dog.' It is elsewhere termed, by the commentary, *draṅyaśwan*, a forest, or wild, dog. *Yáska* interprets it figuratively, and renders *vṛika* by *áditya*, 'the sun,' from whose grasp, or overpowering radiance, the *Aświns* are said to have rescued the dawn, upon her appeal to them.

[a] See p. 291. The story is here more fully detailed in the text. It is only added, in the notes, that *Khela* was a king, of whom *Agastya* was the *purohita*; and it was through his prayers that the *Aświns* gave *Viśpalá* an iron leg.

[b] *Ṛijráśwa* was one of the sons of *Vṛisháqir* (see p. 239); his blindness has been previously alluded to (p. 290); but here we have the story in detail.

[c] The *vṛikí* was one of the asses of the *Aświns*, in disguise, to test his charitable disposition; but, as he exacted the sheep from the people, his father was angry, and caused him to lose his eyesight, which the *Aświns* restored to him.

[d] *Súrya*, it is related, was desirous of giving his daughter *Súryá* to *Soma*; but all the gods desired her as a wife. They

(like a runner) to a goal. When you won (the race), with your swift horse, all the gods looked on, with (anxious) hearts, and you, NÁSATYAS, were associated with glory.

18. When, AŚWINS, being invited, you went to his dwelling, (to give due rewards) to DIVODÁSA, offering oblations, then your helping chariot conveyed (food and) treasure, and the bull and the porpoise were yoked together.[a]

19. NÁSATYAS, bearing strength and wealth, with posterity and vigour-sustaining food, you came, with one intention, to the family of JAHNU,[b] (provided) with (sacrificial) viands, and possessing a third portion of the daily (offerings).

20. Undecaying NÁSATYAS, you bore away, by night, in your foe-overwhelming car, JÁHUSHA,[c] surrounded, on every side, by (enemies), through practicable roads, and went to (inaccessible) mountains.

---

agreed that he who should first reach the sun, as a goal, should wed the damsel. The *Aświns* were victorious; and *Súryá*, well pleased by their success, rushed, immediately, into their chariot.

[a] The *vrishabha* and the *śinśumára*. The Commentator calls the latter, *grdha*, which is, properly, an alligator. But the *śiśumára*, as it is usually read, is, everywhere else, considered to be a name of the Gangetic porpoise. They were yoked to the car of the *Aświns*, the comment says, to display their power.

[b] *Jahnávi*, not *Jáhnavi*. It is here considered as an adjective to *prajá*, progeny (*Jahnoh* • *prajám*). *Jahnu* is called a *Maharshi*. He is a prince of the lunar dynasty, in the *Puráńas* (*Vishńu Puráńa*, p. 398.)

[c] The name of a certain king. We have nothing relating to him, beyond what is stated in the text. [See Vol. IV., p. 154.]

21. You preserved VAŚA, AŚWINS, (that he might obtain), in a single day, a thousand acceptable gifts.[a] Showerers (of benefits), associated with INDRA, you destroyed the malignant enemies of PṚITHUŚRAVAS.[b] Varga XII.

22. You raised the water from the bottom, to the top, of the well, for the drinking of S'ARA, the son of ṚICHATKA;[c] and, by your powers, NÁSATYAS, you filled, for the sake of the weary S'AYU,[d] the barren cow (with milk).

23. NÁSATYAS, by your acts you restored to VIŚWAKA, the son of KṚISHṆA, soliciting your protection, adoring you, and a lover of rectitude, his son VISHṆÁPÚ,[e] (welcome,) to his sight, as an animal that had been lost.

24. AŚWINS, you raised up, like *Soma* in a ladle, REBHA,[f] who, for ten nights and nine days, had lain (in a well), bound with tight bonds, wounded, immersed, and suffering distress from the water.

25. Thus, AŚWINS, have I declared your exploits. May I become the master (of this place), having abundant cattle and a numerous progeny, and re-

---

[a] *Vaśa*, a *Ṛishi*, it is said, received daily presents, to the number of one thousand. (See p. 291.)

[b] We have a *Pṛithuśravas* amongst the *Pauráṇik* princes; but nothing particular is recorded of him (*Vishṇu Puráṇa*, p. 420.)

[c] Of *Sara*, called *Archatka*, or the son of *Ṛichatka*, nothing is detailed.

[d] See p. 293.

[e] We have no particulars of *Kṛishṇa*, *Viśwaka*, and *Vishṇápú*, except their being *Ṛishis*.

[f] See p. 289.

taining my sight, and enjoying a long life. May I enter into old age, as (a master enters) his house.

SÚKTA II. (CXVII.)

Deities, *Ṛishi*, and metre, as before.

Varga XIII. 1. AŚWINS, for your gratification by the pleasant *Soma* juice, your ancient worshipper adores you. The offering is poured upon the sacred grass; the hymn is ready (for repetition). Come, NÁSATYAS, with food and with vigour.

2. With that car, AŚWINS, which, rapid as thought, drawn by good horses, appears before men, and with which you repair to the dwelling of the virtuous, come, leaders of (sacrifices), to our abode.

3. You liberated, leaders (of rites), the sage ATRI,[a] who was venerated by the five classes of men, from the wicked prison, together with his troop (of children), destroying his enemies, and baffling, showerers (of benefits), the devices of the malignant *Dasyus*.

4. Leaders (of sacrifice), showerers (of benefits), you restored REBHA,[b]—cast, by unassailable (enemies), into the water, and wounded, like a (sick) horse,—by your (healing) skill. Your ancient exploits do not fade (from recollection).

5. You extricated, DASRAS, the sage VANDANA,[c] cast into a well, like a handsome and splendid orna-

---

[a] See p. 290. [b] See p. 289. [c] See p. 289.

ment designed for embellishment, and (lying), Aświns, like one sleeping on the lap of the earth, or like the sun disappearing in darkness.

6. That (exploit) of yours, leaders (of sacrifice), is to be celebrated, Násatyas, by Kakshívat, of the race of Pajra, when you filled, for the (expectant) man, a hundred vases of sweet (liquors) from the hoof of your fleet horse.[a] Varga XIV.

7. You restored, leaders (of sacrifices), Vishńápú (his lost son,) to Viśwaka, the son of Krishńa, when he praised you:[b] you bestowed, Aświns, a husband upon Ghoshá, growing old, and tarrying in her father's dwelling.[c]

8. You gave, Aświns, a lovely bride to Śyáva:[d] you gave sight to Kańwa,[e] unable to see his way. Showerers (of benefits), the deed is to be glorified by which you gave hearing to the son of Nrishad.[f]

9. Aświns, who assume many forms, you gave to Pedu[g] a swift horse, the bringer of a thousand

---

[a] See p. 303. [b] See p. 313.

[c] *Ghoshá* was the daughter of *Kakshívat*. She was a leper, and, therefore, unfit to be married; but, when advanced in years, she prayed to the *Aświns*, who healed her leprosy, and restored her to youth and beauty, so that she obtained a husband. [See Vol. II., p. 3.]

[d] *Syáva*, a *Rishi*, had the black leprosy, but was cured of it by the *Aświns*, and, consequently, married.

[e] The blindness of *Kańwa* is not adverted to in any of his hymns hitherto met with. [See Vol. IV., p. 237.]

[f] The son of *Nrishad* is unnamed: he is termed a *Rishi*. [*Kańwa* is meant. See X., XXXI., 11.] [g] See p. 307.

(treasures), powerful, irresistible, the destroyer of foes, the object of praise, the bearer (over dangers).

10. Liberal givers, these your exploits are to be celebrated; and the resounding prayer propitiates you, while abiding in heaven and earth. When the descendants of PAJRA invite you, AŚWINS, come, with food, and grant strength to the sage (who worships you).

Varga XV. 11. AŚWINS, glorified by the praises of the son (of the jar),[a] and giving food, nourishers (of men), to the sage (BHARADWÁJA), exalted by AGASTYA with prayer, you restored, NÁSATYAS, VIŚPALÁ.[b]

12. Whither were you going, sons of heaven, showerers (of benefits), when, on your way to the dwelling of KÁVYA,[c] (to receive his) adoration, you raised up (REBHA),[d] AŚWINS, on the tenth day, like a buried vessel full of gold?

13. You rendered, by your power, AŚWINS, the aged CHYAVÁNA again young.[e] The daughter of the sun, NÁSATYAS, invested your chariot with beauty.[f]

14. Dissipators of affliction, as you were praised, with former praises, by TUGRA, so were you, again, adored (by him), when you brought BHUJYU safe,

[a] We have only 'son' (*súnu*): the Scholiast adds *kumbhát prasútaḥ*, that is, *Agastya*. So, again, the text gives only *viprdya*, which the commentary amplifies by *Bharadwájáya ṛishaye*.

[b] See p. 311.

[c] *Uśanas*, the son of *Kavi*. [See pp. 213 and 329.]

[d] See p. 313. [e] See p. 139. [f] See p. 311.

from the tossing ocean, with swift ships[a] and rapid horses.

15. The son of TUGRA, brought back by you, AŚWINS, (to his father), glorified you, when he had crossed the ocean in safety; and you bore him, showerers (of benefits), with your well-harnessed car, swift as thought, to safety.

16. The quail glorified you, AŚWINS, when you saved her from the mouth of the wolf:[b] you carried off (JÁHUSHA) to the top of the mountain, in your triumphant chariot,[c] and slew the son of VISHWÁCH with a poisoned (arrow).[d] Varga XVI.

17. You restored eyes to ṚIJRÁŚWA, who, on presenting a hundred sheep to the she-wolf, had been condemned to darkness by his indignant father, and gave light to the blind, wherewith to behold all things.[e]

18. (Desiring) that the enjoyment (arising from the perfection) of the senses (should be restored to the blind), the she-wolf invoked you, (saying): AŚWINS, showerers (of benefits), leaders (of sacrifices), ṚIJRÁŚWA, (lavish) as a youthful gallant, (has given me) a hundred and one sheep, cutting them into fragments.

---

[a] See p. 289. For 'swift' we have *vibhih*, to which the Scholiast adds, *naubhih*, ships.

[b] See p. 290. [c] See p. 312.

[d] *Vishwách* is called an *Asura*: the text says, "whose son you killed with poison:" the Commentator explains this to imply a poisoned arrow.

[e] See p. 311.

19. Aświns, your powerful protection is the source of happiness: worthy of laudation, you have made whole the maimed: therefore has the intelligent (Ghoshá)[a] called upon you. Showerers (of benefits), come hither, with your succours.

20. Dasras, you filled the milkless, barren, and emaciated cow of S'ayu with milk:[b] you brought, by your powers, the daughter of Purumitra, as a wife, to Vimada.[c]

Varga XVII. 21. Aświns, causing the barley to be sown (in the fields that had been prepared) by the plough, milking (the clouds) for the sake of Manu, destroying the *Dasyu* with the thunderbolt, you have bestowed brilliant light upon the *Arya*.[d]

22. You replaced, Aświns, with the head of a horse, (the head of) Dadhícha, the son of Atharvan; and, true to his promise, he revealed to you the mystic knowledge which he had learned from Twashṭṛi, and which was as a ligature of the waist to you.[e]

23. Sapient Aświns, I ever solicit your favour.

---

[a] See p. 315. [b] See p. 293.

[c] See p. 294. It is only said, of *Purumitra*, that he was a certain *Rájá*.

[d] *Aryáya*. The Scholiast explains this, *vidushe*, 'to the sage,' that is, to, or upon, *Manu;* but the previous occurrence of *Dasyu* appears to warrant the understanding of *Arya* as its contrast, and to treat it as a national appellative. It may, also, be observed, that the text has *Manusha*, which, the Scholiast says, is, here, a synonym of *Manu*, but which, more usually, designates *man*.

[e] *Twashṭṛi* is, here, considered synonymous with *Indra*. The

Protect all my religious duties, and grant, NÁSATYAS, abundant and excellent wealth, together with offspring.

24. Liberal AS'WINS, leaders (of sacrifices), you gave to VADHRIMATÍ her son HIRAṆYAHASTA.[a] Bounteous AS'WINS, you restored to life the triply-mutilated S'YÁVA.[b]

25. These your ancient exploits, AS'WINS, our forefathers have celebrated; and we offer adoration to you, showerers (of benefits), repeating your praises, accompanied by our dependants.

SÚKTA III. (CXVIII.)

The deities, *Rishi*, and metre, as before.

1. May your elegant and rich car, swift as a hawk, come, AS'WINS, to our presence; for it is as quick as the mind of man, surmounted, showerers (of benefits), by three columns, and rapid as the wind. Varga XVIII.

2. Come to us, with your tri-columnar, triangular, three-wheeled,[c] and well-constructed car; replenish our cows (with milk); give spirit to our horses; and augment, AS'WINS, our posterity.

---

knowledge was *kakshyam vám*,—'a girdle to you both;' strengthening them to perform religious rites.

[a] See p. 310.

[b] He was cut into three pieces,—by the *Asuras*, it is said,—which were reunited into one by the *As'wins*.

[c] See p. 94.

3. DASRAS, (having come,) with your quick-moving, well-constructed car, hear this hymn, (recited by one) who reveres you. Do not the ancient sages say that you are most prompt, AŚWINS, (to avert) poverty from the worshipper?

4. May your quick-moving, prancing steeds, rapid as hawks, yoked to your car, bear you, AŚWINS, (hither), who, quick as (falling) water, like vultures flying through the air, convey you, NÁSATYAS, to the sacrifice.

5. Leaders (of sacrifice), the youthful daughter of SÚRYA ascended, delighted, this your car.* May your strong-bodied, prancing, fleet, and shining horses bring you near us.

Varga XIX. 6. By your deeds, DASRAS, you raised up VANDANA, and, showerers (of benefits), REBHA; you bore the son of TUGRA over the sea, and made CHYAVÁNA young.

7. You (gave relief) to the imprisoned ATRI, (quenching) the scorching heat, and fed him with grateful food: solicitous of worthy praise, you gave sight to KAŚWA, blinded (by darkness).

8. You filled his cow with milk, AŚWINS, for the ancient S'AYU, when imploring (your aid); you liberated the quail from danger; you gave a leg to VIŚPALÁ.

* In this and most of the following verses, we have allusions to the same persons and incidents as have been previously noticed, in most instances, repeatedly, but in general, in this hymn, more summarily.

9. You gave to PEDU, AŚWINS, the white and foe-trampling steed which you had received from INDRA, loud-neighing (in battle), defying enemies, high-spirited, the acquirer of a thousand treasures, vigorous, and firm in body.

10. Earnestly we call you, leaders (of the sacrifice), such (as you have been described), and who are well-born, to our succour,—soliciting, AŚWINS, wealth. Contented with our laudations, come to us, with your wealthy car, to bring us felicity.

11. Come to us, auspicious NÁSATYAS, with the fresh velocity of a hawk. Bearing an oblation, I invoke you, AŚWINS, at the rising of the ever-constant dawn.

SÚKTA IV. (CXIX.)

Ṛishi and deities, the same; the metre is *Jagatí*.

1. Desiring food, I invoke, (AŚWINS), to support my life, your wonderful car, swift as thought, drawn by fleet horses, worthy of veneration, many-bannered, bringing rain, containing wealth, abundantly yielding delight, and conferring riches. Varga XX.

2. Upon its moving, our minds have been raised on high, in praise; our hymns reach (the AŚWINS). I sweeten the oblation: the assistants come nigh: ÚRJÁNÍ[*] (the daughter of the sun,) has ascended, AŚWINS, your car.

3. When devout and unnumbered (men), victo-

---

[*] See p. 311, where she is named *Súryá*.

rious in battle, mutually contending for wealth, come together, your car, AŚWINS, is perceived, on its downward course, in which you bear excellent (treasure) to the worshipper.

4. You brought back, to his ancestors, BHUJYU, who, borne by his own steeds, had perished, (but that you rescued him) with your self-harnessed horses, and went, showerers (of benefits), to his distant dwelling: and great was the succour which, it is known, you rendered to DIVODÁSA.

5. AŚWINS, your admirable (horses) bore the car which you had harnessed, (first,) to the goal, for the sake of honour; and the damsel who was the prize came, through affection, to you, and acknowledged your (husbandship), saying: You are (my) lords.

Varga XXI. 6. You preserved REBHA from the violence around him; you quenched, with snow, for ATRI, the scorching heat; you generated milk, in the cow of S'AYU; and (by you) was VANDANA endowed with prolonged life.

7. Skilful DASRAS, you restored VANDANA, when debilitated by old age; as a (wheelwright repairs a worn-out) car: (moved) by his praises, you brought forth the sage* (VÁMADEVA) from the womb. May your (glorious) deeds be (displayed) for him who, in this place, offers you worship.

---

* The text does not name him. The Scholiast calls him *Vámadeva*: but nothing further is said of him, than that he invoked the aid of the *Aświns*, whilst yet in his mother's womb.

8. You repaired to him who, afflicted by the abandonment of his own father, praised you from afar.[*] Hence your prompt and wonderful succours have been wished to be at hand, (by all).

9. That honey-seeking bee, also, murmured your praise: the son of Uśij invokes you to the exhilaration of the *Soma* juice. You conciliated the mind of Dadhyach; so that, provided with the head of a horse, he taught you (the mystic science).

10. Aświns, you gave to Pedu the white (horse), desired by many, the breaker-through of combatants, shining, unconquerable by foes in battle, fit for every work; like Indra, the conqueror of men.

Sūkta V. (CXX.)

The deities and *Rishi* are the same, except that the last stanza is addressed to the Remedy against bad dreams. Of the thirteen stanzas of the hymn, the first nine are in as many different metres; the three last are in the *Gáyatrí* measure.

1. What praise may propitiate you, Aświns? Varga XXII.
Who may give satisfaction to you both? How may any ignorant (man) pay fitting homage?

2. Thus may an ignorant man inquire the means of worshipping the all-wise; for every (one,) other (than the Aświns,) is unknowing. They, the unconquered, quickly (show favour) to the man (who worships them).

---

[*] This refers, it is said, to the story of *Bhujyu*, whom his father, *Tugra*, had abandoned, or, rather, perhaps, was unable to succour.

3. We invoke you, who know all things. May you, who are omniscient, declare to us, to-day, the praise that is acceptable. Desirous of your presence, I reverence you, offering (oblations).

4. I invite not the gods, immature (in wisdom),[a] but you, DASRAS. Drink of the wonderful and strength-giving burnt-offering, and make us vigorous.

5. (Powerful is) the hymn that was repeated by the son[b] of GHOSHÁ, and by BHṚIGU, and with which hymn the ANGIRASAS adore you. May the sage (KAKSHÍVAT), desirous (of food), obtain it abundantly.

Varga XXIII. 6. Hear the song of the stumbling (blind man);[c] for, verily, AŚWINS, I glorify you, recovering my eyes (through you), who are protectors of good works.

7. You have been givers of great riches; you have again caused them to disappear. Do you, who are donors of dwellings, become our preservers: protect us from the felonious robber.

8. Deliver us not, AŚWINS, to our enemies: never may our cows, who nourish us with their udders, stray from our houses, separated from their calves.

9. Those who adore you obtain (wealth), for the support of their friends. Direct us to opulence

---

[a] *Pákyá*, 'to be ripened;' not yet mature in wisdom (*paktavya-prajnánán*).

[b] Who is called, by the Scholiast, *Suhastya*. [See X., XLI., 3.]

[c] *Ṛijráśwa*. (See p. 317.)

bestowing food: direct us to food associated with kine.

10. I have obtained, without horses, the car of the food-bestowing AŚWINS, and expect (to gain), by it, much (wealth).

11. This (is he who has obtained thee), wealth-bearing (car). Augment (my prosperity). May the delightful car bear the *Soma*-beverage of men (to the AŚWINS).

12. Now am I disdainful of sleep, and of the rich man who benefits not others; for both (the morning sleep and the selfish rich man) quickly perish.

ANUVAKA XVIII.

SÚKTA I. (CXXI.)

The deities are the VIŚWADEVAS, or INDRA; the *Rishi* is KAKSHÍVAT; the metre, *Trishṭubh*.

1. When will INDRA, the protector of men, and Varga XXIV.
granter of riches, listen to the praises, thus (recited), of the ANGIRASAS, who are devoted to the gods? When he perceives the ministers of the master of the mansion, and is to be the object of worship in the sacrifice, he greatly exults.

2. He, verily, upholds the heaven: he, the brilliant, the leader of the (stolen) herd, pours forth the flowing (water), for the sake of food: the mighty INDRA manifests himself after his own daughter,*

* *Indra* is here identified with the Sun.

(the dawn): he made the female of the horse unnaturally the mother of the cow.[a]

3. May he, illuminating the purple (dawn), listen to the invocation (addressed to him) of old, daily bestowing wealth upon the race of ANGIRAS. He has sharpened his fatal shaft: he has supported the heaven, for the good of men, of quadrupeds, and bipeds.

4. In the exhilaration of this *Soma* juice, you have restored the celebrated herd of cattle, hidden (in the cave), for the sake of sacrifice, (to the ANGIRASAS). When, INDRA, the threefold crest[b] engages in combat, he opens the doors of the tyrannical descendants of MANUS;[c]—

5. When your parents, (heaven and earth), the protectors (of the world), brought the nutritious and invigorating oblation to thee, who art quick in act, and when they offered thee the pure and precious milk of the milch-cow.[d]

Varga XXV. 6. Now is INDRA manifested. May he, the overcomer (of his foes), grant us happiness,—he, who

---

[a] *Indra*, in sport, is said to have made a mare bring forth a calf.

[b] Elevated, as a triple crest, in the three worlds.

[c] *Paṇi*, the stealer of the cattle.

[d] That is, the clarified butter of the oblations, from which the nutriment of all things proceeds; for the oblation ascends to the sun, by whom rain is engendered, from which springs corn, the support of living beings. When this has been done, *Indra* opens the doors of the cave, and rescues the cattle, as described in the preceding verse, with which this is connected.

shines brightly, like the sun of this dawn. May the excellent *Soma*, being sprinkled upon the place of sacrifice with a ladle, (exhilarate us), by whom, presenting the oblations we had prepared, it was imbibed.

7. When the bright-edged hatchet[a] is ready for its work, the directing priest is able to have the victim bound in the sacrifice.[b] When, INDRA, you shine upon the days that are appropriated to sacred rites,[c] then (success attends) upon the man who goes, with his cart, (for fuel), the driver (of cattle), or the active (shepherd).[d]

8. Send hither thy horses, the quaffers of the ex-

---

[a] *Vanadhiti*, the instrument that is to be applied to the forest, to cut down the trees.

[b] *Pari rodhaná goh*. The phrase is rather elliptical; and there is no verb. The Scholiast interprets it, *paśo rodhanáya yúpe niyojanáya, pari samartho bhavati*,—the priest, the *adhwaryu*, is competent for the attachment of the animal to the stake. Or the whole passage may be differently rendered; *vanadhiti* being interpreted 'a collection of water' (*vana*), that is, a body of clouds (*meghamálá*): when this is ready for its office of raining, then *Indra*, being in the firmament, is able to remove any impediment to the shower;—*goh* being, also, rendered 'water,' or 'rain.'

[c] *Indra* being the same with the Sun.

[d] The phraseology is, here, very elliptical and obscure, the whole being merely *anarviśe paświshe turáya*, being, literally, "to the carman, to the cattle-driver, to the quick," without any verb. The Scholiast, therefore, supplies the connexion, *abhimatam sidhyet*, "his wish may succeed," and amplifies, or translates, *anarviśe*, 'carman,' as "he who goes to fetch fuel from the wood, in his

hilarating libation: overcome, warrior, the adversary plundering us of our treasure, when they express, with stones, for the increase (of thy strength), the delightful, exhilarating, invigorating (juice), to be overtaken by thee, who art swifter than the wind.

9. Thou didst hurl thy iron bolt upon the quick-moving (*Asura*),—the swift destroyer of foes, that was brought (to you), by ṚIBHU, from heaven,[a]—when thou, who art worshipped by many, striking S'USHṆA, for the sake of KUTSA, didst encompass him with numberless fatal (weapons).[b]

10. When the sun (had emerged) from the struggle with darkness, thou didst break, wielder of the thunderbolt, the cloud that had been his annoyance, and didst sunder the well-fastened covering in which S'USHṆA had enveloped him.

Varga XXVI. 11. Then the vast, powerful, and immoveable earth and heaven animated thee, INDRA, to glorious deeds; and thou didst hurl down, into the waters, with thy mighty thunderbolt, the everywhere-spreading and destroying VṚITRA.

---

cart;" *paświsha*, the driver of cattle; and *turáya*, the active, or quick, *gopála*, or shepherd.

[a] *Divah* * *upanitam Ṛibhwá*. The Scholiast considers the latter to be the same as *Twashṭrá*, "by *Twashṭri*." No doubt, *Twashṭri* is, most usually, considered to be the fabricator of *Indra's* thunderbolt; but we have had it before stated, that the thunderbolt was brought to *Indra* by *Ṛibhu* (p. 285). [?]

[b] This is, most probably, allegorical, if it have any meaning at all. *S'ushṇa* is 'drought;' and this, *Indra* removes, for the benefit of his worshippers, by many drops of rain.

12. INDRA, friend of man, mount the horses whom you cherish, who are fleet as the wind, are easily yoked, and who bear (their burthen) well. You have sharpened the foe-destroying thunderbolt, the slayer of VṚITRA, which inspiring (weapon) UŚANAS, the son of KAVI, gave[a] you.

13. Stop, SÚRA,[b] your yellow horses; for this ETAŚA,[c] INDRA, drags the wheel. Having driven those who offer no sacrifice, to the opposite bank of the ninety rivers,[d] you compel them (to do) what is to be done.

14. INDRA, bearer of the thunderbolt, preserve us from this (poverty) that is so difficult to be destroyed, and from misfortune in war; grant us riches, conspicuous for chariots, remarkable for horses, for the sake of food, of fame, and of truth.

15. Famous for affluence, INDRA, never may thy favour be withdrawn from us: may food ever sustain us. Opulent MAGHAVAN, make us possessors of cattle; and may we, most assiduous in thy adoration, be happy, together (with our families).

---

[a] This is an unusual attribution to *Uśanas*, and rather incompatible with the statement of its having been the gift of *Ṛibhu*.

[b] *Súra*, that is, *Indra*, as the Sun.

[c] *Etaśa* is said to be the name of one of the horses of the Sun. The word occurs, in the *Aitareya Bráhmaṇa*, as that of a *Ṛishi*.

[d] *Nárydṇám*, 'of navigable rivers,' or of such as must be crossed by a boat.

END OF THE FIRST ASHṬAKA.

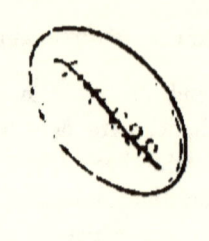

INDEX OF THE SÚKTAS.

ASHTAKA I.—MAŃDALA I.

ADHYÁYA I.

Anuváka I.

Page.		Súkta.	Deity.	Rishi.
1.	I.	(I.)	Agni,	Madhuchchhandas.
5.	II.	(II.)	Váyu, Indra and Váyu, Mitra and Varuńa,	*The same.
8.	III.	(III.)	Aświns, Indra, Viśwadevas, Saraswatí,	The same.

Anuváka II.

Page.		Súkta.	Deity.	Rishi.
11.	I.	(IV.)	Indra,	The same.
13.	II.	(V.)	The same,	The same.
15.	III.	(VI.)	Indra, Maruts, Indra and Maruts,	The same.
18.	IV.	(VII.)	Indra,	The same.

Anuváka III.

Page.		Súkta.	Deity.	Rishi.
20.	I.	(VIII.)	The same,	The same.
22.	II.	(IX.)	The same,	The same.
24.	III.	(X.)	The same,	The same.
27.	IV.	(XI.)	The same,	Jetri.

AA

ANUVÁKA IV.

Page.		Sukta.	Deity.	Rishi.
29.	I.	(XII.)	AGNI,	MEDHÁTITHI.
31.	II.	(XIII.)	ÁPRIS,	The same.
34.	III.	(XIV.)	VIŚWADEVAS,	The same.
36.	IV.	(XV.)	ṚITU, &c.,	The same.
38.	V.	(XVI.)	INDRA,	The same.
40.	VI.	(XVII.)	INDRA and VARUṆA,	The same.

ANUVÁKA V.

41.	I.	(XVIII.)	BRAHMAṆASPATI, &c.,	The same.
44.	II.	(XIX.)	AGNI and MARUTS,	The same.

ADHYÁYA II.

45.	III.	(XX.)	ṚIBHUS,	The same.
49.	IV.	(XXI.)	INDRA and AGNI,	The same.
50.	V.	(XXII.)	AŚWINS, &c.,	The same.
54.	VI.	(XXIII.)	VÁYU, &c.,	The same.

ANUVÁKA VI.

59.	I.	(XXIV.)	PRAJÁPATI, AGNI, &c.,	SUNAHŚEPA.
61.	II.	(XXV.)	VARUṆA,	The same.
67.	III.	(XXVI.)	AGNI,	The same.
69.	IV.	(XXVII.)	AGNI, VIŚWADEVAS,	The same.
71.	V.	(XXVIII.)	INDRA, &c.,	The same.
73.	VI.	(XXIX.)	INDRA,	The same.
75.	VII.	(XXX.)	INDRA, &c.,	The same.

ANUVÁKA VII.

79.	I.	(XXXI.)	AGNI,	HIRAṆYASTÚPA.
81.	II.	(XXXII.)	INDRA,	The same.

ADHYÁYA III.

Page.	*Súkta.*		*Deity.*	*Rishi.*
89.	III.	(XXXIII.)	INDRA,	HIRAŃYASTÚPA.
94.	IV.	(XXXIV.)	AŚWINS,	The same.
97.	V.	(XXXV.)	SAVITRI, &c.,	The same.

ANUVÁKA VIII.

100.	I.	(XXXVI.)	AGNI,	KAŃWA.
104.	II.	(XXXVII.)	MARUTS,	The same.
107.	III.	(XXXVIII.)	The same,	The same.
109.	IV.	(XXXIX.)	The same,	The same.
40 111.	V.	(XL.)	BRAHMAŃASPATI,	The same.
113.	VI.	(XLI.)	VARUŃA, MITRA, ARYAMAN, ÁDITYAS,	The same.
115.	VII.	(XLII.)	PÚSHAN,	The same.
117.	VIII.	(XLIII.)	RUDRA, MITRA and VARUŃA, SOMA,	The same.

ANUVÁKA IX.

118.	I.	(XLIV.)	AGNI, &c.,	PRASKAŃWA.
121.	II.	(XLV.)	The same,	The same.
123.	III.	(XLVI.)	AŚWINS,	The same.

ADHYÁYA IV.

126.	IV.	(XLVII.)	The same,	The same.
128.	V.	(XLVIII.)	USHAS,	The same.
131.	VI.	(XLIX.)	The same,	The same.
50 131.	VII.	(L.)	SÚRYA,	The same.

ANUVÁKA X.

135.	I.	(LI.)	INDRA,	SAVYA.
140.	II.	(LII.)	The same,	The same.
146.	III.	(LIII.)	The same,	The same.

Page.	*Súkta.*		*Deity.*	*Rishi.*
148.	IV.	(LIV.)	Indra,	Savya.
150.	V.	(LV.)	The same,	The same.
152.	VI.	(LVI.)	The same,	The same.
153.	VII.	(LVII.)	The same,	The same.

Anuváka XI.

155.	I.	(LVIII.)	Agni,	Nodhas.
157.	II.	(LIX.)	Agni Vaiśwánara,	The same.
160.	III.	(LX.)	Agni,	The same.
162.	IV.	(LXI.)	Indra,	The same.

ADHYÁYA V.

169.	V.	(LXII.)	The same,	The same.
170.	VI.	(LXIII.)	The same,	The same.
173.	VII.	(LXIV.)	Maruts,	The same.

Anuváka XII.

177.	I.	(LXV.)	Agni,	Paráśara.
179.	II.	(LXVI.)	The same,	The same.
181.	III.	(LXVII.)	The same,	The same.
182.	IV.	(LXVIII.)	The same,	The same.
183.	V.	(LXIX.)	The same,	The same.
185.	VI.	(LXX.)	The same,	The same.
187.	VII.	(LXXI.)	The same,	The same.
190.	VIII.	(LXXII.)	The same,	The same.
194.	IX.	(LXXIII.)	The same,	The same.

Anuváka XIII.

197.	I.	(LXXIV.)	Agni,	Gotama.
198.	II.	(LXXV.)	The same,	The same.
198.	III.	(LXXVI.)	The same,	The same.
199.	IV.	(LXXVII.)	The same,	The same.

Page.		Súkta.	Deity.	Rishi.
201.	V.	(LXXVIII.)	Agni,	Gotama.
202.	VI.	(LXXIX.)	The same,	The same.
204.	VII.	(LXXX.)	Indra,	The same.

ADHYÁYA VI.

207.	VIII.	(LXXXI.)	The same,	The same.
209.	IX.	(LXXXII.)	The same,	The same.
211.	X.	(LXXXIII.)	The same,	The same.
213.	XI.	(LXXXIV.)	The same,	The same.

Anuváka XIV.

219.	I.	(LXXXV.)	Maruts,	The same.
222.	II.	(LXXXVI.)	The same,	The same.
223.	III.	(LXXXVII.)	The same,	The same.
225.	IV.	(LXXXVIII.)	The same,	The same.
227.	V.	(LXXXIX.)	Viśwadevas,	The same.
230.	VI.	(XC.)	The same,	The same.
232.	VII.	(XCI.)	Soma,	The same.
235.	VIII.	(XCII.)	Ushas, Aświns,	The same.
240.	IX.	(XCIII.)	Agni and Soma,	The same.

Anuváka XV.

242.	I.	(XCIV.)	Agni, &c.,	Kutsa.

ADHYÁYA VII.

246.	II.	(XCV.)	Agni,	The same.
250.	III.	(XCVI.)	The same,	The same.
253.	IV.	(XCVII.)	The same,	The same.
254.	V.	(XCVIII.)	The same,	The same.
255.	VI.	(XCIX.)	The same,	Kaśyapa.
255.	VII.	(C.)	Indra,	Várshágiras.

Page.	Súkta.		Deity.	Ṛishi.
260.	VIII.	(CI.)	Indra,	Kutsa.
263.	IX.	(CII.)	The same,	The same.
265.	X.	(CIII.)	The same,	The same.
267.	XI.	(CIV.)	The same,	The same.
269.	XII.	(CV.)	Viśwadevas,	The same.

Anuváka XVI.

275.	I.	(CVI.)	Viśwadevas,	The same.
277.	II.	(CVII.)	The same,	The same.
278.	III.	(CVIII.)	Indra and Agni,	The same.
280.	IV.	(CIX.)	The same,	The same.
283.	V.	(CX.)	Ṛibhus,	The same.
286.	VI.	(CXI.)	The same,	The same.
287.	VII.	(CXII.)	Earth and Sky, Agni, Aświns,	The same.

ADHYÁYA VIII.

296.	VIII.	(CXIII.)	Ushas, &c.,	The same.
300.	IX.	(CXIV.)	Rudra,	The same.
304.	X.	(CXV.)	Súrya,	The same.

Anuváka XVII.

306.	I.	(CXVI.)	Aświns,	Kakshívat.
314.	II.	(CXVII.)	The same,	The same.
319.	III.	(CXVIII.)	The same,	The same.
321.	IV.	(CXIX.)	The same,	The same.
323.	V.	(CXX.)	Aświns, &c.,	The same.

Anuváka XVIII.

325.	I.	(CXXI.)	Indra,	The same.

INDEX OF NAMES.

Adhrigu, 284

Adhvaryu, 18, 101, 214

Aditi, 55, 61, 63, 64, 66, 113, 117, 193, 227, 230, 243, 246, 250, 252, 255, 260, 263, 265, 267, 275, 277, 280, 283, 286, 287, 290, 300, 301, 305

Âditya, 134, 187

Âdityas, 7, 33, 34, 48, 52, 55, 62, 68, 97, 113, 114, 115, 120, 121, 123, 135, 193, 194, 217, 227, 243, 277

Âdityaloka, 35

Âdityamaṇḍala, 17

Agastya, 291, 311, 316

Agnâyî, 82

Agni, 1, 5, 29, 30, 31, 32, 33, 34, 35, 36, 37, 38, 41, 42, 43, 44, 45, 49, 50, 51, 52, 54, 58, 59, 61, 67, 68, 69, 70, 71, 79, 80, 81, 82, 83, 84, 97, 100, 101, 102, 103, 104, 108, 111, 112, 118, 119, 120, 121, 122, 123, 137, 141, 142, 155, 156, 157, 158, 159, 160, 161, 177, 178, 179, 180, 181, 182, 183, 184, 185, 186, 187, 188, 189, 190, 191, 192, 193, 194, 195, 196, 197, 198, 199, 200, 201, 202, 203, 204, 210, 229, 240, 241, 242, 243, 244, 245, 246, 247, 248, 249, 250, 251, 252, 253, 254, 255, 271, 272, 273, 274, 275, 276, 277, 278, 279, 280, 281, 282, 283, 287, 288, 290, 295, 301, 304

Agni and *Soma*, 240, 241, 242

Agnichayana, 191

Âgnîdhrîya, 3

Agnishṭoma, 38, 48, 112, 192

Agnishvâttas, 276

Agnyâdheya, 48, 186, 192

Âhavanîya, 3, 30, 31, 37, 80, 120

Ahi, 65, 86, 87, 88, 136, 137, 144, 164, 204, 206, 266, 267

Aitihâsikas, 228

Ajîgarta, 59, 60

Ambarîsha, 59, 250

Angiras, 3, 34, 40, 79, 84, 91, 122, 135, 136, 160, 168, 197, 201, 242, 256, 260, 261, 283, 294, 320

Angirasas, 4, 17, 79, 136, 140, 167, 168, 187, 193, 198, 212, 250, 261, 277, 308, 324, 325, 326

Anhu, 172

Anjasî, 268

Antaka, 289

Antariksha, 17, 52, 56, 98, 245

Antarikshaloka, 18

Anus, 279

Anuyâjas, 122

Âpah, 57

Apâna, 240

Âpris, 31, 122

Âptyas, 142, 272

Arbuda, 137

Ârchatka, 313

Arishṭa, 188

Arishṭanemi, 229

Ârjîkîyâ, 88

Arjuna, 295

Arka, 18

Arkin, 18, 21

Aruṇa, 220

Aryaman, 66, 100, 112, 113, 114, 121, 205, 227, 228, 230, 231, 233, 271, 272, 277

Âryas, 90, 137, 138, 206, 318

Asiknî, 88
Asridh, 227
Asses of the Aświns, 96, 306
Asura, 94
Asuras, 85, 137, 142, 147, 148, 151, 158, 163, 164, 213, 220, 292, 301, 319, 328
Asurî mâyâ, 216
Aśva, 291
Aświns, 6, 38, 47, 50, 51, 75, 78, 94, 95, 96, 97, 118, 119, 120, 121, 123, 124, 125, 126, 127, 139, 140, 227, 228, 235, 239, 286, 287, 288, 289, 290, 291, 292, 293, 294, 295, 296, 306, 307, 308, 309, 310, 311, 312, 313, 314, 315, 316, 317, 318, 319, 320, 321, 322, 323, 324, 325
Atharvan, 5, 207, 212, 216, 310, 318
Atithigwa, 137, 147, 202
Atri, 122, 136, 290, 293, 308, 314, 320, 322
Atyagnishṭoma, 192
Aupâsana, 192
Aya, 208
Âyu, 147, 231
Âyus, 81, 147

Bala, 28, 141, 142, 193
Bali, 42, 53
Barhis, 9, 32
Bhaga, 31, 59, 120, 227, 231
Bhâgîrathî, 88
Bharadwâja, 159, 292, 316
Bhârata, 52
Bhâratî, 31, 33, 52
Bhayamâna, 259
Bhṛigu, 139, 160, 188, 213, 241, 293, 308, 324
Bhṛigus, 156, 160
Bhujyu, 289, 291, 306, 307, 316, 322
Brahmâ, 33, 60, 101, 244, 261
Brahman, 24, 37, 261, 279
Brahmaṇaspati, 41, 42, 43, 108, 111, 112, 113
Bṛihadratha, 104
Bṛihaspati, 34, 48, 95, 117, 167, 231, 244, 274, 276
Bṛihat, 18, 144
Bṛisaya, 240
Budha, 80

Chakshu, 68
Châpa, 204
Chitrabhânu, 70
Chyavana, 139, 293, 308, 309, 320
Chyavâna, 308, 316, 320
Classes of beings, 20, 230, 314
Cows, 17, 185
Cows of Ushas, 131

Dabhîti, 295
Dadhîcha, 216, 310
Dadhîchi, 207, 216
Dadhyach, 207, 216, 310, 318, 323
Daksha, 34, 227
Dakshiṇâ, 41, 43
Dâkshâda, 37
Dânavas, 87, 136, 147, 159
Danu, 87, 136, 147
Dânu, 87
Daria, 192
Daśadyu, 93
Dasras, 8, 78, 308, 311, 314, 318, 320, 322, 324
Dasyus, 90, 137, 138, 171, 201, 239, 261, 266, 268, 314, 318
Devardia, 60
Dhishaṇâ, 52
Dhṛishṇu, 77
Dhwasanti, 295
Dîrghaśravas, 291
Dîrghatamas, 42, 143, 291
Diti, 302
Div, 246
Divodâsa, 127, 137, 292, 312, 322
Doors, 32
Draviṇodâ, 250, 251, 252
Draviṇodas, 37, 38
Druhyus, 279
Dwita, 141, 142
Dyudevatâ, 78
Dyuloka, 17

Earth, 223, 287
Ehimâyâsah, 10
Ekata, 141, 142
Etaśa, 149, 166, 329
Evayâvan, 231

Gádhi, 27
Gaṇḍakí, 88
Gandharvas, 52, 230
Gangá, 88, 90, 108
Gárhapatya, 3, 31, 37, 80
Garuḍa, 229
Garutman, 229
Gáthin (name), 27
Gáthins, 18
Gayaśiras, 53
Gáyatrí, 164, 205, 241
Gáyatrin, 24
Ghora, 100
Ghoshá, 315, 318, 324
Goddesses, 33, 52, 164
Gomatí, 88
Gopá, 54
Gotama, 155, 161, 166, 170, 173, 197, 201, 202, 204, 208, 219, 221, 226, 227, 232, 235, 237, 240, 308
Grávastut, 37

Hari, 247
Haridrava, 134
Hariśchandra, 59, 60, 71, 73
Haritála, 134
Haviryajnas, 102
Haryaśvá, 181
Heaven, 228
Himavat, 140
Hiraṇyagarbha, 44, 227
Hiraṇyahasta, 310, 319
Hiraṇyastúpa, 79, 89
Hládiní, 88
Homa, 192
Horses of Indra, 18
Horses of the Sun, 98, 133
Hotrá, 32
Hotri, 2, 22, 101, 112, 199, 244

Iḍá, 82
Ilá, 31, 33, 82, 112
Ilá, 82, 122
Ilita, 32
Indra, 5, 6, 8, 9, 11, 12, 13, 14, 15, 16, 17, 18, 19, 20, 21, 22, 23, 24, 25, 26, 27, 28, 29, 31, 35, 36, 37, 38, 39, 40, 41, 42, 43, 46, 47, 48, 49, 50, 54, 55, 56, 58, 59, 68, 71, 72, 73, 74, 75, 76, 77, 84, 85, 86, 87, 88, 89, 90, 91, 92, 93, 95, 102, 111, 112, 118, 135, 136, 137, 138, 139, 140, 141, 142, 143, 144, 145, 146, 147, 148, 149, 150, 151, 152, 153, 154, 157, 158, 159, 162, 163, 164, 165, 166, 167, 168, 169, 170, 171, 172, 175, 180, 191, 193, 197, 199, 204, 205, 206, 207, 208, 209, 210, 211, 212, 213, 214, 215, 216, 217, 218, 219, 220, 225, 228, 229, 231, 232, 241, 255, 256, 257, 259, 260, 261, 262, 263, 264, 265, 266, 267, 268, 269, 272, 275, 277, 278, 279, 280, 281, 282, 283, 285, 286, 292, 294, 295, 309, 310, 313, 318, 321, 323, 325, 326, 327, 328, 329
Indráṇí, 52
Irávatí, 88
Ishíratha, 27

Jahnáví, 312
Jahnu, 312
Jáhusha, 312, 317
Jambúnadí, 88
Jarábodha, 70
Játavedas, 255
Jaundice, 131
Jetri, 27
Jwálájihwa, 203

Ka, 60, 123, 217
Kakshívat, 42, 139, 288, 289, 291, 306, 308, 315, 324, 325
Kali, 202, 203
Kaṇwa, 29, 54, 100, 102, 103, 104, 110, 111, 113, 118, 122, 127, 128, 280, 291, 315, 320
Kaṇwas, 34, 104, 106, 120, 125, 126, 127, 131
Kapardin, 301
Karanja, 147
Karkandhu, 289
Kaśyapa, 87, 113, 225, 229, 255
Kaushítakins, 137
Kavi, 29, 316, 329
Kávya, 213, 316
Kavyaváh, 181
Khela, 291, 311
Kṛiśánu, 295
Kṛishṇa, 260, 313, 315

Kuliśi, 268
Kurukshetra, 216
Kuru, 208
Kuśika, 27
Kutsa, 93, 137, 147, 171, 172, 242, 246, 253, 260, 269, 275, 276, 277, 278, 283, 287, 291, 295, 296, 300, 304, 328
Kuyava, 267, 268

Madhuvidyá, 210
Madhuchchhandas, 1, 5, 27
Maghavan, 85, 88, 93, 144, 148, 151, 157, 209, 210, 218, 263, 261, 265, 266, 268, 329
Mahánámní, 52
Mahí, 33
Maitrávaruṇa, 244
Mandhátri, 292
Mándhátri, 93, 292, 295
Mantra, 18
Manu, 80, 82, 83, 84, 102, 104, 112, 121, 122, 130, 158, 183, 251, 276, 293, 294, 301, 318
Manus, 68, 82, 84, 120, 125, 161, 193, 190, 207, 273, 274, 326
Manus (the), 251
Manusha, 318
Maríchi, 255
Márjáliya, 3
Marudvṛidhá, 88
Maruts, 15, 16, 17, 25, 34, 36, 44, 45, 48, 54, 55, 56, 79, 90, 104, 105, 106, 107, 108, 109, 110, 111, 112, 121, 133, 135, 141, 144, 145, 146, 173, 174, 175, 176, 185, 190, 191, 202, 203, 206, 218, 219, 220, 221, 222, 223, 224, 225, 226, 228, 231, 245, 256, 257, 258, 259, 260, 261, 262, 263, 267, 275, 277, 287, 301, 302, 303, 308
Mátariśwan, 160, 188
Mátṛis, 57
Medhátithi, 29, 54, 58, 135, 168
Medhyátithi, 102
Mená, 130, 140
Mitra, 5, 7, 34, 36, 37, 54, 55, 65, 68, 97, 100, 108, 112, 113, 114, 117, 120, 121, 184, 189, 198, 203, 227, 230, 231, 233, 245, 246, 250, 252, 255, 260, 263, 265, 267, 275, 277, 280, 283, 286, 287, 296, 300, 304, 305
Mortar, 72

Nahusha, 81, 84
Nakshatras, 132
Nakta, 32
Nalini, 88
Namuchi, 147
Nará, 7
Naráśansa, 32, 41, 43
Narya, 149, 293
Násatyas, 47, 96, 97, 124, 127, 306, 307, 308, 309, 310, 312, 313, 314, 315, 316, 319, 320, 321
Naraváhana, 104
Neshṭri, 36, 38, 101
Night, 97, 296
Nirṛiti, 62, 107
Nodhas, 155, 157, 162, 165, 166, 170, 173
Nṛishad, 315
Nyokas, 21

Ocean, 246

Pajra, 308, 315, 316
Pajras, 140, 308
Pákayajnas, 48, 102
Paṇi, 87, 136, 187, 212, 240, 320
Paṇis, 17, 28
Pápadevatá, 32
Paráśara, 177
Parávṛij, 290
Parṇaya, 147
Parushṇí, 88
Paṭharvan, 293
Pávaka, 30
Pávaní, 88
Pedu, 307, 315, 321, 322, 323
Pestle, 72
Pijavana, 127, 294
Pipru, 137, 261, 267
Pitṛis, 140, 230, 276
Piyavana (?), 294
Plakshagá, 88
Potṛi, 101, 199, 244
Prachetasas, 110
Pradhá, 210
Praśástṛi, 244

Prâśitra, 41
Prajâpati, 59, 60, 61, 97, 122, 123, 217, 218, 306
Praskaṇva, 118, 120, 121, 122, 126, 131, 134
Prayâjas, 122
Priests, 17, 37, 101, 107
Prishatîs, 110, 175
Priśni, 56, 105, 107, 219, 229
Priśnigu, 290
Priśnimâtaraḥ, 56, 107
Prithi, 292, 293
Prithivî, 17, 246, 303
Prithivîloka, 18
Prithuśravas, 313
Priyamedha, 122
Priyavrata, 122
Pûrṇamâsa, 192
Purohita, 244
Purukutsa, 93, 172, 290, 292, 295
Purumitra, 294, 318
Purunîtha, 160
Purûravas, 80, 81
Pûrus, 278
Purushanti, 295
Pûshâ, 115
Pûshan, 34, 54, 56, 57, 115, 116, 229, 231, 276

Quail, 310

Rahûgaṇa, 197, 201, 208
Rakshasas or *Râkshasas*, 80, 91, 100, 107, 199, 203, 204, 223, 230, 298

Ram (*Indra*), 135, 140
Rathavîti, 88
Rathantara, 167
Rauhiṇa, 266
Rebha, 289, 313, 314, 316, 320, 322
Ṛibhu, 40, 48, 285, 287, 328, 329
Ṛibhus, 45, 46, 47, 48, 49, 135, 171, 191, 283, 284, 285, 286, 287
Ṛibhukshan, 286
Ṛich, 14, 18, 24
Ṛichatka, 313
Ṛichîka, 59
Ṛijîshin, 223
Ṛijiśvan, 137, 147, 260
Ṛijrâśva, 259, 290, 311, 317, 324
Ṛishis (*seven*), 163
Ṛitashṭubh, 294
Ṛitu, 36, 37, 38
Ṛitus, 38, 218
Rivers, 86, 89, 168, 189, 268
Rohita, 59, 60
Rohits, 36
Rudra, 70, 108, 109, 117, 173, 175, 191, 219, 300, 301, 302, 303
Rudras, 8, 97, 110, 121, 123, 155, 162, 174, 256, 262
Rudrâsaḥ, 109

Śachîpati, 277
Sadasaspati, 41, 43
Sadasya, 206

Sahadeva, 259
Saharakshas, 181
Sahasraputra, 111
Sahasrâksha, 55, 204
Śakra, 20, 135, 148, 289
Śakti, 177
Sâman, 14, 18, 24, 144, 167
Samârohaṇa, 53
Sâmba, 134
Śambara, 137, 148, 149, 150, 260, 261, 267, 292
Śamitri, 206
Sanakas, 90
Santya, 38
Śanyu, 95, 117
Śara, 313
Saramâ, 17, 167, 193
Sarasvatî, 8, 10, 31, 33, 88, 111, 217
Sarayû, 88
Śaryaṇâvat, 216
Śâryâta, 139, 293
Śaryâta, 293
Śaryâti, 139, 293, 308, 309
Śastra, 6, 21, 22
Śatakratu, 12, 13, 14, 24, 39, 76, 77, 271, 295
Śatavani, 160
Śâtavaneya, 160
Satwânaḥ, 173
Śauchîka, 10
Savitri, 50, 51, 59, 61, 97, 98, 99, 100, 103, 120, 272, 277, 284
Śarya, 135

Śayu, 288, 293, 313, 318, 320, 322
Śimyus, 259
Sindhu, 88, 246, 287
Sindhumátará, 121
Śiphá, 208
Sítá, 88
Śiva, 117, 173, 301, 302
Soma, 6, 35, 37, 38, 39, 41, 42, 43, 58, 94, 117, 118, 178, 180, 227, 232, 233, 234, 235, 240, 241, 242, 311
Somapás, 122
Somapálas, 295
Somapati, 109
Somayágas, 101
Somayajnas, 192
Srinjayas, 208
Śroṇa, 290
Śrutarya, 291
Stoma, 14, 21, 22
Stuti, 22
Śuchanti, 290
Suddá, 127, 172, 294
Suddas, 127, 294
Sudhanwan, 46, 49, 283, 284, 285
Suhastya, 324
Sukanyá, 308, 309
Sukratu, 139
Śunahśepa, 59, 60, 61, 63, 64, 67, 71, 73, 75, 78
Sunahśepha, 59, 60
Suparṇa, 99
Surádhas, 259
Súra, 329
Súrya, 51, 54, 99, 118, 131, 132, 133, 134, 159, 166, 247, 261, 304, 311, 320
Súryá, 311, 312, 321
Susamiddha, 31
Śushṇa, 29, 137, 139, 153, 171, 261, 267, 328
Sushomá, 88
Sushumṇa, 217
Suśipra, 22
Suśravas, 147
Śutudri, 88
Swadhá, 140
Swáhá, 31, 34
Świtreya, 93
Swarga, 23, 35, 54, 132, 216, 241, 245, 251
Swarloka, 273
Swaśwa, 166
Świtrá, 93
Świtrya, 93
Śyáva, 96, 315, 319
Syúmaraśmi, 293
Tanúnapát, 31
Tárkshya, 229
Traitana, 142, 143
Trasadasyu, 292
Trikshi, 229
Triśiras, 89
Triloka, 201
Trita, 141, 142, 260, 270, 272, 273, 274, 275, 276
Trivikrama, 53
Tugra, 289, 306, 316, 317, 320, 323
Turvaśa, 103, 104, 148
Turvaśas, 279
Turvasu, 104, 149
Túrvayáṇa, 147
Turvíti, 104, 149, 165, 295
Twashṭri, 31, 33, 36, 48, 51, 85, 88, 143, 163, 207, 217, 221, 240, 310, 318, 328
Udgátri, 18, 21, 101
Ugradeva, 104
Uktha, 6, 14, 21
Ukthya, 38
Upayájas, 122
Urjání, 321
Uśanas, 29, 138, 213, 316, 329
Ushas, 32, 75, 78, 119, 120, 121, 123, 125, 128, 129, 130, 131, 154, 202, 235, 236, 237, 238, 239, 296, 297, 298, 299, 300, 304
Ushasas, 128, 231, 299, 300
Uśij, 42, 291, 306, 323
Vách, 52
Vadhrimati, 310, 319
Vágdevatá, 111
Vágdeví, 52
Vahni, 160
Vaiśwadeva, 192
Vaiśwánara, 157, 158, 159, 254, 255
Vája, 46, 48, 287
Vájas, 287
Vámadeva, 322

Vámana, 54
Vamra, 138, 292, 293
Vanaspati, 31, 33, 72, 231
Vandana, 280, 300, 314, 320, 322
Vangrida, 147
Vál, 18
Vardha, 163, 302
Várshágiras, 255, 257, 259
Varuńa, 5, 7, 37, 40, 41, 50, 54, 55, 59, 60, 61, 62, 63, 64, 65, 66, 67, 68, 97, 100, 112, 113, 114, 117, 121, 184, 189, 198, 203, 227, 228, 230, 231, 232, 245, 246, 250, 252, 255, 260, 261, 263, 265, 267, 271, 272, 274, 275, 277, 280, 283, 286, 287, 296, 300, 304, 305
Varuńání, 52
Varútri, 52
Vala, 201, 313
Vashatkára, 97
Vasishtha, 177, 290, 291
Vasu, 25, 80
Vasus, 97, 121, 123, 155
Vasvokasárá, 88
Váyu, 5, 6, 31, 35, 54, 55, 79, 159, 168, 225, 241, 289
Vayya, 149, 289
Vedhas, 190
Vená, 91
Vibhu, 46, 49, 287
Vikhanas, 293
Vimada, 136, 294, 306, 318
Vipáś, 88
Vírapatní, 268
Virúpa, 122
Vishádpú, 313, 315
Vishńu, 33, 50, 53, 54, 163, 220, 231
Vishńupada, 53
Vishwách, 317
Viśpalá, 291, 311, 316, 320
Viśpati, 29
Viśwadevas, 8, 9, 34, 48, 54, 69, 71, 73, 227, 269, 275, 277, 325
Viśwaka, 313, 315
Viśwakarman, 33
Viśwámitra, 1, 27, 59, 60
Viśwávasu, 180
Vitastá, 88
Vrichayá, 139
Vrishágir, 235, 311
Vrishanaśwa, 139, 140
Vritra, 17, 19, 56, 85, 86, 87, 88, 89, 90, 91, 92, 102, 136, 140, 141, 142, 143, 144, 145, 149, 150, 153, 154, 158, 163, 164, 165, 170, 171, 197, 201, 205, 206, 207, 214, 221, 233, 240, 241, 260, 266, 267, 278, 282, 310, 328, 329
Vritras, 12, 216
Vyushta, 78

Yadu, 104, 149
Yadus, 279
Yajamána, 3
Yajnas, 48, 122, 192
Yajus, 18
Yama, 74, 98, 107, 179, 180, 306
Yamadúti, 74
Yamaloka, 98
Yamuná, 88
Yátudhánas, 100
Yayáti, 84, 104, 149, 279

POSTSCRIPT.

THIS volume, as now printed, will be seen to differ but very immaterially from the original impression. Beyond the correction of oversights in quoting, transcribing, and press-reading, very little indeed has here been attempted.

On reference to the Translator's manuscript, I found justification for changing, at p. 87, line 17, "slept a long darkness" into "slept through a long darkness." The same authority, fortified by the Sanskrit, shows, that, in p. 248, notes, line 1, the term "act" of the first edition should have been "air," now substituted therefor. M. Langlois—see p. 141, note, l. 6,—was formerly quoted as writing "*ou libation qui porte le nom de Trita;*" Dr. Rosen—see p. 255, notes, l. 1,—was adduced for the words "*fac nos opulentos,*" though he wrote "*divitiæ nos opulentos sequuntor;* and, at p. 223, notes, l. 9,—which see,—we were told, that "Rosen has *lance sacrificiis culti;* M. Langlois, *amis de nos sacrifices.*" It will suffice to have thus intimated several categories of improvements which have been introduced in the foregoing pages.

Of proper names and their derivatives the following misspellings, most of which occurred uniformly, have been rectified: Anhas, Árchitka, Chándogya, Dhabhiti, Ghṛitsamada, Kausítaki, Madhuchhandas, Maghaván, Maghavat, Panin, Priyamedhas, Ṛibhukshin, Ṛichitka, S'ákapúrṅi, Sthúláshṭhívin, Suhasti, S'unahs'epas, Vasishṭha, Viśwánch, &c. &c. From the Introduction to III., XXXI.—see Vol. III., p. 42,—it appears that Kuśika was of the family of Ishíratha, not Ishírathi. Vala and Vṛihaspati have here given place to Bala and Bṛihaspati, which the Translator, correctly, came, at last, to prefer. The Vaidik forms have, also, been restored, where he adopted the Pauráṅik, as in the cases of Chyaváña, Manus, and Mandhátṛi. Dadhyanch has, further, been altered to Dadhyach. In commenting on *Nárshada*, Sáyaṅa, as printed,—Vol. I., pp. 940, 941,—twice exhibits the equivalent of "son of Nṛishada," the words of the first edition: but the *Ṛigveda*, as is proved by my reference at p. 315, evinces that some one has herein erred. The scholiast, or his copyists, should have written Nṛishad.

At p. 43, notes, l. 7 *ab infra*, I have replaced "the *Káthakas*" by "*Káthakya*;" and, at p. 272, notes, l. 2 *ab infra*, "*Sátyáyana*," by "the *S'átyáyana Bráhmaña*." At p. 139, l. 3 *ab infra*, S'atakratu has been discarded in favour of Sukratu. Compare Vol. IV., p. 125, l. 3

Under guidance of Sáyaṅa and the *Sarvánukrama*, grounds have offered for modifying the headings of no less than fifteen hymns. It may be added, that it would be an improvement, in the headings throughout, to render *devatá*—here translated "deity" and "divinity,"—by "object of invocation." See pp. 100,

323, where *devatá* designates the sacrificial post and the Remedy against bad dreams. At pp. 275, 277, I have harmonized the headings with the "Index to the Súktas," by giving to the simply transliterated "Viśwadevas"—as Professor Wilson writes the expression,—the preference which it deserves to "all the gods."

Thirty or forty brief references have been incorporated in the foot-notes, for the purpose, with rare exceptions, of pointing out the Translator's own emendations, or additions, especially in Vols. II., III., and IV.

In several instances, it seemed advisable to indicate, by an explanatory "*i. e.*," fragments of elucidation quoted from Sáyaṇa. But for some such indication, it might be supposed,—as in pp. 184, 190,—that phrases extracted from the commentary were taken from the *Ṛigveda* itself.

The statement at the end of note *a*, p. 328, has not been verified, and, probably, arose from misrecollection.

Three passages which I have slightly altered—the second, with warrant from the Translator's manuscript,—are reproduced below, in the form in which they are presented in the first edition:

"We thus find that most, if not all, the deities to whom the hymns of the *Rich*, as far as those of the first *Ashṭaka*, extend, are resolvable into three," &c.—Introduction, p. xxxix., l. 8.

"Who is so brilliant as S'ANYU, who gratifies like gold, the best of the gods, the provider of habitations?"—P. 118, l. 4.

"The red and black coursers, long-limbed, well-caparisoned, and celestial, and harnessed, well-pleased, to the yoke of the chariot in which the showerer of benefits is conveyed, for the enrichment of Ṛijráśwa, and is recognized amongst human hosts."—P. 259, l. 5.

The "Index of Names," has been amended and very considerably amplified.

The Vírapatní river, mentioned at p. 268, l. 7 *ab infra*, I would suggest to be one with the Saraswatí; the word *vírapatní*, "bride of the hero," occurring as an epithet of Saraswatí, the goddess, in VI., XLIX., 7: see Vol. III., p. 483. Compare Soma, for its equivocalness of acceptation, so common in the *Ṛigveda*.

Though nothing approaching thorough revision has here been undertaken, it is hoped that this volume, as now cursorily retouched, will prove acceptable even to those who have profited by the venerable Translator's own edition.

F. H.

London,
June 30, 1866.

CORRECTIONS.

Page	6, line 2.	*Read*	invocation.
,,	10, ,, 8.	,,	(about to be engendered).
,,	176, notes, l. 4, *ab infra*.	,,	*Ṛijíshām*.
,,	180, notes, l. 4.	,,	*Agnyddheya*.
,,	318, line 6, *ab infra*.	,,	Dadhyach.

www.ingramcontent.com/pod-product-compliance
Lightning Source LLC
Chambersburg PA
CBHW020108010526
44115CB00008B/743